WINGS OF ICE

WINGS OF ICE

MIKE STULTZ

Published by:
Grymwolf Press
Spokane, Washington

Wings of Ice
Copyright 2016 Mike Stultz

ISBN-13: 978-0-578-18867-6
Library of Congress Control Number: 2017900781

Printed in the United States of America

Author photo: Tom Dea
Design and production by Gray Dog Press, Spokane, WA

For more information or to contact the author email:
mssmikestultz@hotmail.com

To my sons,

Michael and David

Acknowledgments

"No man is an island entire of itself" is just as true today as it was in 1624 when John Donne penned these famous words. No matter how alone a person feels when he sits down to write the first line of a book, the ocean soon fills with shoals, storm clouds and uncertainties calmed only by the reasoned voices of those trusted enough to be brought into the creative process. *Wings of Ice* first set out to be a modest book to remind my two sons of the life they lived in Alaska, and to quiet my granddaughter, Cayleigh Dea, who made me recite "The Bear Story"—a recounting of a grizzly bear mauling I suffered in Alaska—at every major family gathering. It soon grew into a more ambitious project as the number of pages grew. After writing for six months, I stopped and let others read what I had written. For the past forty years, I had told friends and family members that I would write a book about my life in Alaska, more to get them to move on to another subject than with any real intent of doing so. Now that I had finally started the process I needed feedback.

My wife Colleen Dea read the manuscript and despite the numerous errors told me that I needed to continue writing. I thought that if a woman who hated camping out in anything other than a motel room or a travel trailer could be enthused about my adventures in Alaska, I really did need to continue. However, I decided to take a break of six months, and really think about what I wanted to say. There was no way I could include all my adventures in any reasonably sized book. At the end of those six months I sat back down at my computer and started writing again. In another six months I was finished with the first complete draft.

It was then that the storm clouds of sentence structure, punctuation, spelling and fuzzy grammar made their troublesome presence known. My wife sat down with the manuscript and did the first full edit. When she finished her valiant effort, and I had rewritten the manuscript, we turned to her sister Michole Nicholson. Michole and her husband had once owned a publishing company in California, and she had a broad knowledge of editing and the book industry. Her expertise and encouragement coupled with

Colleen's were invaluable. She read every word, made great suggestions and kept my spirits up through the numerous rewrites. Leah Middlebrook, a professor at the University of Oregon and another family member, soon joined the Stultz Literary Team as cheerleader and sage advocate with her insightful comments and suggestions regarding content. I owe so much to these three delightful and intelligent women for their hard work and unending encouragement and inspiration.

As the ink began to settle, my thoughts turned to the jungles of publishing. What a nightmare! I was thankfully steered toward a Spokane publishing company. Gray Dog Press supported local authors and had been featured in our local newspaper. Colleen and I visited the owner, Russ Davis, and we were amazed at his knowledge and publishing expertise. He made sense of the whole process from the manuscript to the final product. Russ also suggested a copy editor whom he felt was very competent. Thus, Dennis Held joined the team, and began the final step of organizing, editing and making suggestions for the last transformation of *Wings of Ice*. Dennis, with his wry sense of humor and keen intellect, proved invaluable. Not only did he provide a new set of eyes that were not related to me, but his knowledge of the English language and professionalism was a steadying influence in getting the book to the printer. Though my name will be on the book cover, it is the work of these wonderful people who put it there.

Contents

Introduction

THE EVENTS IN THIS BOOK are as honest and clear as I can make them after forty years. I used the names of real people when available in my pilot flight records, and memory. I noted each time I could not remember names of the people I was writing about. Sometimes I made up names for real people I did not want to embarrass in the event they were still alive these many years later. However, in every case, I wrote the story as I remembered living it. The flying, teaching, homesteading, hunting, working for the Alaska State Troopers and the Department of Fish and Game occurred between 1963 and 1984. It was a period in Alaska before oil provided money for large expansions of aviation and law enforcement. There were also no GPS aviation guides for the general public.

Many of the aircraft maneuvers in the book are extremely dangerous and should only be used by pilots with advanced training and skills. No one should attempt them without getting professional instruction from an accredited acrobatic instructor. Do not fly airplanes with the disregard for weight and balance and weather issues I did in the book. Disregarding manufacture's recommendations for their aircraft leads to the death of many pilots each year. There is a reason there are very few of us bold pilots left alive.

I broke many Fish and Game regulations in this book. I was not being a smart or responsible citizen by doing so. Our natural resources are too fragile and scarce for individual citizens to make their own laws. I only included these violations in the book to be as accurate as possible about my actions during that period of my life, not to encourage that behavior in anyone else. Enjoy the book. It was a wild and fantastic journey that I have put off writing far too long.

I am going to spend a lot of time in the beginning discussing my early family life, as it molded me into the young man I became. Later in life the real world had a chance to knock some sense into me, but right out of high school and until my mid-thirties, I was opinionated and cock-sure that my perceptions and beliefs were the only accurate ones. I would realize, as a bear sent me flying through the air, that I should learn something valuable from the experience. Usually, but not always, mind you, I did. God did not provide Stultz men with their arrogance and stubbornness so they could be polite and politically correct or change their behavior easily.

* * *

One of my first childhood memories is of standing by the dead rosebushes outside our white house on Morse Street in Ryderwood, Washington, in the southwest portion of the state, about equal distance between Seattle and Portland, Oregon, and about five miles west of Interstate 5. I was four years old, and tightly encased in a blue jacket with thick winter pants and boots to protect me from the snow still sprinkled on the ground. A chilly wind blew off the surrounding hills. I was looking particularly at the hill we called Baldy Mountain, and wondering what was on the other side of that dark, menacing hill shrouded in mist. Though hardly able to move while wearing all this protective clothing, my young itchy feet felt the urge to trundle me by the telephone office and up past the solitary town store across the railroad tracks that provided this out-of-the-way town its sole source of income, and, finally, move on to explore the seemingly insurmountable obstacle of Baldy. The need to explore and see what was on the other side of a mountain, river or lake was born in those moments, and has stayed with me throughout my adult life. It has led me to many adventures (and misadventures), both in this area of southwest Washington where I was born, and later in the vast wilderness of Alaska. While in Alaska, I would graduate from college; I would then go on to become a father, teacher, Alaska Game Warden, State Trooper, fish and game guide, bush pilot and homesteader.

My story encompasses a journey filled with the beauty and hazards of flying and living in Alaska, and is peopled with the many friends and enemies I made along the way. I will relate my experiences, such as the dissolution of my family, being mauled by bears, crashing planes, falling through an ice-covered river at forty-five degrees below zero, as well as many other personal episodes of Alaskan survival. I will take you with me as I build my homestead on Echo Lake, only to have Bureau of Land Management bureaucrats make me tear it down and fly it to another lake. I will introduce you to the world of being a Game Warden and all the political influences of that occupation. You will hear the difficulties of being the only teacher in single-room elementary and high schools in the Alaskan bush. I'll tell you why I punched more than one school principal in the nose, and why I became so disillusioned with politics within the State of Alaska, particularly within the Department of Fish and Game, that I became an outlaw guide. It is a journey filled with laughter, tears, disappointment and absolute euphoria, and I have put off reliving it far too long.

WINGS OF ICE

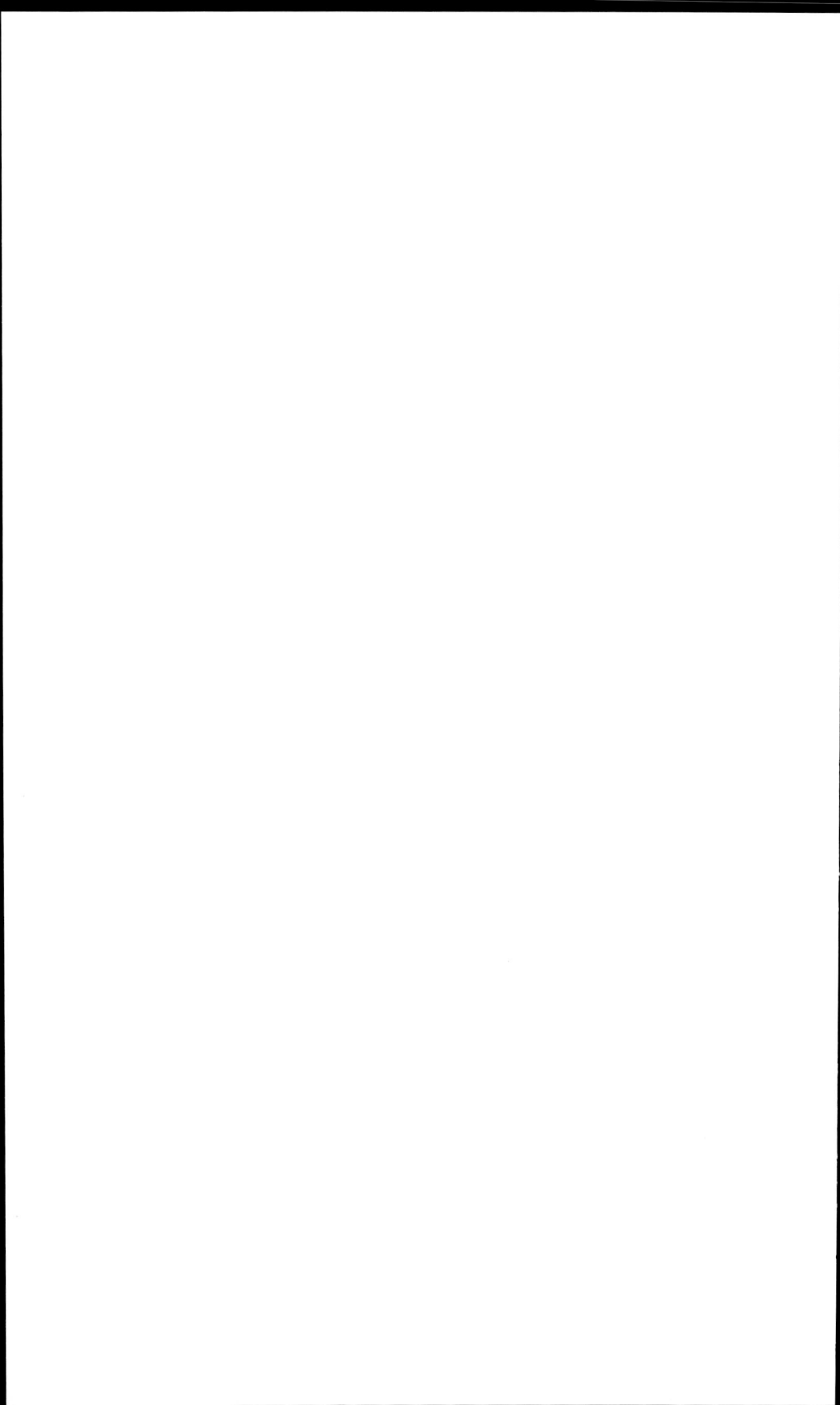

Ryderwood and Winlock

IN ANY ADVENTURE THERE IS a beginning and ending. Mine began when I was born in Chehalis, Washington, to Richard and Bettye Stultz on April 8, 1943. My father was a coach and teacher in Washington State, who became very well known in both professions. He taught in the State of Washington for thirty-six years, and only called in sick one time in all those years. Dad was fond of telling us kids that teaching and coaching was not a job but a passion. Many of his students and athletes admired him decades after he retired from teaching and coaching until he died at ninety-three years of age several years ago. He became a member of the Washington State Hall of Fame for Coaches, with state football championships in Six-man, B, and A level schools. His football teams lost fewer than thirty-seven games during the entire thirty-six-year coaching span. My mother was at first a stay-at-home mom who later became a waitress after divorcing Dad when I was in high school. I had two brothers. Richard was one year older than me, and Jeff eight years younger. My sister Rozan was two years younger.

It is commonly thought that childhood has a direct effect on the person one will become. My early experiences put a brand of behavior on me equal to any hot iron melted into the hide of a cow. Ryderwood was a small town owned completely by the Long Bell Logging Company. It existed solely to support the logging interest of Long Bell. All the city's buildings, including houses, store, post office and telephone house were owned by the company. Anyone who lived in the town was a Long Bell employee or a dependent of one. I am not sure how school employees were classified, but we lived in Long Bell housing.

Loggers are made of stern stuff. They work in a deadly profession that demands attention to detail and great strength. My father was as tough as any of the Long Bell loggers. He was also as mean as a grizzly bear with a sore tooth. A bad combination for a boy who hated to follow orders.

To say my father was feisty is to say an active volcano is warm. The Stultz temper is a blight passed down through generations, and all of the descendants in this particular Stultz family had it in spades. My sister

3

Rozan was not left out of the gene pool either. Getting her mad did not result in the explosive behavior exhibited by my brother. She put off her revenge like a cougar stalking a deer before striking the deadly blow. This usually meant her finding something Dad did spank me for, and tattling for some indiscretion she perceived I instigated. She is still delusional, and claims I caused most of the problems in our childhood to this very day.

Though I have finally learned to control my temper after dealing with the consequences of not doing so for more than seventy years, Richard is just learning to keep his mouth shut. But I like him now, and visit with him regularly. Pat, Rozan's husband, says her temper still gets the better of her. Dad never showed any signs that his temper was cooling until well into his fifties. So I figure I am doing well in the temper department.

Most high school sport referees disliked Dad with a passion usually reserved for ex-wives. Dad was not shy about revealing their ignorance of the rule books, or their inability to see what was in front of their blind eyes. He did so in a boisterous manner that could not be ignored by the crowds attending these events. I can remember in one important football game where Dad decided that yelling at and berating a particularly obnoxious referee had become a waste of his time and voice. He called a time out and told us on the sidelines that, if we wanted to win this game and the State Championship, this referee must be sidelined—preferably on a stretcher! The referee had such an impassioned dislike for Dad and his teams that touchdowns were being called back, nonexistent penalties called, and legally completed forward passes called incompletes.

I never saw eleven boys hit one person so hard with various blocks and tackles at one time in my life. Even our ball carrier, Mike Porter, who led the charge, dropped the ball somewhere in the melee to get in on the action. We won the game after the referee had to leave. I really don't think this was an attitude you should teach young men. Dad always denied this allegation with a twinkle in his eyes, but I know better as I was there on the bottom of the pile.

They say you could hear a pin drop in Dad's classroom. It was true. You could walk down the school's halls in Ryderwood and later in Winlock and Lake Stevens and hear students talking in all the adjoining classes, but never a peep out of Dad's students unless someone in class was asked to participate in a lesson. Students were more scared of missing an assignment or faking a book report with Dad than facing a spanking at home. The flip side of this seemly draconian control is that many of these same students credited Dad with instilling in them the self-discipline and attention to detail that made them successful later in life. Eddie Leonard, one of Dad's students and football players, went on to graduate from the Air Force Academy and become a fighter pilot in the Vietnam War. Eddie was shot down over North Vietnam and spent five years in one of their notorious prison camps. He saved his sanity by recalling the lessons Dad taught. Eddie told himself throughout his long ordeal that if he survived Dad as a teacher and coach, he could endure this torture. He survived to become a successful lawyer and write about his ordeals. The same traits that preserved Eddie Leonard would keep me alive in Alaska while many of my friends, facing the same circumstances, died.

I have lost track of the number of students who told me how scared they were of Dad and how much they admired him later in life. When informed of their fears, I would chuckle to myself, as these students only had my father during school hours. At home Dad ruled the roost with an iron fist. There was no discussing disagreements, work assignments or punishments. If any subsequent discussions were necessary following his judgments, his belt did all the talking.

Not only did we have our own chores to do at home in Ryderwood, but on weekends during the various school sport seasons, our household was filled with vapors from bleaching and washing tubs. All three of us kids helped Mom and Dad wash the team uniforms with an old hand wringer washer. I remember trying to catch Richard's fingers in the wringer when I cranked it as he fed the uniforms into it. When the uniforms were cleaned to my father's satisfaction, we would take them outside to hang on the clothesline to dry. There were also other household chores to be completed in silence and to his eminence's satisfaction.

We worked outside the home as well. I started working at the age of six for Forman's Dairy, delivering milk products to people's homes. Dad would drive me two miles outside of town to the dairy while it was still dark. I would return home sometime in the afternoon when the delivery truck dropped me off. I never received pay for this work, nor did I expect any. Our family received free milk products as a result of my labor. As my father explained, I was simply doing my share as a family member. In later years I would help him paint stores in downtown Winlock during the summer for a winter coat or some other article of clothing. Mostly I would ask for shoes as we were given only one pair a year.

One was a popular number with Dad when it came to gifts. With Christmas or birthday presents, the number was always the same. Mom would sneak in other gifts if she could, but it was like battling a snowstorm with a fly swatter. It usually ended in a fierce argument between the two of them.

Later it was always a mystery to me why the collection money for delivering papers after school always equaled the amount owed the newspaper company for the papers. I thought Richard was probably stealing it, but his math skills were so bad I did not see how he could manage to come out to what was owed the paper. Besides, I never caught him. I mean other kids made enough money to buy bikes and stuff. Me, I was lucky to stay out of debt after a month's work.

Eventually Dad would get fired as coach in 1960 during my junior year in high school at Winlock after removing our varsity baseball team from the field of play during a game at Toledo. This happened when an umpire at our neighbor town rival of Toledo called our players out seven times in a row with some extremely imaginative and whimsical calls. It made no difference if the pitch hit the ground or was two feet outside the strike box, it was deemed a strike. When our players ran the bases they were called out when clearly they were safe by large margins. By the third inning of this nonsense a riot was brewing. I remember telling Fred Norquist if this son-of-a bitch called me out on my next plate appearance I was going to knock his head off with my baseball bat.

My father, seeing a disaster in the making, calmed the situation by removing us from the field of play and had John Poage, our wonderful bus driver, take us home to Winlock. Our shop teacher, Mr. Boe, a former Marine who was at the game, later angrily accused me of giving his wife the finger out the bus window as we drove away. I didn't intentionally insult her, but if she was standing by some cheering Toledo fans she might have gotten flagged by mistake. She should have had more sense than standing next to those low-life Toledoans anyway.

Toledo was Winlock's arch enemy. Being six miles away, they were not privy to our exalted educational system or refined culture. We had a movie theater. They had some pagan celebration called Cheese Day while we, the owners of the world's largest egg, celebrated the widely renowned Egg Day as our day of festivity. We thought the cheese heads uncultured boors while they thought we were full of chicken droppings. The high school sporting events were closely monitored and discussed for years afterwards.

It seemed ironic to me that Dad would be fired for calming down potential trouble instead of causing it. But Winlock's illustrious school board fired Dad from all coaching duties, even though he was by far the most successful coach in the school's history. Their action caused a major uproar in the community for years to come. In my not-unbiased opinion, as well as 95 percent of the rest of the town, these dimwitted city leaders were indeed full of chicken droppings. It was also widely felt they saw it as an opportunity to get even with my father for not giving their sons the playing time or positions of importance in athletics as their societal distinction deserved. Winlock was a town of a little over 800 residents at the time and most of us felt the school board had a pretty exaggerated opinion of their own importance.

Dad stayed fired from coaching but retained his teaching responsibilities. School Board meetings were entertaining for the next year. As for Dad not playing their sons, he told all the parents that when their kids deserved playing time they would get it. He would not penalize anyone on his teams who made the effort to excel just because of some parent's inflated sense of self-importance. Though, I am quite sure his words were not as polite.

To make sure no one could accuse him of favoritism, Dad made Richard and me understand that we had to be twice as good as anyone else in our playing positions to get any game time in school sports. We also had the honor of running twice as many punishment laps as anyone else on the teams. I cannot remember a single compliment from him until I was over thirty years of age, and that came when I was in bed and he thought I was asleep and could not hear him. No matter how many touchdowns in football, baskets in basketball, hits in baseball or races won in track, there was no pleasing him. He would always find something wrong with what I had done. I learned very early that excuses and trying to take the easy way out of any situation invariably led to major confrontations that always resulted a no-win situation for myself. Training myself to keep emotions under control and to only focus on the task at hand, I avoided many negative situations with Dad. It was a trait that saved my life many time in the years to come.

He treated Richard the same way. Richard, being of less durable character than myself, broke much earlier. He called Dad a bunch of interesting names during a basketball practice that led to a fight between the two on the stairway down to the dressing room. Richard was kicked out of school and had to finish high school in Chehalis instead of with his Winlock class-mates. My parents were separated by then, and he moved in with Mom, but that was not surprising as he was always a mommy's boy.

Almost all of my fond memories of my father during my high school years came when we were hunting and fishing. He was a different person with a rod, reel or shotgun in his hand. We spent every available moment we could during the summers fishing the Cowlitz River, dragging a fluo-rescent F-7 flatfish behind his canvas and wood twelve-foot boat powered by a five horse Johnson outboard. We caught many a harvest trout and king salmon along with a few spring steelheads on these trips. I cannot remember him speaking a single harsh word. He did not hunt deer, but took Richard and me on pheasant hunting trips. We would hunt ducks in the fall on a relative's farm outside of Adna, Washington. I rode my first pig and calf on this farm. It belonged to the sister of Grandma Stultz. I forget their names, but I will never forget the hundreds of hours I spent walking the ditches for pheasants or sitting in blinds waiting for duck to fly over.

I graduated from high school with thirteen varsity letters, a couple of sports records, a 2.5 GPA, and delusions of grandeur over my upcoming collegiate and professional sports career. It was a dream abruptly cut short by two broken backs prior to attaining nineteen years of age.

* * *

Growing up in Ryderwood, you learned to use your fists early. Perceived insults instantly became bloody noses. Real insults became fights that could last a lifetime, as the town had more than its share of Oakies from the dustbowl of Oklahoma, Tar Heels from North and South Carolina, and Finns from that frozen northern country, all of whom could hold a grudge for generations. My brother and I grew up fighting not only each other, but anyone else who annoyed us. Some of the few things I liked about being my father's son at this age were the almost unlimited access to the gym and other school sports facilities, being towed behind our car on a large wooden sled in the winter, and going fishing a lot with him. But most of all, he did not care if his sons fought, as he mistakenly believed it built character.

We were never punished for fighting. In our household there was no such thing as "turn the other cheek" or "forgive and forget." You stood your ground no matter the opposition, and always did your best. My father did not even discipline me several years later in Winlock, when I threw a grade school teacher across a desk and punched him for making disparaging comments about my family. He merely asked me if I got in a good punch before I was expelled.

I was certainly no angel in school, and deserved whatever attention my teachers addressed to my bottom or hands. I remember Mrs. York, my first grade teacher in Ryderwood, who tried to break many a ruler over my knuckles in her battle against my efforts to breathe some life into her dull classroom. My behavioral issues had not gotten better by the sixth grade, when an exasperated Mr. Homer W. Stepp told me he had to make a new paddle because there were eleven marks after my name and no room for more. He was not pleased when I told him he just needed to write smaller. So once again he marched me to the boiler room, this time for my twelfth smacking during that school year. In the seventh grade I challenged high school running back Tom Fleming to a fight after he tried to cut in front of me in the cafeteria line. The last spanking I received in grade school was in the eighth grade. My brother Richard and I were writing valentines to our class friends. He was teasing me about some silly thing. Dad was sitting ten feet away, reading, so I could not respond to Richard verbally. I wrote on a blank valentine that he could go do something physically impossible to himself. This message somehow got put into an envelope addressed to Helen Prichard, a girl whom I found very attractive. I was sure Richard did it to get me in trouble. And, as the principal said as he was leading me to the boiler room, there was no mistaking my handwriting on the card.

My last school fight occurred when I was a senior. I was attending a fair in Toledo, Washington, with some friends when we noticed a disturbance. Walking up to the crowd of people, I noticed a Toledo barbarian picking a fight with Paul Elam, a nice Winlock boy. Paul was a smart kid who would later become the quarterback on Winlock's football team, but he was very short and slim, a pleasant, gentle kid who would never insult anyone. Seeing the bully threatening him put my dander up, and I immediately stepped in and challenged him. The fight did not last long, as a couple of my right crosses put the philistine on the ground before it was broken up. His three brothers, figuring their family's nonexistent honor was tarnished, came to my house the following week with about fifty supporters (according to my sister), to put me in my place and see justice done. Unfortunately for them I had to stay after school that week after shooting our bald high school algebra teacher on the back of his head with a perfume-filled squirt gun as he was writing on the blackboard. Later, when I got home, Dad asked how I was going to handle the people showing up at the house. I told him not to worry, they would not be back. The three other brothers were no stronger than the first, and were taken care of one at a time.

My biggest fights, however, were reserved for my bother Richard. We became celebrities in the small logging community of Ryderwood for the length and noise of the battles we waged. Even today, fifty years later, when returning to this area of my youth for reunions, I am still entertained by someone's recounting of a fight my brother and I had. It took me beating the hell out of him in the fifth grade, after he tried to drown me with a toilet plunger while I was taking a bath, for us to stop fighting each other physically. He remembers it differently. It took us fifty years to begin to enjoy each other's company.

Napoleon should have taken lessons from Dad if he had really wanted to get that short-person complex right. If Dad ever weighed more than 150 pounds it was on a wet day with his pockets full of rocks. But he was a dynamo at football practice with all the yelling, butt-kicking and nose guard pulling he believed was needed to accomplish getting us lined up correctly and running in the right direction. Woody Hayes, the famous University of Ohio football coach, was a piker compared to my father. Dad carried on for thirty-six years and was never fired for physical brutality. But back then we did not call pushing, shoving, hitting, kicking, yelling or pulling a player by his helmet brutality. It was called getting a player's attention so the coach could have a teachable moment with him. I know a lot of people in the current generation who could use some teachable moments.

I remember Bud May, a well-known sports writer in southwest Washington who grew up in Ryderwood, telling me of a baseball incident involving my father. Bud was playing the outfield when the opposing hitter hit a high fly ball to him. Bud managed to get under the ball and put his glove up to catch it. Unfortunately for him, the glove was in the wrong position. The ball hit him on the head and bounced over the fence for a home run. Bud was so scared of my father that he threw his glove down, ran through the fence, breaking it, then continued running to his house where he hid in the closet.

Bud also recounted another Ryderwood incident when Dad employed him to watch over us kids while he and Mom had a rare evening out. Dad had told Bud to keep an eye on Richard and me, as we were sneaky. He locked the back door and ensconced himself on a chair in the front room where he could observe both front and back doors to make sure his charges remained in their bedroom where they belonged. Unknown to Bud, there was a large tree outside Richard's room we could climb down. As soon as Dad and Mom left, Richard and I opened his bedroom window, climbed down the tree and went on our merry way. It was not until several hours later when we got into one of our noisy brawls that Bud knew we were missing. He made us promise not to tell Dad as he put us back in bed.

I can sympathize with Bud, as I was a lousy baseball outfielder as well. Unlike Bud, I could not run away and hide. Watching me try to play the outfield drove Dad so crazy that he moved me to first base and gave me a bigger glove. That helped somewhat, but baseball was my worst sport in high school. I did finally end up earning thirteen varsity sports letters and invitations from several colleges to play football or basketball on athletic scholarships. No college offered me a scholarship for baseball, however.

I also discovered condoms in Ryderwood. I always searched Dad's night stand when he was away to find the occasional nickel or dime left behind. I would take these lonely coins, figuring they needed company, to the Merc (the only store serving Ryderwood), for a candy bar. Occasionally I would get caught with the inevitable consequences, but got away with it enough to not break the habit. On one particular day I discovered several aluminum-wrapped packages containing something round. I took them outside, where Richard and I proceeded to unwrap them. Not discerning their intended use, we blew them up like balloons and proceeded to see who could keep them afloat off the ground until Mom came home to stop us.

Mom was not the disciplinarian in our household, but she was decidedly uncool as she quickly popped our balloons and hid them in the trashcan. Normally, she would merely stop the shenanigans and send us to our rooms. This day she did the same, but also promised near-death penalties when Dad came home. I thought this was unfair of her, as we were merely hitting balloons. But, as I found out later in life, there is no understanding a woman. Later, my father, true to form, took off his big leather belt and told us to bend over. This time I was sure I saw a twinkle in his eye as he delivered less emphatic swings of the punishing leather strap, trying real hard not to laugh.

Though I worked all my young life from the age of six on, I would not get a paying job until I was a freshman in high school. I began working for Armand and Dorothy Jeffs on their 600-acre farm outside of Toledo, six miles down the road. They both started teaching at Toledo, but they came to their senses when Ted Hippi conspired against Armand to steal his head coaching position. The Jeffs decided to come to the light side, and started teaching in Winlock. I spent thousands of hours working on their farm, enjoying all of it from cutting the hay to baling, stacking and selling it. Dorothy was a wonderful warm English teacher who gave me my first "A" grade in school and inspired me to continue to read, learn and explore.

Dorothy also employed a fellow Winlock classmate in the summer to help with the cooking for the hay hands, and cleaning chores. Her name was Donna Jantz. Donna would spend time riding on the tractor with me when the household chores were done, but being a shy and sensible young woman would never allow a kiss.

It took me years to learn how to spend that $1.25 an hour I earned working for the Jeffs. Father commented on how thrifty I was, saving all the money I earned. He did not know I was hiding it so no one could steal it.

* * *

In 1953 the logging industry around Ryderwood failed through lack of new harvestable timber, and Long Bell sold the town to Senior Estates, a corporation that would turn the town into a retirement village. We moved to Winlock five miles down the road from Ryderwood, where Dad accepted a job as a high school teacher with the associated duties as coach of the football, basketball and baseball teams.

Life was easier in Winlock, as the school had janitors who washed the uniforms of its sport teams, so I had more time to play and get into trouble with people who would become lifelong friends. Ron Smith lived across the street from us. At the back of Ron's house was a large hillside covered with brush and trees with a small creek running through it, where we spent countless hours playing cowboys and Indians. Fred Mooers, who lived across town, was a fellow miscreant. We would steal railroad ties from the railroad to build rafts to float down Olequa Creek when it flooded during the winter. It was great fun braving the rapids and fallen trees, sweeping quickly down the rain-swollen creek until the violent water tore the raft apart. Fred and I would swim to shore laughing all the way. It was a miracle we never drowned or caught a cold. Eddie Cruse and I had many adventures fishing and doing whatever else we could do to get into trouble.

In the warmer summer weather, Fred and I would hide on the roofs of stores adjoining taverns, watching for loggers who stored gallon jugs of beer in their cars. Taverns at this time sold patrons a gallon of draft beer for $2 if they brought their own jugs. Most of these loggers would go back inside the tavern to continue the night's relaxation after they put the beer-filled jug in their vehicles for later consumption. Fred and I would climb down off the roofs and steal the beer. No one locked their cars or houses at this time, so it was easy to get the beer and run to the creek bank or one of the hillsides overlooking town to enjoy our manly harvest. Many times the fruits of this endeavor were upchucked into the creek while we staggered home sick, but I dimly remember it as being fun.

The town elders in Winlock declared there could be only one tavern in town for each church. This gave us seven taverns to stake out. We knew that if Dick Sutter, the town cop, caught us we would not go to jail. Dick took juvenile offenders to their parents to administer punishment instead of leaving it up to the judicial system. It was much more effective for most kids.

Eddie Cruse, who lived five miles away in Vader, became one of my best friends who enjoyed fishing as much as I did. Bill Berg's house was the home of a thousand basketball games. Sadly, these games used to take place at Bobby Gibb's place, but he died of a heart attack during a basketball practice my junior year. Judi Nicewonger would come over and play house on weekends with my sister Rozan. Somehow the wonderful nests they built usually ended up around my bed. Winlock had many beautiful girls like Anita, Pam, Judy, Marion, Donna, Martha, Helen, and others who made growing up in Winlock so pleasant.

My first broken back happened while working for a Weyerhaeuser Mill in Everett, Washington. Our family moved to Lake Stevens after I graduated from high school. I worked at the mill during the evening while attending college during the day. Unfortunately, one supervisor told me to inspect a railroad car full of lumber while another supervisor told an employee to send a fully loaded railroad car down the track behind me to couple with the one I was inspecting. My back was not up to the challenge of being pinned between these railcars, and I ended up in Everett Community Hospital for a lengthy stay. The only good thing to come out of the incident was that I met my wife-to-be, Sharon Ellis, who was a student nurse at the hospital. She gave wonderful backrubs and sponge baths. She understood men.

Weeks later when I was released from the hospital, and ready to return to work, Weyerhaeuser decided to fire me for stupidity. Just in case this was a family trait they fired my brother Richard, who worked for them as well. The Weyerhaeuser Supervisor in overall charge of the plant had sent my brother with me in the ambulance to the hospital. Upon later reflection, Weyerhaeuser decided that Richard, by following these orders, showed the same genetic imperfection as I had exhibited in following my bosses' orders. It was decided they needed to eliminate any trace of this uncommon obedience lest it infect the entire plant.

Thus, in a few short years, my lifelong distrust and disgust of incompetent people in positions of authority grew by leaps and bounds. This attitude contributed to my fist landing on ego-inflated noses several times during my working life, and a heartfelt wariness of upper management. I felt these punches were fitting exclamation points to our disagreements, though I know from the reactions of the recipients, they strongly disagreed. Looking back, I can see that if my attitude toward supervisors had been more generous and forgiving my life would have been much easier. But then, it would not have been nearly as fun.

The second broken back occurred less than a year later, when I was on my way from Lake Stevens to a spring football practice at the University of Washington. A couple from Fairbanks, Alaska, ran a red light on Highway 99 and hit me head on. My newly acquired Buick went to the junkyard, and I got another red light ride to the Northwestern Hospital. The collision caused the steering wheel to fracture my seventh lumbar vertebra and turn it almost sideways, causing much discomfort, spinal contusion and other big words I did not want to hear, much less comprehend.

Being hooked up to thirty-five pounds of spinal traction for weeks at a time was exceedingly boring and tiring. I would slide down the bed and rest the weights on the floor from time to time. The nurses were not pleased, and after being caught for the third time, they reported me to the doctor, who responded by putting me in a full body cast.

I did not mind the back cast as much as I did the fact that it came down and covered most of my front pelvic region, making conjugal enjoyment of my new wife impossible. After three weeks of frustration I modified my physician's creations to better suit the needs of my wife and me. However, when my doctor discovered this callous disregard of his masterpiece, he showed extreme unprofessional behavior by angrily cutting the cast completely off while giving me the address of someone who would make me an orthopedic brace. He also told me to find a new physician. This back brace would come in handy in the years ahead. Not only did it provide back support but fit tight enough to hold broken ribs in place as well.

It just goes to show you that tempers and bad attitudes do not end with coaches or the Stultz family. I am not sure if the doctor's displeasure with me resulted in his accident on a ski jump a month later that led to his untimely death, but I certainly entertained feelings of guilt that it may have done so. The second set of physicians told me to forget any aspirations of ever playing collegiate athletics again.

As I matured physically, the relationship between Dad and me became more and more tense as it does for many fathers and sons. I became increasingly frustrated with his draconian rules and behavior as well the physical restrictions of my injured body. I had started seeing Barbara Bowman, a former Winlock girl I always admired, a year before I married Sharon. Dad became aware of this and laid down the law that I was to break off the new relationship for some senseless reason. The resulting fight between us was nasty, huge and lasting. I did not want Dad telling me who I could and could not go out with. If I had been well enough to work and support myself I would have departed his home without a goodbye. As it was, we barely spoke to each other.

Later that year I secretly married Sharon Ellis. My mother drove us to Coeur d'Alene, Idaho, for the ceremony. There were two reason for the secrecy. After the blowup over Barbara ten months prior I was not about to share anything personal with Dad. It was also secret because Sharon was studying to be a Registered Nurse at Everett General Hospital. This Catholic nursing institution did not think it healthy for their students to enjoy a well-rounded college experience, and thus forbade any of them from marrying or other sort of fooling around. I did not inform my Dad of my impending marriage. The lingering anger over Barbara Bowman and the fact he was not a person I could have father-son talk with led to my silence on the subject. Asking Dad for advice on anything was like being given a well-defined road map with no detours allowed. I was of the advanced age of not needing maps—especially from my father.

I was still living at his house, as I could hardly walk with my back injuries, when my father found out somehow that I was married. I returned home one Friday evening when he summoned me to the living room where he was having a poker party with six of his friends. He coldly informed me that I was nineteen years old and married and to get out of his house by noon tomorrow. That I was financially destitute, broken physically and had no means of moving out of his house did not deter this edict, nor did the presence of his friends move him to warmth or generosity in his fatherly attitude about my future. The message was clear: Get out of my house now.

My message back to him was not nearly as calm or well structured. I informed him where he could put his blankety-blank house if it would fit in his blankety-blank ass, but as he was so full of himself, there probably was not room for anything else in that particular orifice. I don't remember what else I told him but nineteen years of frustration and anger came pouring out with the accompanying tears. I do know that my tirade was liberally sprinkled with "f" words. He did not blink or look up from his poker game as I yelled at him and stormed out the door. We spoke only briefly over the next ten years. That would occur when neither of us could avoid it. I never informed him of my graduation from college nor the birth of his grandkids when those celebratory events occurred. Did I mention the Stultz temper before? It is violent and cuts both ways, and pride goes before the fall.

I spent that night with my brother Richard, who had an apartment with his wife Carol in Lake Stevens. He was no happier to see me than I was to be at his house. I was able to contact Sharon the following day. I learned she had a couple hundred dollars saved up from working extra shifts at the hospital. We were fortunate to convince a nice older lady in Everett to rent us a furnished apartment within walking distance of the hospital and Everett Community College for $26 a month. I finished my associate of arts degree at Everett Community College, and Sharon received her nursing diploma within several months. We had many meals of beans and rice, and our ride was a 55 hp Honda motor bike. But like many young couples who discover independence and love, we managed.

My lawyer thought I was working for the other side in my lawsuit against the Fairbanks couple that caused my latest broken back, because I refused to act injured. He settled the case for $1,800. Sharon and I used this money to buy a used GMC V6 pickup, some camping gear, and two guns. I went to the lumberyard and bought enough lumber to build a camper on the back of our first real family vehicle. We had decided to move to Alaska.

Several days later we headed for Alaska with $900 in our pockets. That we had no jobs waiting for us at the end of the journey did not trouble either of us. I had been accepted into the University of Alaska Fairbanks for further study. Sharon had her RN degree and felt confident of acquiring a job upon reaching Fairbanks. I was in heaven and thought life could not get better as thoughts of being in Alaska swarmed though my mind.

Moving to Alaska

I HAVE ALWAYS BEEN A PROLIFIC READER. Our town librarian in Winlock told me I was the first kid she could remember who had read every book in the library. Zane Grey and Edgar Rice Burroughs were the authors I mostly hid under the covers and read with a flashlight after the evening's parental command of lights out, but any book or article on the building of the Alcan Highway or stories involving hunting or life in Alaska were high on the list as well. The Alcan was built to free Alaska from the dangers and expense of shipping supplies by boat from the Lower 48, and as a response to Japanese aggression on the Alaskan Peninsula during World War II. The huge project once employed more than 10,000 men. It was completed in 1949 and was comprised of a rough gravel road 1,422 miles long from Dawson Creek, British Columbia, to Delta Junction, Alaska. More important to me, however, was that bear, wolves, moose and caribou could be seen from this engineering marvel.

I could not sleep the night before our departure from Everett. Finally, getting Sharon rousted out of bed and consuming a breakfast of donuts and cold coffee, we were on the road north by 4:30 a.m. The American Customs at Blaine, Washington, consisted of a few question of where we were headed, how long we intended to stay in Canada and our final destination.

Canadian Customs Agents were not nearly as friendly. After examining our drivers' licenses and counting the money we had on our persons the Canadians made us pull over and searched the pickup. The agents were particularly curious about the firearms—a Winchester Model 12-gauge shotgun, a Remington 7mm Magnum and a .357 Magnum pistol. They wrote down the weapons' serial numbers, and sealed the rifle and shotgun in locked gun cases. They firmly admonished us to not unlock the seals for any reason. After learning our destination and length of stay in Canada, they grudgingly let us through the border crossing. Sharon and I both commented on how grumpy and borderline hostile these agents were as we headed north to Dawson Creek, British Columbia.

The trip to Dawson passed through some beautiful country, but was uneventful except the first night when our small two-man tent collapsed in the middle of a thunderstorm. We decided to leave it collapsed instead of resetting it, because we did not want to get wet. Being amateurs at this camping business we did not realize that our bodily contact with the tent material would draw the moisture inside by osmosis. In the morning everything was wet and a goodly amount of time was spent semi-drying sleeping bags and clothes. Full drying would have to wait for a laundromat in Dawson City. Sharon did make some wifely comments about my camping abilities, but I chose to attribute that remark to her not getting much sleep and not because of my manly outdoorsmanship.

We spent an uneventful night in a campground in Dawson City the following night. In the morning our GMC pickup would barely start and when it did was so rough it would not idle. Not really familiar with automotive repairs at this time but knowing that the engine needed air, spark and gas, I opened the hood and examined the fuel lines and sparkplug wires. Fuel was running fine out of the carburetor, but I did find a chaffed sparkplug wire that was shorting out the electrical system.

We found an automotive parts store and bought both new sparkplug wires as well as new plugs. The clerk refused to give us correct change and counted American dollars the same as Canadian currency. He told us that Canadian money was as good as America's even though there was a plus 12 percent value to American money at this time. This was the second time this had happened on our journey. The first was at a gas station the preceding day.

Thus we learned another lesson: we needed to change currency at a bank, as the Canadian clerks we had met so far were somewhat impolite about American money. I repaired the truck while Sharon dried and cleaned clothes. We then found a bank and exchanged $300 of our precious money supply into Canadian currency. It was past noon before we hit the first milepost on the Alcan Highway.

The first hundred miles of the Alcan were paved at this time so the travel was easy. I questioned the waitress at lunch about a good place to fish. She informed me of a gravel road ten miles ahead that ran to a lake with lots of fish in it where the locals went. We located the lake about an hour later. It was a resort of sorts that contained two dilapidated single-room log cabins for rent and a boat half full of water. The cost of a cabin for the night and a boat for the rest of the day was $25 Canadian. We discussed briefly and hotly whether we should spend our limited funds. Sharon did not want to spend the money. I wanted to fish. As my friend Eddie Cruse use to say, "Any time spent fishing makes the day perfect."

Reluctantly she counted out the money to the proprietor, and we took our sleeping and foodstuff into the cleanest-looking of the log cabins. I went back outside to empty the boat of water and asked the proprietor what the fish were biting. I got a terse, "If you don't know how to fish, it ain't my job to teach you." For the first time I noticed this guy not only acted hostile, but he looked funny as well. His right eye was off-color from his left and the side of his head was concave, like someone had hit him with a log. It may have been my imagination, but it seemed to me that he was looking at Sharon way too lasciviously.

We got in the boat and as I rowed away from the dock, I could see thousands of Kootney trout swimming under the boat. Kootney trout are landlocked silver salmon that could not return to the ocean to grow larger. I had never seen so many fish in my life, but no matter what I tried, I did not get a solitary bite. After hours of building frustration, Sharon's complaints, and a hundred mosquito bites, I admitted defeat and headed to shore. So much for Eddie Cruse's intelligence.

While cooking dinner we discussed our situation. We were about sixteen miles off the Alcan Highway on a single lane primitive gravel and dirt road. No one but the owner knew where we were. The proprietor gave us both the creeps, and no one else had showed up at the lake to fish. I went out to the truck and brought in the .357 pistol and loaded it. Our first night in a log cabin was not romantic. I stayed up all night with one hand on my weapon, straining to hear every imaginary sound. We left before daylight in the morning, reflecting that these Canadians were a strange lot.

That day we ran out of pavement on the Alcan and saw why everyone told us to carry spare tires. The washboards and holes in the gravel made going more than 40 mph a physical torture that soon had me putting on my back brace. The freight trucks were moving at more than 60 mph and spraying our truck windshield with gravel and rocks. The first of many cracks appeared on our windshield that first afternoon of unpaved road. At about 4:30 p.m. we decided we had taken all the physical torture we could stand for one day, and turned off the road just beyond a bridge over a creek.

We followed a small dirt road downhill to a flat spot by the creek that showed the remains of a campfire. We slowly set up camp. It looked like a great place to escape from the dust and physical trauma of the Alcan. The evergreens were nicely spread out, providing a pleasant green canopy for the midsize shallow stream gurgling underneath their boughs. I set up our small tent while Sharon was trying to clean some of the dust out of our food stores and sleeping bags when we heard several rifle shots. About an hour later, after enjoying a dinner of corn beef hash potatoes, fried eggs and a drink of Yukon Jack, a Royal Canadian Mounted Police vehicle drove up to our campsite. The young police officer got out and started imperiously questioning us on how long we had been here, what weapons we had, when we last shot them and at what.

I explained to the officer that I had a 7mm rifle, 12-gauge shotgun and .357 Magnum pistol. He demanded to see them. My Stultz ire immediately shot through me, and I started to tell him he could go to hell until he developed some manners, but luckily I subdued these spiking emotions, remembering that I was in a country of very unfriendly folks. I slowly finished my drink while staring at the officer before walking over to our pickup and taking out the .357 Magnum pistol.

He examined the seal and lock on the rifle cases minutely for about two minutes before taking the rifle and shotgun out of their sealed cases. The Mountie then opened the action, looked in the magazines and smelled the barrels before handing them back. He then demanded to know the last time they were fired. I said about four days ago abruptly, mimicking his own bad attitude.

He ordered us to stay by the fire and not move while he searched all around our campsite for spent ammunition cases. After about twenty minutes of fruitless searching he came back and demanded to know why we shot at a car crossing the bridge an hour ago, striking it twice in the driver's door.

This guy was a real jerk, not at all like the Sergeant Preston I had listened to so reverently on the radio when growing up. I replied snottily that he must not know much about firearms or he would know that if I had shot a vehicle crossing the bridge from here: 1) The shotgun would not carry that far; 2) The .357 would not have penetrated the door, and would still be in the metal, if he bothered to look; 3) The 7mm Magnum would have gone completely through the door, killing the driver. Besides that, the rifle and shotgun were still sealed prior to him opening them.

We were both shaking with anger by this time, and stood there, staring at each other with clenched jaws, breathing through our noses like bulls ready to charge. Both of us realized this interview had gone downhill fast. I was no longer in danger of visiting a Canadian jail for the rifle fire, but was in imminent danger of doing so because of the RCMP's unprofessional conduct and my unreasonable reaction to it. It was clearly evident that none of my firearms had been used, but I had been provoked to the point that events were about to get out of control. My Stultz temper and the offensive RCMP interrogation were on a collision course.

Luckily for me, the officer was better trained than I was. He apologized, I apologized, and he explained that two elderly people from California had stopped on the bridge to take pictures of the creek when two shots rang out, hitting their vehicle. They saw our camp below them and figured we had shot. I told the officer that we heard two shots that sounded like they came from a rifle about five minutes after our arrival. I also told him that the shots sounded like they came from the other side of the creek by the pullout on that side.

A quizzical look came over his face, and I wondered if he had considered which way the vehicle was facing and the angle of the bullets when it hit the car. After ten minutes of increasingly pleasant conversation, he left, wishing us a safe and pleasant journey up the Alcan.

Up until this time, most of the Canadians we met on the trip were greedy, suspicious or unfriendly. This was not the case with the majority of the people we interacted with on the remainder of our time there, or on subsequent trips in Canada. For the most part, we found Canadians to be very friendly and helpful people. But at the present moment, we considered ourselves traveling through a hostile foreign country.

Sharon and I sat by our small fire discussing the preceding events as I sipped on another drink of Yukon Jack. Yukon Jack is a blended sweet whiskey much like Southern Comfort. A liquor store clerk had recommended Yukon Jack to me earlier in Dawson Creek. Sharon was berating me for my behavior, telling me she would have been stranded here in the Canadian wilderness if I had been hauled into jail because of my stupid temper. She was right of course, but I was not about to admit it. Seeing this argument was not going any better than my interaction with the RCMP officer, and knowing both of us were weary from the trip, I told her I was going fishing. She could either come with me or lock herself in the truck if a bear wandered into camp. I knew she would not come with me, but I figured both of us could use psychological warfare.

I had never bought a fishing or hunting license in Washington State, so saw no need to buy one here. Because I did not have a fishing license for Canada, I did not want to be seen from the road, so I walked about a half mile down the creek before coming to a place where the creek divided into three branches. I cast a bobber with a black fly attached to it into a deep hole bordered by thick brush. The black gnat had not traveled ten feet in the slow-moving current dotted with emerging insects before it was abruptly jerked underwater by an 18-inch grayling eating the fly. This was the first grayling trout I had ever caught. I marveled at its sparking deep blue-green body and large dorsal fin as I released it. I spent the next several hours catching and releasing many graylings before the sun slid behind a distant mountain and clouds of mosquitoes drove me back to camp. Eddie Cruse was right after all. Fishing did make a bad day better.

Being alone with nature, whether just walking or hunting and fishing, always has a calming effect on me. By the time the softening shadows and I reached camp, I found Sharon asleep in the cab of the truck with the doors locked. I was a dutiful husband, ready to admit the errors of my ways and ask forgiveness from my better half. We spent the rest of the night cuddled up in the tent in one sleeping bag. I may have a temper, but I am not stupid.

We decided the next morning to maximize our travel time and get off the Alcan as quickly as possible. It had gone from an imaginary picturesque journey through God's Land in my mind, to a journey on a road from hell. The scenery was beyond description with the lakes, rivers and mountain we passed calling to my soul for exploration, but the road and my wife's constant complaints about it reminded me of the reality of the bone-jarring and dusty bug-filled ordeal.

We saw our first wolf as we traveled along the Tetsa River one evening beyond the town of Fort Johns. It was grey and white and stood in the middle of the gravel road watching us for several seconds before leisurely departing into the brush along the river. I will never forget that moment of slamming on the brakes, coming to a stop in the middle of the road in a cloud of dust, watching this superb creature. The wonders of this wilderness and my being in it overrode the misery of the highway for several hours. In later years I would have wolves surround my hunting camps in the Alaskan wilderness twice, and entertain me with their mournful songs. However, this first encounter had the most lasting and profound effect on me. It was meeting a dream face to face.

We saw lots of moose alongside or crossing the Alcan. They seemed very ungainly with their long-legged prancing stride. Most of the bull moose we viewed were off the side of the road feeding in ponds. I remember wondering how one person could pack out the meat of such a huge creature. Little did I know that Canadian moose were much smaller than their northern cousins, who would strain every muscle in my body to their absolute limits in later years.

We saw several black bears move quickly across the Alcan in front of our dust laden truck, but did not encounter a grizzly until we were traversing a mountain prior to reaching Muncho Lake. It was on a hillside, about a quarter mile off the road feeding on berries. The sight of it evoked the same reactions in me as the wolf had. We sat watching it for about thirty minutes before the twilight became too dark to see clearly. To this day, fifty some years later, the wolf and grizzly remain my favorite animals of the wilderness. They continue to exemplify the eternal yearning in my soul for places far from human habitat and roads occupied by these wild creatures.

The Alcan of 1963 does not resemble the current highway. The stops for gas, food and repairs were peopled with buildings and residences far more rustic than today. There were also far fewer of them, but you were never beyond several hours of travel for help. The Alcan is paved now, and the people driving it are not weary of the ruts, holes and washboards jarring their vehicles into oblivion. This makes me sad somehow, as if something of this mystic avenue through a land of wonder and dreams is being missed by modern travelers. I have made thirteen trips up and down the Alcan. The thought of driving the now-paved surface is no longer enticing. Somehow the adventure of it is gone with the hardships of past history.

Passing through Canadian and American customs at the Alaska border was anticlimactic. The Canadians checked the seals on the weapons and little else. The Americans asked what we had bought in Canada and where we were headed. The world went silent as we drove the now-paved highway toward Tok, Alaska. The rough road had knocked the truck's front end out of alignment and defeated the shocks making the vehicle difficult to steer. We reached the seemingly supersonic speed of 65 mph when we hit our first frost heave in the pavement.

I was taken by complete surprise when the pavement suddenly disappeared beneath our wheels by a abrupt dip in the road. The truck lost all contact with the highway while Sharon and I, along with maps, coffee cups, food and seemingly thirty pounds of dust, floated weightlessly before a dramatic reconnection with earth. The truck swerved violently upon hitting the highway surface again. I thought we were crashing off the road as I fought the steering wheel for control.

Stopping the GMC after regaining command of the vehicle, I pulled over to the side of the highway where we cleaned up the mess in the cab and caught our breaths. We had met our first infamous arctic frost heave and survived. A frost heave is caused by the ground underneath the highway melting, and the asphalt sinking along with it. We discussed the near disaster and decided to continue to drive to Tok, the Alaskan town nearest to the Canadian border, where we would celebrate conquering the Alcan with a night in a motel, shower and a meal cooked by someone else.

Tok, Alaska, was a small crossroad community where the Alcan continued to its final termination at Fairbanks, and the Glenn Highway started southwest to Glennallen and Anchorage. Most importantly, it contained several more refined garages that could change our oil and filter, realign the truck's front end, and replace the front shocks.

Not even the iron-colored and scented water at the motel could detract from the bliss of standing under a hot stream of water, washing the week's accumulation of grime and dirt from our bodies. A dinner of buffalo steak and potatoes, augmented with a glass of wine, put the finishing touches to our celebration. I don't think either of our heads hit the pillow before we were sound asleep.

The following morning, after a breakfast of sourdough pancakes and eggs, we took the GMC into the adjoining garage for repairs. It cost far more than we anticipated. Our funds were now approaching only $300, so we discussed not going to Anchorage as planned to meet Sharon's father, but heading directly to Fairbanks where she could find a job as an RN.

We finally agreed on Anchorage, because Sharon had not seen her father in years. We also decided to sell our trusty little Honda trail bike upon arrival in Anchorage to supplement our fast-disappearing cash. The trip down the Glenn Highway was an uneventful, pleasant drive. We passed lakes that called out to be fished, saw a lot of moose in shallow ponds beside the highway feeding leisurely on succulent vegetation on the water's bottom, and our first white Dall sheep gracing the majestic snowcapped mountains bordering the Matanuska River. The Matanuska Valley was spectacular with its mountains, glacier and verdant farms. We stopped in Palmer to buy produce grown locally before continuing to Anchorage.

Sharon had telephoned her father from Tok. I did not know what to expect from him, as I had heard stories of his violent temper. My first meeting with Sharon's mother in Everett, Washington, had not gone well. We had taken an immediate dislike to each other that had not diminished with our final visit prior to our departure for Alaska. At our first meeting, when Sharon and I were dating, she looked at me with disdain through faded blue eyes and told Sharon, with a sneer on her face, to remember that, "Blood is thicker than water." She was not invited to our wedding, either.

I wondered, as we pulled up into Dave and Carol's driveway in Anchorage, if I was up to a fight. Mean Dave looked the mean part with cruel grey eyes and a mouth that only pretended to smile. He was tall for his age and seemed to weigh about 180 pounds, all of it lean muscle. Carol was much younger than Dave's sixty-one years, with dark blond hair, and was a little on the buxom side. I never asked how much younger she was, as Dave did not seem the kind of guy you asked this kind of question. The house was a four-bedroom, two-bath, and neatly kept in a nice middle-class subdivision.

Dave handed me a cold beer after introductions were made, and then he led me out to the backyard patio where the male sizing-up ritual commenced. He seemed to like that I did not back down in this process, so we proceeded to drink a second beer. We discussed my plans in Alaska as well as the normal family chatter. Dave did not hunt or fish, but told me to buy a license if I intended to do so, as the game wardens were pretty vigilant in the state. He discussed his background in construction; he worked seasonally on pipeline welding jobs. I seem to remember Dave saying he started welding early in the Oklahoma oil fields and worked his way west, then up to Alaska.

We stayed four enjoyable days with them. Dave taught me how to cook a good steak by searing the outside, trapping the juices inside, and how to tell if the oil was hot enough to cook fish properly. The oil lesson was easy. You just threw a sulfur match in the oil, and it lit automatically when the oil was hot enough. This was before the days of cholesterol and good and bad fats. Vegetable oil was unheard of and everyone used Wesson lard. I used the cooking lessons Dave provided until broiling and barbeque became popular. We made $500 selling our motor bike to a friend of Dave's, and decided to drive up the Denali highway after leaving Anchorage and before heading on up to Fairbanks. Back then, the Parks Highway connecting Fairbanks and Anchorage was not yet built, so we backtracked to Glennallen and then turned north on the Richardson up to Paxon, before leaving the Richardson and turning onto the Denali Highway. On the way out of Anchorage we stopped at a sporting goods store in Eagle River where I purchased a resident hunting and fishing license. I had intended to buy non-resident licenses until I added up the cost of the licenses and caribou tag. It was far more than we could afford, so I lied and told the clerk I had lived in the state for a year, and that Sharon was a nurse in Fairbanks while I attended the university there. Obeying fish and game laws was never a priority in our family or in the crowd I grew up around.

We had an early dinner at the Paxon Lodge where I again questioned our waitress for good fishing spots along the Denali. She informed me that caribou season had started along the Denali, and fish could be caught in any of the lakes or streams crossing the road. We proceeded up the Denali to Butcher's Lodge, about thirty-five miles. The road was gravel like the Alcan, but in much better shape. The small gravel lot outside the inn was crowded with pickup trucks and trailers. I somehow managed to hit Butcher's gas pump, knocking it off its foundation, trying to back into a small parking spot.

The owner came charging out of the lodge with oaths of profanity as I stood surveying the damage. Jim (I seem to remember that was his first name) proceeded to call me some uncomplimentary names while spraying spittle on my face shouting at me. Butcher was a big, well-built, no-nonsense man in his late forties or early fifties. I apologized for the tenth time, and Jim's tirade slowed as he realized I was just a stupid college kid. Somehow the fact that the pump was not leaking gas and there was no apparent damage to it, coupled with my honest embarrassment, stopped the invectives completely as I helped him replace the pump on its small concrete stand. Butcher invited us into the Lodge for dinner, saying there would be no cost for backing into the pump.

Most of the tables were taken up with hunters. We ordered a hamburger, even though we had just eaten at Paxon, to cover some of our embarrassment. Sharon had not said a word to me but just stared at me with that wifely expression that meant, "What kind of cretin have I married?" in wife talk. It became apparent, as I listened to the hunters sitting around us, that Butcher was driving them around in some sort of four-wheel-drive vehicle while they shot caribou off the back. They had each killed a caribou that day, and were looking forward to hunting again tomorrow.

Sharon, knowing how much I wanted to shoot a caribou, looked at me and said, with an emphatic no, we could not afford a guide. Women! They really know how to spoil a guy's fun. However, on second reflection, remembering some snuggling in warm sleeping bags, I thought that perhaps I was being unjust.

After paying for our meal, we continued on the Denali for another twenty miles or so until we came across a stream crossing the road with a good camping spot near it. Figuring this was near enough to where Butcher's hunters were getting their caribou, I pulled over and set up camp. There was firewood nearby from past campers so I gathered it all up and lit a fire. It was one of those magical moments where time seems to stand still, and you just completely relax and enjoy your place in the universe. I'm sure everyone has experienced this deep feeling of calm and of being home. This is what was flowing over and into me at this moment, even though I had never been on the Denali Highway before in my life. This is the life I had sought ever since viewing Baldy many years before.

My wife was not so happy. She complained of the bugs, the rocks under her sleeping bag, and the fact that there were bears in the area. I pointed out that the rocks were not that big, the bugs were far fewer than in Canada, and we had not seen a bear since the Yukon Territories. I should have kept my mouth shut. It was not a night of cuddling in one sleeping bag.

The morning was clear and crisp, as it was late into August. I relit the fire and made coffee. Getting out my Trapper Nelson pack board and Remington 7mm, I headed upstream to look for caribou. Sharon was still in the tent, loudly ignoring the fact that I existed. I was rapidly learning, in my young married life, how women can make the world colder without saying a word.

Soon thoughts of Sharon, the university or the need of employment fled me completely. I am most at home by myself, surrounded by thousands of miles of virgin land. I have never needed the company of others, a complaint that all of my wives in the coming years would expound on to me, neighbors and God. I enjoyed others when visiting or entertaining, but was most content when by myself, with territory around me I had not yet explored.

Throughout the day this section of Denali revealed itself to be one of low rolling hills blanketed with scrub spruce about twenty feet tall, brownish green tundra that was deceptively hard to walk across, and smelly muskeg swamp that was deeper than my boots. I saw my first grizzly track on a muddy trail that Jim Butcher's off-road vehicle might have made. It was a huge track that made every black bear paw print I had ever seen puny by comparison. Most people I would later guide or take into the Alaska bush fishing were afraid of bears. I have never been afraid of them, even when they were charging me or chomping on my flesh. I felt a kindred spirit with bears and wolves since first becoming aware of their existence. We were predator brothers.

I followed the grizzly tracks with a sense of excitement for about an hour before I finally lost sight of it, as the tracks disappeared into the soft tundra. Looking around, I discovered I only had a general sense of where the highway and camp were. I did not have a compass and would not have used it if I had. I was so engrossed in my adventure I was not keeping track of where I was going. I did not worry as I have a compass built into my mind that usually points me where I wanted to go, and started heading in the direction of where I felt camp should be.

I had seen numerous caribou tracks throughout the morning, but was so intent on the grizzly I had not followed them. Suddenly about 200 yards ahead of me, a small group of three caribou appeared. They took off as they spotted me, disappearing over a small hill. I debated following them but decided instead to continuing to head in the direction of camp. All of my ungulate hunting experience to this time had been with the deer of Western Washington. I did not know that the caribou would probably have stopped after they crested the hill, and circled around to get a scent of me.

As I continued on, I heard Butcher's vehicle off to my right. I stopped on a small hill with a clear view of the surrounding valley and ate some blueberries. I heard several shots about 500 yards away. About this time, I saw dust from a vehicle traveling the Denali about six miles away, and knew I was headed in the right direction. Continuing on, I was overtaken by Butcher and his hunters with three dead caribou in their vehicle. They stopped, and I had a drink of their coffee as we discussed the day. They never asked if I was lost, needed help or wanted a ride back to my camp. I never approached the subjects because I wasn't and did not want help or a ride. I was perfectly happy enjoying a brief Moment with fellow outdoorsmen. Years later I would read in the Fairbanks newspaper that an air generator blew up in Butcher's face, badly wounding him. He would never recover, and would be forced to sell the beloved lodge he had built up slowly over the hard years.

But this was a happier day, and I waved goodbye and thanked them for the coffee as they departed. I continued on until I spotted a single caribou in the middle of a muddy swamp. I snuck within 200 yards before putting a single shot though its heart. It dropped dead immediately.

Congratulating myself on a clean kill, I started out into the swamp to retrieve my prize. Within three steps I began to wonder if I had made a mistake killing an animal in the swamp. Within ten steps, I knew for sure I had made a serious mistake. This slimy, smelly, dark-colored wet mud that the caribou traversed with ease was a quagmire to me. It was clutching at my boots, spilling me on my face, and making every step a struggle. It resisted my efforts as I fought toward the dead caribou. I was pleased that I had been smart enough to leave my rifle and gear on firm tundra.

By the time I reached the dead animal I was exhausted, and the work had not even begun. I considered my options of field dressing it here, quartering it and carrying the meat on my pack board as I originally intended, or dragging it through the sticky slime to shore. Knowing that my normal weight had been problematic and that I was a muddy smelly mess, I was really concerned about cutting up the animal in the middle of the swamp and exposing the raw meat to this smelly gunk contaminating it, so I started a two-hour ordeal of dragging the carcass back to the firmer tundra to complete the field dressing.

I later experienced some real ordeals hauling moose, sheep, goat and bears back to camp, but this was the worst experience of my entire Alaskan hunting life. I never again, ever, shot or let any of my hunters shoot a big game animal in a swamp or lake. It was one of those teachable moments that got through my thick Stultz skull and lasted forever. It was that miserable.

It was a journey of pure perseverance. I would pull the caribou two feet, loosen my boots from the mud's suction, take two steps backwards, wipe the swarm of feeding mosquitoes off my face, and pull again. I finally took my boots and socks off and tied them to the backboard. It was easier to kneel down, getting a bigger surface on the mud to lessen the sinking, than try to stand.

I don't remember how long I lay on the tundra recovering from the ordeal upon reaching dry land before dressing out the caribou and tying it to my pack board, but twilight had arrived and the temperature was dropping as fast as my energy level before I took my first stumbling steps toward camp. The sweat on my body finished soaking my clothing that was not already saturated by water and mud, and now began to chill me. My back was telling me it had had enough of this foolishness, and my legs were cramping from the lack of drinking water. I briefly considered the possibility of a grizzly bear smelling the dead animal on my back and tracking me down for a meal. I thought how a bear would have difficulty telling me apart from the dead caribou, if it even cared. I did reload my rifle and put a cartridge into the firing chamber just in case, but I was too damn tired to give much consideration to anything other than reaching camp. I did not remember any of the hunting stories about Alaska that so entertained me in my youth mentioning how difficult the adventure could be. I promised myself on the excruciating trip back to camp to be more careful and smart on my next hunting trip.

Thinking of the mood Sharon was in when I left early that morning, I was not looking forward to any more of my wife's histrionics. I just wanted to get out of these clothes, unload the weight from my back and get cleaned up. I was sure my long absence would have had further deteriorated her mental attitude. I could have not been more surprised when she ran up to me and gave me a big hug and kiss as I neared the burning fire of camp, despite all the grime and blood with which I was covered. She did not complain, helping me wash the caribou and myself off in the stream, and even brought me a stiff drink of Yukon Jack as I put on dry clothes. We cuddled in one sleeping bag that night. I knew then that no man will really understand women.

My first big game hunt was successful, and I learned a lot about the state to which I had migrated. I had received many lasting lessons of what not to do in the future while hunting the wild bounty of this enormous state that I would hereafter call home.

First Year in Alaska

The University Alaska, Fairbanks is about four miles northwest of Fairbanks in the small town of College, situated on top of a series of rolling hills. We were assigned to the married students' quarters, a new dorm with multiple floors. Each apartment consisted of one bedroom, kitchen, small living room and a study. It was very nice, and we quickly made ourselves at home. The next day we rented a frozen storage locker in Fairbanks to store the meat. Within a week Sharon started working as an Emergency Room nurse at St. Joseph's Hospital in Fairbanks.

St. Joseph's was run by Catholic nuns, as was the hospital where Sharon had done her training, so she fit right in. I had more trouble at the university, as I had always relied on my athletic skills in school and had no real experience in how to study. That first year I did play on the university basketball team just to prove my doctors wrong, and earned a varsity letter. I also eventually did learn to study effectively, and even to like the process.

There is really no way to prepare for an Alaskan interior winter. You have to live through it to learn how to cope. The shock of living in minus fifty degree temperatures, driving square tires frozen flat on the bottom by the cold, the absence of daylight, and the ever-present ice fog took a lot of adjusting to before they became the norm. Our first Thanksgiving Day there saw the temperature drop from a chilly ten above zero to a downright frigid minus forty-five. Our truck would not start and had to be towed to a service station to have an engine circulation heater installed. This device hooked up to the vehicle's water system, heating the water and circulating it throughout the engine when plugged in to an electrical outlet. We learned the value of keeping the truck plugged in twenty-four hours a day, when going out visiting or shopping, or just parked at our dorm. Ice fog, formed by an inversion of cold air which keeps the warmer emissions of civilization trapped close to the ground, made visibility severely limited at times. I can remember traveling with the university's basketball team to play in Las Vegas and walking around in shirt sleeves when the temperature was right around freezing, feeling like it was almost summer.

That first winter I found myself fascinated by reading journals of Alaskan old-timers stored in the university's library. I spent hundreds of hours deciphering hand-written penciled accounts of the trials and tribulations of living in the frozen North while searching for gold or just exploring. I kept running across a place called Jumpoff used by dog-sledding miners in the 1890s as a jumping-off place for the booming Alaskan gold fields of that time. I told myself I would try to look up this place in the spring when things warmed up. I was curious about the various descriptions of the mushers' dog-sled journeys in and out of Jumpoff.

Spring finally arrived. Sharon and I sadly replaced our ailing GMC. It had never recovered from the trip up the Alcan and had been a struggle to keep it running over the winter, so we traded it for a brand-new 1964 Chevrolet pickup. It cost us $1,900 for the new ride, but we decided the investment was worth not walking from some remote location.

We both had cabin fever by the time light finally again reigned in the far north, and we badly needed some extended time outdoors. I especially wanted to locate Jumpoff, so we decided to head up the Steese Highway to Circle City, one hundred and sixty miles northeast of Fairbanks, where it was supposed to be located between Central City and Circle City on a waterway called Crooked Creek.

The twelve-mile drive from Fairbank to Fox was paved and made pleasant driving on the balmy fifty-degree day. Outside of Fox the road turned to gravel, and we bumped our way up to Cleary Summit in our new ride. At Cleary we met a construction crew working on the road. We stopped while they told us the road was soft from breakup and advised us not to go further. I listened as attentively as any Stultz, and then, after thanking them, we continued on our journey to Circle.

Within ten minutes our brand new, shiny, white pickup was stuck in mud over its wheels. I swallowed my pride and hiked back through the mess to beg a tow from the construction company. After our rescue by a bulldozer, and many smirks from road workers, we headed back to the university to await firmer road conditions. Breakup is not a time to be traveling on gravel roads in the North Country. As I leaned later, it was not a time to be landing an airplane on gravel runways either.

Later that week while in the Student Center, relaxing after a class and drinking a cup of coffee, I read a notice stating a Fish and Game representative would be on the campus next weekend interviewing students who would like to work the summer for them. There was a contact number listed to make an appointment if you were interested. I wrote down the number and called it when I got home.

Don Roberts, the Regional Manager for the Protection Division of Fish and Game, conducted the interview. Don was responsible for enforcing Fish and Game Regulations from the Alaska Range north to the Bering Sea. This is a huge area geographically. Most people don't know that if you divided Alaska in half, it would make Texas the third largest state. Alaska also contains two-thirds of the coastline of the entire United States. The few roads and remoteness of the villages and towns made Don's job extremely difficult. He asked me questions about my work history; where I was born; did I hunt and fish; was I married, and a whole host of other questions. We talked for about an hour. Don shook my hand at the end of the interview and said I was hired and would receive further information in the mail in several weeks.

I told Sharon that Fish and Game had hired me for the summer when she got home from work. We went out to dinner to celebrate where I immensely enjoyed my first lobster dinner. During dinner she informed me that a friend of hers at the hospital and her husband had driven up to Circle City. The road was rough but passable. We decided to give it a second try that weekend.

Passable is an elastic word. Used in conjunction with the condition of a road, a person would have to take into consideration the familiarity of the one driving it and what they were driving, neither of which I knew to consider when hearing this news. My experience in driving northern roads at this time consisted of driving the Alcan once and one winter driving on the hard frozen pavement in the Fairbanks area. I was also driving a two wheel-drive pickup. In a couple years' time, I would call the Steese passable as well, but by then I would be driving a Toyota Land Cruiser with four wheel-drive and a winch on the front.

We made the trip to Circle, but the journey was neither comfortable nor easy. The rocky, narrow dirt road was very soft and deeply rutted, and my shoulders were knotted in forty miles. There was also the occasional glacier running across the road from spring melt off. This solid sheet of ice was always slanted downslope, toward a drop-off at the edge of the road. At first I tried to creep across these ice fields, only to have the truck start to slide downhill and off the road. Finally, with pounding heart, I learned to gun the engine to race across the ice so we could safely reach the other side. It was hard on the pickup and occupants, but preferable to having the vehicle rolling upside-down off the side of the road.

At the town of Central we stopped for gas at the only gas station and store combination in this small community. We went inside and bought some coffee and talked to the owner, whose first name was Roy. We talked about the road condition and some other stuff before I asked him if he knew where Jumpoff was located. I could have dropped dead when he said that he should know where it was, as he owned it. I told him I had read about it in so many journals written by old timers in the University of Alaska archives that I really wanted to see it. He drew me a map with approximate mileage, stating it was the only narrow muddy path off the road in that area to the cabin and Crooked Creek. He strongly cautioned us not to attempt the drive down the path, as the ground was soft and would swallow our pickup. He did not mention the swarms of mosquitoes biting you every step of the way.

We found the track after much searching, and parked the pickup as far off the road as we dared. Sharon and I walked the mile to the cabin with the irritating company of hundreds of bloodthirsty mosquitos. Being cheechako (newcomers to Alaska) we had not yet adjusted to these pesky insects. The cabin was located on a small hill overlooking Crooked Creek. The well-weathered logs, boards and roof looked like they would fall down in a strong wind. We went inside this rustic cabin and were surprised at how well the interior was preserved, compared to the outside. It was about fifteen feet wide and twenty-five feet deep. Obviously, someone had been living in it in the not-too-distant past. Looking out the dirty glass window you could see that Crooked Creek was high and discolored from the spring snow runoff. The two single beds had springs and mattresses, but I did think I wanted to sleep on them. I wondered how the mushers crowed into this small area in years past. Sharon and I discussed the cabin and location during the rest of the drive from Jumpoff to Circle City. Both of us had fallen in love with it. On our return to Fairbank we decided to stop and see Roy again and ask if he would sell it to us.

Circle City is a small Athabaskan Indian village located on the banks of the Yukon River, about 160 miles northeast of Fairbanks. It was originally named Circle by the prospectors who founded the town during the discovery of gold on nearby Birch Creek in 1893. They thought the city rested on the Arctic Circle, hence the name. The Arctic Circle is really another fifty miles to the north. At the pinnacle of its short-lived prominence this small village was a city boasting seven hundred residents. According to Wikipedia it contained a store, a couple of dance halls, library, school, opera house, post office and an Episcopal church. At the time we first visited Circle in 1965 it was much smaller, and contained a few cabins along the river, a trading post/bar, a single-room grade school, and a small electric company whose total employment was one. We pulled up to the sign at the end of the road, taking the obligatory photo of the end of the road sign, and looked at the Yukon River.

The Yukon was high and muddy. A couple of Native men were working on their flat-bottom river boats along the bank. We walked to the trading post and talked to the owner, and had a beer in the bar. The owner's wife served us the beer in a small room off the back of the trading post. Circle was one of the few small Indian villages that allowed alcohol in the bush of Alaska. The room contained a small bar with five stools. It was about seven feet wide and ten feet long, separated from the store by a wall and door. The bar area was very clean. They sold some of the major whiskey brands and several varieties of beer. Sharon and I enjoyed a Miller's beer, relaxing from the rough journey as we talked to the bartender.

Making small talk, we discovered that a number of black bears were causing some excitement in the village by raiding the community dump. A gravel runway dissected the white one-room school house from the rest of the village. While we were talking, a small single-engine green and white airplane landed. An older couple got out and walked into the trading post. I was envious of their having an airplane and being able to avoid the punishing road we had just traveled.

We stopped at the Circle garbage dump on our way back down the Steese to Fairbanks. There were several pickups containing Native men around the dump, probably waiting for a black bear to show up, but there were no bears visible. Bears in garbage dumps are a problem throughout Alaska. The garbage dump becomes the local grocery store for some of these animals. They don't have to work hard to eat, and these dumps become their daily cafe.

On our way back to Central, I stopped our truck in the middle of the one-lane bridge over Birch Creek, and looked at the fairly large waterway.

I was wondering where it started and ended when my impatient wife made me get back in the pickup, afraid someone would come from the other direction. I thought this was a very small possibility as we had passed only two trucks on our 160-mile journey, but I had learned the hard way not to argue with her unless the topic was more important than stopping in the middle of a bridge.

Little did I know that I would gain intimate knowledge of Birch Creek from its headwaters on Eagle Summit to this very bridge. Years later, Don Roberts and I would haul a canoe over the tundra to the headwater of Birch Creek and float down it to where Crooked Creek entered. We would then head up Crooked Creek to Jumpoff, where we had stashed a vehicle. It was a great three-day journey through pristine untraveled country. We saw moose, waterfowl, beavers, ptarmigan and several black bears. Even when we hit rough water that swamped the canoe and caused us to swim to shore we had a great time. Getting the canoe back to shore and salvaging as much of our equipment and supplies as possible did not dampen our spirits. We just hung all our wet clothes and sleeping bags on the brush, put up the tent and took a nap while the warm sun dried our clothing.

Driving off the bridge and down to Central, Sharon and I again filled our vehicle's gas tank, and asked the owner if he was willing to sell Jumpoff to us. He looked at us like we were crazy and asked why we wanted it. I explained my lifelong dream of owning a cabin in the Alaskan bush and that Jumpoff fit that vision perfectly. I could have fallen over when he told me he would sell it for $500 cash. He explained that the property was five acres total and had been surveyed and titled by the US Government. He further explained that the only reason he would consider selling it is that the State of Alaska was talking about putting in a campground next to it.

We agreed to purchase it for the asking price despite the news about a campground, and told him we would bring the cash up after Sharon's next paycheck. We shook hands to cement the deal. At this time and place in Alaska shaking hands cemented an agreement much more solidly than any lawyer and notary-stamped legal document. A man lived by his word in the Alaskan bush. If he ever failed to live up to the agreement, he was never to be trusted again. This was my kind of country. Even though I was wet behind the ears and knew little about surviving Alaska's weather and wildlife, I felt for the first time in my life that I belonged somewhere.

Thus we became the legal owners of a piece of Alaskan history. I, along with many friends and family, had countless adventures originating at Jumpoff and up and down the banks of Crooked and Birch creeks until years later when I sold it to my good friend, Dr. Glenn Straatsma, to finance my first airplane.

Jumpoff cabin.

End of the Alcan at Circle City.

Author paddling canoe on Birch Creek.

Don Roberts drying out after canoe sank.

Game Warden in Aleutian Islands

MY SUMMER JOB with the Department of Fish and Game started with a weeklong school located at Fish and Game headquarter in Kenai, Alaska. Upon arrival the twenty of us who had been hired for the positions were informed that the classes would consist of wilderness survival, bear encounters, kayaking, camping, weapons handling, and enforcement of state commercial fishing regulations. They explained that every year numerous commercial fishermen netted salmon when the species schooled up at the mouths of creeks prior to spawning. Depending on the salmon species, if these creek robbers hit the creek several years in a row at critical spawning seasons, it could decimate the salmon run in those waters for a long time. Our job would be to prevent this from happening. We were also told that the top eight students would be selected to go to the Aleutian Islands, with the other twelve being sent to other less remote commercial fishing locations.

Was this a class made in heaven or what? I absorbed the lessons presented with the attention and comprehension never given a teacher before in my life. Some were obvious, like "make a lot of noise when walking in bear territory." We were told to sing, whistle or do whatever our chosen method of noise making was, as this would let a bear know we were in his area. The game biologist giving this presentation said the bear would probably get out of our way. The "probably" part of this statement elicited some concern. It sounded like good advice, but did not work well in reality, in my later experience. Bears went where they wanted, when they wanted and how they wanted. I found it easier to avoid them rather than sing to the tone-deaf bruins. Besides, in later years when walking in bear country, I never once saw or heard a game warden or biologist walk along a bear trail singing silly songs or whistling. It was true they made no effort to remain quiet, but only made loud noises when faced with actual bears. Mostly they tried to see the bears first and get out of their way.

We were also given roman candles after the bear lecture, with the explanation this was the preferred method of getting bears out of camp or ending a confrontation. Pepper spray was a joke to these teachers. If the bears got that close to you, the teachers said, you were in real trouble and no spray in the world would get you out of it. Two things I later learned they forgot to give us lessons on were how to keep the roman candles dry in the near-constant rain and fog of the Aleutians, and where we were supposed to carry them when out scouting the bad guys. Roman candles are round tubes about an inch in diameter, and about twenty inches long, wrapped in thin cardboard. There was nothing waterproof about them. Thus the roman candles, for all their appeal, mostly stayed packed inside the tent.

The class eventually covered weapons handling. The teacher handed out our weapons, and I understood why they issued us roman candles. Each two-man team was issued one rifle. The 30-06 rifles given us were rusted and pitted almost beyond recognition. I don't how many years clueless, would-be game wardens like ourselves packed them through the saltwater environment of coastal Alaska where we were headed, but it had to have been generations. They were a mess. Weapons care had been pounded into me from the age of six when I got my first .410 shotgun. Any dereliction of duty on my part such as not cleaning or properly oiling it after using, resulted in the weapon being taken away for a month. Even at that early age I learned the value of caring for and using a firearm safely. After examining the action and bore of this 30-06 issued to me, I saw that no cleaning or oiling would salvage it. I determined to never use the weapon except as a last resort. I was surprised that the rifles fired and did not blow up in our faces as we tested them.

A game warden took us outside Kenai to shoot the rifles. He filled a coffee can with rocks and rolled it down a hill. We were to fire twice while it was still moving. The only person to hit the coffee can was a person I will refer to as Will out of respect for the feelings of his mother. Actually, I will refer to him as Worthless Will. WW hit the moving can cleanly in the center twice. I can remember thinking at the time that I wanted this guy as my partner.

The other major class that I really enjoyed was kayaking. We were using Klepper kayaks. Klepper had been making these folding kayaks in Germany for about seventy years. These were the two-person folding model, making them ideal for our purposes. The boat could be dismantled. The frame folded into several pieces, allowing it and the kayak skin to be a put in a compact bag. This made it possible to carry the kayak in an airplane with our other gear.

The kayaking class was held on a beach near Kenai City, located on the shore of Cook Inlet. Most of the students got wet during their first excursion in this wobbly and tippy invention of a mad German scientist. I was the only exception, and managed to paddle it successfully without getting baptized in the frigid water. My smugness ended when we were doubled up with a partner in the flighty two-man craft. My partner, as luck would have it, was Worthless Will.

Will was as incompetent with the kayak as he was competent with the rifle. I would try to counteract his uncoordinated gyrations without success as we again and again got soaked in the cold waters of Cook Inlet. Finally, our instructors felt mercy and hauled us all back to warm showers and dry clothing. I began to worry about Will as a partner, thinking I may have been too hasty after the rifle demonstration. The wetter and colder we became the more panicked was his reaction in the kayak. If we were to be teamed up together I vowed never to get in a kayak with him.

The sleep of our next-to-last night in Kenai before being shipped out to our summer locations was rudely interrupted with unearthly screams and shouts. The loud noises and physical struggle awoke even the soundest sleepers among us, as Fish and Game personnel tried to get one of our fellow students under physical control. Finally, they subdued and sent him off to a mental hospital in Anchorage. We learned the following day that the guy was a manic depressive and suffered a breakdown after not taking his medication. So much for the employment selection process. I wondered about the mental stability of whatever partner I was assigned. I should have packed my bags and headed back to Fairbanks right then. The next day I was called into a private interview and told I was one of the top students in the school and had been selected to go to the Aleutian Islands. My partner would be Worthless Will.

The eight of us selected to enforce commercial fishing regulations along the Alaskan Peninsula and Aleutian Island chain packed our gear and were met at the Kenai airport by John Klenbile. John was the head pilot, and in charge of all things involving aircraft for the Protection Division of the Alaskan Department of Fish and Game. John was flying us to Sand Point in a Grumman Goose.

The Goose is a twin-engine amphibious aircraft capable of landing on both land and water. It was originally designed by Grumman to carry eight businessmen in the Long Island area of New York. During World War II it was used by the military to carry passengers up and down the Alaskan Peninsula and Aleutian Islands. It is a very durable aircraft powered by two Pratt & Whitney air-cooled 450 hp engines and had a useful load of eight thousand pounds. Because of its short body and high wing design, the Goose was tricky to land on pavement. Many pilots who forgot to lock the tail-wheel upon landing would ground loop or crash. It was very tail sensitive, especially in a crosswind.

John explained all this to me as I sat next to him in the co-pilot's seat on the journey as we flew the Goose from Kenai to Sand Point. The Sand Point Fish and Game complex was to be our base for the summer. It had its own gravel runway, electric generator, showers, bunks and cooking facilities. It is located on Popof Island, about 575 miles southwest of Anchorage, and it is part of the Shumagin Island group off of the Alaskan Peninsula with one of the largest commercial fishing fleets in the Aleutians. The Fish and Game complex was located remotely from the town and harbor. I was only in Sand Point City proper one time during this summer, but I was groggy from forty-eight sleepless hours and a rough sea voyage, during which I was concerned that the ship's crew would murder me if I slept. So I don't remember much of the city.

The flight from Kenai to Sand Point was the beginning of my love of flying. John let me take the controls several times as we traversed southwest over Kalifornsky and Kachemak bays. John got more serious as we left the headland of Kachemak for the long over-the-water flight to Kodiak Island, then over more water to the Alaskan Peninsula and down to Sand Point.

I had read so many books in which Kodiak Island was featured that I was in awe as we traversed its shoreline and bays. Here I saw my first brown bear feeding on a whale carcass on the rocky shore. The bear looked huge to me, but John dismissed this observation, saying it was only a three-year-old. I remember thinking, if this was a small bear, what would a large one look like? I would see many of them up close and personal in the next two months, and could indeed testify that this first bear was but a small representative of the species.

I remember being really disappointed in the geography of Sand Point after we landed in the rain and wind. It was high barren tundra in which the majority of habitants were sea birds of one species or another. A small herd of buffalo lived on the island, but I never saw them. I read they were transplanted there in 1930. I have no idea why. In the 1930s buffalo were introduced by the federal government to several places in Alaska to help supplement the locals' food supply, and to entice farmers to move to Alaska during the Depression. It never made much sense to me, as Alaska had many game animals native to the area. There were flocks of ptarmigan on the island as well. Ptarmigan are small grouse-like birds that inhabit most of Alaska. But mostly I remember the rain, fog, wind and lack of trees or blue skies, and the constant noise of the camp's diesel generator.

We arrived at Sand Point several weeks prior to the opening of commercial fishing, so John had us busy repairing, painting and sprucing up the Fish and Game complex. John asked me if I had any experience painting and repairing buildings, as he knew I grew up working on a farm. I replied that I did. John said he had a job for me tomorrow getting a small plywood shack ready for biologists on Pavlof Bay. I was excited at the prospect of getting out of the compound and into the rain-soaked wilderness that surrounded me.

It was a fairly short flight from Sand Point with a low overcast and moderate winds, causing John to pilot the Goose within several hundred feet of the ground. I was amazed at the speed so apparent when this close to terrain, and was completely engrossed in the flight. When we landed, John pointed out the small shack as he taxied the lumbering aircraft toward shore, and asked if I had all my survival gear packed. I took this to mean did I have my sleeping bag, clothes and rifle with me. I informed him that I did. John said he would be back early the next day to pick me up.

It did not dawn on me that what John was really asking me was if I had packed a complete survival gear outfit, including matches and food. I was so excited about the trip that I had not even considered bringing food, though it was emphasized time and time again in the Kenai class to never fly or get out of an airplane without proper survival gear because of the possibility of accidents and the unpredictable, rapidly changing weather conditions in the state. I was so excited to get out into the wilderness that I had completely forgotten Rule Number One in Alaskan survival. It was a huge mistake that penetrated my thick skull, never to be repeated again in the rest of my days. In less than a year I was already having many of these teachable moments.

John hand-pumped the landing gear down as we neared shore, and using one engine, pivoted the airplane to face back out toward open water. As I got out, John asked me if I was comfortable being alone here. I replied that I was very contented with it, and he, departing, said he would return in the morning. After John left, skipping the Goose across the small waves, I anxiously looked around for bears, sure that this area contained one every square mile. Seeing none, I concentrated on hiking to the small one-room plywood shack that I was to get ready for fisheries biologists. I walked up to the plywood shack to see what damage the weather and bears had done to it over the winter. This one-room plain cabin was located about 300 yards from Pavlof Bay and half a mile from Canoe Lake, which emptied into the Bay.

Bears had scratched the door and windows, and I could see their teeth and claw marks on the corner of the structure, but no major damage was apparent. The long nails driven through the stout bear shutters covering the windows and door had many long brown hairs on them from curious bears, but they had not done major damage or gained access inside.

I spent the rest of the afternoon removing these nail-encrusted shutters, cleaning the floor, table and bed of the cabin, and puttying several windowpanes with the tools John gave me before he left. Having accomplished this, I took my fishing pole and rifle and headed to the shoreline for some fishing. I greatly enjoyed several hours of catching and releasing Dolly Varden trout in the grey, wind-tossed ocean. I saw salmon rolling and jumping in the bay but did not catch any.

Getting hungry and being tired from the excitement of the day, I headed back to the cabin for dinner and my warm sleeping bag. I stopped on the way to watch a very large brown bear with two cubs work the shoreline for food. Back at the cabin I opened the cupboards and discovered, to my dismay, that there was no food. There were dishes and cooking utensils, but no food. In retrospect, it made a lot of sense to not leave any kind of food in the structure that would entice wildlife to break in during the long period of vacancy between commercial fishing seasons. Kicking myself for not bringing food supplies for myself, I remembered the propane tank I had hauled up from the airplane. I attached it to the outside fitting and went inside to light the stove. There were no matches. Catching a fish for the evening meal was no longer an option. I was going to bed hungry whether I wanted to or not. At least, I thought, I was dry with a roof over my head and besides, John would be back in the morning.

The next morning, I lay in bed as long as possible before my sore back drove me to my feet. The night had been uneventful. No bears had come calling. The lack of wind buffeting the cabin and rain on the roof quieted the interior of the structure. After dressing, I opened the door to be greeted by a world of white. Fog had descended on my Alaskan abode. It was not the normal fog I was used to in Washington State, but the kind of fog where you can't see your hand in front of your face. It was so thick that ten feet outside the cabin I lost complete sight of the structure. Not wanting to get lost, I hurried back inside after emptying my bladder.

I surveyed the inside of my small domicile and wished I had thought to bring a book. Not finding any reading material, I did calisthenics to loosen my sore back. Finally, bored out of my mind, I retreated to my sleeping bag for the lack of anything better to do.

Fog is formed when air density and temperature equalize. When air is no longer able to absorb more water it becomes clouds. On the ground we call these clouds fog. Normally, fog disappears when the sun heats the air enough that it can absorb more water vapor, or when wind disperses it. I waited for the sun or wind to clear the air while anxiously listening for the sounds of John returning.

I waited and waited. Finally, it got dark, and it was still so foggy I could only see a few feet in front of me. I thought that maybe conditions would improve overnight as I took my angry and empty belly back to a now very hard and unwelcoming bed.

I was also very thirsty. Dehydration can kill a person faster than hunger, and my last drink of water was twenty-eight hours ago. I was surrounded by water. Even the air was full of it, but I had none to drink. I was afraid to walk to the creek for water even though it was only half a mile away, fearing I would not be able to find my way back to the cabin. There were no trails from the cabin to any drinkable water supply that I could see or remember from the prior day.

Looking around the cabin, I spotted several sheets of plastic. I took one outside and formed a water still by attaching one end to the roof of the cabin, and using the bear shutters to elevate and secure three other sides. I cut a small hole in the center of the plastic sheet and weighted it down with several rocks. Underneath the hole I put a cooking pan from inside the cabin to collect the condensing water. This process took several hours. I thanked my Boy Scout days for teaching me how to make the water still, and went back inside to wait for the water condensing on the plastic sheets to collect in the pan.

The night was a miserable experience of tossing and turning on the bed, getting up and doing calisthenics to burn time and energy, and checking my still for water. I greedily gulped the first cup as soon as the pan collected it. I scolded myself, knowing I needed to drink more slowly next time. The next day was more of the same. I had some water to drink but no food. If I could have seen the shore I would have been able to go down and catch fish. The thought of eating them raw turned my stomach, as I was not yet familiar with sushi. Every fish I had eaten in my life had been cooked. My mind this third night was consumed with thoughts of food. No matter what I did to distract myself, thoughts of food keep flooding back and ending my troubled sleep.

Intellectually I knew I could survive a week or longer without food, as long as I had water. My mind and body were not agreeing with each other, though. Knowledge is a poor source of nourishment. I was a fit one hundred and eighty pounds with no fat to sustain my body in the absence of food in my digestive system. I thought I knew what being hungry was about prior to this, but little did I know how physically and mentally pervasive these hunger pangs could become.

As I lay restlessly in my sleeping bag, monitoring this war between intellect and body, I was brought wide awake by a gust of wind so strong that it shook the cabin. I raced outside to see my water still being ripped apart by a strong wind. I could see the bay again as the angry wind had dissipated the fog. I debated going down to look for food along its shores like any self-respecting bear or fox, but convinced myself to wait until morning as it was also starting to rain very heavily. The wind and rain were so strong that the rain came in horizontal sheets. I drank all the water in my pot and placed pots under every corner of the roof that had water running off of it in case the fog returned. I restored the bear shutters under the cabin and brought the sheet of plastic inside where I had found it. During the night, unable to sleep, I filled every container in the cabin with water.

At first light I put on rain gear and collected my fishing rod and a couple of large fishing lures, as well as my rusted rifle, before heading to the bay. I was weak from lack of food, and walking in the gale-force wind was a real challenge, as I was very dizzy. It must have been blowing between 40 and 70 mph, and the heavy rain cut visibility to less than a mile. Trying to cast my lure far enough into the bay to catch one of the salmon I saw jumping here three days before was impossible. The wind blew my lure almost back into my face after every cast. Not even the Dollies were biting.

Frustrated, angry and hungry, I gave up fishing and walked the shore-line looking for other sources of nourishment. I was famished. I came upon some blue-shelled mussels clinging to rocks above the receding tide. I used my Gerber knife to pry them off the rocks and open their shells. Their pale flesh was the most succulent four-star meal I had ever eaten. I don't know how long I scoured the rocks and ate these small clams before my stomach rebelled, and I gave it all back to the sea. Reading about eating small amounts of food after going a long time without any was one thing; resisting the temptation to eat more quickly was another.

I collected about thirty blue shelled mussels, stuffing my pockets with them, and headed back to the protection of my plywood shelter. Inside the cabin, I deposited the clams in a pot after I emptied the water out. I ate several of them, and forced myself to stop while I sipped some water. In the next several hours I slowly consumed fifteen of the mussels, forcing myself to stop to allow my digestive system to adjust to food. It was nice going back to my bed with a full stomach, even though the bed seemed made of concrete because of all the time I had spent in it. I knew now that I would not starve and the thought of eating raw meat was no longer a problem. I would eat what I could find and survive until John returned.

The storm did not let up that day or night, and it was still blowing and raining just as hard the following day. The mussels were dead in the pan, so I was afraid to eat more of them. I collected my gear and, heading to the shore-line again, I dumped my dead blue-shelled friends back into the sea.

Following the shore toward the end of the bay, I came upon the river connecting Pavlof and Canoe bays. The tide was ebbing and I could see salmon schooled in clear water that was not being torn by the wind. I was not any better protected from the wind as I headed toward Canoe Bay, but at least now it was blowing toward the direction I wanted to cast. After several casts I hooked a bright salmon of about four pounds. From the Fish and Game classes in Kenai, I knew it was a pink salmon. I cleaned the fish and carried it back to my cabin. There I filleted it, and threw the head, bones and guts as far away from the cabin as I could. Inside I slowly

49

ate some of the rich flesh before lying down and resting. Even though my system was now digesting food, I was still very weak and not up to any major tasks. I stayed inside the cabin the rest of the day while the storm raged outside. The only thing I was missing was heat. If I was careful not to get wet or let my body heat fall below normal, I could wait out the storm, even if it lasted a week. I was learning important virtues that were key to wilderness survival. I call them the Three P's: patience, planning, and perseverance.

In the middle of the night I was awakened by a loud scratching on the cabin door. There were no trees or bushes nearby that could rub against it and make that noise. I was wondering, in my sleepy state, what was going on, when an enormous dark shadow blocked out the only window. My now-awake mind registered that a very large brown bear was looking inside the cabin.

All bears are immensely strong, even a small, months-old cub. This was a fully grown, mature bear that could easily come through the wall, if so motivated. I immediately wondered if the fish I had disposed of before retiring had somehow attracted it, or if the bear was just investigating my remaining fish. It roamed around the cabin for about twenty minutes, snuffing and scratching, before finally disappearing into the rainy gloom. I had survived my first close encounter with a brown bear. It is amazing how insignificant these large animals can make a man feel when up close. I was not afraid, but my senses were heightened by the adrenalin rushing into my system as the bear roamed around outside the plywood shack. I kept my rusty 30-06 close at hand, and did not sleep much the rest of the night.

The storm was still at full force in the morning of my sixth day. Donning rain gear, I went outside to see if the bear was still in the neighborhood. There was no sign of it, but the spot two hundred feet from the cabin where I had thrown the remains of the fish I had been eating was freshly torn up. Examining it and the fresh pile of bear scat nearby revealed the bear had dined here. I thought I had disposed of the fish well enough to avoid attracting bears. I was wrong. Another lesson learned about a bear's incredible sense of smell. I resolved to carry any uneaten fish or clams to the bay shore in the future, instead of burying them close to the cabin.

The temporary twenty-four hour stay at this cabin lasted nine days before I heard the deep roar of the Grumman Goose coming to pick me up. I had learned many valuable lessons about wilderness survival and about myself during this lonely, cold ordeal. Even though I saw many brown bears during my nine-day stay, I never had another problem with them. The remains of fish and clams I left on the shore were often gone the next morning as I took my daily walk, having been eaten by fox, bears or sea gulls, but I was never awakened again by a bear. I would also never go unprepared into any wilderness again, and would be better equipped to meet its challenges. Slowly but surely my bumbling experiences were shaping me into an Alaskan.

John was concerned when he got out of the Goose after taxiing up to shore, explaining that the fog and storm had kept him grounded. He asked if I was okay. I said I needed a shower and some hot cooked food. He thought I had gotten tired of the rations provided by the Department when away from the main complex, but when I explained that I had neglected to bring any food along and that there were no matches in the cabin, he looked at me in astonishment. John said, "I asked you if you had your gear packed and you said yes." I replied that I had been stupid, and that my gear did not contain any food or matches. I assured him it was a lesson I would never forget, and that raw fish, clams and seaweed were not too bad a food source, but the lack of variety became challenging after a while. John was still shaking his head in disbelief at my stupidity as he readied the aircraft for takeoff. I am sure he was telling himself that he would have to more closely monitor us in the future. It would take me another twenty years to learn to tolerate sushi.

The days following were filled with grey skies, rain and wind, as all of us would-be fish cops checked and rechecked our gear between card games of hearts and spades. All eight of us were relieved when John informed us we would be heading into the field tomorrow, weather permitting.

The weather the next day was gorgeous, with blue skies and low wind. As we were loading our gear into the airplane, John informed us that two teams would work together on this first assignment. Tom would be in charge, as this was his second year. Tom was a friendly, outgoing guy, always joking around in both the school and here at Sandpoint. The only thing I remember about his partner was that he was a tall thin boy with brown hair who rarely spoke, but exuded a sense of competence.

I have no idea where John flew us, but upon landing, he handed each team a portable radio and told us he would be back in six days. We had to hike about half a mile with all our gear and kayaks to get to the targeted bay with a strong salmon run in the rivers emptying into it. The commercial salmon season would open in the morning. All commercial fishing was closed within various distances of a stream terminus into a body of salt water to allow the fish to school up prior to running up the river to spawn. The closed areas were plainly marked with large signs.

Tom took us to an area about a quarter-mile from the stream mouth. We were hidden from the bay by low hills of sand and alders. After setting up tents and putting together the kayaks, we snuck up to a place where we were still hidden from the fishermen but had a good view of the complete bay, including the closed area. With our binoculars we looked at all thirteen commercial fishing boats anchored just outside the closed area. After writing down the names of all the boats, I spent some time watching huge schools of salmon as they jumped and rolled, loosening up the roe in their bellies prior to their journey up river to spawn. The other three members of our team had returned back to camp to make dinner. I remained to enjoy the weather and scenery.

The weather remained calm and clear, with deep blue skies the rest of the day. A couple of bald eagles were being harassed by small black birds as they floated on updrafts of air. Getting hungry, I decided to join my fellow protection officers back in camp for dinner. All the boats were still anchored and it did not look like any would attempt to rob the fish in the mouth of the river.

Will handed me a tin plate with rice and beans as I sat down with the others. I told them everything was calm with the fisherman. We were still eating dinner when we began to hear skiffs and large boat motors starting up. This was followed by sounds of power takeoffs. We looked at Tom for guidance, as he was experienced at this enforcement business. Tom said to relax and finish our meal. Even though he said these were not the sounds of boats fishing, I did not believe it, and started to go back to observe what was going on in the bay. Tom called me back and said he would tell us when to leave. John had made it clear that Tom was in charge of this group. I looked at him intently trying to decide whether to challenge him before sitting back down. Though I was not experienced with commercial fishing, it sure sounded to me like the boats were fishing. Even if they were not putting their nets in closed waters, the season had not yet opened.

After a while, Tom got up and told us to stay where we were while he checked out the bay. All the boat sounds had stopped by this time. I got up and followed him. I was furious when, looking over the bay, I saw that there were no fish jumping and a number of the boats sat lower in the water. The long seine nets piled at the rear of the fishing boats were shiny and wet. It was obvious that while we were eating, the commercial fishermen had set nets in the closed area, harvesting most of the salmon there. Tom had to have known this, and he had deliberately misled us.

Back in camp, I confronted Tom. He had to have seen what I had. He said I was over-reacting, when the sounds of another boat and skiff starting their engines floated over us. I grabbed the end of my kayak and asked Will if he was coming with me. Will looked away and did not respond. Tom told me to stay in camp while he and his partner checked the situation out. I was in no mood to trust Tom. After they left I confronted Will, asking why he had not backed me up. It was to no avail, as he would neither look at me nor reply to my question.

Angrily telling Will he was as worthless as tits on a boar, I grabbed my kayak and started to follow Tom and his partner. I was halfway to the bay, trying to maneuver the long kayak through a thick patch of alders when Tom's partner returned. He told me that a boat was fishing in closed waters, and Tom was paddling out to arrest them. We both pulled my boat to the shore where we watched Tom on the deck of the commercial boat, talking to the crew. After about twenty minutes the boat skiff brought him to shore where Tom had told his partner to pack their equipment. They would both travel with the boat back to Sand Point where the fishermen on board would face a magistrate for commercial fishing during a closed season in a closed area. I could plainly hear the captain yelling about the other boats getting away with fishing illegally.

I fretted that evening in camp about the day's events. It seemed apparent to me that the only semi-honest fisherman of the bunch had watched the other twelve boats fish illegally, catching the majority of the salmon near the stream mouth, and had refused to join them. Getting mad after watching this crime and seeing no Fish and Game personnel coming out to arrest them, he decided to follow suit and got caught. His angry cursing of Tom and all Fish and Game Protection Officers was heard clearly by me and Tom's partner, as we had waited on the bay's shore for Tom to finish citing the boat's captain.

I decided to have it out with Will. He had not once left camp during the entire day. I asked him what he thought of the day's events. Will replied that we had caught a boat, so the day was successful as far as he was concerned. I asked him if it bothered him that eleven boats had done the same thing and were not apprehended. He shrugged as if to say it was no skin off his nose. Glaring at him, I asked why he had applied and accepted this job if he did not care if the salmon run in this stream was ruined. Looking away from me he replied it was none of my business. I asked why he stayed in camp all day instead of doing his job. He got up and entered the tent, zipping it closed behind him. I imagined what my dad would have done if Will worked for him with this attitude. It was certainly a foreign concept to me and the kids I grew up with, to accept a person's money and not do the job you were hired to perform.

I sat that evening, considering the problems I had with Will. My life, to some extent, would depend on Will in the following month, and I wondered if I would be able to count on him. I seriously doubted that I would be able to do so, and made a commitment to myself that night to not put myself in a position of needing to trust him.

Thus Will became Worthless Will, or WW as I would refer to him the rest of the summer. His inaction and disregard for the job he had been hired to do would become more set in concrete, endangering me several times. He also had a real fear of bears, and I was to later learn of his incapacity in their presence. I can usually find something good to say about people even if I do not like them, but with WW, I came up blank, other than the fact that he was a good shot. He was not interested in the geography, fauna or wildlife around us. He did not read the commercial fishing regulations or anything else in my presence, and he certainly had no intention of enforcing those regulations. His only interests that I could see were cooking and shooting. I decided to have a serious conversation with John Klenbile about Will at the first opportunity.

In the morning all commercial boats had left the area, as there were no more salmon to catch. I fished the river, catching some large Dolly Varden trout, one of which I cooked without sharing with Will. There were plenty of bear signs around, but we did not see any. We did not talk to each other in the next five days, before being picked up, any more than absolutely necessary to perform some critical chore.

John picked us up later. The following afternoon, I told John I wanted a private conversation with him. In his office, I relayed what had happened the previous week. He seemed surprised by the fact that more than one boat had fished illegally without being cited or even investigated. He asked if I had gone out to the boats I suspected of fishing illegally and inspected their fish holds. I told him that I did not even consider it, as I thought we had to catch them in the act itself. I then told him I would not partner with Will in the future, and why I had such distrust and dislike of him. John said no one else wanted to go out with Will either so I was stuck with him, and to make the best of it. I told John to keep him in camp, and I would go out by myself. He replied that was not an option, and to get used to Will being my partner.

On our next trip, John dropped us at a place on Unalaska Island in the Aleutian Islands chain. It did not contain much of a bay, as the river emptied into a long, sandy stretch of shoreline. A small mountain extended on the east side out into the Bering Sea, but the shoreline to the west was flat and covered with tall grass. The river ran south several miles into a lagoon.

John suggested we stay on the east side of the river, up on the slope of the mountain where we would have good visibility of the closed area, but far enough back that fishermen would not see us. Will and I set up the kayak in uncomfortable silence and hid it in the alders, where it would be close to the sea but not visible unless someone actually walked up on it. Finding a camping spot was more difficult. The only way to traverse the thick alders was to follow bear trails. That thought did not instill peace of mind. It soon became apparent that any camping spot would be connected to these same trails. It would be the same for the rest of the summer. All camping would be in wide spaces of bear trails within alder thickets. Anything else would make us visible to commercial fishermen and end any chance of catching them fishing illegally. We set up camp about a quarter of the way up the small mountain, about 700 feet above and a half mile away from the closed area, in an alder patch surrounded by thick grass. We had a view of the bay from the edge of the alders, about twenty yards from camp.

No fishermen were in sight, so I decided to go down to the river and fish. At high tide the water was so deep you could not wade across it, but at low tide it was possible to get across to the big meadows of grass and alders on the other side. I caught and released several salmon and trout before the river level dropped enough for me to cross.

Contentedly fishing my way upstream toward the lake, I was suddenly confronted by a large brown bear fifteen feet away. We took each other by surprise. He was coming down the river while I was fishing my way up.

When it rose on its hind feet, peering at me, the bear looked twenty feet tall and half a mile wide. It was the closest I had ever been to any bear, with the exception of my night encounter on Pavlof Bay. However, at that encounter, there was a wood wall between us. Now there was only air, as time stood still and we took the measure of each other. If I were a bug I would have crawled under one of the nearby rocks. We had but one rifle. Will had kept it with him in camp. I had a .357 Magnum pistol on my hip, but the thought of trying to kill such a large animal with a pistol this close seemed ludicrous.

My heart was pounding as adrenaline flooded my system. Strangely, I was not frightened. I found myself retreating to a state of calmness, where I immediately assessed all my options and decided what to do next. I tried backing up slowly to give the bear room as I talked to it, but the huge animal came back down on all four legs and took several steps toward me. I stopped and shouted at it as loudly as I could. It immediately reacted by running fifteen yards away from the river, then stopped to face me again. Repeating the shouting had no effect on the animal, and when I again tried backing away from it, the bear started following once more, coming within fifteen feet. The beast showed no inclination of leaving me. Remembering the Fish and Game bear expert telling us to do the unexpected in these circumstances, I charged the bear, shouting and waving my arms and fishing pole. My legs felt like they weighed 500 pounds apiece, but I made them obey my mind.

The brown bear, not knowing what kind of unreasonable creature was coming at it, immediately departed. It was not until I lost sight of the retreating animal that nerves took over. I sat down to collect my breath and relive the encounter. I could only imagine what one swipe of those enormous claws would have done to me,

I was lucky. I had not been paying attention to my surroundings, but enjoying the weather and fishing as I went up the stream. Bears have tremendous senses of smell and hearing, but do not see well. The slight breeze was blowing down river, so it did not smell me coming, and was just as surprised as I was when we met. Standing up on his hind legs was not a sign of aggression, but mere curiosity concerning the identity of the strange two-legged animal in front of it. My later experiences with all species of bears in Alaska revealed that when most bears become aggressive, they lay their ears down flat and they stay on all four feet, usually clicking their teeth before charging, with their head low to their shoulders. The most dangerous situations involving bears were walking up on their food supply, or coming between a sow and her cubs. Neither of these had occurred this time.

This brown bear's action was expressing the curiosity that I later observed in many of the species. I have been charged by bears many times during my Alaskan years, and only had to kill five in the act of charging. Of those five, I was actively hunting four of them. I would be bitten and clawed by two bears. The first was a black bear that charged as I was walking out the door of a log cabin Bill Spear and I built on the Toklat River in central Alaska. It bit me and knocked me back into the cabin before following me inside. The other bear that mauled me was a grizzly that had been shot in the stomach at close range and not killed by a hunter I was guiding.

At this time, I was young and green and had little knowledge of bear habits, so I sat on the banks of that unknown stream thanking God for delivering me from being a meal while regaining my composure. I also wondered why I was not afraid during the encounter but had legs of wet noodles afterwards. Losing all interest in fishing and exploring, I re-crossed the river and walked back to camp. Will was sitting on a small knoll with binoculars when I arrived and told him what happened. He told me he knew, as from his vantage point he could see both me and the bear approaching each other a long time before we met.

I was struck dumb by his statement. How in the world could he sit there and watch this unfold without trying to warn me? I angrily knocked the binoculars out of his hand and punched him in the nose so hard he rolled ten feet downhill. When I caught up with Will I grabbed him by the chest with two hands and jerked him to his feet, demanding to know why he had not fired a shot in the air or shouted to warn me. His fearful stuttering answer, that I should stay in camp and not wander around, was so incongruous that I let him go and walked disgustedly back uphill to camp muttering to myself. What could I expect from someone so scared he would not leave camp or warn me of danger, thinking only of his own personal safety?

The next two days passed uneventfully, as no commercial fishermen came to our location. We saw lots of brown bear feeding on salmon in the river, but were not bothered by them in our small camp. Our routine was interrupted the morning of the fourth day.

Hearing a boat cruising the shoreline, Will and I crept to the edge of the alders in which our camp was located. I was surprised that Will had followed me, but did not comment on it. Focusing my binoculars on the vessel, I saw three men on the stern holding rifles. Thinking they were going to shoot some of the seals fishing in the area, I continued to watch them. It dawned on me they were not looking at the seals, but at the mountain we were camped on. Suddenly all three men started firing their rifles at our alder patch on the mountain side, focusing their rifle fire on our camp site.

We crawled backwards into our alder patch when bullets started cracking the trees above us. This time I did not blame Will for covering his head and laying as close to the ground as possible. I counted fifteen bullets zinging through our camp before the fusillade stopped and the boat departed.

We were told in Kenai this might happen. Fish cops were not beloved by most commercial fishermen, thinking we were preventing them from paying for their boats and feeding their families. There were even stories told of temporary officers like ourselves disappearing, never to be found during their summer employment by the Department. I did not know how true those stories were about disappearing, but it was readily apparent this particular boat and crew had no love for us and had not cared if they killed us.

I left Will digging a foxhole outside our camp, and went to where we stashed our kayak. Launching the kayak into the bay, I paddled a quarter mile out to sea and looked back at where our camp was located. I was wondering why the fishermen focused their rifle fire on the alders in which we were camped. It became readily apparent, looking back at our camping location. Grass! We had left trails through the two-foot-high grass leading right to our camp. The trails came from four different directions, all leading directly into our camping site. These were so visible from the sea that it was almost comical. We had taken such pains to hide it, but left a roadmap for anyone who wanted to know where we were located. We were lucky neither of us was injured. It was another valuable lesson learned about this magical but unforgiving land and its inhabitants

That evening, becoming restless from my lack of exercise, I decided to take the kayak out for a night jaunt to a small island about three miles off shore. It was a calm night, with small swells on the gentle ocean surface. The few clouds gently crossed the full moon on their leisurely flight across the land below. Upon reaching the island, I found it did not offer a place to land the kayak. The shoreline was composed of a high rock face and large encrusted rocks around its entire perimeter. There might have been several places for me to put ashore at low tide, but I did not see any in the dark at high tide. The winged inhabitants squawked loudly at me as I paddled away.

I spent five hours of pleasurable paddling on the sea that evening, observing seals and other sea life. Occasionally the ocean would light up with green illumination as I paddled along. I would later learn this light was phosphorescent plankton. It was intriguing watching these ocean lights as I slowly moved back toward camp, thoroughly entranced and relaxed by this night's journey.

Suddenly, without any warning, something very large came out of the water right beside me. I caught a glimpse of a huge dark shape moving beside me before I was upside down under water. Either the wave caused by the creature's breach or my physical reaction to the large mass suddenly interrupting my solitude caused me to jerk uncontrollably and turn my kayak upside down. It was disconcerting to suddenly be upside down under water in the Bering Sea two miles off shore.

At first I thought a shark or some large sea mammal had attacked the kayak. I tried three or four times to roll the kayak right side up, and failed. The slim two-man craft was so long and partially water filled that I could not right it. I untied the canvas around my waist that was designed to keep water out of the craft, kicked myself out, and swam to the surface.

I gently climbed on top of the upside down kayak. It was in this position I saw a whale breach about 200 yards away, and knew what had tipped me over. The whale may have been feeding on the plankton I had been observing, and upset me unintentionally.

Looking around, I saw I was quite a way from shore. There did not seem to be any ocean current moving me away from my desired direction. I sprawled on top of the half-submerged boat with a leg and arm on each side, carefully balancing myself as I paddled toward the coastline. It took a little time to work out the proper rhythm of rowing with the double-bladed kayak paddle while kicking my legs to get forward movement without the threat of tipping over again. But after a bit I was heading to shore at a steady pace. It was a slow trip. I was freezing cold before touching the sandy beach.

Beaching on the far side of the river away from camp, I took off my wet clothes and boots after emptying the kayak. I spread my clothes on the kayak not to dry, but to keep them out of the sand. It was a warm, windless night for this part of the world. Despite that fact, I was shivering from the cold water. I ran, naked, up and down the dry, soft sand of the beach above the high tide mark, generating heat for my trembling body. I remember hearing myself laughing and thinking that if anyone could see me I would be immediately taken to the nearest mental institution for a psychological evaluation. My laughter was not insanity however; I was just enjoying myself and the world around me. I had survived another dangerous situation and learned more about the environment with which I interacted. I loved this place and the life it provided for me.

I arrived back in camp at 3 a.m., after dressing in wet clothes and paddling back up the shore and across the river to store the kayak. I hung my wet clothes on alder branches around the tent. While doing so, I wondered about being able to survive so long in the cold Aleutian waters long enough to get to shore. I had heard and read so many accounts of people dying after a few short minutes in these waters. I finally attributed it to a combination of my being in great shape and the fact that I was mostly out of the water and engaged in physical activity. I didn't know if the warmer waters of the Gulf of Alaska and the influence of the Japanese Current mixing with the cold water of the Bering Sea had anything to do with it, but decided it did not matter, as I was alive. I crawled into my warm sleeping bag after putting on dry clothes. It had been a great night's adventure. I immediately fell into a deep sleep.

Our next trip out of Sand Point was again down the Aleutian Islands to an island containing a large natural harbor. The bay was full of salmon in their pre-spawn phase, rolling and jumping on the surface of the bay by the hundreds. The river and the creeks merging with it were also full of spawning salmon. In some places the small waterways were so full of fish and so shallow you could see thousands of fish backs wiggling in the current. The banks and streams were littered with hundreds of dead and dying salmon, and the bones of their passing spread across the shorelines like pale ghostly lichen.

For a boy who grew up hoping to catch five salmon in a year, this was paradise. I put the kayak together while WW started making camp. We selected a wide spot in the fifteen-foot alders with room enough for a tent and our gear. The prerequisite bear trails were all around us. We were becoming used to this, and we had not been bothered by bears in our previous two camps. We did not need to dig a fox hole here, as the sandy shore contained several high dunes that would block any rifle fire from the water.

As the day wore on, several commercial boats arrived in the bay and set anchor outside the closed area, waiting for the week's fishing to legally open in the morning. By morning the number of commercial boats increased to eleven. None of them started fishing prior to the legal opening. Bears outnumbered fishing boats by a large margin. They seemed to be everywhere, from large solitary boars to sows with cubs. The animals had an insatiable appetite for fish and often slept in the alders around the river shore to be close to their next meal. Needless to say I did not walk this stream to fish, but stayed close to the shore of the bay where the water was too deep to allow easy fishing for the animals.

The commercial boats stayed in legal waters and seemed to be catching a lot of salmon. I lay in the tall grass below the apex of the sand dunes watching them fish by the hours. It was interesting watching the boat and skiff work in a coordinated dance to encircle the schools of fish with their seine net. The skiff would circle back to the mother boat and transfer its end of the purse seine back to it. The deck hands on the larger boat worked feverishly, shooting bubbles of water into the open ends of the net under the boat to scare the fish back into the closed sections, while the captain and other deck hand closed the bottom of the net by pulling in a rope running though large rings at the net's bottom. When the bottom was completely closed they would start pulling in the rest of the net, stacking it on the stern until only a small section was left in the water. This was referred to as the money bag, as it contained the majority of the fish caught. From here they would use a large power-operated bailer to remove enough fish into the hold to reduce the weight of the remaining fish. The money bag was then pulled onboard and fish deposited in the fish hold. It was both a calm and frantic ballet to observe. Between the saltwater and the stinging jelly fish raining on the men as they stacked the net, being a member of the deck crew on a seiner looked like a nasty job, despite the grace with which they performed.

After watching the commercial boats, bears and eagles fishing for several hours, I went back to camp. Will had cooked dinner. We ate in silence as the world slowly darkened around us. When it became too dark to read anymore of Farley Mowat's book, *Never Cry Wolf*, I joined Will in the tent.

In the middle of the night I was awakened by the sound of thunder. Thinking of our gear outside, I listened to hear if raindrops were falling on the tent. As I lay there wondering if we had left anything out that could get wet, I became aware in the dim light that my side of the tent was caved in about six inches. The thunder was loud and it moved a little. I suddenly woke up enough to become cognizant that I was not listening to thunder, but the growling of a bear's stomach. The animal was laying against my side of the tent, with my head touching the side of its stomach.

I held my breath trying to decide what to do next. I moved the bottom of my sleeping bag with my feet and nudged Will awake, afraid to move my head laying against the bear. Will came awake and asked what was wrong. I put my finger to my lips in a shushing motion to quiet him, and mouthed "Bear" while pointing at the caved-in tent. He looked confused for several seconds then dove back inside his sleeping bag, covering his head, refusing to come out again. I don't know what I expected Will to do, but it would have been nice to have some help handling this situation. His cowardice really angered me. Besides, if the bear decided it wanted inside the tent, covering his head up with his sleeping bag would do Will little good. We would both be a snack after following its main course of salmon.

I slowly moved my head away from the bear, fully expecting it to jump up and tear into the tent, killing us both. For whatever reason, the bear completely ignored my movements and kept sleeping. With my head now physically clear of the bear, I lay there thinking what could I do next to get the bear out of camp without anyone getting injured. My hand closed around the 30-06 rifle, but I discarded it, thinking if I even got out of the tent without disturbing the bear, I would be within several feet of it; too close to be sure of getting off a clean killing shot. I had heard so many stories of brown bears absorbing many rifle rounds without dying that I had no faith in being able to stop it fast enough.

I decided my best bet would be using the roman candles. They put out balls of fire and smoke. It might frighten the bear enough to chase it off. Unzipping my sleeping bag and tent seemed to take forever, and the zipper opening my sleeping bag sounded 1,200 decibels loud. I was sure the bear would hear it, but again, it did not move. Locating the roman candles, I removed one but could not find matches to light it. I hoped Will had not put them outside after cooking dinner.

Pushing his sleeping bag did no good. I finally reached inside and grabbed his hair, twisting it while I pulled him out. Will was now as mad as I was. I whispered that I needed him to light the roman candles. He did not say anything, but rolled over to his personal gear and took out a box of matches. The first roman candle was so damp it would not light. We were on our third candle when the fuse sputtered. Jumping outside the tent barefooted in my long johns, I screamed at the large brown bear laying against the tent five feet away and pointed the roman candle at its face. The enormous bruin became instantly enraged. Its ears were flat against his head. His mouth, as he opened it to growl at me, looked like it could swallow me whole. The now fully awakened bear gave out a challenging roar and jumped to its feet, facing me. It swung its huge paws toward me in a quick blurry motion, tearing a hole in the tent where I had been laying.

I seemed like an eternity before the first ball of fire shot out of the candle, hitting the bear in the nose. I have never seen anything move so fast in my life as that astounded animal tearing through camp and knocking down alders as it fled. It seemed like we could hear brush crashing for a mile before everything except our breathing got silent again.

I looked at Will, smiled, and said, "Thanks, I could not have done this without you." He smiled back, and we shook hands. I thought that maybe the partnership would work out after all. Boy, was that happy thought short-lived.

We spent part of the next day unsuccessfully trying to dry out the remaining four roman candles. It would take a large fire to accomplish it. We could not do that. Every fisherman in the bay would see the smoke and come to investigate. I decided to dry out the rest of the roman candles at the Fish and Game complex when we returned after John picked us up. I would melt candle wax over the fuses and parts of the body, hoping they would keep dry enough to light if we ever needed them again.

The rest of the week passed uneventfully. I could not fish myself, but enjoyed watching other denizens of this island getting their energy replenished and stored for the leaner times of winter. After being picked up by John and flown back to Sand Point, we rested for several days, taking a shower and catching up on washing clothes before getting ready for the next trip. The normal card games and camaraderie with the other teams was ongoing. The only arrest that had been made so far in the Sand Point

District was the original one by Tom. We discussed this amongst ourselves as we completed chores and relaxed.

We flew over the Cold Bay settlement on our next trip out of Sand Point. John explained the lives of the residents of Cold Bay to me as I steered the lumbering Goose along the island's shore. John, like most pilots, liked to share his love of flying with others. He made fun of my hands, clenched so hard on the control wheel that I had white knuckles. Telling me to relax, he shoved the rudder sideways with one of the pedals, laughing as I swallowed my breath and tensed up even more. Finally, I got his message and relaxed my hands and arms, but I did not put my feet on the rudder pedals. I was more than happy to listen to him explain the function of the various gauges and controls, but I really liked best the times when he would let me steer the aircraft. At this time, I had no thoughts of becoming a pilot myself. The mystique of pilots and the art of keeping a heavy loud hunk of metal in the air were beyond my comprehension or dreams.

John landed and deposited Will and me at the end of a long bay, about seventy miles west of Cold Bay. The weather was overcast and threatening to rain as John departed. After the normal duties of putting the kayak together and setting up camp in the alders about a quarter-mile inland from the inlet, I left Will in camp to find a good location to observe fishermen. Finding an area protected on three sides from the wind but offering a view of the bay through some tall grass, I set up the spotting scope to become familiar with the closed fishing markers and areas open to commercial fishing. The fishing would open tomorrow, but there were no vessels visible. I had not seen any during the flight in on the Goose, either.

There were two sets of closed markers that I could see from my location, as more than one stream emptied into the bay containing salmon runs. The far marker was about a mile from my position on the north side of the bay. The second and larger stream was to my right as I lay glassing the area. A fair number of salmon rolled and jumped at the mouth of each stream. It began to rain, with increasing wind and fog. Getting cold after several hours of being inactive, I walked over to the stream to my right. It was deep even at low tide and would take the kayak to cross it. I debated going back to camp and getting my fishing rod, but decided on a warm dinner and early night instead.

Arriving back in camp, I smelled burning rice and stew on our Coleman stove. I called Will several times without an answer. Swearing at the thought of having to start dinner all over again, I removed the ruined food from the stove and started to take it to the stream to dispose of it and wash the pans. On the way out of camp I noticed Will crouching at the top of some alders about one hundred feet away.

I knew Will was weird, but this was abnormal behavior even for him. I called out, asking him what in the world he was doing up there. He put his fingers to his lips telling me to be quiet, and pointed to the other side of the alders he had climbed. Alders on the Aleutian chain are only tree-like bushes. They are small at the base; a big one may have a twelve inch in circumference. They only grow about fifteen feet tall, at the most. The sight of a 150-pound man crouching as far up one as he could climb was comical to say the least, as the alder was swaying and threatened to deposit Will on his head at its roots. Will was scared senseless, which was a normal state for him, but the burned dinner and the sight of the 30-06 laying in the sand halfway between camp and Will's precarious perch in the alder made me think bears had scared him into trying to escape by climbing the tree.

Only WW would be stupid enough to think he could escape a full-grown brown bear in this manner. A bear could easily either pull him out of the alder or just knock it down. They are extremely strong and agile for such large animals. I started to laugh and order Will down when I smelled bear and heard one grunt. Taking out my .357 Magnum pistol, I started walking toward the hastily abandoned rifle looking through the brush trying to locate the animal.

I was talking loudly to Will to let the bears know I was near as I bent down and picked up the rifle. Will was almost crying and making frantic motions for me to be quiet. I finally spotted two large bears about ten feet from Will on the other side of the alder in which he was perched, looking up at him as if trying to understand what they were seeing. They were circling around a bit, and snorting. They showed no signs of aggressive behavior, but with these animals that could change in a heartbeat. Mostly they looked perplexed.

I checked the rifle barrel to make sure it was not plugged with sand, and chambered a round. I also considered going back to the tent to get some of the roman candles I had prepared prior to this trip. I finally discounted taking the time to get the candles, thinking Will might do something stupid and get himself seriously hurt or killed in the time it would take me to locate them. Continuing to make loud noises, I backed slowly away from the animals then shot two rounds into the air. They quickly left the area, looking back over their shoulders as they departed.

It took me another fifteen minutes to talk Will out of the alder. When his feet were steady again, I asked him what in the hell was he doing in the tree, because either of the two bears could easily have ripped the small tree out of the ground. I also yelled at him for letting me walk nonchalantly to within fifteen feet of them. Will was shaking from fright and had tears in the corners of his eyes. I might as well have been yelling at a two-year-old instead of a nineteen-year-old man. Handing Will his pacifier, I went back to the stove and picked up the burned pans and told him I was going to the river to clean them, and that he should reload and clean the rifle I had just given him. I was both disgusted and amused. Will belonged in a city where the trees were big enough to climb or hide behind. I would try to help him survive long enough to go back there. It would not be easy.

For two days the rain, wind and fog made camping miserable. It is really tough to stay dry and warm in this situation, when you cannot build a fire big enough to dry things out. Finally, one boat did enter the bay we were camped in, and anchored out by the far stream. It was outside the closed waters as far as I could determine, but with the fog and rain it was hard to tell. I tried to read the name of the boat without success. My binoculars and spotting scope kept fogging up, keeping me from seeing clearly. I thought the first part of the boat's name was Sea, but could not make out the second part.

As I was straining to see what the boat was doing, it raised the anchor and moved toward the illegal fishing area. When the boat and crew started setting the net in closed waters, I ran back to Will and explained I was taking the kayak out to arrest them. I told him to follow me back out so he could observe what was taking place from the shore. To my surprise he followed me and helped launch the kayak.

The mile-long trip out to the boat fishing illegally was difficult with wind, fog, rain and four-foot ocean waves blowing salt spray into my stinging eyes. The fishermen were so busy they did not see me approach. It was not until I was climbing aboard, on the far side of the boat from where their attention was focused on the seine net, that they became aware of me. The looks they shot my way as they became aware of my presence were as cold and unforgiving as the waters they fished.

After tying my kayak to a cleat, I asked who the captain was. A scruffy, tall thin man in rain gear stepped forward and asked, "Who wants to know?" I identified myself and stated I was issuing a citation to them for commercial fishing in closed waters. They were instructed to release the remaining salmon in the net. I wrote out the citation and told the captain he was to make ready to go back to Sand Point, where he would have an opportunity to explain the boat's actions to a magistrate. As I observed the crew releasing the fish in their net and stacking the seine on the stern, the captain disappeared back inside the cabin.

He reappeared shortly thereafter, pointing a rifle at my chest. The captain informed me I had made a big mistake. He and his crew were not going anywhere. From his demeanor and two deadly, intense eyes glaring at me, I took this to mean I had the choice of getting off his boat or being shot. The crewmembers quickly assembled by the stacked seine net out of the line of fire. None of them looked like they were about to help me in any way. I debated getting in the kayak and departing, but thought that would probably get me shot in the back anyway. I had left my .357 pistol wrapped in an oil rag in our tent to keep it from being rusted in this weather, and forgot to get it when I went back to get Will. Besides, even if I had had it with me, it would have been stupid to try and use it with a loaded rifle pointed at me.

Again I felt my mind retreating back into that calm place, considering my options. I informed the captain that he was making a big mistake. I told him my partner and I had already radioed the name of his boat into headquarters at Sand Point before I came aboard, which was a big lie. Our radio only transmitted five miles, when it worked. If he shot or caused harm to me in any way, the charges against him and the crew would be much more serious. The captain sneered at me and asked in an icy voice what the name of his boat was. I was stupefied into silence by my mistake in not looking at the boat's name as I approached, but bluffed and said, *Sea Ranger*. The captain continued to look at me for several seconds before lowering his weapon. I told the captain if he gave me his weapon for the trip into Sand Point, I would not use his pulling it on me against him. This may have been an ill-advised promise, but I wanted the weapon out of his hands and in mine. He reluctantly handed me the rifle and asked if I needed anything from shore. I told him I needed to get some of my gear and inform my partner that we were headed back to Sand Point.

The captain told the skiff operator to take me to shore. During the trip into camp I noticed the skiff operator had armed himself with a pistol. I wondered if it was his job to see if I had a partner and to eliminate me if I was alone. On second thought, I did not believe this to be the case. I had checked the captain's rifle and it was unloaded. He had been bluffing as well.

Upon beaching the skiff, we proceeded to our spotting location where I retrieved my abandoned binoculars and spotting scope. I called Will's name but got no reply. The skiff operator was looking at the tracks in the sand. It was apparent from the numerous tracks there were two different boot sizes. I informed him that my partner had obviously seen the rifle the captain had pointed at me and would not reveal himself. I was thinking that for once Will's natural inclinations were working in my favor. Though I called his name several times, WW did not appear. The crewmember accompanied me to our campsite where I collected my gear. I observed the man taking in the two sleeping bags as I did so. There could be no question in his mind that two people were camped here.

The eleven-hour trip back to Sand Point in the *Sea Ranger* was tense. The boat crew ignored my presence, not even offering me coffee or food. There was no question I was the enemy in their eyes. The adrenalin from apprehending the *Sea Ranger* and its crew left me very tired as it dissipated from my body. I was afraid to go to sleep or let down my guard in any way. Finally, as we approached Pavlof Island, I told the skipper I needed to use his radio to notify headquarters we had arrived. John answered my call. I informed him that I was on board with the crew of the *Sea Ranger* I had radioed about earlier for fishing in closed waters. We were entering Sand Point harbor and needed him to meet us at the dock.

John and an Alaskan State Trooper met the boat as the crew tied off at the Sand Point dock. John ordered the captain to remain in Sand Point until his hearing the following day. He drove me back to Sand Point where I told him of what happened and wrote out my report before falling asleep. When I awoke the following day, John informed me the District Attorney said we could not use the fact that the captain had pulled a weapon on me in the hearing as I had promised him I would not do so. I was glad to hear it. Neither he nor his crew had harmed me in any way, even though they outnumbered me. The man was in enough trouble. The trial went smoothly. The captain and crew were fined heavily and warned if they were caught fishing in closed waters again, they would lose their commercial fishing license and boat. That threat probably meant more to them than the loss of thousands of dollars.

After the court hearing John flew out and brought Will back to the Fish and Game complex. Will was sheepish when asked why he did not assist me and refused to answer any questions about his behavior. I looked at John and again requested to patrol by myself again. Again John refused. I did not bother approaching Will. He should have never been hired.

Two trips later, as my summer employment was approaching its end, I had my final bear encounter. After setting up camp on a hill overlooking a bay we were to watch, I decided to take my 8mm Rolex movie camera and get some movies of brown bears. I already had film of bears fishing from a distance, fox, seals and salmon, but no real close-up movies of bears.

I paddled across the stream to a large meadow of grass where I had seen four brown bears earlier. After walking about 75 yards into the meadow, the four bears came out from behind some brush about 200 yards away. The two adults looked almost identical and were accompanied by two first-year cubs. They either did not see me or were ignoring me as I filmed them. Suddenly one of the adults looked my way and stood on its hind legs. I had not noticed that the wind had changed, allowing the bears to smell me.

The one staring at me suddenly dropped down on all four legs and charged. I continued filming as I backed rapidly toward the stream, still facing the bear. I pulled out my pistol and shot two rounds into the air while doing so. The charging bear stopped about fifty yards away and stood up on its hind legs again. I stopped filming and looked behind me at the river. When I looked back at the bear it was again on all four legs, but now the ears were flat, and it was growling and snapping its teeth as it charged. Noting the difference between a curious animal and a furious mother, I dropped my camera and pistol, ran to the river and dove into the deep channel next to the bank. I am a very good swimmer and scuba certified. I had no trouble swimming fifty yards downstream under water and emerging next to the bank, hiding behind some willows.

The noise the mother bear made tearing up the area where I had dropped my camera, gun and pack was deafening in the silence of this remote wilderness. I remained submerged in the frigid water for ten more minutes before the tearing of willow brush and infuriated growls subsided. Finally, after another five minutes of silence, I emerged from the river and cautiously approached where I had dropped my belongings. The packsack was completely demolished. Only one shoulder strap was recognizable. My movie camera was untouched and lay under some torn-up tundra where I had dropped it. Despite looking for over an hour, I never found my .357 pistol. I was amazed at the devastation the mother brown bear made of the area that I had been standing on before diving into the river. Not a willow was upright, and the ground looked like a farmer's plow had gone through it. In all my subsequent years in Alaska, I never again saw a bear do so much damage. I later caught wolverines in traps that did as much destruction over a larger area than this, but never a wounded or angry bear.

This incident cemented forever in my mind just how dangerous bears could be, and how much respect they deserved. Thinking back later over the incident, the strangest part was the two adult bears traveling together with cubs. Males often eat newborn cubs, so sows usually don't let them close to their young.

The film of the charging bear and the damage to the terrain was so dramatic it was a hit with everyone who saw it, until the whole reel was stolen years later by the owner of a construction firm I once worked for. The loss of the history, terrain and animals I filmed that summer has bothered me for more than fifty years. I wish the man who claimed he had lost it somehow was still alive so I could punch him in the nose again.

The next several trips out of Sand Point to watch over closed fishing waters went smoothly, and I soon was back in sunny warm Fairbanks, getting reacquainted with my wife, Sharon. We bought an eighteen foot Grumman square stern canoe, 10 hp Mercury outboard motor, and a lift to attach the motor to the back of the canoe. We headed up the Steese Highway to our Jumpoff cabin to celebrate my return. I had certainly had my share of adventure in the past months. Some of it was due to my inattention, some to my natural love of exploration and some due to the nature of the job. All in all, it had been a great summer. I was safe and much more knowledgeable about Alaska. Will also had survived and was home with his family.

First Moose Hunt

OUR NEXT YEAR WAS MORE SETTLED. We knew what to expect from the weather. We spent a lot of time at Jumpoff fishing, hunting black bear and exploring Birch Creek. I shot my first black bear on the river, and several more on the gravel road connecting Circle to Fairbanks. We also moved out of student housing into an old, one-room log cabin on the banks of the Chena River that had not been lived in for years.

When Sharon approached me about the cabin I was dubious. We thoroughly enjoyed the Jumpoff cabin that fall, but I was reluctant to spend a winter in it. I had had my fill of camping out working for Fish and Game. The log cabin she wanted to move into had no electricity, running water or modern bathroom to make the extreme weather more livable. She was so excited about the prospect that I agreed to go look at it.

The cabin was a typical log structure, about fifteen feet wide by twenty feet long, located about forty feet from the Chena River about mile below the winter ice bridge crossing the Chena by the International Airport. The one window needed glazing. There was no stove or bed, and the roof needed work. I also would have to dig a new outhouse and build the frame for it. I did not know it then, but this was a tremendous experience and helped in the following years when we moved away from civilization. At this time, I was a little ticked at Sharon. She had all these great ideas but I had to do all the work. Autumn was approaching. I wanted to go moose hunting, not work on an old worn-out log cabin.

The roof and windows were the easiest to correct. Shake shingles and glazing compound quickly fixed them. For the bed, I found four empty fifty-gallon drums and built a wood platform above them for the mattress and bed. The area below became storage shelves for clothing. I made a Yukon stove out of another fifty-gallon barrel with a kit readily available in Fairbanks. Copying a friend's stove, I cut off a side portion of the barrel with an arc welder, and welded a flat plate of one-eight-inch steel to the remaining portion for a level place to keep food, coffee and water hot. For the kitchen area I built shelves with a solid top to put the Coleman stove

71

on, as well as room to wash and stack dishes. Dishes, pots and pans were stored in shelves below, as well as food. The outhouse took more work. Digging a deep hole in the frozen ground by hand is labor intensive.

By the time the outhouse was dug and the two-hole enclosed toilet walls and roof were built, I was more than ready to head up to Jumpoff for my first Alaskan moose hunt.

Sharon was working and not interested in going hunting in the increasingly chilly weather, so I headed up the Steese Highway alone. My canoe and outboard motor were stored at Jumpoff, leaving me only clothes, food and hunting gear to prepare. The drive up the Steese was beautiful. The birch trees were in shades of gold and red, and sometimes stretched for miles before disappearing over distant ridges. I stopped twice to shoot grouse along the road and arrived at my destination about three hours after leaving Fairbanks. After cooking the three grouse breasts for dinner I settled into my sleeping bag, anxious for morning to arrive.

Early next morning I slid my canoe into Crooked Creek and silently paddled down the slow moving stream. Mist was rising off the cold river water like wraiths above a graveyard. The river was liberally sprinkled with gold and red leaves dropped from trees preparing for the long winter. Once in a while I would pass a few ducks that had not gotten the memo to head south. I paddled the canoe instead of using the motor, because I wanted to be silent and not broadcast my presence.

I passed several cow moose with their calves. The mothers watched with twitching ears and unmoving eyes as they munched willow leaves along the river bank, while the newborns stared wide-eyed as the stranger in their midst glided silently by. Parking my canoe at the mouth of sloughs that were once part of this meandering stream, I would hunt as quietly as possible the rest of the closed-off waterway. It was below freezing and every step resounded with the crunch of ice. Walking silently inside the tree line was difficult as well. There were so many dead branches on the ground it was impossible not to make noise. Once in a while I would find a moose trail that made the hunting easier, but not often.

I heard several moose that could have been bulls crash off into the brush ahead of me, but never got a good look at them. Finally, at about 9:30 a.m., as I was having a cup of hot coffee to warm my hands as much as to drink, I heard a moose call in the back of a slough I was passing. It sounded like a bull in the rut calling for cows, so I quickly paddled to shore and beached the canoe as my cooling coffee lay spilt and abandoned on the bottom of the boat.

Putting the pack board on my back and chambering a round into my 7mm, I crept as silently as possible to the source of the noise that had drawn me to shore. My first sighting of a large bull moose standing on the banks of the slough took my breath away. It was huge, by far the biggest moose I had ever seen, with extremely large antlers. The moose was aware of my approach and stood watching me with twitching ears. When I stopped, the bull did an about face and disappeared into the forest behind it. I did not pull the trigger despite my desire to do so, as I did not have a clear shot.

I made myself sit down, as I knew the animal would be monitoring anything moving behind him for a while. His eyesight and sense of smell were far superior to mine. He knew where I was, so I wanted to give him time to relax before following him. I desired this animal so badly it was pure torture to remain still and silent. Finally, after twenty minutes of watching my breath condense into fog as I exhaled, I rose to follow the trail left by this superb animal.

I forced myself to remove branches on the ground and crawled underneath higher branches for another fifteen minutes before I caught sight of movement in the trees ahead. The moose was standing in a group of tamarack, watching his back trail. He had not seen me, but would if I moved. We both played the waiting game for minutes that seemed like hours before he began slowly walking again.

At last the bull walked into a small clearing, giving me a clear shot at his heart. After I pulled the trigger, I saw through my nine power Leopold scope the branches of a bush I had not noticed before sharply dip as my bullet hit it instead of the moose. The 7mm Magnum is a wonderful weapon, but the sectional density and speed of the bullet makes it a terrible weapon in brush. Anything that it hits in its path deflects it from its aimed spot. I quickly chambered another round and waited for another shot to present itself. Finally, about 200 yards away, the moose slowed and looked back. This time I put the bullet right through his heart and he dropped immediately.

Breathless and with shaking hands I approached the animal that would feed us for over a year. It was even bigger than I had thought, and was wedged between two trees. I checked to make sure it was dead before taking out my camera to record and honor his death for the rest of my life.

When I look at the pictures of this magnificent animal all these years later, I am still struck by its size and the amazement on my own face.

Reality is a bitch, and I soon had to face it. Reading about shooting an Alaskan moose while warmly snuggled in a bed is a far different proposition from really doing it. I had a dead one-thousand-pound animal at my feet, over a mile away from my canoe through thick trees and brush. The largest animal I had ever field-dressed in the woods this far from transportation before was a hundred and forty-pound deer. Even then I had someone to help by holding its legs, keeping the animal centered so I could clean it and get it ready to pack out. Think of the largest domestic bull you have ever seen, wedge it between two trees and try to figure out how to skin and butcher it with a four-inch knife blade, then carry it a mile on your back through difficult terrain. As I said, reality is a bitch, and only I could make this situation right. Any hunter who kills a big game animal is obligated to treat the beast with respect and take all the meat out.

In later years, I would try to never shoot a moose that I could not drive my airplane, boat or vehicle up close to, partly as a result of this hunt. I learned another valuable lesson here. The temperature started to warm with the awaking mosquitos arriving by the thousands. This was no longer fun, but a duty to complete as quickly and as efficiently as possible.

I tried unsuccessfully to move the animal to gain access to its belly and chest. I could not budge it, as it was stuck between two trees. I cut the jugular vein to let the animal bleed out as I walked back to my canoe to get an axe to remove the small trees. After cutting the trees down and moving them out of the way, I started on the real work of getting my animal to the canoe. No matter how much effort I put into it, I could not move the large inert mass of meat into a position where I could remove the guts and internal organs. After pondering the situation for a while, I wedged one front leg behind the antlers and tied the other front leg to a tree with a rope. I tied the two hind legs to different trees to stabilize the bull on its back, and got to work.

Several hours later I had the animal skinned and quartered, with back strap (New York steak for those who do not butcher) and tenderloin ready to be packed out. Only the skin, part of the rib cage, head and neck bone would be left behind. The trophy—the antlers—would come out last.

I was so excited to get started that morning I had not eaten breakfast, and was beginning to pay for the oversight. I needed to eat something.

Determined to pack a front quarter out to my canoe before sitting down to lunch and coffee, I tied a front quarter to my pack sack. It was so heavy that I could not raise the pack to my shoulders. Lying down, I slipped my arms through the shoulder straps, and tried to stand up. The weight was still too much; I could not get to my feet. With cramps starting to build in my legs, I rolled onto my stomach and crawled to a tree to help pull me to my feet. I had spent most of my adolescent summers working on a farm, throwing sixty pound bales of hay high over my head onto a trailer, but getting to my feet with this front quarter was almost more than I could handle—and it was only the first trip. I had four more after this.

Once I got to my feet and figured out the best posture to walk with the weight, I started for the canoe. When I got so tired I could not walk further, I would lean the meat against a tree, standing instead of sitting down, as I was afraid I would not be able get back up again. Arriving at the canoe, I lost my grip on the front shoulder while lowering it into the craft. It fell so hard into the canoe a piece of bone went through the bottom of the vessel. The puncture was large but so tight water did not leak into the canoe until I removed the last quarter at Jumpoff, and I came back to find it sunk.

Hours later I could barely stand, but gave out a large sigh of relief and satisfaction as I started my outboard motor to begin the trip back up Birch Creek to Jumpoff. Not only was my first moose hunt successful, but I had managed to solve all the problems of getting the meat out. It was not until I stopped to gas up at Central that I realized just how big this moose was. Roy commented as he was filling up my truck with gas that he had never seen a bigger moose come out of this area of Alaska. Roy should know, as he had lived and hunted there most of his life, and most people stopped and got gas or coffee on their way back to Fairbanks after their hunt. He went inside the garage and brought out a tape measure. The antlers were seventy-four inches wide with large palms, and fourteen points. I never shot a bigger moose in all my remaining time guiding and hunting in Alaska. I only saw one bigger, shot by one of my drop-off hunters from California, that measured eighty-two inches.

Sharon was ecstatic when I returned home with a truckload of moose meat the following day. We drove into Fairbanks and dropped it off at a local meat market to be cut and wrapped, as well as having fifty pounds. made into hot dogs and sausage. Following this, we rented two large meat lockers to store the processed meat from a Fairbanks moving company that rented lockers out to the public, because we did not have electricity at the cabin.

Sharon and I probably experienced the best time of our relationship during the following winter. We bought five cords of wood to heat the cabin. We also purchased a number of five gallon jugs to fill with water at a local spring for cooking and cleaning. I would get up early each morning to make a fire, perk coffee, and put a Coleman stove under the motor of our pickup to warm the oil enough for the engine to start. Then off to work and school we went, as clumping tires tried to regain a round form on a stiff, cold truck that resisted all efforts to steer.

Sharon had quit her job at the hospital to work for the Northern Biology Institute on campus, making this morning drive much easier. At school I would plug our truck's engine warmer into one of the many electrical outlets the university provided in its parking lots. We would take our weekly showers at Sandy Jamieson's log house. Sandy was an accomplished artist who would later became very well known for his art and his log home construction business. At this time, we were just a bunch of college kids meeting at his log cabin tucked into the woods, taking off our clothes, having a sauna, then jumping into a snow bank to cool down. The nudity part bothered me the first time. I was not used to a bunch of men and women running around undressed together. That discomfort soon passed, never to return.

* * *

When summer finally arrived I was contacted by Don Roberts, who wanted me to work for him as a temporary game warden in the Fairbanks Region. That temporary summer job led to a permanent position, prompting me to leave college prior to earning my degree.

I used my personal canoe that first summer to float the Chena River. I loved the river systems in the state more than the roads, as they took you away from civilization faster and more completely. I always carried my badge and citation book with me on these trips, as I would find more people fishing without a license on remote portions of the stream than those sections along the roadways. My sister, Rozan, visited us that summer. She still remembers seeing me walk up to check on fishermen while on a canoe trip down the Chena with the back of my jeans split open. I did not mind the fishermen looking at my bare behind as long as they had a licen Gissberg se to fish. On another trip down the Chena that fall, my stepbrother, Tom Gissberg, grabbed a branch of a sweeper as we rounded a sharp corner in the middle of a fast rapid, causing us to overturn. We clung to the overturned canoe until we hit calmer waters and could get it to shore. We lost some gear but not our sense of humor before continuing on down the river. My trusty 7mm Magnum rifle found a home on the bottom of the river until I retrieved it two weeks later on a subsequent trip.

Alaska seemed to be a magnet for my family. Mom would visit us later. Both my brothers, Richard and Jeff, came to visit and also stayed with us. Richard was not a stranger to Alaska, as he worked for Foss Tug out of Seattle and sailed into many Alaskan ports. He also spent a year at Dutch Harbor and later several years at Clear Air Force Base as a fireman and EMT. Rozan came up in the summer of 1966 and stayed until January. I was still not talking to Dad, so he was not invited.

Working for Fish and Game was the best and worst job of my entire life. I loved my summer in the Aleutians, so when Don Roberts asked me to work as an assistant for him in the summer of 1966 in the Fairbanks region, I jumped at the chance. Working for Don was a pleasure. He was fair, just, and expected certain performance standards from his employees.

This was illustrated later, after I cited a hunter for the wanton waste of three caribou. He shot three caribou on Eagle Summit on the Steese Highway, eighty miles north of Fairbanks. After shooting the caribou, the hunter drove to his home in Fairbanks. The next morning his truck was repossessed by the bank financing it. The bank called the Fish and Game office the following Monday stating the truck had three rotting caribou in it. Don asked me to investigate.

It was a difficult decision. Who was at fault, the hunter or the bank? After investigating, I decided it was the hunter's fault, as he shot the caribou and did not even field dress them. He had also had an opportunity to get the animals before and after the truck was repossessed, but refused to do so, saying the bank took possession without his permission. If the hunter had acted responsibly and taken good care of the animals after shooting them, I would not have cited him.

In a large city like Fairbanks, the District Attorney decided if charges would be filed. The DA, after reading my report, decided that his office would not file, as the bank was in possession of the truck when the caribou spoiled. My hunter ethics warred with my common sense; this was a very difficult judgment and legal call. In the end, the fact that a hunter has a responsibility to care for any animal he harvested won out.

I told the DA I understood where he was coming from, but disagreed with his decision. We argued. I insisted they file charges. He said no. I said I would file them without his support, and I subsequently filed the paperwork with the court myself after our meeting. That Stultz temper again! At the arraignment the DA got up and excused the DA's office from further legal proceeding in the matter, as they did not believe there was enough evidence for the State of Alaska to proceed. I got up and told the judge in my opinion, there was enough evidence to prove the defendant's culpability at trial. I told him I would represent the Department of Fish and Game and the State of Alaska in the matter. The judge looked at me as if I were crazy, but allowed the arraignment to proceed after noting the DA's decision on his file. The defendant pleaded not guilty. His lawyer, after listening to the DA and seeing the judge's reaction to my request, asked for a trial by judge instead of jury.

Don Roberts also looked at me like I was being irrational when I told him the results of the arraignment. He asked me if I was absolutely sure I did not want to drop the case. I replied that someone needed to pay for the waste of three caribou. He backed me up saying to proceed, but that I was probably making an enemy of the DA, and that I would regret it in the years to come. In my arrogance I dismissed it, thinking that DA would be just one of many.

In Alaska what I did was legal. Foolish, but legal. In smaller communities without a DA office present, Protection Officers routinely wrote and filed the legal paperwork with the local jurisdiction, which was usually a justice of the peace. I did so many times in the following years.

The trial had been set for a month from the date of arraignment. Doing a detailed and lengthy investigation of the defendant, I found that he had been convicted of two Fish and Game violations in the state of his residence prior to moving to Alaska. He was also charged for hunting without a license in another state.

I took this information to the DA, after apologizing for my youth and eagerness in the prior proceeding, in case it had caused him any embarrassment. I said I would like him to represent the State of Alaska in the upcoming trial. The DA looked at the new information, and at me, for a while. Finally, he told me he would represent the State. He congratulated me on the completeness of my research, but stated in no uncertain terms that his office and I needed to be on the same page from now on. We shook hands and in the months following we became friends. The defendant was found guilty of wanton waste at the trial.

The point of this was that Don Roberts stood behind my decision despite the fact that he knew I was letting my emotions get the better of me. He wanted me to learn to curb my impatience. Very few supervisors would have risked the ire of the District Attorney by doing so. Don was the only supervisor in Fish and Game ever to do that for me. Most of those I had direct interaction with were political creatures, more concerned with their careers than protecting Alaska's animal resources when conflicts arose.

The Fairbanks Protection Division of Fish and Game was responsible for enforcing Fish and Game regulations in an immense area stretching from the Alaska Range to the Arctic Ocean. At the time, most of this area was without roads, meaning the largest part had to be covered by air. I did not have a pilot's license in 1966, so most of my flying was as a passenger, but I learned a lot from Buck Holt, the primary pilot for the region at the time. He did not hesitate to give me stick time and explain the intricacies of bush flying.

One of the most important lessons I learned from Buck occurred when he was not even talking to me, but was explaining a landing approach to a mystified bush pilot. We had stopped on a small gravel bar in the Alaska Range to check on this pilot, who asked Buck how he could bank his Super Cub so deeply and rapidly, and come in for the landing without stalling out and crashing. The pilot was a noted guide in the area and had thousands of hours flying Alaska's dangerous mountains in Super Cubs. Buck said, "It's simple. Just don't hold the nose of the aircraft up while banking." That stuck with me forever, and I later puzzled many pilots while using the same approach.

It is beat into every beginning pilot to never let the nose of the aircraft sink toward the ground during a turn. You are judged on your ability to keep the airplane at the same altitude throughout the turn, and made to practice until you are able to do so. The descending final approach into airports is made in a very controlled manner, with wings banked no more than a thirty to forty-five degrees and letting the aircraft lose altitude by the power setting. Nothing should be forced or abrupt and all maneuvers should be accomplished in a smooth, controlled manner.

There is a very good reason for this. A pilot who lets the nose drop more than thirty-five degrees below the horizon cannot get the airplane back into level flight by pulling back on the yoke or control stick. Doing so only tightens the turn radius, ending in what is called a death spiral. You are taught that, if this occurs, you can simply level the wings out of the bank and pull the nose up, gaining level flight again. Unfortunately, some pilots panic, especially when close to the ground, and keep pulling back without leveling the wings until they and the craft they are flying meet the ground with tragic results.

So Buck's landing approach technique ran counter to what most pilots were trained to do. I later took this a step further by raising my aircraft nose, pointing almost straight up, prior to starting the approach when I needed to make a one hundred and eighty degree turn at the same time. Reducing power, I would apply full rudder, push the stick full forward and to the side of the direction I wanted. The aircraft would roll over on its back and the nose would quickly point toward the ground, holding the pilot and passengers in a weightless embrace. When the nose was pointed in the direction I wanted, I would level the wings and pull up into level flight before my airspeed built up. I could pull the nose up, having lost only about one hundred feet, while completing a one hundred and eighty degree turn going in the opposite direction in an extremely small radius. It is a modified "split S" turn that is normally done much higher in the air. It is definitely not something any pilot should attempt unless it is to perfection at a high enough altitude to safely recover from a stall or spin. Buck's method was another option when a simpler approach was required. The trick in both maneuvers is to know your airplane intimately. All aircraft tell pilots, without use of stall horns, if they are being mishandled or asked to do things they were not designed to accomplish. Good pilots learn their aircraft's language. Bad Alaska pilots who do not usually end up dead or horribly injured.

In most landings or turns, this would be a dangerous approach, especially in controlled airspace around airports. But it was useful to learn because in Alaska there are gravel bars or small lakes in narrow canyons. It was also useful when you found yourself unintentionally going up a narrow canyon in bad weather, and you needed to turn back quickly. However, if you miscalculated, you were most likely to be standing or lying beside a crumpled airplane.

In Fairbanks I spent most of my time the first year on the roads in a green Ford station wagon with the Fish and Game logo on the doors, enforcing fishing and hunting regulations in the greater Fairbanks area. The Chena River attracted a lot of sports fishermen from both the Fairbanks area and Fort Wainwright. Hunting was popular on the Chena Hot Springs Road, Steese, and Elliott highways. There was always somewhere to patrol twelve months of the year. I would happily spend seventy to eighty hours a week enforcing Fish and Game regulations without thinking of it as a job.

This led to hard feelings from some officers. They felt I was making them look bad by writing so many violation citations and working long hours. The most notable of these was by a man I will refer to as "Sergeant Joe," my immediate supervisor. He ignored me as much as possible, and was borderline hostile when he couldn't. He told me he would get me fired one of these days. When a report came in of caribou being shot and left where they fell on Eagle Summit, he told me he knew I had done it when I patrolled up there that weekend, and he would prove it. He was definitely not happy when I was offered a job as a full-time warden.

Things came to a conclusion with Sergeant Joe when, on the opening of the hunting season in the Fairbanks area, Don Roberts assigned the Sergeant and me to patrol the Steese Highway. John was to patrol Eagle Summit to Central, and I was assigned Central to Circle City. During my hunter checks, several people told me there was suspicious hunting activity between Eagle Summit and Central. When I told them that an officer was already patrolling that area, they replied they had not seen any evidence of Fish and Game patrols, and asked me to check it out.

Driving back to Central, I saw Sergeant Joe washing his patrol vehicle at the gas station. It was 12:30 p.m., and evident that he had not been out patrolling. I stopped to tell him about the reports of illegal hunting in his patrol area, but he would not look at or speak to me. I thought the hell with him, and drove to the area where the hunting violations supposedly happened. I found two men driving a Jeep Wagoneer, loading the last of a cow moose into their vehicle. Cow season was not open. I took statements from the hunters, issued citations and confiscated the meat and their rifles.

Monday morning, after reading my report on the incident, Don called me into his office and asked me to explain why I was patrolling out of my area. Fed up with the situation, I told Don exactly what had happened. He dismissed me and called Joe into his office. Several days later Sergeant Joe resigned from Fish and Game.

Sergeant Joe had the last laugh, however. A year later he found out, somehow, that I had bought a resident hunting license the first year I was in Alaska. He reported it to the Records Division in Juneau, who investigated and found out it was true. When Don Roberts called me into his office to ask about the complaint, I admitted it. It cost me my job, but I had no hard feelings. I broke the law and paid the price. It was back to the University of Alaska to finish my degree in education.

* * *

In 1967, after being fired from Fish and Game, I returned to the University of Alaska to finish my education degree. Our first son was born on December 1 of that year. We named him Michael Stewart Stultz Jr., or Little Mike. Sharon had previously had six miscarriages, so Michael's arrival was a blessed event. Up to that point, we had tried everything medically available without success to allow her to carry a baby to full term. We even tried sending her outside Alaska to her mother's house once when she became pregnant. Her mother, deciding blood was not thicker than water after all, kicked her out after several months, resulting in another miscarriage. Michael was a joy to us. He was a happy kid who never woke us up in the middle of the night or cried without good reason. I loved being a Daddy and playing with him.

So we were really looking forward to having a second child when David arrived in April of 1970 just before we moved to Yakutat. Even though it was late April when he was born, it was almost minus forty degrees outside. We were living in a modern house on the outskirts of Fairbanks three miles upriver from our old cabin on the Chena River. It had a coal furnace that quit the day we brought David home from the hospital. I could not contact the owner or get anyone to come out and repair it, making it necessary to move into a hotel downtown. Even though David's homecoming was a mixed bag of joy and consternation, we felt very lucky to have two beautiful healthy sons after all the sadness of Sharon's not being able to carry babies to term. David right from the start was not as easy to please as Michael. He complained immediately if things were not to his satisfaction no matter if it was in the middle of the day or night. He knew what he wanted, and he wanted it right now.

*   *   *

My first teaching job after graduation was at Clark Junior High in Anchorage in 1968. I taught a three-hour block of English, History and Reading. That year was memorable on three counts: 1) The class consisted of mostly female students; 2) We bought a new 1968 Toyota Land Cruiser with a winch on the front, and our first snowmobile; 3) We met a wonderful couple, John and Kathy Peterson.

I was shocked when all those young females filed into my classroom that first morning. I was soon begging the principal to transfer any male student into my class he could find, no matter if they were problem students or not. Teaching was easy compared to handling a gaggle of eighth-grade girls.

My father's sternly disciplined manner of teaching was not my style. The vivid memories of returned papers cluttered with red ink and disparaging comments made me more sympathetic to students who were struggling. Instead of trying to correct every spelling or punctuation error, I would try to find something original or positive with each paper. I emphasized what was good about the student's work, while holding to a minimum pointing out errors in spelling and grammar.

I would even purposely misspell words on the blackboard and give extra credit to students who discovered them, thereby providing incentive to study spelling more intently. I made sure even the lower-level students could catch the errors. Students who were further along in their studies could assist their friends who were struggling. It worked surprisingly well. I maintained this approach to teaching at every school where I taught. It was unconventional and did not receive some of my fellow educators' approval, but students who had seldom had a teacher give them compliments began to enjoy school and studied harder. Brighter students learned deeper concepts and more material by helping their friends. In the end, every student gained from the process, not just the brightest kids in class.

Not to say I didn't have rules. My biggest rule was that students were to treat each other with respect at all times. The first fifteen minutes of each day they were to come in quietly and read. I did not care if it was a magazine, a car repair manual or a novel. I just wanted them to learn to enjoy reading. Students who handed in every assignment would receive a passing grade on their report card, no matter what they scored on tests. Mastery of the subject matter was secondary to the student learning the right way to study and enjoy school. Mastery could come later. The bright kids would learn the lessons no matter how I taught.

My last rule was put in later, when I became aware that some of these kids came from very dysfunctional families and may not have been able to sleep the night before or eat breakfast before coming to school. That rule was that any student who did not feel he or she could participate in the classroom could go to the back row and sleep for the first hour. I would also privately tell students that, if they were not getting breakfast, a free lunch ticket would be available to them. All they had to do was leave a note on my desk.

A lot of teachers and some parents did not approve of my teaching methodology. I was called in by the principal more than once that first year, for a conference with an upset parent who wanted me to follow all the traditional classroom rules. The principal would listen sympathetically to the parents, but after they left he would pat me on the shoulder, saying, "Keep up the good work." He would also quietly transfer some of the students who were having problems in other classrooms into my class.

John and Kathy Peterson were also teachers. John taught shop at Clark, so I got to know him first. When we first met in 1968, they lived in a double-wide trailer before building a very nice house in the hills outside Anchorage proper. John was my type of person. He was direct and honest, and loved to fish and hunt as much I as did. I don't remember where or what Kathy taught. When I was invited over to their trailer the first time, she came across as a quiet and classy lady. That image never changed. I have never seen her lose her temper, even when her eyes were darting fire, in all the years I have known her. I liked her immediately, as well.

The Petersons came from Colorado and arrived in Anchorage several years before Sharon and I did. John knew all the fishing places around Anchorage. We spent many a weekend fishing, even if that meant hiring a local bush pilot to fly us out to remote lakes and rivers. John taught me how to catch red salmon with flies on the Russian River; to use ice from glaciers in coolers whenever possible, as it is much colder and lasts four times as long as commercial ice; how much fun snow machining was. We caught red salmon in Swan Lake, king salmon on the Deshka River, and trout in Bonnie Lake. We smoked much of the salmon we caught.

The Deshka River trip was one of those things in life I could do over and over. There were four of us on the trip: John, Curt Henning, Barney Kay and me. We all taught at Clark Junior High. We hired a floatplane out of Lake Hood in Anchorage. They flew us and our gear out to a small lake close to the upper reaches of the Deshka, and agreed to pick us up five days later where the river emptied into the Susitna River. After packing our gear over to the banks of the river, we inflated the rubber rafts and started down this medium-sized, crystal clear stream. It is a short river, only forty-four miles long, lined with tall pines and bushy willows, but it contained a large run of Chinook salmon. The resident rainbow were present in abundance as well, but our main focus was salmon. The river today does not much resemble the Deshka we fished in 1968. Now it has a fishing lodge, gated access, and special regulations because of motorboat wake damage to its banks. We did not see another person on our trip, while today you would have to dodge motorboats.

We started out fishing by casting lures, but as soon as we caught a female Chinook bulging with eggs, I switched over to the roe. I can vividly remember trying to get the fresh salmon eggs through the swarms of rainbow trout that followed the Chinook to feast upon their eggs when the salmon finally reached their spawning grounds. Nine times out of ten they would clean my hook of bait before I could get it low enough in the water for the salmon to have a chance at it. It was maddening to watch the constant jiggle of the rod tip, trying to decide whether it was a trout or salmon. The reactionary strike as I sharply jerked the rod tip to set the hook usually came up empty. These fish were playing with me and getting a free dinner. When I would finally hook a salmon, all hell would break loose. The Garcia spinning reel would screech in protest as the large fish would test it and the eighteen-pound line, in a mad dash for freedom. I would frantically adjust the tension of the reel, trying to adjust the drag to compensate for the energy of the fish. Sometimes I won, but just as often, the Chinook would pull free or break my line. It was a battle fought with finesse, glee, and my fishing laugh, often followed by a groan of disappointment and a bow of respect for these magnificent fish.

Chinook salmon usually spawn in the deeper rivers of Alaska, but can run up smaller rivers as well. I usually think of them as having a seven-year life cycle, but actually they can return to the stream of their origin anywhere from one to eight years. They are the largest of the Pacific salmon, and can reach a weight of over one hundred pounds in extreme cases. Alaska Department of Fish and Game set the weight of a trophy Chinook at fifty pounds. Of all the hundreds of Chinook I caught in Alaska, only eleven were over fifty pounds, with the largest topping the scales at eighty-five pounds. Some rivers, like the Kenai, were noted for having larger Chinook. In the Deshka, I think the largest any of us caught was a little over twenty pounds.

We were not here for trophy fishing, however. We were here for fun and relaxation after a long year of teaching. The best thing about teaching was not the salary (my first year I only earned $8,000), but having the summers off to do things like this. Slowly our coolers filled with salmon as we wound our way slowly toward the Susitna River.

The upper portion of this short river contained faster water and was liberally sprinkled with large boulders. I lost more than one fish that ran my line around a boulder while we quickly floated down the opposite side. It was not long before I wished I had brought another spool of line, because the line on my reel was rapidly getting shorter. I remember being down to about fifty yards remaining on my reel, after beginning the trip with 220 yards. I hooked one salmon at the end of our journey, while waiting for the floatplane to pick us up. It ran me around a snag on the bottom of the river. Being desperate for line, I took off my clothes and dove into the river. Following the line down twenty feet to the bottom, I unwound it from the stump. The water was freezing cold. I needed fishing line more than body heat.

At the end of the first year of teaching in Anchorage, I transferred to Lathrop High School in Fairbanks. I had missed spending time at Jumpoff and wanted to be closer to it. I would continue to see John and Kathy for many years and have other adventures with them.

While teaching at Lathrop High School, I started taking flying lessons and took the FAA written test for a pilot's license. Getting a license to fly the bush of Alaska became more important to me each year. Every year my adventures had progressed further from the road systems. I had graduated from a two-wheel to a four-wheel drive vehicle with a winch. Tiring of that, I got a canoe with an outboard motor on a lift to get into places my four-wheel vehicle could not take me. The final step in my mind was to get a pilot's license and my personal airplane to open the entirety of Alaskan wilderness to me.

The school system in Fairbanks sponsored a two-month evening class for teachers who wanted to take the written test and become private pilots. At the end of this class I was amazed that over 50 percent of the college-educated teachers failed the final exam. I passed the written exam with only one wrong answer. I immediately began the process of getting a flight instructor to complete actual flight qualification. My flight instructor was named John Seale. He guided me through the flight proficiency portion of becoming a private pilot.

I scoffed to myself when my instructor told me that when or if I finally got my license I should remember that I was just learning to fly. The next 200 hours after passing the flight examination would become the most dangerous of my flying career. Since I could land and take off without difficulty and passed my written test with the highest score in the class, I mistakenly believed I was better than most beginning pilots and smiled politely at his comment. However, John turned out to be much smarter than I.

I had not completed taking my flight check at forty hours of flying before realizing how smart my instructor was, and how dumb I was to question his judgment. The first incident happened when he told me to fly to Fairbanks International Airport from the small dirt airstrip where I was learning to fly. John wanted me to be comfortable landing at a large modern airport. I called Fairbanks Flight Control prior to getting permission to enter the downwind path for landing. I was mentally congratulating myself on how professional I was handling this new process. The tower cleared me for final approach, advising that a large jet was landing ahead of me, and to use caution. I watched the jet land and then turned from base to the final approach when everything went to hell.

The first indication something was wrong was when the small Cessna 150 I was flying jumped violently up, then down, before rolling over on its back. Cool I was not, as my instructor yelled to give him control of the aircraft. He somehow got the airplane upright before bringing it to a halt on the runway. He looked at me in exasperation and said, "I told you before about vortices behind large aircraft. You need to learn to listen and think instead of thinking you know everything." I was truly contrite as I cowered beneath his fierce gaze. This was a flying mistake never to be repeated. It was that terrifying.

The second incident that made me aware of how little I knew about controlling an aircraft occurred on my first cross-country flight. This flight is one of the two mandatory cross-country flights required before an aspiring pilot can get his license. The destination airport must be a minimum of two hours away from the student pilot's departure point. On first flight, an instructor accompanies you and checks your route planning, flight plan, weight and balance, and other intricacies pilots must handle before flying on a long journey. The second cross-country had to be completed by the student alone in the airplane. I considered two possible airports for my first cross-country: Tok and Tanana. I finally chose Tanana because it was off the road systems and mirrored the type of flying I wanted to do. That is, I would not have any roads to follow and my ending point was a wilderness village not much affected by civilization or connected to a road system.

It was a typical interior Alaska summer afternoon when we took off. The few white cumulus clouds were still puffy and not close to gaining the energy needed to transform into thundershowers. Everything went smoothly as I consulted the map on my lap to keep track of our location. Following the Tanana River past Nenana, I set the nose of the aircraft toward some grey cliffs bordering the Kantishna River, not having any idea that in the years ahead I would build a homestead twenty miles beyond this river. Passing the mouth of the Kantishna, I again followed the Tanana down to its conjunction with the Yukon River.

About five miles from where the two rivers met, I saw towering clouds of blowing sand. Looking at my instructor I asked what caused it. He told me that the blowing sand was where the Tanana River met and became the Yukon River. Wind from both rivers converged and mixed there, and that I should exercise caution. Knowing that the airport was five miles beyond the blowing sand, I headed to the airport. I added power to fly above the sand.

Not knowing how much energy the winds from the two rivers were generating, I was taken by surprise when the aircraft started bouncing all over the air. My rate of climb instrument was cascading from plus 2,500 feet a minute to minus 2,500 feet per minute. I was having an extremely difficult time keeping the nose of the aircraft pointed in the general direction I wanted to head. It was as though I flew into a mix master, which in reality, I had. John told me not to fight the wild winds, but to reduce speed and average out the rough direction changes. We were almost five miles beyond the Tanana Airport before I felt I had control again. The flight back to the airport took a long time, bucking 40 mph headwinds and moderate turbulence.

After we landed and drank a cup of the FAA station's coffee, my instructor asked me what I had done wrong and how I would correct it in the future. Thinking about what happened, it seemed to me there were two choices: 1) Climbing much higher above the blowing sand, or 2) Cutting across the Yukon before it met the Tanana, and coming in from the other side of the runway. He accepted both alternatives, but added a note of caution. Flying in Alaska is not like flying in other states. There are so many variables to weather and flying conditions, a pilot must always be alert to the conditions around him and think about what they mean to his flight. Inattention to details could be deadly here, because it can be extremely difficult to find missing aircraft. He ended by saying that when I got my pilot's license, I was not yet a pilot. It was just a piece of paper that allowed me to start learning how to be a pilot in Alaska. He was so right.

Author and first moose.

First moose.

David refusing to come out of the rain.

David eating by campfire on upper Birch Creek.

Curt Henning, author and John Peterson.

Alaska State Troopers and the Department of Fish and Game

IT WAS NOT LONG before I began to feel constrained by the four walls enclosing my classroom. I loved teaching kids, but I hated being inside a small room all day, so in my second year teaching in Fairbanks I applied to the Alaska State Troopers for a patrol position. The qualifications for the Alaska State Troopers positions were very high. I did not think there was much chance of obtaining a job with them. You had to be one of the top three candidates in both the written intelligence test and the oral interview to be offered a job. There were hundreds of applicants for these positions from both inside and outside Alaska. Extra points were given to veterans of our Armed Forces. I had not served in Vietnam because of the two times I had broken my back. I was surprised when the offer of employment came in the mail several months after taking the intelligence and oral exams.

The Alaska State Troopers was a great organization. I loved the dedication and work ethic of everyone with whom I came into contact. There was none of the office politics or backstabbing I had witnessed in Fish and Game. However, it was just a job for me. I was happy to be outside and not enclosed in a four wall prison, but I did not have the passion for being a Trooper as I had as a Game Warden.

Almost everyone with whom I interacted in both organizations was armed with a weapon. In the State Troopers many of the people were impaired or angry that I contacted, while as a Game Warden they were mostly friendly unless being cited for a violation of Fish and Game regulations. Yet, despite being alone without backup, in most of the encounters with armed citizens, there were not incidents of unprovoked or unwarranted shooting by law enforcement personnel that I now read about in my home town and on national news.

One of the many incidents I had with an angry armed individual occurred in Nenana. I was told by the dispatcher to assist Wayne Walters, the town marshal, who had received information that a man armed with a rifle was headed into town with the intention of shooting his ex-wife and her current boyfriend. I met Walters outside the town café where he explained that the man was driving a Ford station wagon and was known to have a bad temper.

A short while later the guy drove by us and parked down by the Tanana River at the tug boat depot. We approached him as he exited his vehicle with Walters taking the lead. This was his town. I separated from Walters so we would not be standing next to one another making ourselves an easy target if the man opened fire. He was obviously upset and ignored Walters's attempts to communicate with him. Walking to the back of his station wagon, he opened the back door and pulled out a rifle hidden under a red and black blanket.

I was behind and to the side of the agitated man and immediately drew my .357 Magnum pistol. I could have shot the man as my training told me to do, but gave Walters a chance to calm the person down. I kept my eye on the man's trigger finger which was on the trigger guard and not the trigger itself. If he moved his finger to the trigger, I would shoot. Walters, who was a big burly man, did not draw his weapon, but told the man in a loud commanding voice to put the weapon down. Talking to him and calming the situation, he was able to get the guy to hand him the rifle without anyone being injured. Another incident involved driving a vehicle at high speed on frozen roadways. I was patrolling the North Pole area when the dispatcher radioed for me to respond to the report of gunfire at a tavern outside Fairbanks. It was about 1:30 a.m. and the weather -45 degrees outside, with some isolated ice fog. The Ford Inceptor's powerful engine soon hit 125 mph on the empty four-lane highway, with lights flashing and siren howling. When I let off the gas to slow down well before turning off to the bar, the patrol vehicle started spinning donuts down the middle of the highway, just from the compression of the engine slowing down. There was nothing I could do to control the situation, as the spins were too rapid. I just held the steering wheel straight and braced myself for the impact of crashing. Surprisingly, I ended up facing the wrong way in the middle of the highway, no worse for wear, other than an accelerated heart rate. Arriving at the bar, I found the report of shots being fired was not true.

I enjoyed the job of being a State Trooper, but found my personality changing. The constant interactions with drunks, belligerent drivers and other civilian personalities at odds with law enforcement was slowly altering me. One night, after stopping a swerving vehicle for a possible DUI violation, I was confronted by the angry and profane wife of a local politician. I could not smell any alcohol on her breath, her eyes were not blood shot, and she passed the walking sobriety test. I made her "walk the line" and do other sobriety tests simply because she made me mad by her profane abuse and the fact she told me I could shove my Breathalyzer up my ass. She said the vehicle was swerving because she had dropped her cigarette and was looking for it. She also stated any half-trained monkey could see she was not drunk, and would quit bothering her.

My Stultz temper was boiling as I found myself looking at her license plate light while writing down the number. I twice had to fight the overwhelming urge to break it, thereby faking a vehicle code violation and haul her sorry, pampered ass off to jail for driving without a license plate light. I had never lied in court, cheated on investigational facts or been untruthful in any circumstance involving charging a person with a crime. This was not me. I faced the fact that I was probably not psychologically suited for this type of law enforcement position. I have the utmost respect for honest police officers and the State Trooper organization; they have an extremely difficult job. But when Don Roberts later offered me a chance to rejoin the Fish and Game Protection Division, I jumped at it.

Don had probably forced the Director to hire me back by arguing that the State Troopers had hired me, and that I was, from all appearances doing a good job for them. There was bad blood between Don and the Director that I thought at the time had to do with the competition for the Director's position. He never stated this, but from what Don both said and did not say about the Director, I had the feeling there was tension between them.

I really enjoyed being a Game Warden. It was my calling in life. I have never been happier on the job than when patrolling in vehicle, airplane or boat for the Department. I also respected and liked working for Don. By this time, I had my private pilot's license, so I got to fly along on many more enforcement patrols off the road system as Fish and Game instructors prepared me for being one of their pilots. Phil Connors had replaced Buck Holts as the primary pilot for the Fairbanks Region. Phil was from Texas and was a past contract instructor for military pilots in Texas. He was both an excellent instructor and pilot. He taught me a lot about bush, instrument and float flying. He was more reserved than Buck, but we got along okay.

I got to fly along with and learn from some of the best bush pilots in Alaska. We flew from the Alaska Range to the Bering Sea. Flying in Alaska is extremely challenging and results in many crashes every month of the year. I remember one time Phil and I were flying the Brooks Range when the weather turned bad on us. I was flying a Cessna 180 on floats and started up a creek in a heavy snow storm that came up unexpectedly. I thought this creek led to a lake where it had been reported personnel from oil companies were illegally harvesting large amounts of lake trout. I was wrong. This was not the correct creek.

I was making a mistake that kills many Alaska pilots. You never fly up a creek in bad weather unless you are absolutely sure you will not end up in a dead-end canyon you can't climb out of. I was doing that. Phil asked me if I knew going up this creek was safe. Having fished the lake several times, I replied yes. Too soon, however, I was adding power to the engine to stay above the terrain. This was not right. I turned to Phil and said I made a mistake. This is not the correct creek.

He did not say anything, other than telling me to give him control of the airplane. He banked so we were flying on the left side of the canyon we were traveling up, reduced power while applying flaps, and did a one hundred and eighty degree turn back down the canyon. The weather had cleared enough that halfway through the turn I could see that if Phil had not acted when he did we would have crashed. We were in a dead end canyon on the wrong side of the power curve. Flying up a pass or approaching a mountain ridge you always want to carry excess speed to allow you to climb or turn if it becomes necessary. Being behind the power curve means you have already expended all the speed and energy needed to accomplish this and your airplane is struggling to stay airborne. As it was, the stall warning screamed throughout the turn. There are few things in life that rivet your attention as being in an airplane in a ninety-degree bank on the verge of falling out of the sky watching a mountain fill your windshield. Phil missed the opposite side of the canyon by no more than twenty feet. Both Phil and I thought we were dead. Very few pilots could have made that turn. Later, after we had landed safely, he informed me that he could not have pulled back any more on the control yoke without stalling the airplane. He did not have to tell me I made a bad mistake. It was another lesson learned and never repeated.

Back then there was neither GPS nor the number of weather reporting locations now available. If you were going to fly in Alaska, you had to learn to fly in bad weather, as it changed so frequently and so quickly. On the longer flights you invariably flew through weather you had not anticipated.

Some of the rules were so simple you would think they were common sense, like never fly up a creek in bad weather, always fly on the right side of a mountain pass and never the center or left side, and never try to turn in a small canyon in extreme weather. You should always turn before you get into an extreme visibility or turbulence situation if you can. If the conditions change so quickly you can not avoid them, keep going the direction you are flying or land straight ahead.

Pilots must fly on the right side of a mountain pass, because airplanes approaching one another head-on have very little time to react to avoid a fatal crash. This is especially true as weather worsens, so it is important for pilots to fly on their side of the pass. Not doing so is akin to two motorists driving down a freeway at one hundred miles an hour in fog in the same lane approaching from different directions. Only bad things can happen.

I had many experiences with such circumstances. In my years of flying the Alaska bush, I saw the remains of many crumpled aircraft in mountain passes where pilots had tried to turn back when conditions said otherwise. I know from experience that reading or being told what to do is much simpler than following through on the advice when you are in the middle of fighting for your life. One other rule I leaned from Phil is that when you become lost in bad weather, find a creek and fly down it. The creek will eventually run into a river that will have inhabitants along its bank where you can land and find out where you are.

Don told me I had the highest rate of finding fish and game violations and later convictions in court of any Protection Officer in the state. I prided myself on being thorough and fair. I think the judges picked up on this, because when a defendant or attorney brought up something I had not considered in my investigation, I would admit it instead lying or trying to cover it up. I only lost two court cases in my career as a State Trooper and Fish and Game.

I lost a DUI case as a State Trooper. The guy was driving the wrong way on a four-lane highway leading out of Fairbanks. He was weaving over the two lanes in a manner consistent with being seriously impaired. I became aware of him when I saw the vehicle he was driving traveling in the same direction I was on the wrong side of the median strip. I put on my siren and lights, and drove as quickly as possible to a crossover location to pull him over before an accident occurred. He completely ignored me as he drove past, weaving all over the road.

When I finally got him stopped he was so drunk he could not stand up to take even the most basic sobriety tests after refusing to take the Breathalyzer. The man's speech was so slurred I had a hard time understanding him. He was more incapacitated than anyone I had ever pulled over. During the trial his lawyer somehow convinced the jury that the man had a bad leg, and that was the reason for his stumbling. He also claimed that his client was trying to turn around when I stopped him. The judge gave me a look and a shrug of the shoulders after the jury read the "not guilty" verdict, as if to say the process is not perfect but it's the best judicial system we have. I had done my job by getting him off the road. The jury did not do theirs.

The second case I lost had to do with a dog while working for Fish and Game. A woman in Fairbanks wanted to breed and sell Australian dingoes. Dingoes are wild dogs in Australia, and are pure pack animals. A biologist working with Sharon at the Arctic Biological Institute brought this to my attention, and asked me to talk to the lady and confiscate the dog if it was true. There were Fish and Game laws prohibiting bringing dangerous foreign animal species into the state and/or breeding them without a special permit. Sharon told me that the Northern Arctic Biological Institute had studied the shorthair dingoes and found them to be even more cold-weather tolerant than Alaskan wolves. A couple of researchers had put a dingo into a cage with a wolf to see what would happen. The dingo had the much larger male wolf on its back in a few seconds. I am not sure if this was true, but it was the information I had at the time. I do know the Game Division of Fish and Game and the University of Alaska were worried about dingoes getting loose and forming packs.

I talked to the dingo owner, and discovered that she owned a female she planned to breed, and that she intended to sell the pups without a permit. She would not tell me who owned the male dingo she planned to breed with hers. I confiscated the animal and put it in a local shelter while the trial took place. Her attorney opted for a trial by judge instead of by jury. The DA informed me we faced an uphill battle, as the female judge assigned the case was a well-known supporter of animal rights. He was right. We lost the case. Not all was lost however, as the female dingo somehow died while under the care of a local veterinarian while the trial was going on.

Don would assign every case to me that required a high level of investigation. I had solved a number of difficult cases that required those abilities, so he would always call me into his office when he became aware of a case more difficult than normal. One of the two hardest cases Don assigned me involved a report from a local taxidermist of helicopter pilots shooting animals from the air on the North Slope. The other involved an Army four-star general.

Don called me into his office and said a local taxidermist had overheard two helicopter pilots bragging about shooting wolves and wolverines out of their helicopters, and asked me to investigate. He told me the investigation was very sensitive, as our Governor, Wally Hickel, had just made a statement to the national media that there was no truth to the rumors of oil company helicopters hunting illegally on the North Slope.

I called the taxidermist who had talked to Don. He was also a friend who did all my taxidermy work. We agreed I would work undercover as his assistant when the pilots were due to return with more skins. That day came and went without the pilots coming into the shop. My friend was worked up over the situation, so I decided not to delay the investigation, but go the North Slope and see for myself. I had the names of the helicopter pilots and the oil company they flew for.

I flew to Dead Horse and interviewed oil company executives who said none of their pilots would ever do such a thing as shooting animals out of their company's helicopter. Besides, it was against company policy. When I asked to talk to the two pilots, the executives became evasive, claiming the pilots were out flying geologists around the North Slope from camp to camp. When asked to see their schedules to determine when they were due back in Dead Horse, I was told there was no schedule, and they did not know when either of the two would come back to Dead Horse. When I asked for the names of the geologists they were flying, I was told they did not know, as it changed from day to day. Okay, I was being stonewalled.

I asked my pilot if he knew where these remote camps were located. He replied that he had flown into them. I told him to start with the closest and work out from there to see if we could find out where the pilots were. He was not really comfortable doing this as he earned a lot of his income flying for the oil companies, but finally agreed to take me, as long he was not brought into the investigation.

At the first four camps we checked, they all knew the pilots but did not know where they were or when they would fly back into the camp. They all denied knowing anything about shooting illegally from a helicopter. At the fifth camp, I got lucky. After all the interviews and subsequent denials someone slipped a piece of paper in the parka I had hung up when entering the camp. The note said to check the freezer in the generator shed.

After reading the note, I asked the camp manager to show me all the freezers on the station. He took me to two of them, one in the kitchen and one in a storage locker. He told me those were all the freezers they had. When I told him I wanted to look in the generator shed he became visibly nervous. I had to threaten to get his boss involved before he opened the shed for me. Opening the freezer, I immediately saw a fresh large walrus skull and tusks. It was illegal for anyone but an Alaskan Native to hunt walrus. They could not sell the tusks, but could use the ivory in making jewelry and other Native craft items.

I confiscated the skull and the tusks, and informed the manager I would now seriously consider charging him as an accessory to the crime unless he stopped lying to me. He finally told me the truth. I found out the walrus had been shot by one of the pilots whose names I had been given. I have forgotten the guy's name. The manager told me the pilot and his lead geologist were due back in camp before dark. I did not have to remind him that he had lied to me earlier about both the pilot and the freezer. I told him that he should very carefully consider his answers to subsequent questions or in any court case in the future.

When the helicopter landed an hour later, I waited for the pilot and his mechanic to secure the aircraft before approaching them. I introduced myself and explained why I was here. The pilot at first denied any knowledge of the walrus until I told him I had sworn statements from several people, including the camp manager, that they had seen him take the walrus out of his helicopter and put it in the freezer after bragging about killing it to camp personnel. He then tried to tell me he bought it off some Eskimos he saw out hunting for walrus. I informed him it was not the season Eskimos hunted walrus, as they were migrating too far beyond the villages. Besides, I informed him, they were hunting mostly for meat and hides when they did hunt walrus. If Natives had also wanted the tusks they would chop the ivory out of the skull instead of hauling the heavy head back to the village.

Finally, the pilot admitted to shooting the bull walrus out of his helicopter. I confiscated the helicopter and had the pilot fly me in it to Nome the following day, to be formally charged in court. The District Attorney in Fairbanks led me through the exact legal wording for the complaint, and I took the case before the local judge. I was surprised the pilot pled guilty. I understood later there was a deal between the District Attorney's Office and the oil company who chartered the helicopter that if the pilot pled guilty, the State of Alaska would release the helicopter back to the oil company.

The story of my arresting the pilot for illegally hunting out of the helicopter and the confiscation of the helicopter somehow hit the national news. I am sure Governor Hickel crossed me off his Christmas card list.

The second notable case I investigated concerned General William Westmoreland of Vietnam fame. Don called me into his office stating he just received a call from Fort Wainwright that General Westmoreland had reportedly shot a grizzly bear, Dall sheep, moose and caribou from a helicopter over the past three days. The person calling refused to identify himself, because he was afraid of repercussions. For the same reason, he did not want to report it to the base wildlife office. The man informed Don of the times and places the animals were taken, which lent credibility to his report. Don was also informed that the General would be bringing the meat and skins into a local creamery to be packed in dry ice the following morning at 8 a.m., prior to being shipped by army transport back to the Lower 48. It was pretty obvious to Don that the man calling him had been on the helicopter with the General when the infractions occurred.

At 7:45 a.m. the following morning, I drove to the creamery that was located next to the banks of the Chena River on University Avenue close to where it crossed the Chena River. The man who opened the door for me explained that the person who had brought the meat and hides in to be packed in dry ice had already left. The workman explained that the person who brought them in was not a General, but he could not remember the name and rank of the person. Asking to see the paperwork, I was informed there was none. It was strictly a cash deal that they did for a lot of hunters. I gave the workman my card and confiscated the meat, hides and bear skull pending further investigation. None of the trophies had the required state non-resident seals for big game species. The skull belonging to the grizzly bear hide had not been brought to Fish and Game for sealing, either.

I informed Don of what had happened. I explained that after dropping off the confiscated items at the office, I would head out to Fort Wainwright to contact the base's Wildlife Officers and talk to the General and whoever was in charge of the base helicopters. I was stunned when the MPs at the front gate refused me entrance. They told me they had just received orders that no State Fish and Game personnel were to be allowed on base. I took that to mean that the creamery had a contact telephone number for whoever had come in for dry ice earlier and had notified them that I had confiscated the meat and hides.

I never did get to talk to anyone on base about the incident. I have no idea if General Westmoreland was even in Alaska. It was impossible to check without access to the base. No charges were ever filed against the General or anyone else. Two days after I was denied entry onto Fort Wainwright, Don received a registered letter from the Alaskan Army Command informing him that enforcement officers from Fish and Game would not be allowed on any Army facility in Alaska for the next two years. Although I never got to bring the case to conclusion, someone high enough in the Army with enough clout to deny Fish and Game entry onto all Army Facilities in Alaska was somehow involved.

I asked Don what to do next as I wanted the General or whoever was responsible for these flagrant violations of Alaska's Fish and Game regulation to be held responsible for the crimes. Especially since they felt so entitled that they banned the department from their bases. Don told me the situation was forwarded to Juneau for further consideration because of the politics involved. Seeing that I was not satisfied with that decision, Don said that the meat was donated to local charities and the grizzly bear hide tanned and donated to the Fairbanks chapter of the Boy Scouts. I was never contacted by Juneau about the situation. Nor was there any publicity in the newspaper. The whole incident was swept under the rug as far as I know.

* * *

After getting my pilot's license, I had joined a Fairbanks flight club to build hours in an airplane less expensively. I flew to Circle City, Tok, Nenana, Tanana as well as the Minto Flats and Alaska Range areas. Though I was building hours, they were not the type of hours I really wanted. That would require access to a floatplane or a bush taildragger, not the front-wheel aircraft I was flying. The front-wheel variety was not suitable to landing off maintained airstrips. Often, I dreamed of owning my own aircraft, but that was a sore point between my wife and me. One thing I was learning was how little I really did know about bush flying. It was challenging, in Alaska's ever-changing weather, to land airplanes during thunder and snowstorms as well as mastering crosswind landings on short narrow airstrips.

Being rehired by Fish and Game was a dream come true on two fronts. First, it was the job I was most suited to do and most enjoyed. Second, it provided access to the very type of flying and aircraft I dreamed of. I set about getting one hundred hours of flight time in department aircraft so I could take the department check ride, allowing me to fly their aircraft without being accompanied by one of their pilots. Besides flying every minute I could with Phil and other Fish and Game pilots, I flew the Fairbanks Flight Club Cessna 150s and 172s.

I asked Phil Connors how to log the time we spent flying together, as he was my instructor. Phil said to log the entire time of the flight, as I was learning, no matter who was at the actual controls. This made sense to me. Learning to fly, I logged the entire flight time the instructor was with me whether I had the controls or the instructor did.

Don Roberts called me into his office one day and said he had a request from the Department Director to transfer me to the Yakutat office to be the officer in charge there. Don advised me not to take it. He told me the Director and his best friend Claude St. Alman (I'm uncertain of the correct spelling, so I'll go with this) only wanted to get me down to St. Alman's region to find a reason to fire me. This made absolutely no sense to me. I did not know either of the men, having met Director Stewart briefly once when he came to Fairbanks to get checked out in a Cessna 180 on floats by Phil. I had ridden along on the flight in the back seat. When we got back to the office I told Phil I was not going to log the hours as I did not touch the controls. He said to log it, as the department was only interested in me observing weather, flight techniques and weather effects on aircraft performance when riding with one of their certified pilots. I did not feel right doing this, but logged it against my better judgment which turned out to be big mistake. You would think by now I was old enough to trust my instincts over someone else's word.

Don told me he would get me into one of his remote offices as soon as one came open if I would stay in the Fairbanks Region. I told him I would talk it over with Sharon and let him know. I was puzzled by Don's reluctance to have me go to Yakutat and should have given it more thought and credence, but it did not make any sense that someone who did not know me would go to the trouble of moving my family and me all the way down to Yakutat on the Alaskan Coast between Cordova and Glacier Bay just to fire me. It seemed ludicrous. I did not consider that Don had pushed through my rehire despite the objection of the Director. I should have. Several days later I told a disappointed Don Roberts that I would accept the transfer to Yakutat.

Yakutat is located on the coast of the Gulf of Alaska, about halfway between Cordova and Juneau. It is a sportsman's paradise. The strip of land between the Gulf and the Costal Range has rivers and streams home to Pacific salmon and trout. The Situk River five miles east of Yakutat is a gem in the sport fishing world. The two local roads in Yakutat both allow access to the river. One road runs to its mouth as it enters the Gulf of Alaska, and the other has a bridge crossing it halfway to the site of its origin in Situk Lake. It was one of the premiere steelhead fisheries in the state at the time I was there in the early 1970s.

State Fisheries biologists would fish the Situk every winter I was there to take scale samples of steelhead running upriver to spawn. Unlike salmon, which die after spawning, steelhead can return to the ocean afterward and continue growing. I remember one biologist telling me they had scale samples of some Situk steelhead retuning to spawn seven times. This was unheard of in other state rivers. I'm sure this was partly due to the lack of commercial fishing at the mouth during the time of their major run, and the fact that the river was a well-kept secret of those few sports fishermen who returned to fish for them year after year. I only knew of five people who would return each year to fish the Situk for steelhead, not counting me and a few local residents.

Yakutat Bay is the only large bay between Glacier Bay, by Cape Spenser, and Prince William Sound. It was known for its halibut, king and silver salmon fishery. All other salmon could be caught in the bay as well, but among the local fishermen king, silvers and halibut were the targeted species. The bay is bordered on the west by Malaspina Glacier, a huge glacier that moved so far and fast the first year I was in Yakutat that it threatened to cut off Russell Fiord, the headwater of the bay. Scientists from all over the world came to study the phenomenon. They wanted to study the process of Russell Fiord slowly becoming a freshwater, land-locked lake. That never happened. The glacier slowly retreated enough to allow the fiord to remain salt water.

Most of the many rivers emptying into the Gulf from the Coastal

Range had at least one species of salmon running up them to spawn. Some were targets of commercial fishermen, while others were left to evolve naturally. It was a great playground for me and my eighteen-foot patrol boat.

Ken Lewis was the Fish and Game Protection Officer in Yakutat before my arrival. He showed me the facilities, which contained a double wide trailer for my family, and a large bunkhouse complete with kitchen and office for visiting Fish and Game personnel. There was also a separate house for a Commercial Fisheries biologist aide who came each summer to monitor their programs. The compound stood by itself, about three quarters of the way between the town of Yakutat and the Yakutat Airport. A logging compound was across the road from it.

Ken showed me the garage in the compound that contained so many cases of beer I could not count them all. A barge full of that summer's supplies for cannery operations along the Alaskan Peninsula had lost its motors crossing the Gulf of Alaska a few weeks before and had gone aground between Yakutat Bay and Icy Bay. Locals in Yakutat competed with each other to see who could harvest the most of this bounty. As Ken did not fly, how he got as much beer as he did was a mystery, but I knew better than to ask.

What was also in the garage that did interest me, however, was a wrecked 7-AC airplane. It was all in pieces. Ken told me a pilot had wrecked it trying to land on a nearby beach and sold it to him for $500. When Ken asked if I wanted to buy it from him for what he paid for it, I wrote out the check before we left the garage.

I was now the owner of my own personal aircraft. The fact that it was built in the 1940s and was in many pieces was just another challenge to overcome. How great was this? My job was to spend as much time as possible in this coastal Alaskan wonderland and given the tools to do it while having my own personal aircraft.

This wrecked airplane is how I came to meet and become friends with Terry Holliday. Terry and his dad were well-known pilots in the Cordova and Prince William Sound area. They flew for various commercial fishermen, providing the latest aerial information on fish location and boat numbers in the Sound. At this time, he was flying commercially for Dick Nicholes, who owned Yakutat Air Taxi. Dick later told me there was not enough business to hire Terry, but Terry wanted to build hours and flew for free.

When I learned that Terry was also a licensed aircraft mechanic, I asked him to come over and look at my 7-AC. I wanted an estimate on what it would take to put it back together. Also, if I did the work myself as planned, I needed a licensed mechanic to sign off on it. After inspecting the aircraft, Terry told me it needed to be rebuilt from the frame on up. All the fabric covering the frame was so old it was brittle. The metal tubing on the frame itself was rusted in places and needed to be inspected carefully. He also said it would probably cost around $2,500 in materials to accomplish the rebuild. This was quarter of my entire year's salary. I told Terry I needed to think it over, as I knew nothing about rebuilding an airplane. I changed my mind when he told me he was planning to spend the winter in Yakutat and would help me for free if I would help him. The help he required was hunting for wolves, wolverines and coyotes from his airplane along the forelands and rivers between Yakutat and Glacier Bay. He would get to keep all the fur. I agreed.

I knew nothing about aerial hunting except what I saw on TV and read in Fairbank newspapers. I was still pretty much influenced by my reading the fairytale sold as non-fiction by Farley Mowat called, *Never Cry Wolf*. Asking Terry what was expected of me, he replied I would be his rear seat gunner. This was legal at the time, so I agreed, even though I had compunctions about the fairness of killing wolves this way. I should have saved my compunctions about the fairness part. The wolves were more than equal to the challenge. I also discovered that winter that Mowat's portrayal of wolves was far from the truth, and hunting them from an airplane was challenging, dangerous and was far more likely to fail than succeed.

Claude St. Alman, my new supervisor, was scheduled to fly up to Yakutat to go over my duties and responsibilities a couple of days after my arrival. I was excited to meet him. I wanted to make a good impression to get our relationship off on a positive note. I met Claude at the airport upon his arrival from Juneau. Smiling and introducing myself, I was shocked by his demeanor. He was coldly indifferent. He never stated he was glad I came to Yakutat or gave any indication that I was welcome in his region. The entire day I spent with him he did not smile or show any indication there was to be anything but a strict supervisor-employee relationship, in which he was the alpha male.

Maybe Don had been right, but I was determined to prove myself to the man and show him I was an excellent employee. The only other time I can remember him coming to Yakutat to see me was right after a huge snow storm had dumped about three feet of snow in two days, collapsing the roof of my patrol boat. When I reported this to him, he stated he would be down the following day. He arrived to tell me how incompetent I was to allow the snow to damage my patrol boat. The fact that I had kept the snow off almost all the equipment I was responsible for most of the winter and the fact that the Yakutat area had about twenty-seven feet of snowfall that winter did not faze him. This made me angry. He ignored all the thousands of hours I worked overtime for free, and all the hard work investigating and prosecuting violators in the region, just to tell me how incompetent I was over a boat roof that I would easily fix with a couple of two-by-fours.

I pointed at our trailer house buried under mounds of snow, and told him I wanted the Highway Transportation employees in Yakutat to bring some equipment and remove the snow off the roof and around the edges. The house was completely buried under snow. The front door opening was more of an ice tunnel than a free access entry. I was really concerned for the safety of my family in the event of a fire. The one operational door was out the front of the house, while the bedrooms were in the back. The furnace was located between the two. It was a fire-trap.

Claude looked at it and said snow was one of the occupational hazards of living in Yakutat, and that I needed to handle it myself. I understood then that a collapsed boat roof was more important than my family's safety to him. I talked to the people at the road department after he left. They had kept a parking area in front of my house plowed that winter so I could get into my driveway and park, but were afraid to try and remove snow from the roof and sides. The Fish and Game department had built a secondary roof over the trailer's flat roof to keep to keep it from collapsing. However, this steep roof shed snow off to the side, covering all side door access. This winter had dumped so much snow that there was still a thirty-foot stack of it piled along the airport's parking area in the middle of July for airline passengers to photograph. Yakutat receives the second most precipitation in the United States. I was extremely relieved when I could finally shovel snow away from the other doors out of our department house.

Claude was transferred out of Juneau shortly after this to Big Lake. He passed away within a year from a bad heart. I don't know if those health issues affected our relationship or not, but I do know that his replacement was ten times as bad.

The boat harbor in Yakutat Bay was surrounded by rocky reefs at low tide, so I had a local commercial fisherman show me how to navigate those dangerous waters. I would be going in and out of the harbor at all different tides and times. I was especially concerned about returning to the harbor after dark, when I could not see the rocks and reefs. I was not a proficient saltwater sailor, and needed all the help and information I could get. The bay was the source of commercial and subsistence fishing to residents the entire year, so I would be using the harbor all twelve months.

My first trip patrolling those waters happened several weeks after my arrival, on a wet gloomy grey day. After carefully navigating the entrance reefs, I opened up the large Mercury outboard and zoomed across the still water protected by several smaller islands. I wanted to check the waters between the harbor and Knight Island for fishermen. Once leaving the protection of the islands, I found myself slowing the boat dramatically and quartering waves that were building from the unhindered wind. I found the switch for windshield wipers and slowly made my way to Knight Island. The island was home to a local family who farmed the land and fished the water surrounding them. I did not stop and introduce myself, as I saw no boats or people. I did find a small inlet protected from the wind and waves that would become my favorite king salmon fishing spot in the years to come. On my trip back to the boat harbor, I found it was much easier to drive across following seas than head into them. I arrived back at the dock before dark with a sore back and neck from the pounding waves and a profound respect for the power of the ocean.

I was beginning to build a knowledge base for boating in saltwater in the same manner I had in learning about flying. I enjoyed both equally, and understood that carelessness in either environment could quickly doom you. I resolved to read, ask and learn as much about the sea as I had the air.

Yakutat had a limited local road system. I don't remember how many miles they comprised, but it could not have been more than forty. The main road was between the small city and the airport, followed by the road out to the mouth of the Situk River. I traveled these incessantly whenever I was not in my patrol boat or in the air. At the mouth of the Situk I would check commercial and sports fishermen, and I wrote many citations to the sports fishermen there.

Most sport citations were the result of the fishermen using illegal gear or catching more than the daily limit allowed. It was popular to tie a heavy weight on the end of the line with several large treble hooks tied further up. This setup would be cast into the river and brought back to shore in jerks. Red salmon did not usually bite lures during their spawning run, so the intent was to snag the fish in the side. Two parts of this were against Fish and Game regulations. It was illegal to sport fish in the Situk with more than one hook having over a half-inch gap between the shank and hook point. It was also illegal to keep any salmon caught by snagging.

After writing a fish or game citation, I had to type up the complaint on an official Department form and present it in court. I got to know and develop a good relationship with the local justice of the peace. I remember her one-hundred-year-old mother sitting in her favorite front porch chair, wrapped in many blankets, giving me a toothless smiling welcome whenever I came to their house for business or pleasure.

I easily spent eighty-plus hours a week during fishing and hunting season, patrolling this sportsman's paradise. In the winter when things calmed down there was not that much to do, other than take care of equipment, fight with my compound's water pump, and check whatever trapping was going on along the road system. I would also play on one of the local basketball teams. Once in a while I would perform State Trooper duties, if necessary, but this was not often and only by necessity. Like many Native American cultures, some locals had issues with alcoholism that would cause problems, but by and large, the winter was a peaceful time.

My family and I spent numerous hours on the bay and the Gulf of Alaska in the patrol boat fishing for salmon and halibut. I even tried to commercial fish for halibut with a friend in his personal boat. The Natives in Yakutat had shown me a shallow bar about forty feet deep surround by water a hundred and eighty to two hundred feet deep where halibut came to spawn during certain times of the year. One night, after a few too many beers, the friend and I decided to use my expertise as a scuba diver to shoot halibut with a spear gun. We figured this would be a much faster and easier way to harvest the fish than setting out long lines.

The following weekend, after my patrol ended, we met and motored out to the spawning area. After anchoring the boat, I put on scuba gear and jumped into the water. Jack handed me my spear gun, which we had modified to hold one hundred and fifty yards of heavier line that I attached to my weight belt. The idea was for me to shoot a halibut with the spear and then inflate a balloon with a compressed air cylinder tied to the other end of the long cord, and let it rise to the surface where my friend would pick it up and pull in the fish. Ah, the best laid plans of mice and men.

Following the boat anchor line down to the bottom, I saw several large halibut moving slowly on the sandy bottom. Picking out the largest, I carefully approached, not blowing out any air bubbles, and shot it with the spear right behind its eyes, figuring it would stun the fish. The large fish was not stunned but exploded into frenzied activity, quickly swimming in a circle around me. With my spear stuck through its head, the halibut disappeared in a shower of sand and dove off the shallow bar for the deeper water below. I tried to get the excess line off my weight belt to inflate the balloon, but all I accomplished was to wrap the line around my legs and fins as I swirled around in the water, trying to follow the fish with my eyes. Suddenly the line tightened around my lower body as the large halibut reached the end of the slack, pulling me over the edge and into the deeper water. Attaching the line from my spear gun to my weight belt was big mistake, as I could not get it free.

I thought that this was a hell of a senseless way to die as I doubled over, trying to reach the diving knife attached to my leg, fighting the jerking motion of the fast-moving fish. My eardrums felt like they were going to rupture, because I could not equalize the pressure against them as fast as I was being pulled downward. Finally getting my knife free, I cut the line to my spear in the halibut's head. Looking at my depth gauge, I was one hundred and fifteen feet deep when I got free. Swimming slowly back up to the surface, I climbed aboard the boat to the questioning look of my friend. I explained to him that this was one of our more stupid ideas, and that I needed a drink of Yukon Jack as fast as we could get to shore.

Sharon and I had many conflicting emotions before deciding to sell Jumpoff to finance the rebuild of our airplane. We contacted Dr. Glenn Straatsma, a friend in Fairbanks, and asked if he wanted to purchase it. He and the rest of his financial investment group bought Jumpoff for $2,500. We were sad to see it go, but had few options available for finding the money to rebuild the 7-AC.

Terry Holliday and I cut all the fabric off the fuselage and wings of the airplane to see how much work was ahead of us. By prior agreement, I would do as much of the work as possible, with Terry supervising and signing off on it when he was satisfied with the quality of my work and the structural soundness of the aircraft. Unlike automobiles, all aircraft maintenance had to be inspected and signed off by a licensed FAA mechanic for the airplane to be deemed airworthy. I wanted to learn how my airplane functioned from the inside out, so I was more than happy to do the work.

I sanded the metal frame free of all rust, and painted it with a white aircraft-approved hardened enamel. This added a few more pounds of weight than using the normal rust inhibitors, but gave it much more protection from salt. I used white so I could more easily inspect the frame later. The wooden ribs between the frame and the fabric that would later cover the aircraft wings and fuselage were such a mess that I had a hard time finding one complete enough to use for a template. I called John Peterson in Anchorage and asked if I could use his shop to cut the wooden ribs, as nothing was available in Yakutat. He agreed. I flew to Anchorage, bought aircraft plywood, and cut the ribs under John's supervision. I would become an accomplished wood worker later in life, but at this time I barely knew one type of saw from another.

Slowly but surely, through the winter, the airplane began to take shape again. Soon Terry and I were attaching the fabric and shrinking it to the frame with my wife's hair dryer. The process of attaching the fabric and shrinking it to the frame with heat was fascinating to watch. Some people would probably compare the process to watching a rock grow, but I was enthralled. It was a dream coming to fruition before my eyes. We briefly discussed converting the engine from 75 hp to 90 hp, but I was running out of funds. As spring arrived and the snow melted, we loaded the completed wings on a trailer and towed the rest of the airplane to the Yakutat FAA hanger where we finished the rebuild and attached the wings.

Not many people have flown or ridden in a 7-AC. It was produced from 1944 to 1948. There are several variations of the aircraft, mostly based on horsepower. The original was produced with a 65 hp engine, but mine had a 75 hp. It had a two-seat configuration, with the passenger sitting behind the pilot. There was no battery or electrical system. To start the craft, you had to hand-prop it. That is, you turned on the magnetos, primed the engine, pushed the lean control all the way in, set the throttle, then stepped outside and spun the propeller by hand. It is important not to wear rings on your fingers during this process, because the engine has a propensity to spin backwards if it does not start. The interior is very utilitarian, with basic instruments on the dash.

111

The dash contained airspeed, turn and bank, altimeter, artificial horizon and lean and prime controls. The throttle was located on the left side of the aircraft, along with the magnetos. The magnetos controlled spark to the engine spark plugs. Airplanes have two separated magnetos in case one fails during flight. The gas tank was thirteen gallons, and sat in the nose behind the engine. The gas gauge was a thin metal rod attached to a cork that floated on the gas and ran through the engine cowling. You guessed how much gas you had by how far the rod stuck out of the cowling. It was developed as a basic trainer.

The 7-AC was 21.6 feet long with a wingspan of 35 feet. It weighed about 720 pounds empty, and would carry a legal load of about 460 pounds. I weighed one hundred and eighty pounds, and when combined with the seventy-eight pounds for a full load of gas, that gave me a little over 200 pounds to legally carry behind me. Depending on the pitch of the propeller, it would cruise at 85 mph and had a range of 270 miles. As basic as an aircraft could be, to me it was a thing of beauty. The new fabric with its blue and white paint symbolized newfound freedom to explore and come to know Alaska more intimately.

My first flight in N1254E occurred on April 20, 1971. It was far from uneventful, even though it was a rare bright and sunshiny day in Yakutat. I talked to friends operating the control tower at the Yakutat Airport on the process of landing and taking off without a radio. Prior to taking off, I went to the control tower to get the reports on current weather, as well as local and anticipated aircraft in the area. On takeoff, I did the run-up short of the active runway, and then looked at the control tower. If I was free to take off they would shoot a green light at me; if not, a red light. The process on landing was to enter the traffic pattern and look to the tower for the red or green light. If it was red, I would go around the traffic pattern until I was given a green light. The FAA personnel operating the airport stated I needed to get an aircraft radio as soon as possible. After this first flight, I saw how important a radio would be, so I ordered a handheld radio that contained all aircraft radio frequencies. There was no possibility of installing an electrical system in the airplane.

By the date of this first flight, I had accumulated 354 hours of flight time in a wide variety of aircraft. Fish and Game had checked me out to fly their Beavers, Cessna 180s and Super Cubs. However, it had been a while since I had flown a tailwheel aircraft, so I had a difficult time taking off.

N1254E wanted to go anywhere but straight down the runway. I wobbled my way into the air in a few hundred feet, and then climbed to traffic pattern height. I told the tower prior to takeoff that I would remain in the traffic pattern until I was sure the airplane performed as intended. That meant that the engine continued to run and the ailerons and rudder were attached correctly and controlled the aircraft as designed. Most importantly that the wings stayed on.

Everyone at the FAA compound knew I had spent the winter rebuilding 54E in my garage and this was its maiden flight, so the control tower was full of people observing. Some hoped everything went all right, and a few whom I had cited for Fish and Game violations probably hoped I crashed.

After about ten minutes of slow turns, I decided to do some touch-and-goes. They did not go as planned. The airplane had heel brakes that were operated with your heels while you controlled the rudder, which also has directional influence on the airplane, with the balls of your feet. I had bad knees from football and skiing. That made it difficult for me to bend my knees in such a way that I could operate both controls with any sort of light and deft touch. As soon as the tailwheel came into contact with the pavement, I overcorrected and ground looped. I came to a stop in the middle of the runway facing the wrong direction in a cloud of blue tire smoke. Embarrassing!

I could almost hear the derisive laughter in the control tower as the tire smoke cleared. I said, after I caught my breath, "Okay, great and mighty bush pilot, get your head out of your ass and do better." After checking the landing gears and tires, I took off and landed again. This time I knew what to expect and only wobbled a little. I did ten improving touch-and-goes before heading to the Gulf of Alaska. I intended to fly east down the beaches away from Yakutat Bay.

I had just crossed the Situk River when a loud flapping noise almost gave me a heart attack. I froze on the controls, expecting the wing or tail to fall off. After about two minutes of flying straight and level with everything still attached, I again took a breath of air and looked cautiously at all of the aircraft I could see from the pilot's seat. I could see nothing amiss, but the loud flapping noise continued. I began to wonder if the fabric was coming off the airplane. I did not want to be a brick falling out of the air, so I immediately made a cautious turn back to the airport. Upon arrival I did not enter the flight path or look for a red light, but after visually checking for other air traffic just landed, much to the consternation of the control tower. They made it apparent to me this was not to happen again, or I would hear from Big Brother by official nastygram.

I inspected the airplane after getting out at my tie down location. I could find nothing amiss. The fabric was trim and tight everywhere I looked. In exasperation, I got a ladder out of the hanger to look at the top of the cabin. Sure enough, right above where I sat in the pilot's seat, the end of a small piece of patching tape had come loose. It was only two inches wide and three inches long; just enough to vibrate loudly and scare away two years of my life. Well, that's enough for one day, I thought, as I drove home to a large glass of Yukon Jack on the rocks.

I took Sharon for a ride down the coast in 54E on the next good day. We landed on several sandy beaches, found glass floats hidden among the unpicked driftwood, and other questionable treasures tossed into the sea by boats crossing the Gulf of Alaska. We enjoyed a leisurely sun-blessed picnic before heading back to Yakutat. Soon I was loading all four of us into the little blue and white airplane for fishing, picnicking, and exploring all over the Yakutat area. When flying alone, I used the 7-AC to rapidly expand my flying expertise. I landed in so many off-runway places that Dick Nicholes, the owner of Yakutat Air Taxi and a good friend, told me to knock it off. Dick had flown a little J3 Cub up from the Seattle area and started his flying business in Yakutat with only a student pilot's license many years ago. He had flown the area for more than thirty years and knew it better than anyone.

Fish and Game had a contract with Dick to fly me when I patrolled out of town. I flew hundreds of hours with him and learned many valuable lessons. He taught me to read coastal winds; how to decipher from blowing sand or spray off ocean waves which way and how hard the wind was blowing. Sand was the main runway away from the Yakutat Airport. He taught me to read sand colors and composition from the air, to tell which was safe to land on. How to lock my brakes and ski across water on wheels to land on short sandbars. How to get back to the airport if the weather closed down unexpectedly fast by following the fluorescent white line of ocean waves breaking against the sandy shore. Or following the sand and rock moraine locked within the icy embrace of glaciers if I needed to fly through low visibility fog to get back to the beach. That bald eagles and white geese

114

were two of the biggest dangers of flying in low-visibility following breaking waves, because they would not get out of your way. Dick also explained how to determine if it was safe to land in low-lying grasslands.

So when Dick told me to knock it off, as he expected to find me and my airplane rolled into a ball someday, I took him seriously. I asked him what he meant. He said I was flying my little airplane to the very edge of its flight envelope. Someday the engine would cough, the wind change, or a rock or soft spot in the sand would result in a crash. He told me, "Look at me; I was just like you! I was invincible, and could land and fly anywhere until the one time I made an error in judgment, showing off for friends on the beach. The resulting crash caved in my head and led to leg injuries so severe I will never walk normally again. The months spent in the hospital taught me to wise up and stop the nonsense of flying on the edge if there was no need." I listened to Dick and stopped some of the flying I was doing. There would be times when I would need to take risks, but not on every flight. Such caution does not last long in a Stultz's behavior. I was on my way to becoming a bold bush pilot. In Alaska, or anywhere else, that is not a good thing.

Aerial Wolf Hunting in Yakutat

When I was off duty and not working at rebuilding 54E, Terry and I would fly in his red Super Cub, hunting on the beaches and flats between the Situk and Alsek rivers for wolves, coyotes and wolverines. I really had no idea what this would entail. I had watched the TV documentary, *Wolf Men*, about aerial wolf hunting years before. It did not do justice to the difficulty of actually accomplishing it; the program had been meant to rile conservationists in the Lower 48 to unite against the practice.

The idea is for both the pilot and gunner to look for live animals or fresh tracks in the snow or sand. Once spotted, the animal would be tracked close to a location where the airplane could land. If the animal was already in such a location, the pilot would set up a pass for the gunner to try and shoot it, with the airplane moving 60 mph through the air and the animal dodging on the ground.

Sounds easy right? No, it is extremely difficult and dangerous. A mistake by the pilot or gunner could end in the death of both. This happened many times in Alaska when this type of hunting was legal, and even after it was banned. The pilot had to control the airplane at low speeds, trying to get the gunner a good shot, while the prey used trees, hills, brush and everything else in the vicinity to avoid being shot. The gunner had a split second from the time the running animal cleared the propeller until it passed under the wing struts to shoot. The gunner had to correct for speed, wind and the direction of the animal in this split second, while fighting the numbing effects of a freezing wind blowing on his hands and buffeting the weapon. The gunner could wear a hat but not gloves. He also had to safely handle a loaded firearm inside the cabin of the aircraft. Shooting the propeller or wing strut ensured a short and dramatic ending to the flight, while shooting a tire was a more prolonged drama.

Most hunters have a hard time shooting pheasants and ducks with the birds going in one direction while the hunters feet are firmly on the ground. Think of trying to do so out of a boat going 60 mph across bumpy water, in which you have one second to spot the bird and fire, and you have some idea of the difficulty of hunting wolves from an airplane. Hunting from the speeding boat is far easier, as it does not have propellers, wing struts or landing gear, and the bird is not dodging through brush, trees and stumps. You also do not have to find a safe place to dock the boat once the prey is downed.

In later years I would learn to be both the pilot and gunner at the same time. I would control the rudder with my feet, the ailerons with my knees, and gas with my elbow while leaning out the window to shoot the running animal forty feet above the ground. It was difficult, dangerous, and stupid, but I was immortal. During this first year aerial hunting with Terry, I missed far more animals than I hit. However, we did end the year with eight wolves, sixteen coyotes and three wolverines. We were far more successful than Fish and Game several years later, trying to thin the large wolf population in the Yakutat area with a helicopter. They only killed one wolf despite weeks of flying. It is not an easy feat, even in a more stable helicopter.

I flew this little lightweight airplane over 400 hours doubling my flight hours in the six months I owned it before selling 54E to a flight club in Anchorage. My family was growing. Both Michael and David were gaining height and weight, and refused to be left behind if I was flying for pleasure and the weather was good. I needed a larger airplane with an electrical system and more advanced instruments if I was going to fly them safely. The

7-AC was a great aircraft for someone just developing bush flying skills, but the lack of modern instruments and a weak engine limited its usefulness. A fellow game warden in Cordova was selling his PA-20. I decided it would be a perfect airplane for us, so I called Mac McKinley in Cordova and told him I wanted to buy his airplane. He agreed to hold it for me while I sold mine.

I advertised my airplane in the Anchorage paper and sold it that week for $4,000 to the Anchorage Flight Club. The only condition they put on the sale was that I had to deliver it to Anchorage. I was concerned about this, but agreed in the end. It was a long flight, with much of it over water. I was also concerned about landing at Anchorage International Airport, a large modern airport with lots of jets and other big aircraft landing every minute. I did not know how my top speed of 85 mph would fare there. I talked to my FAA friends in Yakutat about landing in Anchorage. They told me not to worry, and when I got within ten miles of the airport to call approach control and identify myself. They would talk me into the airport. They then called their cohorts in the Anchorage Tower and explained the situation. Anchorage promised to treat me as an overwhelmed student pilot on his first cross-country flight. Landing at Anchorage proved to be the least of my worries.

I took off for Anchorage from Yakutat several days later. The weather was overcast with little wind and no precipitation. As always, there was a low pressure system in the gulf, but it was not expected to influence my flight to Cordova where I planned to spend the night. After removing the back seat and tying down a ten-gallon container of extra gas, I took off.

The first part of the flight across Yakutat Bay was an eighteen-minute journey that in my little airplane seemed like two hours. During the flight across the Bay, you knew that if your engine quits you are dead. Breathing out a sigh of relief upon safely reaching the Malaspina Glacier on the other side, I dropped down from 5,000 feet to a couple hundred above the sand and followed the beach toward Icy Bay. The wind was picking up as I flew west. By the time I reached Icy Bay it was blowing me around pretty badly. Icy Bay was covered with four-foot whitecaps blowing out of the glacier at its head. This was mixing with the winds from the low pressure system in the gulf and creating a flying condition of absolute chaos, much like I experienced on my first cross-country flight to Tanana. Only this time my instructor, John Seal, was not there to help.

The 7-AC is in some ways like flying a kite. Its large wings, light body and underpowered engine makes flying in high wind conditions a real problem. Fighting the severe turbulence, I flew across Icy Bay to the lowlands on the other side where a logging camp and small gravel runway were located. I briefly considered landing and waiting out the weather, but convinced myself the moderate-to-severe turbulence I was flying through was the result of the mix of winds and would soon abate to just head winds. Besides, I could also return to the Icy Bay logging camp if it was too dangerous to continue.

Big mistake! By the time I came to the conclusion that I needed to land at Icy Bay, I had only flown three miles up the coast from the camp. My forward progress had almost stopped. The headwind had picked up to over 70 mph in those three slow miles. Deciding enough was enough, I tried to turn back to the camp. I could not turn the airplane. Every time I banked and tried to turn, the wings and tail would wash out, sending me into a mini stall toward the ground. My engine and tail surfaces were not strong enough to counter the power and turbulence of the wind. I had read about this phenomenon, but had never experienced it. I tried for fifteen minutes, in increasing desperation, to turn back but could not.

I could neither go forward nor turn back to the logging camp. I could land on the beach, but the wind would blow my airplane away before I could find anything to tie it to. Considering my limited possibilities, I decided the only option I had was to let the airplane fly backwards to the gravel runway by reducing power and flying with forward airspeed that was less than that of the wind blowing down the beach. If the winds abated in this backward flight I would just turn and land on the lumber camp runway.

I climbed to 2,500 feet before reducing power. Sure enough, my ground speed was negative, although my airspeed indicator was bouncing around 55 mph. I was flying backward. This was very disconcerting, as I could not see behind me. I maneuvered the airplane to where I thought the runway was located behind me. It was a constant battle with the turbulent and shifting winds as I added and reduced power, trying to keep myself in the air before the runway started to slip past on my right. I could see loggers on the ground waving at me; they had noticed my plight and were working to help me. Allowing the airplane to slide to the right in the wind so I was over the runway, I concentrated on getting on the ground and bringing this nightmare to an end.

The loggers had put a pickup on each side of the runway, and were motioning me to land between them. There would be no landing roll upon touching down. The loggers would have to get the rope they had attached to the trucks tied to my airplane before I could reduce power and shut down the engine. It was a battle of the elements against my will to survive before my tires touched earth for a final time, and the loggers could get control of 54E, safely lashing it between the two pickups.

Just opening my airplane door was a challenge in this wind. Finally, a large burly logger held it open long enough for me to get out. On our way to the bunkhouse one of the loggers accompanying me told me I owed him $20. To my puzzled reply that my billfold was still in the airplane, he chuckled and said, "No, you survived." Logging operations had shut down because of the high winds, so the entire camp was aware of my situation after I flew over the first time and did not land. They bet each other when they saw me flying backward toward the airport as to whether I would crash and die, crash and live, or land safely. Only one logger bet I would land safely. He was considered the least intelligent logger in camp.

I spent two days at the camp before taking off again. They filled my gas tank prior to my leaving with automotive fuel. No aviation fuel was available, but most lower powered aircraft engines operated on normal automotive fuel. It is the reason so many Alaskan pilots landed on roadways and taxied up to gas stations. I could not get current weather reports between here and Cordova, but decided to take off in the light falling rain. Visibility was okay as far as I could see, at about five miles. Most important, the wind had died down.

The weather all the way past Cape Yakataga was fine. A light rain was streaking across my windshield, but there were no significant fog banks I could see, so I continued past the Yakataga airport toward Cordova. The rain and the fog rolling down from the Bering Glacier begin to make the flight more difficult the further I flew. Soon I was flying fifty feet off the ground, with breaking waves on the left and sand on my right. The skies had opened up and the rain on the windshield and fog were blinding my forward visibility. I knew it was an only a small squall, and if I could get through it, I would be able to see in front of me again.

Suddenly, the white breaking waves and the sand beneath the airplane disappeared. I could see only the angry breaking waves of the ocean a few feet below my wing. I immediately remembered that there was a long narrow spit of land short of Kayak Island, and thought I had flown off the end of it. I had been looking for it, intending to swing northwest when I reached the place where it swung toward the open Gulf and Kayak Island. The almost zero-zero visibility prevented me from seeing that I was flying down this long narrow spit, and not along the main shoreline.

I had only the most basic of instruments, and no way of telling where Cordova was in this soup. Luckily, the winds were not a factor, so I increased my altitude to several hundred feet, turning northwest as I had intended to if I had spotted the spit in time. I was basically flying on the simple instruments on my dash with only brief glimpses of water below. I hoped I would be able to see the low grasslands when I reached them somewhere ahead.

Breathing a sigh of relief, I saw mud and grass underneath my wings about fifteen minutes later, and turned to a westerly heading as visibility greatly improved. Soon I could see the mouth of the Copper River and the hills leading to the Cordova Airport, where I landed safely within thirty minutes. I stayed in Cordova for another two days until another low pressure system moved on and blue skies again ruled the Gulf. The stay also allowed me time to talk to Mac McKinley, and inspect the new airplane I planned on purchasing.

After filling up with gas and checking the airplane carefully for what I had thought, at the beginning, would be the most perilous part of the flight to Anchorage, I took off. I climbed to 5,000 feet and started across the 115 miles of open water to Portage Glacier Pass. Islands dot the surface of Prince William Sound, but, flying with wheels, they were of no benefit to me if I ran into trouble.

The weather was perfect and visibility unlimited as I nervously droned over the Sound at 85 mph. I was more than relieved to finally see the mouth of the fifteen-mile-long pass into Cook Inlet and Anchorage. The closer I got to it, however, the more anxious I became. From ten miles away I could see whitecaps shooting from the mouth of Portage Pass well out into the Sound.

Portage Pass is short, but well-known in flying circles for its severe turbulence if any wind was blowing. If there was a pressure difference between Cook Inlet and Prince William Sound, the pass acted as a natural venturi tube for the wind flowing from the high-pressure to the low-pressure area. If I could see whitecaps from this far away, I was in for a really rough ride. The closer I got to the pass, the slower my speed across the water became. Five miles from Portage Pass, my airspeed across the wild white waves dwindled to almost nothing. When it seemed as if my forward progress stopped, I had had enough of wind and turbulence, and turned to the right toward the Valdez Arm. An hour later I landed at the Valdez airport to refuel, reflecting on the fact I had been flying for over two hours that morning and only made about fifty miles of headway. I had been within thirty minutes of Anchorage when forced to turn back, and now faced a three-hour flight on the alternative route. It certainly reinforced my desire to sell this airplane for a more powerful one.

This much longer flight took me up the Richardson Highway out of Valdez, across Thompson pass to Glennallen, and then on into Anchorage. I amended my flight plan with the FAA, and took off. At Glennallen I noticed gas leaking out of the carburetor as I was refueling. I observed when propping the airplane to start the engine that the leak disappeared with the engine running. Talking to the locals, I found that the only aircraft mechanic available was in Anchorage for several days. I should wait for him to return, but I was more than tired of this flight already. I restarted 54E's engine. When I did not see any gas leaking out, I jumped in and taxied toward the main runway. I hoped that if gas started leaking out of the carburetor again, it would not be ignited by the airplane exhaust pipe that was located close to the gas leak. The paint covering my airplane had a high concentration of nitrate in it, the same chemical used to make gunpowder. Any type of fire, no matter how small, would quickly become a deadly inferno. Shutting this thought out of my mind, I lined up on the center of the runway and took off for Anchorage.

The flight was long and uneventful. I thought back to the sense of wonderment I had felt as Sharon and I drove the highway when we first arrived in Alaska ten years earlier. Life moves in strange, unbelievable circles. The beauty of this part of the flight was such that before I was ready for it to end, I was crossing the Big Susitna River and contacting Anchorage Approach Control, identifying myself. They directed me to the airport before handing me off to the control tower.

The only issue I experienced was when landing. I stopped within 300 feet of the end of the runway, resulting in the Control Tower telling me to immediately expedite off the active runway as there was jet traffic behind me. So I took off again, flying five feet off the runway until I reached a taxiway where I could get off. Two guys from the flight club drove up as I was tying 54E down in the transient parking area. They had followed my flight all the way from Yakutat through the FAA. They handed me the check as I gave them the airplane logs. They commented they were glad I was flying and not them. I wasn't. It was a miserable flight during which I was reminded again that Alaska weather had many tricks up her sleeve she could use to make you one of her many conquests.

Later that winter I would again get to experience the pleasure of flying backwards in an airplane. Only this time Dick Nicholes would be flying, and we were in a Cessna 180. Two hunters had landed on the small strip at Harlequin Lake to hunt mountain goat. While they were out hunting, the winds came up and blew their airplane fifty feet from where they had parked it, onto its back. Commercial air traffic heard their emergency beacon going off and reported it to Yakutat. The control tower called me after a flight plan became overdue.

I called Dick Nicholes to arrange a flight to check up on them. Dick told me there were terrible winds blowing out of all the mountain passes, and it was probably not possible to make it up to Harlequin. It was not uncommon for drainage winds (williwaws) to exceed 200 mph out of the mountains. We agreed to give it a try, as we did not know if they had crashed or were safely inside the Forest Service cabin at the lake.

The winds were calm at Yakutat when we took off. The closer we got to the mountains, the more Dick was fighting the controls, and the slower our ground speed became. Flying at 7,000 feet, we got close enough to Harlequin Lake to see the overdue airplane upside down near the cabin before our forward speed stopped completely, and we were going backward. Thinking that the two guys were safe in the cabin, we turned back to Yakutat. We tried to rescue them three times in the subsequent week before the winds died down enough to allow us to land. Even then Dick had to continue flying the airplane on the ground while the two stranded hunters and I struggled to get the airplane door open enough for them to climb in. It was a great feat of flying by Dick.

The day after I sold the 7-AC I booked a flight on Alaska Airlines to Cordova where I met Mac McKinley and took possession of N2358A. The PA-20 had much different flying characteristics from the 7-AC. It was more tail-sensitive on landing and takeoff. I had to be very careful on the rudders and brakes landing and taking off to avoid ground looping the craft. A major plus for my bad knees was that it also had toe brakes on the rudder pedals instead of heel brakes, making it much easier for me to control the landing and takeoff. Other than that, it was a great flying airplane. With flaps, battery, toe brakes and full instrumentation, it was much more manageable on longer flights. It was a rugged four-place aircraft, right at home in the bush of Alaska.

The new airplane cruised at 127 mph, making the flight from Cordova to Yakutat a breeze compared to my last trip up this coast. Being a four-place airplane, my family was much more comfortable flying in it. There were several variations of the Pacer, notably involving wheel placement and engine size. Some had a nose wheel and were called a PA-22, which was mostly useless for off-runway flying. Others, like mine, had a tail-wheel. You could convert the engine with an FAA approved conversion kit, from 125 hp to 180 hp. The one I bought from Mac had a 135 hp engine. I would convert it to 150 hp in a few years, as well as lengthen the wings two feet on each side after I had an engine failure. In the later configuration, the airplane was almost impossible to stall.

I had problems landing 58A in the sand right after I brought it home from Cordova. Its shorter length and heavier engine would not allow me to land in places I had been landing before. Also, the landing speed was over 10 mph higher. This made a big difference in landing roll distance. In the first month landing on beaches, I put the airplane up on its nose twice. Once I did minor damage to a wing tip and bent the propeller. I took the propeller off and bent it back to as close to normal as I could, wedging it between two stumps. The airplane shook so much on the short flight back to Yakutat that I was worried the engine would vibrate off its frame.

I had to ship the propeller off to a propeller shop in Washington to have it reannealed and painted before flying again. The original owner of the company I sent the propeller to would take bent airplane propellers and fix them. I think I sent him six propellers from various airplanes before he retired and his son took over. His son refused to continue his Dad's practices because of liability issues associated with fixing badly damaged propellers. I liked the old man much better.

John and Kathy Peterson came to visit us in July of 1972, the second year I was in Yakutat. We flew into the Italio, Lost and Alsek rivers, and looked at the mountain goats around Harlequin Lake, and at seals resting with their newborn pups on the ice floes from the glaciers in Russel Fiord. We also fished the Situk river by truck and canoe.

Fishing was not that good in the Situk so I decided to take John to Italio, because red salmon were still running fairly well there. Kathy was pregnant but wanted to come too. I agreed that the fishing trip would be more enjoyable with her along. I could land on the beach bordering the Gulf of Alaska and walk over to the river, but we'd have to climb some large sand dunes to reach it. Considering Kathy's condition, I decided to land on a short and narrow sand runway that ran beside a pool in the river that held a large number of fish.

At 500 feet long with willows bordering its sides, the runway was normally long enough to get onto and off safely with three people. But you had to be careful. Unfortunately, this day it was eighty-five degrees with a 15 mph wind blowing in the wrong direction. You could only take off and land in one direction as there was a large hill bordering the southeast end of the runway. The heat and tailwind made landing there inadvisable.

Taking a pass over the runway, I thought it was too marginal to land. Pulling up into the air again, I looked at the sand bar beside the pool we wanted to fish and decided to land there. I had landed on it many times with my Champion 7-AC without any issues. Unfortunately, being a fairly new pilot with only a little over 800 flying hours, I did not consider the different circumference of the wheels on the 7-AC versus those on the PA-20. On a difficulty scale of one to ten, landing on this bar rated about a seven. Difficult, but manageable. Most importantly, I was landing into the wind on a hot day. Air temperature, altitude and wind direction greatly affect an airplane's performance. We were landing at sea level, so altitude was not an issue. The other two factors were prime concerns, but not the only ones, as I soon learned.

Because of the direction of the wind I had to land upstream, and that meant a sharp ninety-degree bank following the curve of stream and the side of the 250-foot sand hill bordering it. It was necessary to keep the right wing tip just a few feet above the river. Then, with a quick leveling of the wings, I set the airplane down where sand met water.

I accomplished that superbly. But shortly after touching down I realized I had made a major misjudgment, as the tail of the airplane began to climb higher in the air than the nose. I recognized abruptly that I was in the process of tipping the airplane over and landing on its back with a very pregnant woman in the back seat. I had not considered that the wheels on this airplane were smaller than on my 7-AC, and sand would pile up in front of them. The nose slowed faster than the tail, and over we went. Luckily we did not go all the way over, but ended up nose first into the ground with the tail high in the air.

I had landed the PA-20 probably a hundred times on the sand without an issue after the first two months of owning it. The sand on this bar was obviously softer, not having had the pounding benefit of ocean waves. John and I jumped out of the front seats as the aircraft stopped to survey the damage. I inhaled a sigh of relief upon seeing there did not appear to be any real damage. I would not know if the propeller was bent until we pulled it out of the sand. Getting on opposite sides of the fuselage, we pulled it back off its nose so the tail wheel was again on the ground and not twenty feet in the air. In our male chauvinism, we had completely forgotten about Kathy in the back seat.

As the tail wheel banged into the ground with a puff of sand, we heard a loud groan from the back seat. Both John and I said in unison, "Ah, shit" as we darted to the back seat to see if Kathy was all right. Being buckled in with a seat belt across her swollen belly during this whole fiasco was not helpful to either her or the baby's well-being. As we helped Kathy out of the plane, she remained as regally composed as ever, but her eyes darted fire at her husband. Life is a dance we learn as we go, and this was one of the more difficult steps.

The PA-20 has less wingspan and is shorter in overall length than Super Cubs, Citabrias, or Cessnas. This makes the craft harder to take off and land, and more likely to go up on its nose under these circumstances. Luckily the propeller was not bent, so after cleaning the sand out of the vents, I taxied it up onto the runway, and we proceeded to catch red salmon. The takeoff when we were done fishing was a little longer than I wanted. The wind had died down somewhat, but it was still very hot. I held the brakes and revved the engine until reaching a high rpm. After releasing the brakes and lifting the tail wheel off the ground, I was concerned we were not picking up speed quickly enough. To be on the safe side, I held the airplane on the ground until we reached the end of the runway, then lifted the nose and applied full flaps, quickly gaining altitude above the river passing below. By the time we got home I was sure John and Kathy were wondering if it was safe to fly with me.

The three of us flew out to the Lost River the next day where I practiced takeoff and landing in the sand while they enjoyed the warm weather and sandy beach bordering the Gulf of Alaska. Once I was sure I knew exactly how the PA-20 acted in different types of sand, I joined them for a picnic. Kathy later delivered a healthy baby boy they named Eric.

During the first several months of owning the PA-20, I figured out where and how to land it, and had no more issues until John and Kathy Peterson's flight. After that incident, I put larger tires on the aircraft. That solved the problem.

The year before, while making a Fish and Game enforcement patrol in my 7-AC, I had landed on this same bar for the cameras of a movie star. One evening after returning from a long boat patrol of Yakutat Bay, Sharon told me she had sold a fishing license to the movie actor John Wayne. The next day while flying a patrol, I saw a crowd of people and several helicopters fishing the same hole where John, Kathy and I later experienced the problem landing on the sandbar. I knew Wayne had a fishing license, but no idea if the other people did. The helicopters were parked in a way that was blocking the use of the runway. The number of people and their location made using the whole sand bar unfeasible.

Dick Nicholes, the owner of Gulf Air Taxi in Yakutat, had taught me how to land on a very short sand bar by locking your wheel brakes and skiing on the water until you hit land. You have to maintain an airspeed over 20 mph, but that is no problem if you are careful. The biggest concern is the initial contact of the wheels on the water. You need to be fairly level so you don't nose the propeller into the water or jerk the control stick hard enough to sink the tailwheel into it. I would have to use landing with wheels on water for this landing. I was a little concerned as I had not practiced it much. It is not something you routinely practice, like doing stalls. I lowered my airspeed below 40 mph and touched down on the water with the brakes locked, skiing on the river surface around the corner, then coming to a stop on the sandbar about fifty feet from the edge of the water.

I got out of my airplane and went over to check fishing licenses, and was met by an astonished group of fishermen. I easily recognized John Wayne, though his face and neck were much more wrinkled than when seen on the movie screen. He approached me with a wide grin on his face. I shook his hand as he said that was the most amazing airplane landing he had ever seen, and he asked me if I would I do it again so they could photograph the complete landing. It was really not that amazing for an Alaskan, but I told him sure, once I had checked licenses and he had the helicopters moved so I could use the runway to take off. When that was accomplished, I did as he requested. I was smiling as I flew away, thinking who would ever believe one of the most famous movie stars in the world would take pictures of me.

Anyway, I always thought of that sandbar as Kathy's bar, and not John Wayne's bar.

Frank Moser, an Air Controller for the FAA in Yakutat, asked me to fly him and two relatives across Yakutat Bay to moose hunt. I flew them to an area between Yakutat Bay and Icy Bay, and dropped them off with their gear. I had met Frank right after moving to Yakutat. I knew him by name prior to arriving, as I had chased him all over the North Slope of Alaska after it had been reported to the Fish and Game Office in Fairbanks that he was shooting big game from a helicopter he was flying for oil companies in their search for oil. Frank had heard I was looking for him, so when we finally met at Yakutat, the circle was closed and we became good friends. He took me out on his boat shrimp fishing, so I felt obligated to fly him out hunting.

I flew back to their hunting camp a day later, intending to check up on them and fly any moose they had shot back to Yakutat. Upon landing, I discovered they had two moose down and were in the process of packing the meat back to camp. I decided to help them. While we were completing that task and putting it in my airplane, the weather turned bad. Looking at the increasing wind and rain, I decided to spend the night with them instead of trying to fly back to Yakutat. I had an important meeting the next day I had to attend, but figured I had plenty of time to wait out the weather.

We had a great evening draining bottles of alcoholic beverages and eating fresh moose backstrap around a blazing driftwood fire. I woke up in the morning to silence. On the Gulf of Alaska, the noise of wind and rain was the norm. Getting out of the tent after dressing, I saw the camp was suspended in a sea of fog. Not normal fog, but thick pea soup fog, much like I had experienced years before in the Aleutian Islands. Unfortunately, my mental faculties had diminished in the ensuing years. I should have stayed in the tent like I had in the cabin.

I could hear waves breaking on the shore a hundred feet away, but could not see ten feet in front of me. I followed our tracks down to my airplane, because I was concerned a brown bear would smell the two moose we had put into it the evening before, and tear up the aircraft to get to it, not an unusual occurrence in the bush of Alaska.

The airplane sat safely undisturbed where I had tied it to driftwood the night before. The fog was so thick I could not see the nose of the airplane while standing at the tail end. Thinking it would burn off shortly, I returned to camp for hot coffee and breakfast. By 10 a.m. the fog had not dissipated one bit. Like any young fool thinking that a meeting was more important than dying, I walked back down to the beach to look the situation over.

I could tell the fog did not ascend too far above the ground, as it was brighter looking at the sky than straight ahead. How thick it was I did not know. The big problem in my mind at the time was how I was going to see to take off. I could not see driftwood, holes in the sand, or the ocean to give me a clear takeoff path.

In a moment of insanity, I decided to solve the problem with sticks and toilet paper. I tied one-foot lengths of toilet paper to small pieces of driftwood I found lying on the high tide line. The guys helped me put the sticks with toilet paper at ten foot intervals in what we thought was a straight line. We soon had 500 feet of sand marked that we thought was a fairly straight line. I figured I would be able to follow the toilet paper until I had the speed to take off. I removed one of the moose from the back of the airplane to lighten my load, just to be safe. Unfortunately, what seemed like a straight line of toilet paper and sticks on the ground was in actuality bent. Because of our limited visibility in placing them, we had inadvertently turned my runway toward big driftwood logs, tall trees and a cliff above the high tide mark.

I got the engine well warmed up and myself primed to go immediately on instruments upon gaining flying speed before applying full power. I could see the white toilet paper of the first stick as I lifted the tail wheel and increased my speed. Soon, my left wheel started digging into the sand, causing my airplane to want to turn in that direction; the direction in which disaster awaited. Recognizing that we had not laid the sticks and toilet paper in a straight line, I had to steer the struggling aircraft away from the sight of the markers. In a split second I was flying blind down the beach not knowing if I was heading toward rock, driftwood, ocean or trees. It was not a good feeling. It made me realize way too late this meeting was not so important after all.

Somehow, out of pure luck, I held the airplane straight enough that when I saw the white spray of breaking waves closing fast on my right I could pull on full flaps and get airborne. I flew close to the waves underneath me until my airspeed allowed me to lower the flaps and climb up into the fog. Climbing on instruments up into clouds is not nearly as big a deal as descending into it when you don't know what is underneath you. But because I had not had time to set up correctly in the chaos of the takeoff, it was several minutes before I got the instruments and myself settled enough to reach the sun-drenched skies above.

I'd had another close encounter on the same beach the previous year flying my 7-AC. I wanted to put an emergency stash of gas and kerosene on this side of Yakutat Bay in case I needed them some time in the future. I had two five-gallon cans of sealed aviation fuel and one of kerosene in the baggage area. My assistant wanted to come with me, because he was tired of driving on the limited road system around Yakutat. He had been assigned to me for the summer by my supervisor in Juneau.

I relented and let him buckle up behind me. A short trip became much longer when he asked to see more of the Malaspina and Bering glaciers, as well as the logging camp he had heard about. We flew for several hours looking at moose, brown bear, seals and sea lions before flying back toward Yakutat. I was not comfortable with the amount of fuel I had left, so I decided to land again where I had stashed the gas on our way over. Besides, I really had to go number two badly. I landed and told my assistant to put five gallons of the red marked aviation fuel in the tank while I attended to nature. I had plainly marked the cans so a person would not put the wrong fuel into the airplane. I hurried off to the alders with my roll of toilet paper.

Upon completing this necessary call of nature, I returned to the aircraft and checked that he had put the fuel cap on correctly. He had and we both climbed in and took off. Shortly after takeoff upon reaching about 100 feet of altitude, the airplane engine coughed and started to sputter badly. I immediately started turning back toward shore. Upon completing the turn, I was down to twenty feet above the waves, as I had had to lose altitude to keep the airplane from stalling.

Flying just a couple of mph from the airplane falling out of the sky in a stall, I realized I would not be able to make a safe approach, but had to land straight ahead toward the driftwood and trees that bordered the beach—if I could make it that far. I ran out of airspeed and altitude as my front wheels just about cleared a receding wave, and we landed in a spray of saltwater. Where my wheels touched down it was only several inches deep, and the airplane continued up the beach toward dead trees and driftwood. I jammed on the brakes as hard as I could. When we hit softer sand the airplane turned violently up on its nose, burying the propeller in the sand.

I thought the engine had blown a cylinder or developed some type of engine failure while the incident was occurring. My passenger was pale white and sitting on a driftwood stump as I pulled the airplane back on all three wheels. I took the engine cowling off and cleaned out all the sand. I did not see oil or any other indication of a major engine failure, so I checked the propeller next. The propeller was fine because the engine had quit before the crash, and it had stopped in a horizontal position instead of vertically.

The engine would heavily sputter upon trying to start, but it would not catch and run. It acted more like a fuel problem than an engine failure. I looked inside the fuel filter. The liquid inside was clear instead of colored red. My assistant had put kerosene into the fuel tank instead of aviation gas.

I won't repeat what I said to him. We were not close before this, but had a far colder relationship afterward. You would think a student of law would be able to read and tell the difference between aviation fuel and kerosene. Well, maybe not, remembering some of the lawyers I have met. I almost always personally fueled aircraft I was flying. Twice I did not, and I paid for it. This was not the last of my problems with this jerk.

Going to the bathroom while piloting an airplane can be a tricky endeavor. Going number one is no big deal if you are male, as most pilots have a can in the back seat just for this purpose, but doing number two presents too many difficulties. You are better off just letting number two happen and clean your pants later than trying to find a bush landing spot in a panic. I tried to land once in dire straits instead soiling my clothing. I did not wreck that time in a poorly planned and executed landing, but when I saw the rocks and holes I had narrowly missed, I was so stunned that I got my first pair of eyeglasses on the next trip to town. I am positive there are air crashes in Alaska each year as a result of this predicament, which remain unknown because it is not cool to tell the FAA, your wife and friends that you wrecked an expensive airplane because you did not want to crap your pants. An engine failure sounds much more manly and dramatic.

I flew hundreds of hours each year with Dick Nicholes, doing patrols at all times of the year. One of the most awe-inspiring sights I ever encountered in nature occurred on one of these trips. We were flying down the beach east of Yakutat when we noticed a large number of seals on the shore. I remarked to Dick that this was strange as I had never seen a seal here before. I asked Dick to fly closer when I saw more seals scampering out of the water as fast as they could.

It was then I noticed a killer whale swimming just behind the seals who were frantically seeking the safety of the shore. I asked Dick to climb to 5,000 feet so I could see a larger area of the sea. Dick and I were stunned to witness a large pod or several small pods of killer whales in a two-mile circle around a large number of desperate seals. The whales slowly tightened the circle until it was only hundreds of yards across. The slaughter commenced at this point, as the killer whales rushed into the packed seals, killing them in large numbers. I won't say the sea ran red with seal blood, but many were killed. We witnessed the large predators tossing seals high into the air and killing them as they hit the water again. It was an amazing lesson in nature's cycle of life. I never gave killer whales the high appreciation I accorded my two favorite predators—grizzly bears and wolves. But it was readily apparent that nature has well-defined their role in the balance of life in the ocean.

I thought I had understood the lectures on the balance of nature while attending college. In real life, I saw no balance. Where predators were few or nonexistent, prey thrived. When predators killed off the prey their numbers declined until the food source could again recover. It was a scale that only balanced in the middle of the cycle. The balance of nature was really this wild swing between predator and prey, and was never a static number. Unfortunately, nature did not account for man becoming armed with powerful weapons that would put her whole process in jeopardy.

I have buried the name of the man who took over for my first supervisor so deep in my memory that I cannot retrieve it. It was the same guy who had been working in the Juneau office and researched the illegal hunting license I had bought when I had just come to Alaska, costing me my first permanent job with Fish and Game. That violation should not have affected our relationship, as I was told he had been fired from the Department previously himself for shooting a moose for his personal use while driving a Department patrol vehicle. For the purposes of identification, I will refer to him as Supervisor Dip.

I knew that Mr. Dip had been made Supervisor of the Juneau District, but gave it no thought until he flew down to Yakutat to see me. I had put in a mileage reimbursement request for the use of my personal vehicle on Fish and Game business while my department vehicle was out of commission for repairs. I bought gas at the local gas station and paid for it out of personal funds. Supervisor Dip thought this was reason enough to spend over one hundred dollars on an airplane ticket to question my seventy dollar request for reimbursement. He could have just sent me a letter or called by telephone to refuse me. It would have ticked me off, but that would have been the end of it.

Instead, he went into a red-faced rant when he entered my office, accusing me of falsifying documents for an illegal claim. He said I should have used a Department of Transportation vehicle available instead of my own personal one. I told him I requested one when I took mine in for repairs. The foreman told me that they did have one available, but he would not even drive it home, it was so old and broken down. I drove a lot each day on bumpy gravel roads doing sport fishing patrols, as my logs reflected, and did not want to take a chance of breaking down, so I opted to drive my personal Toyota Land Cruiser.

Mr. Dip stated he did not believe me and again accused me of lying as well as falsifying documents. I showed him my department daily logs and pointed out to him I had flown hundreds of hours in my personal aircraft, at my own expense, doing Fish and Game business plus all the miles I drove on the road system, and that I had not requested reimbursement from the state on the thousands of dollars I spent on gas. I told him if I was going to put in a false reimbursement request, I certainly would not limit it to seventy dollars. He refused to believe me and stormed out of my office.

I found out later he went to the owner of the gas station and tried to browbeat him into signing a paper stating I had never bought gas there during the time I had claimed. Mr. Dip then went to the foreman of our highway division and got a statement that there was a truck available during the time I drove my own vehicle. There was no note attached saying the vehicle was past its useful life.

Arriving back at the compound, he showed me the statement from the foreman, and told me the gas station owner had no recollection of me buying gas there. That was completely false, as I found out later when talking to the gas station owner. Supervisor Dip then accused me of stealing gasoline out of the department storage tank on the compound for my personal use. By now I was mad as a wet hen, and told him he was full of crap. If he could prove it do so or shut up. The large 1,000-gallon department gas tank had not been filled to my knowledge since I had been in Yakutat. The gas I had tried to take out of it for my patrol boat had as much rust and water in it as gasoline.

Telling him to get off his butt and follow me, I emptied some gas from the department tank into a glass container, showing him how contaminated the gas was. I told him I would not use this gas in anything I owned, but if he wanted me to use it in my patrol vehicles to put it in writing, as I would not be held responsible for any resulting damage. Supervisor Dip caught the afternoon flight back to Juneau after still refusing to approve my reimbursement request, telling me never to falsify department documents again. I loved Yakutat but was really questioning my move there. It had become apparent that Don Roberts was right. Someone in the Department wanted me fired.

The next time I met this delightful supervisor was when someone in the Protection Division of Fish and Game wrote to the State Department of Labor filing a claim of being forced to work overtime without being paid for it. I am sure he thought that I had made the complaint, but it was against labor laws to come right out and question me. I asked why he flew all the way to Yakutat when he had the records detailing how many hours I worked. They were listed in my weekly and monthly reports. I did not say so to him, but to me this was not overtime but part of the job I loved. I would never even have thought of complaining about the hours. Mr. Dip told me they did not have the records. We both knew that was a lie, but he kept a straight face.

The Department just did not want to show the Labor Department how many hours employees worked beyond forty hours a week, so they came up with a form for all their employees to fill out and sign. The form was a monthly statement for the prior year asking us how many hours of paid and unpaid work we performed for the department. My work week from spring hunting until the end of the fall season averaged between seventy and ninety hours per week. Winter hours, from late October to April, were far fewer and probably did not average forty hours a week. Mr. Dip told me that was not documented, and to put something more reasonable down. I signed the form and handed it to him saying he had my reports, and if he didn't want to use them, put down whatever number he fancied. However, if the Labor Department contacted me, I would not lie to them. He again took the evening flight home without saying goodbye. It was another attempt at harassment, and another matter that could have been easily handled by telephone or mail.

The next time I became aware of his evil designs was when he assigned the law student who put kerosene in my airplane instead of aviation fuel to be my summer temporary. Yakutat had never had a temporary Protection Officer, nor had I requested one. This was not from the goodness of Supervisor Dip's heart. The guy was there to spy on me and to provide reasons for my second termination. Mr. Dip was determined to remove me from Fish and Game again.

Most temporary hires I knew of at least tried to get along with their supervisors. Mr. Important-Lawyer-To-Be started off by telling me what hours he would work. He also stated that, as a student of law, he would personally handle all court cases going to the justice of the peace. I just laughed in his face and told him to get back on the airplane to Anchorage in the morning. Until then he could stay in the bunkhouse. He replied that he was hired for two months and he would stay that long. Seeing who set this up and what they wanted from it, I told him okay, but he would patrol forty hours a week where and when I told him. He could also accompany me to court on any case he generated, but I would type the case out and present it. If he did not like that, he could still get on the airplane in the morning.

Mr. Wannabe stayed the two months, and was almost as incompetent as Worthless Will. He did write one violation citation during the time he was in Yakutat and threw a fit when I refused to let him present it in court. How anyone could spend two months patrolling the Situk River and only write one citation was beyond me. Almost every time I did an enforcement patrol there I saw something against Fish and Game regulations.

The whole situation involving this temporary hire was so sad it was funny. I would find him poring over any report, expense statement or paperwork relating to the management of the compound that was not locked up. I had bought a new .243 Mauser rifle for Sharon during the time he was there. He questioned me about how I had paid for it. I told him it was none of his business. Sure enough, his report to Mr. Dip after his job ended stated that Dick Nicholes and I had falsified flying reports, overbilling the department to get the money to buy the rifle. He listed a bunch of other supposed transgressions I committed that Supervisor Dip would use to try and fire me. Most of these accusations were so silly I forgot them.

I had known for a long time that important people got special treatment from Fish and Game. Besides the episode with General Westmoreland, I had cited the Lieutenant Governor of Alaska for fishing without a valid license in the Paxon Lake area while I worked for Don Roberts out of Fairbanks. The Lieutenant Governor told me he left his license in his room at the Paxon Lodge after purchasing it that morning prior to going fishing. I wrote out the citation but told him if he would bring me his license later I would void it. Unbeknownst to him, I immediately went to the Paxon Lodge and asked to look at their sport fishing license book. As I figured, he was lying and had not bought a license there. Not only that, he was not even staying at the Lodge. Don Roberts told me when I returned to Fairbanks three days later that the citation had been voided by the Juneau Offices, saying the Lieutenant Governor had brought the citation and a valid sports fishing license to them. I told Don how I had checked the records and the guy had lied to me on two counts. Don just shrugged and told me that at least I had forced him to go buy a fishing license. He could no more fight Juneau politics than I could.

In Yakutat I was involved in two more blatant examples of political favoritism. The first one involved a very well-known Alaskan big-game guide. I was patrolling Yakutat Bay in my patrol boat when I saw a fairly large yacht. I had never seen this boat before, so I veered toward it for a closer look. No one was fishing from it, but there was a fresh black bear hide hanging from the stern. I swung around the bow of the yacht, signaling the person at the controls to stop so I could board. Upon boarding I was met by the guide. Introducing myself, I asked to see the license and tag of whoever shot the black bear and anyone else on board who happened to be hunting or fishing.

The guide produced both the nonresident person he said shot the bear and his out-of-state hunting license. The nonresident license did not have a black bear endorsement. Upon closer examination, the black bear was not tagged with a non-resident seal either. I told the guide I was citing the client for both violations. The guide told me I could not do that, as none of his big-game hunting clients had to buy either tags or licenses until after they actually shot an animal. I almost burst out laughing because this statement was so outlandish. You bought licenses and tags for the privilege of hunting the animals, not after you killed one. The license did not come with a money-back guarantee if you failed to actually get what you hunted.

The guide was not amused and told me he would see me in Yakutat later that evening where I would be returning his client's bear hide and voiding my citations. After saying I would check into it, I departed. Later I called Supervisor Dip to let him know Juneau would probably be receiving a complaint about me from the guide, and the circumstances of the citation. He told me it was true this guide's clients did not have to purchase tags until they actually harvested big game animals. He added that I was to go to the gentleman's hotel room to apologize and return his bear hide. I told him he must be wrong; that such a practice would make a shambles out of Alaska's revenue from hunting, and make enforcing regulations impossible. He replied to just do it and hung up on me. Later that evening I went to the guide's room to return the hide and retrieve the citation I wrote his client earlier. I was angry and embarrassed to be put into this situation, but accepted their offer of a drink to show I was a bigger person than the witless state politicians who wrote this addendum into law.

The second incident in Yakutat involved a commercial fisherman on a river east of Yakutat fishing for salmon without a license, without his gear being marked as required, and fishing outside legal time periods. The person making the complaint fished the same river close to the illegal fisherman. He was a straightforward retired colonel from the Air Force whom I had met before. I tended to believe him, so I had Jerry Wells, who was flying for Dick Nicholes at the time, fly me out to the river after dark. After landing on the gulf beach I walked over the sand dunes separating the river from the Gulf of Alaska to observe night fishing activities. The current fishing period would end at 8:00 in the morning. I wanted to see if anyone was fishing after the commercial fishing period ended. Hiding in a place where I could see both fishing operations, I spent the night watching.

Both nets were out of the water before time ran out, but when I went up to inspect the nets and boats, I saw one of them was not licensed. Also, the buoy at the end of the net inside the boat did not have the number of the fisherman's license written on it as required. Both were violations of Fish and Game commercial fishing regulations.

I approached the cabin of the person using this boat and gear. I knocked on the door. The man opening the door was upset that I had interrupted his breakfast. I identified myself and told the guy why I was there. He told me that he did not have to license his boat or gear. I replied that I did not agree, and wrote out citations for both violations. Upon notifying Supervisor Dip of the incident, I was again told to void the citations. The gentleman in question was exempt from following commercial fishing regulations. Being exasperated to the extreme, I asked who else in my region was exempt from the regulations that everyone else in the state had to follow. Mr. Dip was not amused and told me to void the citations, hanging up on me again. When I saw the colonel several weeks later, I explained that my supervisor in Juneau told me I could not enforce regulations on his neighbor. He stated what I felt, that this was political bullshit.

I strongly believed that this favoritism was wrong. There was nothing I could do about it but treat everyone equally. I stopped writing citations to anyone in my District who commercially fished without licensing their boats or writing their license number on the end of their buoys. I just made sure they had a valid commercial fishing license. It made my job harder, as I had no way of identifying nets set in the water and left unattended. Fortunately, I never saw another guide that failed to tag and seal their client's big game trophies.

Sharon and I were having serious issues. I had suspected for the last four years that Sharon was being unfaithful in our marriage. The sickening feeling of betrayal by my wife, whom I loved and trusted above all others, was being replaced by growing anger. I had asked her about strange encounters of other men in my house after being gone for multiple days on long patrols. She always had a reason for the men being there and could lie with a straight face, blue eyes beaming love for me, and hurt at my accusations. In Yakutat her affair with the base commander of the Coast Guard Station became so blatant I decided we needed to divorce. This and this deteriorating situation with my supervisor left me sleepless for many nights trying to decide the best course of action. I was also concerned for Michael and David and what a divorce would mean for them.

I had become so depressed with both my marriage and my Fish and Game Supervisor that I was no longer enjoying my work. Something needed to change. I called Don Roberts and asked if he had an opening for me back in Fairbanks, figuring if I transferred back to work under someone I admired, half the battle would be won. Don said he had an opening and would love to have me back, but had to get Juneau's approval. I put in a written request for transfer after calling Don, and within two weeks I received a letter approving my transfer back to Fairbanks.

Prior to leaving Yakutat I received a call from the airport manager requesting that I come out and seal a brown bear skull and hide. This momentarily puzzled me, as she was the town magistrate and could seal them herself. I figured there had to be something wrong with the kill for her to call me. I immediately departed for the airport to check it out.

I recognized the dead bear immediately upon seeing it on the airport tarmac. It was a female brown bear with three cubs that I had seen many times that summer in the vicinity of the Italio River. Shooting a sow accompanied by young cubs was illegal. Checking the hide, I found that she had indeed been lactating. I questioned the hunter, whose distinctive airplane I had seen camped on a sandbar alongside the Italio, as to the circumstances regarding shooting the sow. He told me he and his partner saw the bear walking alone on the Italio and watched it for about an hour before shooting it. They thought it was a young male, because there were not any cubs that they could see. Upon discovering it was a female, they brought it in to be sealed.

If this were true, I would have written a warning. It is difficult to tell the sex of a young bear if it is not accompanied by cubs. I did not believe him, so I confiscated the hide and wrote him a citation for killing a sow with cubs. I had never seen this particular sow without her cubs nearby. I immediately had Dick Nicholes fly me out to the Italio where I had seen this brown bear and her cubs many times. The tide was starting to come in, but from the air, I saw tracks in the sand of a brown bear with three cubs walking down the beach from the direction of the Alsek River. After having Dick land, I took my camera and followed the tracks on foot. It was easy to see that the sow was following the tide line looking for food while the cubs wandered in and out of the driftwood that littered the beach. By the tracks, I could tell they were never further than thirty feet from her at any time. I photographed this and where the sow's tracks dug sharply into the sand as they veered toward the trees higher up the dunes, with the cubs' tracks following. The sow's tracks ended in a pool of blood sunk into the dry sand. The cubs' tracks spread out at this point, before disappearing into the woods. There was no body, but drag marks in the sand led me to where the body of the dead bear had lain inside the tree line, out of sight of passing airplanes. I took more pictures.

I knew what had happened as surely as if I had watched it unfold in person. The sow, with her cubs, was walking up the beach when she was shot. She died before reaching the trees. The man shooting her dragged her into the trees where he and his partner proceeded to remove the skin and head as required by law, thinking that the carcass would never be found. He then flew to Yakutat, and tried to have the bear sealed by the station manager of the Yakutat Airport instead of bringing it into a Fish and Game office, not knowing she was also the justice of the peace for Yakutat.

I sent a detailed report along with pictures I had taken to Juneau, with copies to the Anchorage Fish and Game office where the man would be arraigned. About a month after moving back to Fairbanks, Don Roberts called me into his office and told me the man had hired a lawyer and the trial date was set.

Before the trial I met with the Anchorage District Attorney handling the case and went over the report and photographs I had taken. He wanted to enter the photographs into evidence during my testimony and wanted to make sure I had taken them and in what sequence. It was a trial by jury that the DA told me we would have lost without the photographs, as it is very difficult to tell the sex of a bear without cubs accompanying her. I was pleased when the guilty verdict was read; the man had not only killed the sow but her three cubs as well. They would not survive without the sow to protect and feed them.

Within days of arriving back in Fairbanks from the trial I was called into a private meeting with Supervisor Dip. He had flown up from Juneau to talk to me personally, instead of having Don Roberts do it. Mr. Dip had waited for the trial to be over. He suspended me from duty prior to termination for my supposed actions in Yakutat. This miserable excuse of a supervisor stated I had falsely submitted records of flights with Dick Nicholes and used the money to buy a .243 rifle for my wife. He was subpoenaing my bank records and Dick Nichole's flight records to prove it. I told him he did not need to go to the trouble as far as I was concerned, as I would provide them to him. I also told him I was sure Dick would do the same because neither of us had anything to hide. He told me not to be so cocky—he had a witness. I replied that his witness would make a good lawyer when he graduated, if he was willing to lie in court. He asked how I knew who this witness was. I just looked at him and said, "Next time you hire a temporary to spy on one of your game wardens, make sure they at least show more interest in the job itself than the person they're supposed to watch."

He went on to state that I had not taken care of my patrol truck, and he had had to spend a day removing tar from the body. I replied that was partially true. The truck had some road tar on it because the highway crew had just tarred the roads the morning I was scheduled to leave Yakutat, and I needed to turn the truck into them before I transferred to Fairbanks in a few hours. There was not enough time to clean the truck as well as get the rest of the compound ready for my transfer. The next thing he accused me of really made me angry.

Mr. Dip stated that I had disconnected the toilet in the house and was urinating and defecating in the rear bedroom. I was absolutely stunned. This was so farfetched and stupid I could only stare back at him before asking him to repeat what he just said. He repeated the accusation, adding there was water on the back bedroom floor as well as dried feces in the room.

I completely lost it and yelled at him that not only was he the worst supervisor I had ever seen, but he was stupid as well. If he had looked at the carpet he claimed was wet from urine, he would have seen imprints of the two freezers located along that wall. We had defrosted the freezers prior to them being shipped out, and had placed pans to catch the defrosting ice. We had also set up a portable heater and fans to dry the damp carpet from the water the pans did not catch. If there was any moisture still there, it was because of the defrosting process. I did not dignify the defecation claim with a response. He shouted at me that I was suspended, and to turn in my badge and revolver. I carefully put my revolver on the desk and flipped my badge at his face. I told him I would be happy to meet him in court if I was fired, so I could show everyone just how stupid and dishonest he was; that went for his little spy, as well. It was all I could do to restrain myself from punching him in the nose.

Sharon was a lousy housekeeper. I knew that. It was one of our many growing problems. But the accusations in the complaint were untrue. I called Dick Nicholes and told him to expect his flight records to be inspected. He told me that Supervisor Dip had already spent a day in his office before going to Fairbanks, combing over the records and trying to get Dick to admit that he sent false flight reimbursement requests to Juneau and split the money with me. Dick said he just laughed at him and replied that I was probably the most honest officer the Department had ever sent to Yakutat. He would also be happy to testify to that in court.

Mr. Dip knew this before talking to me, but tried to bluff me into admitting wrongdoing during our meeting. That was not a bad tactic if you were smarter and better prepared than the person being questioned. He was not. Mr. Dip tried to get me fired by taking random facts, applying some written statements from his dishonest spy, and planting false evidence (if there were indeed any dried feces in the trailer's back bedroom). His entire time as my supervisor was spent collecting evidence against me in this pursuit. To him it was personal. I never did learn why this was the case.

The next day, after being suspended, I went down to the Fairbanks School District's Administrative Office to apply for a teaching position. Two weeks later a young game warden I did not know showed up at my apartment with a typed letter on Fish and Game Department letterhead supposedly written by me stating that I had requested the previous two weeks off for vacation. I laughed and took the letter to our kitchen table not to sign but to write that I was being lied about and railroaded out of a job. I also wrote on the letter that if I were subsequently fired, I would sue the State of Alaska and the Protection Division of Fish and Game for slander and illegal termination. The guy turned a little grey when he read what I had written, and left. Two days later I received a letter from Don Roberts, telling me to report back to work. I learned later that the District Attorney from Anchorage had raised hell in Juneau about my termination, stating that whenever the Department had anyone who could conduct a cohesive investigation, they ran them out of the job.

Ever since I returned to the Fairbanks Office, Don Roberts had treated me fairly. He even had one of his pilots tutor me in the department aircraft so I could get a Fish and Game permit to fly their aircraft. I had previously flown to Anchorage while I was in Yakutat and passed the check flight for flying department aircraft, which was denied later by Juneau. This was unheard of in the Department. Even though I had passed every check ride given by the Department, including one by John Klenbile, and had more than ten times the required air hours, I was never granted pilot privileges. I was told in a meeting with Don Roberts, Director Stewart and John Klenbile that it was because I had falsified my hours. They gave as the reason the time I had flown in the back seat of the Cessna 180 when the Director of the Protection Division was being checked out in the airplane by Phil Connors. I had logged the time of the flight in my pilot logs. They asked why I had logged them. I explained that Phil had instructed me to do so. Phil was called in to meet with them after I was dismissed. Phil told them it was a lie, because he had instructed me to only log time I was pilot in command. When he was asked why he signed off on my total flight hours as being equal to the hours the airplanes I was in were being flown when he was the pilot in charge, he replied he never touched the controls during those flights. All three of them knew Phil was lying and yet they still denied my request. I was depressed at this treatment. It was apparent to me that no matter what I did, I would be persecuted while I remained an employee.

This whole process of providing special exemptions from Fish and Game regulations for a precious few friends and politicians along with their persecution of me left such a deep anger that I began to hate the job and the people who ran the Department. I would never again strictly follow the letter of the law regarding Fish and Game regulations. The Department had lost my complete respect, eventually leading me into becoming a rogue guide in the state.

I wrote the following article several years later expressing my feelings. It appeared in the *Alaska Wildlife Digest*, Vol. 2, Number 2, Spring Edition, published in Fairbanks, Alaska in 1975. The front page has a picture I took of a four-year-old cow moose standing in a pool of blood, waiting for the wolves surrounding her to finish the process of killing her.

Yakutat Moose Problem
Told by Mike Stultz

(EDITOR'S NOTE) In 1964 Mike Stultz came from a farm area in south-western Washington to the University of Alaska to finish a bachelor of education degree. Since graduation he has taught, served in several sections of the state as a Protection Officer for the Department of Fish and Game, and is now back to teaching at Circle City. He has two children and his hobbies are flying, photography, hunting, fishing, scuba diving and canoeing.

The Alaska Department of Fish and Game in releasing figures to support the predator control program reported here, placed the Yakutat moose herd at a high of 2,600 animals which had diminished to 400. They placed the number of wolves at about forty and were going to attempt to take half of them.

I arrived in Yakutat, Alaska, in November of 1970 with my wife and two children to take the position of District Game Warden of the area reaching from Cape Fairweather on the south to Katella to the northwest. This is a 300-mile stretch of land with the Gulf of Alaska on one side and the mighty Coastal Range crowning the other. It is one of the most beautiful places in the state with the immense peaks of the Saint Elias Range towering 18,000 feet above dense forests of spruce intermingled with fjords, glaciers, and river systems. Inside Yakutat Bay lies a string of islands with white sandy beaches that provide refuge and food for deer, bears, and coyotes along with other species of small game. Fishing in the Italio and Situk rivers was some of the best to be found anywhere. The forelands which start at the base of the Coastal Range and extend five to fifteen miles west where it ends in the wide sandy beaches bordering the Gulf of Alaska, teemed with big game such as moose, black, glacier, and brown bear. The mountains are dotted with mountain goat. It was at that time one of the most sought after districts in the state as far as Protection Officers were concerned—it was an outdoorsman's paradise.

143

Little did I realize that I would personally witness the destruction of one of the great moose populations in Alaska through the forces of nature and the blind stupidity of the Department of Fish and Game, and that the experience would leave me with a feeling of frustration so great I can never work for the department again.

Predating my arrival in Yakutat by about forty years, moose, the largest member of the deer family, had begun a slow migration through the Chilkat Pass in Canada, down the Tatshenshenini River and finally along the Alsek River into Alaska and the Yakutat forelands. Here they found a habitat ideally suited to them. There was plenty of food—willows, sedges, pond weeds, and lots of alder. The vicious costal winds kept snow blown off the willows and alders along the major rivers providing abundant food even in years of large accumulations of snow. The moose continued northwest to Yakutat Bay and here, thanks to their dense long hollow hair which acted as both a life jacket and warm insulation, swam across the bay and established herds around Malaspina Glacier, the largest icefield in the world outside the polar icecaps, to Icy Bay. Here the moose was separated from his perpetual nemesis, the wolf. Wolves, not having the long buoyant insulating hair of the moose, could not swim the frigid waters of Yakutat Bay. Neither could they walk around Yakutat Bay because of Russel Fjord, impassable glacier, or the five mountains surrounding the bay that run from water's edge to heights of over 15,000 feet. The moose that crossed the bay, free of wolves, contentedly spread westward and multiplied, while those to the south were left to a far different fate.

South of the bay wolves came by the same path as the moose and multiplied. What they saw they liked. Things begin to change. The Indians, used to a diet of seal and fish, began to acquire a taste for moose. People from the larger population areas discovered the treasures of Yakutat and came in increasing numbers to enjoy its hunting and fishing. The U.S. Forest Service put in cabins and airstrips to accommodate people. The Alaska Department of Fish and Game established a three month either sex hunting season.

This was the scene I so unsuspectingly stepped into upon my arrival in Yakutat. There were moose everywhere. You could fly in any direction and see literally hundreds of moose. Who would ever suspect that something was about to happen? Who would ever think that within a few years moose hunting would be just a memory in Yakutat?

That winter, flying with Dick Nicholes and Terry Holliday of Gulf Air Taxi based in Yakutat, I began to see things I found very difficult to believe. Everywhere we went south of Yakutat Bay I observed large numbers of moose kills by wolves. Like many people I was of the belief wolves did not nor could not kill healthy moose. I was worried and upset that the moose in the area were suffering from a serious food shortage or ailment that made them so weak they fell prey to wolves.

Going to Juneau and discussing the problem with the game biologist who was supposed to study and control the animals in the Yakutat area, I met only polite indifference and disbelief concerning my observations of the moose situation. You only had to look at the computer printouts from returned harvest tags to see the moose population there was in great shape. Yes, he would try to get up to Yakutat sometime this winter and explain why healthy looking moose were falling over dead for the wolves to eat. I really didn't believe that wolves could kill healthy moose, did I? How long had I been there? Wasn't I imagining just a little? I left this important man's office and went back to Yakutat determined to make right my grievous error in suspecting the poor wolf.

Flying with Holliday every hour we could get into the air I examined dead moose, live moose and the stomach contents of dead wolves we shot. I visited the fenced-off moose browse study areas the Department, along with the U.S. Forest Service, put in the more densely populated moose areas. I also observed from the air my first battle between a live healthy four-year-old cow moose and five wolves. It wasn't a battle really. The wolves just took so many fist sized bites of meat out of the rump, side and shoulders of the cow that within fifteen minutes the snow was red in a thirty-foot radius around her, and in twenty minutes she was dead. It sickened me then as it still does now. I landed and examined the dead cow. I took a tooth, looked at the heart, lungs, and liver. I cracked a leg bone to examine the bone marrow, but I could not see anything wrong except she was dead from wolf bites. She appeared to be a fine, fat, healthy moose that was in the wrong place at the wrong time.

There had to be a key somewhere, yet I couldn't find it. The browse was in good shape—it was hard to tell the difference between the fenced-off study plots and the foliage surrounding it. The stomachs of the wolves I found contained large concentrations of moose hair, bone chips and big chunks of rotten meat, some deer hair, and an assortment of smaller bones. The moose from both the air and ground appeared to be heathy, vigorous animals. Why was I seeing up to twenty fresh moose kills a week?

Summer came and went. I was so busy with commercial and sports fishermen I didn't have time to think about either moose or wolves. Even if I had the time to work at the problem I wouldn't have been able to see anything of value. The heavily forested area hid what I would have been looking for. Wolves, difficult to spot in the winter, are impossible to see in the summer. The biologist must have felt the same way, because he still hadn't come around. Apparently no one cared until that fall's hunting season rolled around and the previous winter's predation by wolves began to show its effects.

I flew hundreds of hours during that moose season visiting all the hunters and their camps. Almost everywhere I went the questions and statements were the same: "I have been hunting this spot for five years and never failed to get my moose within a half mile of camp the first or second day out. I haven't even seen a moose this trip, and I have been here a week." "What are all those big dog tracks doing on all the river bars?" "If thing get worse I will have to go to the interior to get my moose next year." "If there aren't many moose around here anymore, why do you guys have a three month either sex season on them?" "I don't see how hunting can get much worse."

That last statement was wrong. The hunting would be much worse next year as the wolves kept right on killing moose when the hunters quit and went home. Two years from this time hunting would be stopped by the Department on the south side of Yakutat Bay. Right up to the dying gasps of this herd the Department maintained a three month either sex season.

By this time the difference became very noticeable between the moose herds on the north and south sides of Yakutat Bay. This was the key I had been searching for. The moose on both sides of the bay received the same human hunting pressure. The food situations, cover and terrain all were almost identical on both sides. The only observable difference was in the presence of wolves. In one area wolves enjoyed a twelve month either sex moose season and on the north side of the bay moose hunting was closed to this four-legged predator.

**I have not included the last section of the article in this book as it is a repeat of information already provided.

I am aware that I was not really being fair to the biologist in charge of Yakutat hunting district when writing this article for the Alaska Wildlife Digest, as he could have flown a moose survey from Juneau without my knowing. He could also have petitioned his supervisors to reduce the hunting season in Yakutat and been denied. The fact remains that the long either sex hunting season for moose in the Yakutat area remained in effect until the once-plentiful herds of moose were almost decimated.

Author with Alsek River kings in Yakutat.

Kathy Peterson with Situk River steelhead.

Author with rebuilt 7-AC on Yakutat beach.

Fish and Game house in Yakutat buried under snow.

Author hunting glacier bear in Yakutat.

Author on Yakutat beach.

Author introducing Michael to David.

Yakutat beach.

Teaching in One-Room Schools

DURING THIS SECOND SUSPENSION after transferring back to the Fairbanks office I had been visited by the principal and vice-principal of Eielson Air Base High School offering me a teaching position. I told them I would think about it and let them know. I accepted, and within a few months of going back to work for Don Roberts, I resigned from Fish and Game for the last time to begin teaching again.

After the mess with Fish and Game and my problems with Sharon, I needed to get away and be alone for a while to think about my marriage and my life. While waiting to start teaching at Eielson, I decided to fly to the North Slope to hunt wolves, fox and wolverine. I would stay at a hotel in Kotzebue and hunt during the day. A friend of mine had just returned from the area after a successful hunt.

The two-hour flight to Bettles was uneventful. I landed there to re-fuel and check the weather in the Brooks Range, because I planned to fly through Anaktuvuk Pass to reach Kotzebue. There was a low-pressure area building, but I should be on the leading edge and flying away from it. Bettles weather was sunny and clear at -5 degrees. The FAA said a pilot had just flown through the pass and reported slight turbulence and a few isolated light snow showers. Kotzebue was clear with unlimited visibility. The weather was good enough for the flight, so after eating lunch at the lodge, I departed.

Approaching the Brooks Range, the weather was as the previous pilot had told Bettles Flight Service. I flew through some light snow showers. The weather had deteriorated by the time I flew over Anaktuvuk village half an hour later. I would have landed and spent the night if the village had a runway. I did not want to fly all the way back to Bettles only to wait there for several days while the low pressure system settled into the area. Deciding to push on to the better weather on the other side of the pass on the North Slope, I banked 58A to the right side of the narrowing canyon in case there was another pilot flying my way from Kotzebue.

I entered a snow shower, expecting it to be like all the others I had flown through earlier. It was not. Visibility became less than a quarter mile. I concentrated on the ground below and the mountain to my right, expecting at any moment for the snow shower to end and my forward visibility to improve. It got worse instead. Dropping down to within a hundred feet of the snow-covered ground below me, I could barely make out the terrain flashing beneath my wings. I edged closer to the mountain on my right. Its grey granite walls provided some relief to my eyes, which were straining to see the white snow-covered ground ahead and below me. The wind and turbulence increased to the point where I could not turn around safely even if I wanted to. I was also worried about the ice that was building up on my windshield and the leading edges of my wings.

Soon, the ice completely covered my windshield, blocking any forward visibility. My airspeed indicator began a slight fluctuation, indicating that ice was also building up on the pitot tube. If ice covered it completely and shut off the air flow and vacuum, I would not only lose my airspeed instruments and turn and bank indicator, but artificial horizon as well. Bad at any time, but deadly in this narrow pass and these weather conditions. The mountain on my right suddenly disappeared into the grip of the swirling storm. Looking out my side window to my wings I was shocked to see they appeared to be wings of ice instead of fabric and metal. All too soon I was flying an ice cube completely blind with failing instruments in a narrow mountain pass that had claimed the lives of many Alaska pilots.

I had no choice but to land straight ahead before my airplane quit flying or I crashed into something. My vision was completely blocked. I would not be able to see if the pass made a turn or if the ground ahead of me rose. Not being able to see what lay in my landing path and hoping it was not too late, I pulled on flaps and reduced power, keeping my rate of climb indicator at a minus 200 to 400 feet-per-minute. Fighting the wind gusts in the turbulent air, I concentrated on my failing instruments to keep the nose of the aircraft at a positive angle to the ground. Whatever was ahead of me, I wanted to hit it with my skis first, if possible. If I hit the side of the mountain that would not matter.

I had no idea when I landed. I neither saw nor felt the snow-covered ground as my skis settled gently into it. The turbulence stopped except for the rocking of my wings by the wind, and my rate of climb and airspeed all said zero. I was on the ground. I jumped out into the freezing snowy wind and fought the hostile elements to get my wings and engine covers in place. I lit and placed my small heater on the fast-cooling engine before buttoning up its winter cover. I did not know how long the storm would last, but I wanted to be prepared to fly as soon as it ended. Standing in the storm beside my rocking airplane, I again felt relief at being on the ground. Like many flights before, the safety of the ground brought comfort to me.

Back inside the cozy cocoon of my aircraft cabin, covered in layers of warm clothing and sleeping bags, I waited out the storm. I thought about all the times I had escaped the dangers of Alaska that had killed so many of my friends, and wondered why I was able to survive. I finally decided it was the result of my hated father pushing me to be perfect in everything I did. Failure was never an option. Growing up with him, I had learned to shut out all fear and emotions and to concentrate only on the task. During my flight today, that trait had allowed me a chance at survival when the odds were stacked heavily against me. No matter what situation I got myself into, my mind was always clear as I sorted my options and sought a remedy. Thinking about this, bundled up in an airplane grounded in a snowstorm in the vast mountain wildness of Alaska, I decided that, after more than ten years, I needed to forgive my father and make contact again. He was not perfect, but he was my Dad. He had given me life in more ways than one.

I spent all the rest of the day and night waiting before the weather cleared enough for me to continue onto Kotzebue and my planned hunt. Getting out of my aircraft the following morning, I was amazed to see that I had landed on a small plateau. If my landing path had been 500 feet shorter I would have crashed into the side of the steep slope leading to the top of the hill on which I was parked. Not only that, a quarter mile ahead of where I had landed, the pass took a turn to the left that I would not have been able to see. It was as if God had been my co-pilot and placed my landing path in the only location that would not have led to disaster.

* * *

There was no classroom available for me the rest of the first year at the high school on Eielson Air Force Base, so they sectioned off an area of the cafeteria for my use. It was a difficult experience trying to teach freshmen in this setting, but the students and I successfully made it through the noise and confusion of others eating and chatting a short distance away. One of the classes they had me teach that first year was New English. Plain English I knew well. This new method had to have been made up by some overeducated and underemployed eggheads with nothing better to do. It was gibberish as far as I was concerned. Thankfully the experiment was dropped the next year at Eielson where, in the quiet peace and comfort of my own classroom, I could again teach traditional English.

Driving the thirty miles each day out to and back from Eielson AFB was tiresome, so I bought a brand-new Toyota Corolla. We had the new vehicle for less than a month before it was totaled in a wreck. Sharon, the kids and I had driven down to Anchorage over the Christmas vacation to visit friends. One evening David and I were going to the store when a four-wheel-drive Ford pickup with a full load of firewood in the bed lost control rounding a corner on the icy road and hit us head on.

Luckily for me, this happened right in front of Providence Hospital. I was unconscious from head injuries for over three hours before coming to in the hospital emergency room. David was uninjured except for bruises, but he was traumatized emotionally from the wreck and what followed. Every time he heard a siren for the next several years he would start crying. After I woke up, I started trying to convince the hospital staff to let me go back to our friends to stay. They wanted to keep me overnight for observation, but after talking to Sharon and learning that she was an RN, they released me. The following morning, I had an extreme headache and dizziness. I had developed a subdural hematoma from the crash. Back to the hospital I went.

Sharon and the kids eventually flew back to Fairbanks several days later, when it was apparent that I would recover. The doctor attending me would not let me fly back with them, as I was still experiencing severe headaches and spells of dizziness. I had also reinjured my back in the accident, and had a hard time walking. I hounded him that I needed to get back to work until he relented several weeks later, telling me he would only let me board an airplane if his nurse accompanied me in case of an emergency due to my brain injury. I agreed and told him I would pay for her roundtrip ticket.

That nurse was Becky Spear. During the flight to Fairbanks, between bouts of headaches and back spasms, she told me her boyfriend had recently moved to Fairbanks to work as the business manager for the Jim

Thompson Ford dealership. His name was Bill Spear, and he had just bought a PA-12 aircraft. He had his pilot's license but did not know much about flying the bush and wanted to learn. I promised Becky I would look him up when I could.

Thus I met Bill and Becky Spear. I meet a lot of people with whom I have friendly relationships, but only a few become lifelong friends. Bill and Becky Spear, Kathy and John Peterson, Bob Widmann and Dr. Glenn Straatsma were six from my Alaskan days who are still close friends today.

It was springtime before I recovered fully from the car wreck. I looked up Bill Spear at the Ford dealership and introduced myself. He remembered Becky telling him about me. I liked Bill right away. He was a little taller than I was, with brown hair and a quick smile that put people at ease. We discussed many things, including flying and hunting. I had started flying again several weeks prior to meeting Bill, so told him I would be happy to teach him about flying in the bush of Alaska. We spent hours discussing weather, flying techniques and mountain flying. We were both surprised when his secretary came in to tell Bill it was quitting time, and she was going home. The hours had flown by. I departed after agreeing to fly with him into the Alaska Range that coming weekend for a caribou hunt.

Bill had hunted in Washington and Montana before moving to Alaska, so he was well versed in hunting wild animals. Remembering all the hard lessons I had to learn by myself gaining the knowledge of flying and hunting Alaskan animals, I was more than happy to help Bill out. We agreed to fly separate airplanes, as Bill was nervous about flying two people and dead caribou off a mountain ridge. We met at Fairbanks International Airport, and after writing down the radio frequencies we would use to communicate with while in the air, took off for the Alaskan Range. We flew wingtip to wingtip as I radioed areas of interest, what to look for if you needed to make an emergency landing, mountain cloud formations and what they meant, while we bored holes in the air on the hour-long flight to our destination.

Climbing to 5,000 feet, we flew until we spotted a small herd of caribou on a snow-covered ridge. I told Bill to follow me as I turned toward a canyon intersecting the ridge to locate a place to land. High mountain winds blow snow off the ridges, and it collects in side canyons protected from the wind. They were safe places to land if there was enough snow in them, even though you had to land uphill. After making a pass and seeing it was safe, I told Bill I was landing and to follow me.

I landed and taxied up onto the flat surface of the ridge where I saw Bill about to touch down on the ridge itself. I screamed on the radio for him to pull up and not land. He heard me and after a brief contact with the ground pulled back up into the air. He had seen me land in the canyon and thought it was too dangerous. This is certainly understandable for a new pilot. It looks more difficult than it really is.

New pilots are taught to land at minimum speed when landing off-runway, but while landing uphill in the narrow confines of a small canyon you want to land with a faster ground speed, as the last thing you want is a stalled landing. The ridge, by comparison, looked like it was smooth and covered with snow, so he opted to land there. Little did he know that the snow was very thin this late in the spring, and underneath it were large rocks and holes that he would not be able to see. Even when the snow was deeper you still had to be careful landing on ridges.

Bill went around and made a perfect landing in my tracks. He got out after pulling up beside me and asked why I called him off. I explained why, but I could tell by his expression he really thought I was showing off and did not believe me. We discussed how to get close to the caribou and started the stalk. We each shot two of the animals, dressed them, and then walked back to our airplanes to taxi up to the animals and load the meat for the trip home. Just taxiing across the ridge was rough on the airplanes because of rocks and uneven ground underneath our skis. After reaching the caribou we had shot, Bill got out of his airplane and thanked me from stopping him from landing. Thus the long, costly and difficult process of learning to fly and land on the varied terrain of the Alaskan Bush began for Bill. Like me and many others, he would suffer bruises and broken aircraft along the way.

It was illegal in Alaska to fly the same day you shot a big game animal. I would continue to buy the proper licenses and tags and follow most Fish and Game regulations, but for anything associated with flying and hunting the same day, Fish and Game would have to catch me to stop me. I don't know if Bill ever got comfortable landing on mountain ridges, as I never saw him land on one again in all the years we flew together. He did become very proficient at wheel landing on river sandbars, as well as float landing on rivers and lakes. Like many others, Bill would wreck several airplane during the journey of becoming a proficient bush pilot.

About this time, I got a letter from the FAA telling me my flight physical had been cancelled due to my head injury the preceding winter. The only way they would have known that is if either Sharon or my lawyer in Anchorage, whom I will refer to as Steelhead Hank, had told them. I had Dr. Glenn Straatsma and a neurologist examine me after receiving the letter to see if there were any underlying problems with my brain that would prevent me from flying safely. They found none.

I took those results to the Fairbanks FAA office to try and get my flight physical reinstated. They said they would look into it and get back to me. Two weeks later I received a letter from them stating my physical would not be reinstated, and to apply again in two years. After my experiences with Fish and Game I had had enough of government bureaucratic nonsense. I tore up the letter and said to hell with them; I was not going to stop flying. If Dick Nicholes could start a commercial flight business in Yakutat on a student pilot's license with the FAA looking the other way, I could fly without a physical. I really thought Sharon and/or Steelhead Hank in Anchorage had put them up to it to get more money out of our car accident lawsuit. This thought was backed up when later Hank was disbarred by the Alaskan Bar Association.

I knew it was not beyond Sharon to report me. We had several fights about her going behind my back and talking to Hank about the lawsuit. It was no surprise to me that when the suit was settled, Hank wanted to write a check to Sharon for 60 percent of what I was to receive, because she "had to care for me" during the aftermath of the accident even though we were in the process of divorce, and I no longer lived with her. I had stayed in Officer Housing at Eielson Air Force Base the past winter. They both argued about whether or not to accept the offered accident settlement and whether Sharon was entitled to a larger part of the settlement than I was, even though I had suffered the injuries. I was more than fed up with Sharon's ability to manipulate facts to suit her imagined wrongs at my hands. I told her to have her attorney address the issue at our divorce hearing, and told Hank that the lawsuit was filed in my name only and to write the entire amount out to me. I had to buy a new car, pay medical bills, and make up for lost wages out of the settlement, besides what I paid Sharon each month for child care.

*   *   *

Frank Moser called me from Yakutat later that summer as I waited for the school year to start, requesting that I fly to Spokane, Washington, to look at a PA-12 airplane he wanted to buy. Frank said he would pay all my expenses for the trip. I had not seen my dad for more than ten years, and after my experience in Anaktuvuk Pass, I decided I would accept. My mother lived in Spokane, and I would see her when I checked out the aircraft. I would then fly the airplane through the Cascade Mountains and land in Snohomish to visit my dad in Lake Stevens to see if our relationship was reparable.

The PA-12 was in great shape when I inspected and flew it, so I gave the owner the check Frank had provided for its purchase. I visited Mom and her husband, Virgil Krupa, before taking off from Spokane for Snohomish. I was flying above Highway 90, wondering why anyone would live in these countless miles of nothing but sage brush and wheat fields, when the flight controls for the tail elevators and wing ailerons began to get harder and harder to move. Looking at the map open on my lap, I saw there was a small airport fifteen miles away at a town called Ritzville. I used the control stick and rudder pedals as little as possible because every time I moved them they got tighter and tighter, making it difficult to control the airplane.

I made my way to Ritzville. There was a mechanic at the airport, and I pulled up to his shop. He examined the airplane and found the problem. The owner had, for whatever reason, put light foam padding in the fuselage between the fabric and the cables running to the controls. The cable rubbed the foam and it slowly collected in the control pulleys, jamming them. The more the cables rubbed the foam, the harder the pulleys jammed. The mechanic, trying to move the stick, asked how I had flown the thing, let alone land safely. I told him I was used to every airplane I got in trying to kill me. The mechanic took out all the foam and cleared the pulleys without charge, and soon I was back in the air.

Dad had remarried a woman named Sue Gissberg, the ex-wife of a Washington lawyer and politician. Sue was of Swedish descent with three kids from her prior marriage. Her son Tom and daughter Kris were still living at home, so I got to meet them. During my visit with Dad, Tom asked if he could fly back with me to Alaska. I agreed, if it was all right with his mom. The back seat was empty and it would be nice to have someone to talk to on the long flight. Dad and I visited pleasantly during the week I spent with them. As he took me out to eat, I wondered what had happened to the bastard who raised me. We mended our troubled past and would continue to have a close and warm relationship from then on until he died at age 93, many years later.

I decided to fly Frank's PA-12 up the coast after closely examining my aerial maps at Dad's house. This route was much shorter than flying up the interior of Canada to White Horse and then down the Alsek River to Yakutat. I felt comfortable flying in coastal weather. Besides, if the weather got too bad we would just land on a beach and camp out until it cleared. Little did I know there would be no sandy beaches to land on the whole trip. Hugging everyone goodbye, Tom and I took off and headed northwest.

After clearing Customs, we flew up Vancouver Island and landed at Port Hardy to refuel and spend the night. Sitting down to dinner that evening, Tom got a taste of the wilder side of life. I heard a couple of men arguing at a corner table while eating my steak and sipping Yukon Jack. Suddenly I heard one of the men yell, "Fuck off, Bob," shortly followed by the crashing of their dinner table and dishes breaking on the café floor as the men engaged in the long-held manly ritual of beating each other about the head and body. I paid no attention to it as their friends picked sides and joined the falling bodies and blood in pursuit of the honor of standing up for their friend. Tom's eyes got bigger and bigger as the grown men proved they were still little boys until the Mounties showed up and escorted them to an iron-barred bedroom. Tom asked me why I did not join the fight. I told him it was not my fight unless they spilled my Yukon Jack. If they had done that, I, too would have spent the night in a cell. Some things are sacred.

The next morning after the fog cleared, we took to the air again, heading to Prince Rupert, the next airport on the coast of Canada. It would be long flight, more than four hours, and would stretch our fuel. I had a five-gallon spare packed with our survival gear, and planned to land somewhere between Port Hardy and Prince Rupert if we were running low on fuel because of headwinds. The wind did blow, knocking us around to the point where I seriously started looking for a place to land. I even looked closely at a fishing dock at one of the villages we passed along the coast. There was absolutely no place to land a wheeled plane between Port Hardy and Prince Rupert. It would continue this way the rest of the trip. If I had known there was nowhere to land anywhere but on runways, I would have flown the interior route. We made it into Rupert with very little gas left in the PA-12's tanks.

The view was spectacular flying up the Inside Passage to Alaska from Washington in a small airplane at 2,500 feet above ground. We went from the rural checkerboard farms of Western Washington to the first open water crossing of the San Juan Islands to Friday Harbor for American Customs and then across the Strait of Juan de Fuca to Canadian Customs at Victoria. I preferred to fly up the inside of Vancouver Island to keep out of the restricted military airspace of the mainland. Both pleasure and commercial boat traffic dotted the water of the Inside Passage until the numbers thinned above the well-known salmon fishery of Campbell River. The cultivated farms gave way to large clear-cut areas of the Island the further north you went. The big sandy beaches disappeared, becoming rocky outcroppings above the high-tide mark, interspersed with a few small patches of sand. The last town on Vancouver Island was the medium-sized city of Port Hardy, home of a Canadian fishing fleet.

After Port Hardy it was a long, 275-mile flight (if the weather was good enough to fly a straight line) over the increasingly rugged Canadian coast to Prince Rupert. There were a few isolated fishing villages. Huge pine trees untouched by chainsaws towered over the cliffs and bays as we weaved in and out of the smaller islands. Prince Rupert airport was large and modern with all the services required of bush and commercial pilots. The next landing spot for us on this flight was 316 straight miles to Juneau, Alaska, across long stretches of open water.

The morning after Tom's introduction to the short tempers of commercial fishermen I checked the weather, and we took off heading toward Ketchikan and then on up the Inside Passage to Juneau. At Fredrick Sound we hit a solid wall of fog, rain and wind. The old axiom about weather on the coast, that what you see is not what you would get one hour later, proved true. It was much clearer off to the west, toward Sitka. It was either Sitka or go back to Prince Rupert; there was no way to make Ketchikan, let alone Juneau, on my intended route. We were closer to Sitka, so I headed that way. I did not want to go to Sitka because it opened onto the Pacific Ocean and was more susceptible to unruly weather. I wanted to stay on the Inside Passage all the way to the closest wheel-landing airport at Juneau. At least that was the plan as we took off.

Only a pilot can understand the constant movement of legs and arms it takes to keep a small plane flying in bad weather. This is not counting the mental stress of fighting limited visibility and turbulence. I had been doing this for three days while trying to follow the map on my lap. I saw I could cut across Chatham Channel to Gut Bay, fly through a short pass to Whale Bay, then up the coast to Sitka.

The first part was only hindered by high winds and turbulence. Visibility was a good fifteen miles. Flying through the small pass to Whale Bay, the rain increased and visibility proportionately decreased. Clouds were not an issue, so I continued flying at 2,000 feet, bucking rain and headwinds. Clearing the low pass, I tuned the VOR to follow the radio beacon to Biorka Island upon reaching the Pacific Ocean. When we reached Biorka Island, I was flying in a solid storm of rain, the intensity of which is seldom seen, even on the coast of Alaska. Reaching Biorka, I turned north to follow the zero degree heading from the VOR radio signal north to the Sitka Airport. I called the Sitka Flight Service to amend the flight plan I had filed for Juneau before leaving Prince Rupert. The rain was so heavy I did not see the airport until it was underneath me as I flew across it.

When we landed at Sitka I had been flying over sixteen hours since leaving Washington. Talking to Flight Service, I found the weather had just moved in and was expected to last another four days. I called Frank and told him I was leaving his airplane in Sitka, as I was not going to spend another four to five days waiting for weather to clear. He had been worried about us as he was following the weather and knew how bad it had become. When we did not report in at Ketchikan as our flight plan said we would, and knowing that the Juneau Airport was closed due to weather, he was worried we had crashed somewhere. Still, Frank being Frank, he tried to talk me into staying in Sitka until the weather cleared. I told him if the weather cleared before a commercial flight out of Sitka to Yakutat arrived, I would continue flying his airplane to Yakutat where I had left my personal airplane. If not, I would fly to Yakutat commercially. His airplane was now parked only a little over one hour's flight from Yakutat. He could fly it himself that far, as he was a commercially rated pilot. That is, he could fly it himself if he had the guts to fly across the open water of the Pacific Ocean to Cape Spenser and then on up the coast to Yakutat. If not, he could find someone else. I understood Frank's hesitancy. Coastal weather can be very intimidating.

In later years I would fly up and down the coasts of Alaska, British Columbia and Washington while flying support for my friend Bob Widmann's commercial fishing operation in Prince William Sound, but never again in a wheeled aircraft. I would only attempt it on floats. Larger planes, like a Cessna 180 or 182, would be much safer, as they fly faster and have a much longer range of flight. There are more roads to land on now and more airports, but the weather is the same. It changes quickly, and any wheel pilot has to be prepared to handle it. Flying an airplane on floats, you can duck into many of the saltwater bays and camp until the weather clears. There all you have to contend with are bears, bugs and tides.

A commercial flight arrived the next morning, so Tom and I boarded it for Yakutat. At Yakutat, Frank paid me for my expenses. Tom and I spent the night, and then flew to the Italio to fish for red salmon. After a pleasant day of catching salmon in a light drizzle, we loaded everything the following morning in 58A before heading to Cordova then up the Copper River to Fairbanks. After resting in Fairbanks for a couple of days, Tom and I headed up the Steese Highway for about seventy miles where we had parked my Toyota Land Cruiser. We hiked from there up to the summit of some higher hills to shoot caribou. I shot two. We made camp on the top of a small mountain to spend the night before hiking back down to the Cruiser, heavily weighted down with dead caribou on our backs.

While Tom and I camped on the unnamed ridge that night, we experienced a rare phenomenon, even for the far north. We were aroused from sleep almost simultaneously, and peered out of our sleeping bags in the middle of the night to strange buzzing sounds. The sight we saw around, above, and below our sleeping bags both delighted and amazed us. We were completely surrounded by a vast display of northern lights. It was awe-inspiring as we lay, with mouths open, witnessing the wildly swirling and changing colors of the light show. Some scientists say that northern light displays are silent, just being light reflections of electrically charged particles from the sun entering the earth's atmosphere. All I can say is that Tom and I were both awakened at the same time by a strange sound I had never heard before or since. I have witnessed thousands of spectacular instances of northern lights, but nothing approaching what Tom and I saw that night.

Tom departed Fairbanks back to Lake Stevens a week later. He finished high school in Lake Stevens and went on to become a lawyer. This was the last adventure we were to share together.

* * *

As spring in 1973 approached, Bill Spear and I flew the Tanana Flats and Lake Minchumina area looking for black bears coming out of hibernation during the mild spring weather. We discussed building a cabin along one of river systems west of Nenana, far enough away from normal flight traffic that we would not be bothered. It would save us hours of flying time to hunt and fish this area, as well as serve as a weekend retreat out of the city. I greatly missed Jumpoff and wanted to establish another wilderness cabin.

On June 14, 1973, Bill and I, flying our separate airplanes, took off from Fairbanks International Airport to look for a place to build this wilderness cabin of our dreams. We found the perfect location on the Toklat River. The Toklat runs out of the Mount McKinley National Park for about thirty miles before becoming part of the Kantishna River. We wanted to locate a building site out of the park itself, but close enough to it to allow good hunting and trapping. Like many Alaskans, we would just build a cabin without getting permission or land permits from either the State or Federal Government.

We found a possible site about seven miles below the park boundary. There were big pine trees right next to the Toklat River with a sandbar close by that might make a good landing strip. I told Bill I would land and check out the sandbar. It was safe, so Bill followed me in. A creek ran between the sandbar and where we wanted to build the cabin. After wading across it, we found a good location to build on. It even had enough straight pine trees to construct a log cabin.

Going back to our airplanes, we took out fishing rods to see if there were any fish in the small creek. We were delighted to learn that there were plenty of grayling trout to be caught in it, and spent several hours catching medium-sized grayling. We discussed the situation and decided to erect tents on the sandbar to live in while we built the cabin. Becky, who was riding with Bill, seconded our idea, so we set about the process of making this dream come true.

The following weekend we flew our families out and set up a camp again on the sandbar. Bill had his daughter from a previous marriage, Becky, and their dog with him. Becky had moved up to Fairbanks to be with Bill full time since she accompanied me to Fairbanks. Sharon, Michael, David and

164

Toklat, our dog, came with me. Looking at the creek again, we decided to build an Alaskan bush bridge over it. We felled several trees big enough to span the creek with both ends firmly anchored on each bank. Then the branches were trimmed so you had a way to cross the creek without getting wet, if you did not fall off the logs.

We worked all summer on the cabin and had it completed by late fall. Bill knew far more than I did about construction, so he was the boss and I was the laborer. My brother Richard was working as a fireman and EMT at Clear Air Force Base at the time. I would land on the main highway and taxi up to his trailer house to fly him out to help us build the cabin. Richard loved flying and the bush. He was a great help when he could get out to help, as was my younger brother, Jeff, who was visiting us that summer while attending mechanic's school in Fairbanks.

One evening around a Toklat River campfire Bill ask me if I had ever shot a black bear. I replied that I had taken many of the bruins for their meat, hide and fat. Black bear is a tasty food source if they are feeding on berries or vegetation. They taste like some of the finest pork you could buy and were a staple in my household. If they were feeding on carrion, neither your family nor your dog would touch the meat. Bear fat, when, rendered to oil, is prized by all Alaskan cooks. You could tell immediately if any dessert you tasted was made from it.

Bill said he had never shot one and would like to try. We agreed to go hunting after working on the cabin the following day. Black bears are plentiful in the interior bush. It was only about fifteen minutes after take-off that I spotted one feeding in a small slough off the Toklat River. We landed on a sandbar and snuck through the trees toward the animal. Upon sighting it, Bill downed it with one shot. A half-hour after takeoff Bill had killed his first Alaskan bear. An hour later we were back at the camp with a skinned bear hide and meat.

The next weekend after Bill and Becky had eaten bear meat for the first time, they asked if we could hunt bear again to get more meat for the winter freezer. Becky wanted to come with Bill this time on the hunt. Bill knew what to look for and how to hunt bear now, so I did not take off with them, but finished hauling and cutting wood for the camp. A half-hour later, after finishing this chore, Michael and I took off to look for them. By the time I spotted Bill's PA-12 parked on a sandbar near the Kantishna River, Michael had fallen asleep in the back seat. I saw the bears they were probably after from the air before landing. I was surprised they had not shot one yet. There were four black bears feeding on a large area of blueberry bushes about a quarter-mile off the river. I could not see either Bill or Becky in the trees and brush along the banks of the river, so I landed. I figured they were getting into position to shoot.

Deciding to leave Michael sleeping in the back seat, I removed my .444 Marlin carbine and packsack out of the back seat and took off through the trees toward the feeding bears. I still had not seen any traces of Bill and Becky before I was in the middle of the feeding animals. When they spotted me and started to run away, I shot three before the final one disappeared.

Wondering where Bill and Becky were, I started skinning and dressing the first bear before they showed up. Bill was used to hunting in Montana where hunters tried to get above their prey before shooting. He and Becky had climbed a nearby hill to get above the bears when I walked into the middle of them and ruined their plan. I told them I was sorry for spoiling their hunt, but had not seen them from the air. They helped me skin the animals and pack them back to the airplanes.

As we walked back toward our parked airplanes, I became concerned as I saw Michael's small tracks following the trail I had made through the trees on the way to the bears. He had awakened during my absence and tried to follow me. I should have woken him and taken him with me on the hunt, but he was so dead tired from a day of playing and swimming with David I had decided not to. I was relieved to find him back at the airplanes and not lost in the wilderness. We hung the meat and hides up when we arrived back at camp. The meat would be split two ways and provide welcome table fare along with caribou and moose in the coming winter.

* * *

That fall I had two serious incidents at the Toklat cabin: an airplane wreck and a black bear attack. The airplane wreck occurred on a small sandbar on the Toklat River. I saw a nice bull moose from the air and landed to hunt it. After shooting the moose and carrying it to where my airplane was parked, I decided the bar was too small to fly all of the moose meat out at once. I loaded the lightest parts of the moose in my PA-20, leaving the hindquarters behind. I wanted to see how the airplane performed getting airborne in the 300-400 feet I had to take off in. That would tell me if I could fly both hindquarters out together, or have to take them separately.

It took the entire sandbar to get airborne, so I decided to fly the hindquarters out one at a time after landing back at the Toklat cabin and offloading the meat I had with me. Accomplishing that without any drama, I flew back to where I had shot the moose to get one of the hindquarters. The wind had picked up and was blowing some dust off the bar as I approached. I figured this was a plus, as the wind would cut down on both my landing and takeoff distances.

I had to land over an abrupt five-foot ridge carved by the floods of the spring break-up at end of the sandbar. Flying back over the sandbar I thought it would have been much nicer if the wind was blowing out of McKinley Park instead of toward it. That way I would not have to risk shearing off my landing gear on the small ridge, trying to land as close to it as possible in the short distance I had to land and stop. The river edge would have been a much easier landing as it was smooth, but that was out of the question with the current wind condition. Setting up my final approach, I applied full flaps and reduced power to land within the first twenty feet of the sandbar. Everything was normal until I almost reached the abrupt drop-off.

Without any warning a strong gust of wind hit the airplane, dropping it fifteen feet and into the face of the small ridge. In one second I went from being on an ideal landing approach to being in the chaos of a crash. My airplane slammed into the end of the bar, tearing off my landing gear and throwing me forward, hitting my head on the airplane dashboard. I saw stars as the airplane came to deafening halt in the sand-filled air. After I caught my breath and the stars subsided, I climbed out of my crumpled aircraft to see how much damage it had suffered.

My propeller was destroyed, as well as the nose cowling and one landing gear. One of the landing gears was bent but salvageable. The other one was a complete write off. The struts on the wing that suffered the most damage were bent and needed replacing as well. Luckily the main fuselage seemed okay, as I did not see any wrinkles in the fabric. There was some major tearing of the aircraft belly fabric, but I did not see any damage to the frame, thankfully. I would not know if the engine was damaged until a new propeller was installed and I could turn the engine over. A great start to moose hunting on the Toklat River, I thought disgustedly.

I checked my emergency beacon and saw that it was operating normally over the emergency frequency that all overhead aircraft could hear, including jet liners, letting them know I had crashed. I sat down on a log by the moose meat, still on the sandbar, and started making a list of all the parts I would need to get the PA-20 off the sandbar and into a repair shop. I figured it would be a minimum of two hours before a helicopter flying out of Eielson Air Force Base could find me after hearing my emergency beacon. It could be longer, but I was close enough to the jet flyways between Anchorage and Fairbanks that I felt pretty positive my distress signal would be discovered soon. I had taken my survival gear out at the Toklat Cabin to be as light as possible for flying the rest of the moose out. I would have to hike back to the cabin if a rescue did not happen before dark. I did not want to hike back to the Toklat cabin to spend the night, but wanted to be at the site of the wreck when the rescue helicopter arrived. I knew the Air Force personnel in the helicopter would not fly out anything but myself. I would have to leave the moose meat and my rifle until I could get a ride back.

Three hours later, with a stiffening back and neck, I listened to the thumping approach of the Huey rescue craft. They circled me twice before landing on the sandbar. The medic got out and asked if I was okay and then helped me inside for the flight back to Fairbanks International Airport. He examined me during the flight and only found what I had already told him: that I had suffered minor back and neck injuries, along with a growing bump on my forehead when I hit the dashboard with my head.

Upon being dropped off at Fairbanks International Airport, I thanked the crew and walked to the hangar of a local flight charter business to schedule a Super Cub to take me back to the crash site the following afternoon. They would also fly the moose meat back to Fairbanks on their return trip after dropping me off at the crash site.

I then telephoned Bill Spear and told him what had happened. Bill said he would drop everything, and help me get the aircraft parts and fly back to the Toklat cabin to get the moose front quarters that evening. Tomorrow he would join me at the crash site.

Scrounging all the aircraft repair facilities in Fairbanks, we located used landing gear, wing struts and engine cowling, as well as purchasing a new propeller. The landing gear was not set up for my larger tires. There were also no brake fittings in Fairbanks that I could use to adapt it to my airplane that would enable me to have brakes on both wheels. I would have to make do with only one brake and two wheels of different sizes. This was disturbing, as the PA-20 was tricky enough to land and take off with two brakes and the same circumference wheels. The smaller tire on one side was a concern. It would dig into the soft sand deeper than the larger tire, increase drag and add instability to the takeoff. Not good choices, but the only ones available to me without waiting for parts to be shipped to Fairbanks from the Lower 48.

The following afternoon we loaded the parts into the Super Cub and Bill's PA-12, and flew back out to the crash site. I noted as I watched Bill land that his skills as a pilot had greatly improved. I was relieved to see that my airplane radios had not been stolen and that the moose meat had not been eaten by a bear. The Super Cub departed back to Fairbanks after we loaded the hind quarters into it. Bill commented that I needed to find longer landing sites in the future. Dick Nicholes was right. When you fly on the edge of your airplane's flight envelope, bad things will happen. It is just a matter of time. Father Time had finally caught up with me.

The first task for Bill and me was to construct an A-Frame to lift 58A off the ground so temporary repairs could begin. Taking our axes into the woods, we cut down and dragged three trees to the airplane, two for the main A-Frame, and one to steady it. This took three hours to get it in place. Attaching a lifting ratchet and cables from the A-Frame to the airplane wing bolts, we gently hoisted it three feet off the sand before replacing the twisted wing struts. Raising it higher, we replaced the landing gear and straightened the other one as much as possible before lowering the PA-20 back onto the ground.

Now came the moment of truth on whether I would be able to fly it out today. After removing the mangled propeller and replacing it with a brand new one, I climbed into the old girl and started the engine. All the gauges were in the green, indicating the engine was operating normally. Climbing back out I stood alongside Bill and watched the propeller as it tracked over the small stick we had placed underneath it. It tracked perfectly. The crankshaft had not been broken or bent. Only the takeoff and flight would reveal if it had been cracked. The engine would either run normally, or suddenly seize and fly apart in flight if it was cracked.

After shutting down the engine and putting on the new engine cowling, Bill and I sat down to a small lunch and discussed what to do next. Bill had not gotten out the night before to get the moose meat from the Toklat cabin, so he would fly over and pick it up after watching to make sure I took off safely in my crippled aircraft. Looking at the belly of 58A, we decided to patch the holes with duct tape to prevent further damage before taking off.

The wind was again blowing upriver, so I would be able to attempt my take-off downriver. Strapping myself in, I started the engine and taxied to the end of the sandbar I had crashed into the day before. I was only able to turn to the right, the side of my one brake on the landing gear we had straightened and not replaced. Getting lined up as best I could, I pushed the throttle all the way in and started my takeoff roll. I was able to steer for the takeoff using only the rudder for directional control. It was a surprisingly easy takeoff, allowing me to pull on full flaps well before the sandbar met the river, and fly downstream gaining altitude and airspeed.

Circling over the sandbar until Bill took off safely, I followed him to the Toklat cabin. Instead of landing as we planned, I circled overhead until he took off with my emergency gear and moose meat. I did not want to land on soft sand with the borrowed landing gear from a wrecked airplane. Looking anxiously at my oil pressure and oil temperature gauges, I was relieved to see them stay in the green. I had not noticed any vibrations from the engine that would signal impending crankshaft problems, so I headed toward Fairbanks International Airport where I landed and left my airplane at an aircraft repair shop. The mechanics told me it would be about three weeks to a month before the new parts came and the aircraft was repaired.

* * *

I had my first bear attack later that fall after getting 58A out of the repair shop. I was at the Toklat cabin alone, clearing brush for a trap line I wanted to use the coming winter. After waking in the morning and deciding to catch some fresh grayling for breakfast, I opened the cabin door while tying a fly on my fishing line, stepped outside, and saw a starving black bear chasing a rabbit fifteen feet in front of me. It was immediately apparent the bear was in bad shape. The bear stopped chasing the rabbit, seeing me as a bigger meal, and turned on a dime to charge me.

This all happened in a few seconds, and before I could react, the bear hit me so hard it knocked me all the way across the interior of the cabin. Luckily for me, I came to a stop right beside my bed at the rear of the one-room structure. My .444 was leaning against the wall beside where I had landed. It was loaded. I always kept a loaded rifle beside my bed when sleeping at the cabin. Half dazed, I picked up the rifle and shot the bear dead as it came into the cabin after me.

I suffered bruises, abrasions, a strained back, stiff neck and a few small claw cuts from the brief attack. I felt I was lucky to have so little physical damage as I dragged the dead bear out the front door. Looking at it in the strong sunlight, I could see my first impression that the bear was starving was correct. The hair covering its hide was patchy and dull, with ribs showing beneath it. Whether from disease, old age, or accident, the animal had been desperate to find any food source. I was glad it was not me. I threw the bear into the Toklat River, as neither the hide nor meat were any good. I needed the river to take it far away from the cabin so it would not attract others of its kind.

*　*　*

Becky and Sharon surprisingly never became friends like Bill and I had. I asked Becky about this later. She said Sharon was more like one of the kids than an adult. Thinking about it, I had to agree. Sharon did not have any white female friends that I could remember, but gravitated toward males and female Native Alaskans. The male part became the big issue in our marriage that I could not work around. Our divorce had become final the previous summer. She was awarded custody of David in the divorce, and I was awarded Michael. I lived in the Officers Quarters on Eielson AFB that school year. She lived in Fairbanks with both boys, as Michael was not allowed to stay with me on the base. I took all of them out to the Toklat when I could as the boys loved to be with me while playing and fishing at the cabin. Sharon and I had an understanding after the divorce that our separate personal relationships with others were our own business. However, when we were together, we would be circumspect for the sake of the kids until either of us remarried. It was a bittersweet process, this divorce thing, as you grew further apart from the person you planned to spend your life with.

Michael and David were very close growing up. I never saw them fight as Richard and I had. They had a ball on the Toklat fishing, swimming and camping out. I really enjoyed being with both of them. Sharon not so much, but she was the price I had to pay to be with the kids. I could have left David with her in town and just taken Michael, but I loved them both and wanted to be around them together. The Toklat would become the location of many memorable get-togethers with family and friends. It was also the location of another of my memorable escapes from the icy clutches of the grim reaper.

I wanted to trap up the Toklat River to the McKinley Park boundary and down to the Kantishna along the Toklat River the coming winter. I had been preparing this trap line, several months earlier, when I was attacked by the black bear. To trap as long a line as I planned, I would have to get a snow machine into the cabin. It was now mid-December, and the northland was solidly frozen. I decided to use Big Blue, the one-cylinder snow machine I bought in Anchorage for my winter expeditions with John and Kathy Peterson. The nearest road location to the Toklat cabin was Nenana. There was no GPS at the time, so I flew along my proposed snow machine route to get some idea of what to expect.

After locating a plausible snow machine route from Nenana to the Toklat from the air, I got everything ready for the trip. When I left Nenana the following weekend it was a fairly comfortable -30 degrees. Pulling a sled behind me with survival gear on it, I started off in the general direction of the Toklat. The weak sun hiding on the horizon did its best to illuminate the white wonderland across which I slowly crept, trying to keep warm from the biting wind and cold. It was a fairly pleasant journey across the deep snow-covered tundra except for the uncertainty of where I would actually have to turn to intersect the Toklat River. If I missed where I wanted to swing left, I would end up somewhere along the Kantishna. By then I would have run out of daylight in the short four hours of winter light, and have to make camp out in the cold.

I wanted to make it to the Toklat cabin and a warm bed. Everything looks much different from the ground than from the air. After several hours of traveling in the increasing cold, I thought the trees ahead of me looked familiar. I turned left as planned and slowly worked my way through the black spruce and western pine trees to the bank of the creek that entered the Toklat River by our cabin. Looking at the creek, I figured out I had turned too soon and was about ten miles above our cabin. Congratulating myself on at least finding the creek, I sped down its smooth icy white surface at a much faster pace than I had been traveling. You really cannot completely protect yourself from the elements when going this fast on a snow ma-chine, so I huddled behind the small windscreen on the sled, wishing the journey would end soon. I knew where I was now, and was looking forward to a fire, meal, and warm bed.

The first sign of trouble was when the snow machine started bogging down, sinking further into the snow-packed surface of the icebound creek. I applied full throttle to try and ski across the overflow that was now trying to pull me and my snow machine down into the water beneath the snow. Overflow is water-saturated snow and is common to all interior Alaska rivers and some lakes. The current of the stream coupled with the expan-sions and contractions of the ice forms cracks in the ice covering the river. The pressure and weight of the ice and snow forces water upward, mixing with the snow above the ice. A lot of times you could see a different color of snow, indicating overflow, and avoid it. In an airplane, I would make a pass over the area of the river I wanted to land on, pushing the airplane skis through the surface crust of the snow while keeping up airspeed. Getting airborne again, I would circle around and look at my tracks in the snow. If the ski tracks were dark there was overflow on that section of the river, and I would look for another place to land.

River overflow is bad enough by itself, but sometimes the river's cur-rent would completely eat away the ice, leaving just a patch of snow over the river. Alaskans crossing these open holes usually died, the driver and machine disappearing forever. These deadly sections were impossible to see in time to avoid, as the snow covering the open river did not look any dif-ferent from the area around it.

I quickly applied full power to Big Blue, looking for a place up the steep riverbank to get off the river's surface. There was no place to get out of the river, and the heavy waterlogged snow slowed the underpowered machine, pulling it down into the water along with its rider. My first thought, as the machine under me came to a complete stop, was to thank God it was not an open hole swallowing us completely. My second thought was that I was standing in waist-deep water with all my survival gear under that water.

I looked around in the fast-fading daylight and figured I was still five miles above the Toklat cabin. The temperature had dropped to less than -45 degrees, and was still dropping in the diminishing light. The obvious solution of getting out of my clothes quickly and building a fire was not possible because of my submerged survival gear. I knew that the minute I stepped out of the water my clothes would almost instantly freeze to my skin and my core temperature would begin a rapid decline, quickly ending in my death. I remember thinking, as I stood in the water, that freezing to death was supposed to be a fairly pleasant way to die.

The calm part of my mind took over as I formulated a plan to live. I had never heard of anyone trying what I planned to do, but I could not think of any other options. Making my way through the deep overflow, I climbed up the steep bank and immediately began doing jumping jacks and squat thrusts. The outer water on my clothing immediately froze and sloughed off from the jumping and bending, leaving me able to move. I definitely weighed more with the water and ice in my clothes, but I could move. The clothes next to my body were still wet, but as long as I could keep my outer clothes flexible, I could move. The fight now was to keep my core temperature warm enough to not shut down blood to the outer portions of my body.

I started running and doing jumping jacks with an occasional squat thrust through the two-foot-deep snow. Every time I felt increased resistance to my efforts from freezing clothes I would stop running and do more stationary bending and twisting exercises. My past conditioning coaches would have been proud of the effort I put into the activity. Any animal observing this would think I was in the last stages of delirium. Twenty minutes later I saw Bill and Becky flying overhead looking for me, but they could not see me through the thick pine trees. After several circles they flew on toward the Toklat cabin. I thought the cabin would be warm if I could just reach it in time. The deep burning in my chest told me my violent workout and running in this frigid temperature was freezing my lungs. The warmer temperatures beneath the snow helped keep my feet and ankles from freezing solid. Using all my willpower and strength, I fought my way to the cabin and stumbled through the door to the lifesaving warmth within.

Becky, being a nurse, immediately took charge. Quickly, she and Bill removed my boots and clothing and, after helping me get into some spare dry clothing I had stored there, started massaging my hands and feet to get circulation going again. She was surprised there were no frozen body parts. With the help of a roaring fire, blankets, and hot water, I began to recover. I would be susceptible to pneumonia for the rest of my life due to my damaged lungs. This was much preferable to the alternative. As I lay in my bunk that evening with every muscle twitching from the effort I had expended in reaching the cabin, I wondered why I had so many of these encounters. Most of my friends had, at most, one or two close brushes with death. With me it seemed to be a monthly occurrence. True, some of them never survived that first skirmish, so maybe I should consider myself lucky.

Bill and I walked up to my sunken snow machine the following morning and were able to get it back up the bank and out of the creek. Surprisingly, it started up right away before the ice and snow in the tracks froze solid. I slowly made my way back to the cabin following the trail I had previously cut. I trapped this location for the rest of the winter getting lynx, fox, marten and wolverine.

I became tired of Eielson AFB and living on a road system during the ensuing school year. When an opening in the state school system came up at Circle City, I applied and got the position. Circle City had a one-room, one-teacher grade school. I taught all eight grades at the same time. The road between Fairbanks and Circle City was closed by snow in the winter, as the State Department of Transportation did not maintain it after the first snow fall. I talked Sharon into coming with me, as I wanted to be around my sons. I had not been able to convince the judge to give me custody of both boys, and I felt it was really important that David have a father around to counteract some of the bizarre behaviors that Sharon was more frequently exhibiting. My personal feelings were not as important as the health of my sons.

I really enjoyed teaching the Athabaskan Native children of Circle City. The only Caucasian students were Michael and the son of the white man who ran the city's electrical plant. The kids were shy, but eager to learn. I used some of the techniques I had learned teaching at Clark with success. I also bought Michael a silver German shepherd puppy he had been bugging me about before the road to Fairbanks was closed for the winter. He named the puppy Toklat.

I had taken Toklat out for a bathroom break after school one afternoon. While he was attending to business, I saw a pack of huskies run across the gravel aircraft runway that crossed in front of the school, toward us. I could tell they were after poor little Toklat. He was only ten weeks old, so I lifted him above my head to keep the pack from him. The dogs surrounding me became tired of trying to reach Toklat, so they began to attack me. As I would yell and kick one, others would circle around and bite me from behind. With both hands occupied in controlling a frantically struggling puppy, their numbers were preventing me from reaching the school house door.

I was just coming to the realization I would have to drop Toklat to save myself when Michael burst out of the school house with a snow ski, screaming at the dogs and hitting them with the ski. He was all of seven years old, and maybe weighed fifty pounds, but between the two of us, we had the dogs running away in seconds. I really don't know if he was more worried about the puppy or his father, but I was relieved to have his help. Michael had saved both mine and his puppy's life, or at least prevented me from being seriously injured. I learned that evening, after Sharon patched the wounds, that the dog team had gotten away from a local dog musher. The dogs were not friendly or tamed. They were bred and used for one thing only: to pull a sled. They were not fed well either.

Several maulings by loose dog teams happened every winter in Alaska. In larger towns it usually resulted from military personnel being transferred out of the state and not finding someone to take the animals they had bought for their dog teams. They turned their dogs loose rather than putting them down. Mauling usually led to fatalities or disfigurement among children until the loose dogs were hunted and shot by law enforcement or concerned citizens. Many villages and towns had standing orders to shoot any loose dog that was spotted for just this reason.

The second time Michael saved me was several years later, taking off from Wein Lake. Sharon had filed for a homestead on Wein after I filed for one on Stultz Lake. Michael and I were flying back to Stultz Lake, about ten miles away, while Sharon and David visited Dale, a man who was living at her cabin at Wein. After taking, off I pushed the flight stick forward to level the airplane at about 150 feet in the air. When I tried to pull back on the stick to complete the leveling maneuverer, it would not move. The nose of the airplane continued past level flight until it was pointing steeply toward the ground. I could not raise the nose because it was somehow jammed. Pulling the elevator trim all the way back had no effect on our direction of flight. I yelled to Michael in the back seat that something was jammed in the controls back there. He immediately dropped down to the floor boards and removed a screwdriver that had somehow come out of the pocket where I stored tools and become wedged in the back seat controls. I was just barely able to raise the nose of the airplane in time, and we missed the ground by less than ten feet. That crash would have killed us both. People almost never survive when an airplane crashes nose-first into the ground. I survived all of my crashes by making sure I carried enough airspeed that the wheels or floats always hit first after an engine failure.

* * *

The school year at Circle was fun until it wasn't. The airport runway ran right past the front door of the school. I hauled a 500-gallon gas tank to Circle and put it off the edge of the runway where I parked my airplane. I hunted moose and caribou that fall after school, and on weekends I ran an airplane trap line for wolves and wolverine. It was a nice combination of teaching and wilderness living. The teacher's quarters were part of the school, so I did not have to worry about starting a car or traveling when the temperature plummeted and the snow fell.

That first fall at Circle I was told by Dick, the owner of the electrical plant who was also a pilot, about a lost kid at Circle Hot Springs, about thirty miles from Circle City. It was a popular place for local residents to take a hot bath and have a meal they did not have to cook themselves and people traveling up the Steese Highway. I had loaded the family into 58A and flown there for a relaxing hot bath and lunch in the restaurant many times. Dick said they were asking all bush pilots to come and look for the lost boy. The kid was not from Alaska but from Chicago, so he probably did not have the minimum survival skills for being alone in the Alaska wilderness. I was the only available pilot they were able to contact so I loaded some extra survival gear into my airplane and took off.

The Hot Springs had an airport cut inside a pine tree forest. I had to get on the controls heavily to keep from crashing in the thirty-five knot crosswinds on landing. The wind boiled off the tall trees forming the borders of the runway, creating significant turbulence with the accompanying up and down drafts, shaking the airplane up, down, and sideways.

Talking to the parents and their companions, I noticed several things beside the fact they were desperately worried about their ten-year-old son who had wandered off two hours ago. All the men and women were of Italian heritage, and the eight men were armed with pistols under their jackets. They spoke with a heavy Italian accent that was most noticeable in the frantic mother. Alaskans who wore side arms had them on their hips for easy access, and they did not carry the small-bore weapons these guys were carrying. The hackles of my police mentality immediately raised with one word coming to my mind—Mafia. There was not any Mafia in Alaska that I knew of, so it did not make sense until I remembered the lost kid was from Chicago. The FBI had been cracking down hard on the Mafia in the Lower 48. I wondered if the bosses had scheduled a meeting in the bush of Alaska to get away from the FBI's attention.

Putting my law enforcement instincts aside, I listened to what the mother was saying. The family had also called for a helicopter from Fairbanks to help in the search, but it had not arrived yet. I was the only pilot to show up. The woman had reason to be worried. Being lost in the Alaska bush was problematic for veterans, let alone a kid with a light jacket and no food. The kid's biggest problem was not bears eating him, as the mother was moaning about, but mosquitoes and dehydration. The difficult wind condition was also going to be a concern in the search, because I would have to fly up and down canyons at a low altitude. The turbulence as well as up and down drafts would require taking attention away from looking for the boy. The only good thing about the weather was that it was clear and sunny. It was also August, so I would have plenty of daylight.

I flew up and down canyons, fighting the turbulence, until I saw something white move in the thin trees about forty-five minutes later. Flying overhead, I saw the kid waving his white tee-shirt. I flew over and waved my wings so he knew that I saw him. I would not be able to land anywhere close to the lost boy, so I climbed higher. I had prepared a small packsack prior to leaving Circle, containing a locator beacon, candy bars, water, and mosquito repellant. In the calmer winds, I wrote out a note for the kid to stay where he was and not move, and put it in the pack. After attaching surveyor's tape to the straps of the pack, I flew slowly back over the boy and dropped it.

I watched the kid run to the pack sack and open it. After reading my note he waved that he understood. I turned my aircraft radio to the emergency frequency to make sure the beacon was still working, and flew back to let his parents know I had found him, and that he was safe.

I don't think a grizzly bear could have hugged me tighter than the mother at hearing the news. The helicopter from Fairbanks landed five minutes later. I told the pilot where the boy was. I hopped into the helicopter and flew with him to the lost boy's location. The pilot found a small clearing he could land on, about a hundred yards from the boy, who was sitting on a rock waiting.

Landing back at the airstrip, I got my locator beacon and pack from the kid. He had drunk the water and eaten three of the candy bars, which I would replace when I got back to Circle City. After telling the kid I was glad we had found him and shaking hands with the father, as well as surviving another hug from the mother, I flew back to Circle City. I had not told them my name, so I was surprised to receive a Christmas gift that year from the family: an expensive hand-blown Italian glass set with eight shot glasses. The decanter and glasses were decorated with 18 karat gold.

* * *

The first inkling I had that things were not going well that year in Circle City was when I was told, during the village Christmas party, to take Sharon home immediately. She was not drunk, but had been propositioning the guy who ran the electric company in front of his wife. This was the second time this sort of thing had happened. The year before, in Fairbanks, she had done the same to Glenn Straatsma in front of his wife, and I was asked to remove her from that Christmas party. Several years after this episode I was told by Joe Chandler, a wolf-hunting friend who lived in Anchorage, I was welcome in his house anytime, but Sharon was never to come back after she had propositioned him in a movie theater.

We were not married. I did not particularly like her anymore, but put up with her antics to keep David close by. I now knew how wives put up with unfaithful spouses just to keep the family together. My respect for them and the mental anguish they suffered in their sacrifices for the family greatly increased.

I did talk Sharon into seeing a psychiatrist the preceding summer, but it did no good. She told me the psychiatrist said the reason she acted out was because my standards of behavior were too high and beyond the normal expectations of a husband. Again, everything wrong in her life was my fault. At this point I did not care who she slept with, I just wanted her to be circumspect in front of the children and not embarrass me in front of my friends.

The year at Circle City deteriorated after the party. The man who ran the trading post controlled the Natives in the village by use of their lines of credit at his store. If they did something he did not like, he called them in and told them their line of credit was cancelled and they had to pay up before they could purchase anything else. The owner was a friend and, although I did not approve, I did nothing about the situation until late March, when a group of five men and women from the village came to the school one evening to complain.

A local school board election was coming up. Sharon had gotten involved in convincing the citizens to throw off the yoke of the trader and elect who they wanted instead of who they were told to vote for. The group told me the store owner was stealing cheese meant for the food program at the school and selling it to them in his store. One of the people making the complaint was the school cook, who should know if this sort of thing was happening.

I did not know that Sharon had put them up to it, and was riling the villagers to rebel against the trading post owner. I told them I would inform the Yukon Region School Administrator I worked for of their complaint. I wrote a letter outlining the above, stating I did not know if it was true or not, but was bringing the situation to their attention.

All hell broke loose after the Yukon School District notified the store owner of these allegations. The owner of the store brought all the villagers involved into the store and told them to deny my accusations if they wanted to continue to buy food at his store. He had the school cook and my teacher's aide resign. The aide also removed her son from school. All the lights around the school were turned off, making it pitch black outside after dark. The kerosene I put in my aircraft heater was replaced with flammable gas in an attempt to burn it up.

Luckily, the resulting fire only burnt a hole in the engine cover and did minor damage inside. The tracks to and from the airplane in the fresh snow were size thirteen boots. The only man who had that size of foot in the village was the husband of my school aide, and the person who ran the electrical plant. All of Sharon's Native friends were told they could not visit or be friends with her anymore. After several weeks of this, Sharon took off with both boys, unbeknownst to me while I was teaching, and fled to Fairbanks. She told Glenn Straatsma the reason she had to leave was because I was beating her. Although I felt like doing so many times, I had never struck a woman in my life and would never do so

So there I was, alone in a village that now hated me, in charge of a school without a cook or aide. In retrospect, I should have either taken the complaint to the trading post owner and asked about it, or ignored the whole thing and just done my job. I was no longer in law enforcement. I finally told the cook if she wanted her son and daughter and other children in the village to have a school lunch, she would have to come back and cook it. I was not going to cook on top of everything else. She would never talk to me again, but she did return to her job. I finished the school year, but was told I was being transferred to teach in Ruby next year. Small village politics are the same as everywhere else. Reason was in short supply when the person in power had economic control.

* * *

The Homestead Act in Alaska was ending the summer after school closed in Circle City. Bill Spear and I discussed it one weekend at the Toklat cabin. We decided we needed to find a place to file on before the opportunity was lost. We both wanted our own separate places. We got along well, but wanted to live in an area where there was no one else nearby. We would search for isolated lakes apart from each other, but close enough to help one another if needed.

Bill found a lake about five miles from Wein Lake that fit his needs. I found Echo Lake, fifteen miles north of where Bill and Becky were filing, toward Moose Heart Mountain. Since most of the building would take place during the summer, we each needed floats for our airplanes. Bill accomplished this first and started building a log house on the lake they now called Becky Lake.

I decided I needed to sell my PA-20 and buy a new airplane, as 58A's engine had a tendency to quit on takeoff. The engine had done this three times. No one could figure out why. It had something to do with the fuel pickup, but aircraft mechanics could not put a finger on the reason.

The first time it happened I was checking my trap line between Circle City and Fort Yukon while teaching at Circle. I had landed and taken a nice wolf out of one of the traps. It was fairly warm at -25. I had taken off my glasses upon entering the warmer airplane cabin when they frosted over. The run up and takeoff were normal, but at forty feet in the air, the engine just quit. You have almost no excess airspeed at forty feet, as you are climbing for altitude. Trying to turn back to where I had taken off would result in a crash and a casket. I put the carburetor heater on immediately, and switched the fuel system to both tanks. The engine caught again, just as my skis were hitting the tops of brush and small trees. I gently eased upward, gaining both altitude and speed.

The second time this occurred was at the Toklat cabin. Again, at fifty feet, the engine quit. The air temperature outside was a hot eighty-five degrees, so I knew carburetor icing was not the problem. I switched the fuel system to both tanks again, and again, the engine restarted right off the ground. There was nowhere to land. I was at the end of the small sandbar we used as a runway. I also could not climb high enough to avoid the trees ahead of me. Directly in front of the struggling airplane was the Toklat River, and on the other bank were 150-foot-tall pine trees. The only option was to try and turn 58A 90 degrees up river, without either stalling or putting the wing tip into the water. It took every ounce of skill I had to accomplish this. I think the only thing that really saved me was the two extra feet I had built into each wing. I was able to turn just on the edge of a stall. I could feel when the wings were losing airflow, and let up backward force on the control wheel each time I was about to fall out of the air. Dear old 58A made the turn and then climbed to clear the trees.

The third time was not a charm. Bill and I were hunting one cold winter day up by Lake Minchumina. We were looking for wolves and wolverine. We had landed on a small lake for a cup of coffee and to get feeling back into our compressed butts. I took off first when, at fifty feet, the engine quit. This time there was no escape route. Ahead of me, at my altitude, were jack pines. I did not have time to even try to switch the fuel system before my skis were crashing through them. I just concentrated on keeping the nose of the airplane elevated as my airplane made thousands of matchsticks out of the pine tress it was demolishing.

You experience a lot of loud sounds in life, but none louder than trees bashing in your wings and fuselage as you crash through them. The resulting silence, when I came to a stop still in one piece, was deafening except for the ticking of my hot engine cooling down. My first thought was that I had survived. My second thought was to thank God Bill was right behind me and had seen me crash. My third thought, as Bill flew over the top of the crumpled airplane but did not circle back, was unrepeatable.

I got out and looked at the damage. The leading edges of the wings were beaten flat. The wing struts still held the wings up, but one was badly bent. There were holes in the sides and bottom of the aircraft. I was lucky these were small trees, only twenty to forty feet tall, and three to six inches in diameter. I radioed Bill to let him know I had crashed on takeoff, but my aircraft radio antenna had been ripped off, and I could not reach him.

After twenty minutes of ever-deepening cold silence, I came to the conclusion I was going to spend the night on this lake in a -45-degree temperature. I got out my survival supplies after setting off my emergency beacon. I had just finished setting up my tent and sleeping bags when I heard the drone of a familiar airplane engine. Bill flew overhead and circled twice before landing.

Bill had not seen me crash. The snow and ice crystals blown into the air on my takeoff run had obscured his vision. When he took off he did not notice the splintered trees leading to 58A. This is not as unusual as it sounds. He could not see my takeoff run. He was occupied with getting his own airplane off the short lake and over the trees. He had looked for me once airborne, but was looking in the sky. After he did not see me, he tried to radio. It was only when he tuned his radio to the emergency frequency thirty minutes later that he knew I had crashed. It took Bill a while to find me, as there are hundreds of small lakes around there with no distinguishing features.

I had decided to sell the PA-20 after having it rebuilt again. In the meantime, while 58A was being rebuilt, I headed down to visit my friend, Bob Widmann, in Santa Cruz, California. I had met Bob one winter when Sharon and I were living in the log cabin on the banks of the Chena River while attending the University of Alaska. One day, sitting in the Student Union building drinking coffee and waiting for my next class to start, I read a notice on the bulletin board advertising an advanced scuba diving class to be held in the university pool. I called the number on the board and made reservations.

Bob and I hit it off right away. He was originally from New Jersey. After getting his PhD in physical education, he began teaching scuba diving at the University of California, Santa Cruz. He also had a commercial seiner fishing boat in Cordova, and commercially fished Prince William Sound during the summer. A friend of his living in Fairbanks had asked him to come to the university to teach a scuba class. I had gotten my original scuba certification while working at the World's Fair in Seattle before coming to Alaska, and continued to dive by myself in various lakes and rivers in Alaska. I thought it would be neat to meet some fellow divers, as it was not a popular sport in Alaska.

At the end of the class I had Sharon make Bob a jockstrap out of mink and beaver I had trapped. That cemented our friendship. In later years I flew him around interior Alaska and up to and around the North Slope, Kotzebue and Nome. He and his wife, Dotty, would visit us at Stultz Lake, and I would visit him in California. We also went on diving trips to the British Virgin Islands and other places Bob arranged for friends and students. It was a comfortable relationship.

After school was out for the summer in Circle City, I found out that Sharon had both kids in Yakutat. I decided to go visit Bob in Santa Cruz and see my sons on my way back up to Fairbanks. Upon my arrival in Santa Cruz, the first thing Bob did was take me to a nudist beach. I mean, what else would a good friend do for a guy who hadn't seen a woman in a dress, let alone nude, for many months. We had that kind of a relationship.

We discussed my situation with Sharon and my concerns about what to do with Michael. I could not leave him alone as I flew long hours getting building supplies for the proposed homestead on Echo Lake house. Bob suggested putting an ad in the college paper for someone (female) to accompany me, all expenses paid, for a summer in the bush of Alaska. The adventure would include canoeing, flying and living in a wilderness setting. After placing the ad, I was so swamped by the number of women replying that I had to spend more time interviewing them than I had planned. Bob knew the type of companion I was looking for so he was able to conduct many of the telephone interviews. After narrowing the list to ten women, whom I interviewed face to face, I selected Jennifer Wesson. Her father was a famous weapons builder. Besides her other talents, I felt that being around weapons all her life would bode well for her in Alaska.

After hiring Jenny, I flew from Yakutat on a commercial flight back to Fairbanks to talk to Sharon. Not to my surprise she was living with Dick Nicholes. I had decided to stop there and get Michael. David was so upset he was not coming with us I convinced Sharon to move to Anchorage so he could spend time with Michael and me. Later that summer I received a letter from John Peterson, after his fishing trip at Echo Lake, stating I had to get David away from her. I went to Anchorage to see what was going on. The apartment they were living in was an absolute mess, with clothes, dirty dishes, and garbage all over.

Sharon had degenerated from a bad housekeeper to an absolute slob. John was right, it was no fit place for a human to live, certainly not a young boy. We argued about my taking David from her. She threatened to get a lawyer and sue me for alimony and child support if I tried it. For the first time, I seriously thought about taking another human's life. I felt that angry at her and upset at how she was treating David. In the end, we compromised. I would take both her and David back to Fairbanks where I could keep a closer eye on things. When Jenny left I brought them both out to Stultz Lake. I needed someone to watch the boys while I was flying. Unsurprisingly, Sharon was at her best isolated from drugs, alcohol and men. She was still a bit crazy, but tolerable. She really loved the boys as much as I did and was a good mother when sober.

PA-20 checking out building location for Toklat cabin.

Bill and Becky Spear fishing at Toklat cabin.

Bill and Becky Spear unloading author's airplane at the Toklat.

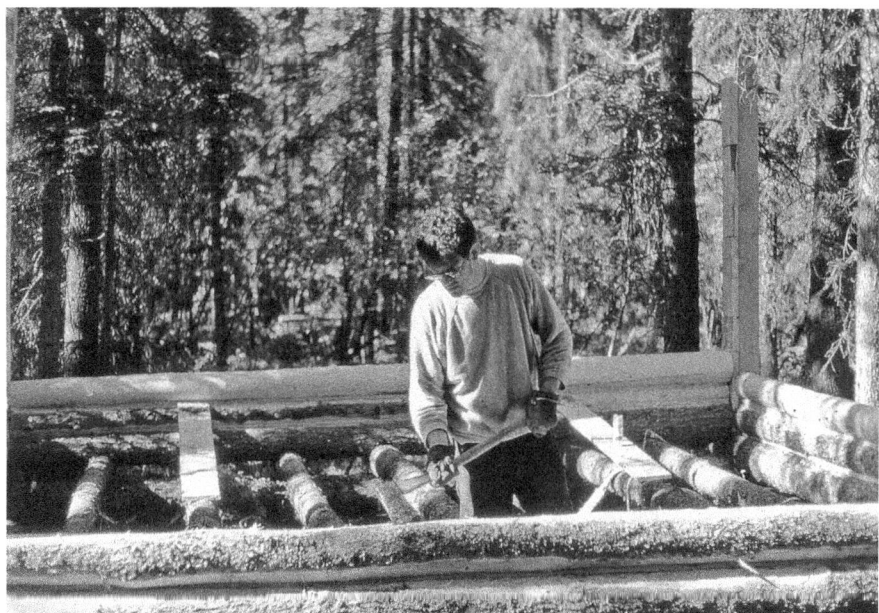

Author leveling logs with axe.

Author with Bill Spear on his first black bear hunt.

David admiring Michael's grayling.

David's first grayling.

Three black bear hunting trip.

Crashed PA-20 on Toklat River hunt.

Recovering snowmobile from the overflow.

Jenny Wesson loading canoe for trip to Toklat cabin.

Jenny and Michael at Toklat cabin.

Bob Widmann admiring grayling on our trip to Kotzebue.

Marshal Wayne Walter helping me fuel up in Nenana.

Author at Toklat cabin recovering from falling through the ice.

Putting in lawn and garden at Stultz Lake.

Bill and Becky Spear looking for homesite.

Looking for a Homestead Site

JENNIFER WESSON WAS ATHLETIC AND ADVENTURESOME, but right from the start, things did not work out as anticipated. I had everything set up to take my canoe from Nenana to the Toklat cabin prior to her arrival in Fairbanks. It was to be a long journey down the Tanana River, up the Kantishna and finally up the Toklat to our cabin. I picked Jennifer up at the Fairbanks Airport. Upon opening the door to my pickup, we discovered that Toklat had thrown up all over Jennifer's seat. One look at Jennifer's face told me this was not the adventure she had planned. After cleaning the seat, we drove out to Bill and Becky's house to spend the night.

The next day we drove to Nenana, where I loaded the canoe and we started our journey down the Tanana River. It was a pleasant day's float as we leisurely made our way downstream on the large, glacial, silt colored river past moose, Indian fish wheels, bears and birds of all variety. That evening I set up our tent and made camp as Jenny cooked dinner, the results of which made both of us question the sanity of our being together for the summer. I had dropped her off at a supermarket earlier that day and gave her money to buy supplies for two weeks. We had discussed prior to her coming to Alaska that part of her duties, beyond watching Michael, was to cook while I flew and constructed my house on Echo Lake.

Jenny handed me a plate of tofu and sprouts. I had heard California girls were a little strange, but TOFU AND SPROUTS? My reaction of throwing the plate and its contents into the Tanana River did not meet with her approval. Off to a good start we were not.

I could be pleasant and always tried to be a gentleman around women, but I did still, at this time, possess a few traits of a male chauvinist. This was before the women in my life would make me realize there was a larger reality than the small one I inhabited. At this time, I would not allow strange foods, such as onions, avocados and other green vegetables in my kitchen. Green beans were okay, but such foods as asparagus, bok choy, broccoli, spinach and other leafy green things were only eaten by the French and Italians. Being a manly Alaskan, this insult of tofu and sprouts was beyond the pale. It was another one of those cold, uncomfortable nights I seemed to experience around some of my female friends.

The rest of the trip became more pleasant, as the following day we silently floated down the Tanana observing the wildlife along its banks. At the mouth of the Kantishna I landed the canoe and made a white arrow with toilet paper held down by rocks so if we had an accident, people would know to look for us beyond this point. The bush of Alaska is huge. Finding someone missing in it is very difficult, as so many things could go wrong. Bears, capsizing the canoe and drowning, or getting lost and running out of food were but a few of the misadventures that could transpire. The only two people who knew where Jenny and I were and what we were doing were Bill and Becky Spear.

Jenny was enthralled by several white swans that landed ahead of our canoe and slowly drifted past us in their stately elegance. The difference between us could be summed up in that she saw beauty and grace while I saw dinner. I was beginning to understand that the questionnaire I had for the women who wanted to accompany me this summer had been lacking a few important topics.

I found a buyer for my PA-20 a short while after Jenny and I had reached the Toklat cabin. Bill flew 58A out to the Toklat. Upon landing on the sand bar, he asked how I flew the damn thing. He had almost wrecked on both takeoff and landing. It was much more tail happy than his airplane, requiring a lot of attention. Bill had not enjoyed the singular privilege of flying her.

The buyer was the son of the original owner of my airplane. His father had owned the Bettles Lodge and had used 58A to fly supplies to the lodge from Fairbanks. As a kid, he had spent many enjoyable hours flying in it with his father, who had passed away. He wanted the airplane as a reminder of those times. I had greatly improved the airplane his father flew, with a new and bigger engine, longer wings, and better instruments and radios. He was more than happy to pay the $8,500 I was asking, even after I explained that the engine quit at times. He stated the same thing had happened when his father owned it, and he knew how to prevent it.

I took ownership of a brand new Citrabria GCBC a week after selling 58A, and immediately had the dealer put Edo 2,000 floats on it. The Citabria is a two-place airplane, in the same general classification as a Super Cub. Alaska pilots argue vehemently about which is the better aircraft.

Having flown thousands of hours in both, I don't take either side. The Super Cub will fly slower, as well as land and take off shorter, but the Citabria is faster, warmer and will hold more because it has a bigger cabin and smaller camber built into the wings. Though, in all the years I flew my Citabria hunting and fishing with friends who flew Cubs, they never landed anywhere I could not. I just had to work harder at it and take more chances.

I chose the Citabria because I could not get Jenny, two kids and a 130 pound German shepherd into a Cub. They couldn't legally all fit into a Citabria either, but legal issues were the FAA's problem, not mine. The Citabria was my station wagon. Shortly after taking delivery, I ordered floats for it, increased the horsepower from 150 to 160, and installed a constant speed propeller, at the cost of over $18,000. You need a flat pitch propeller for short takeoffs, and a deeper pitch for cruising in the air fast. I intended to haul heavy loads in the Citabria, and wanted as much boost on the ground and water as possible. I also wanted to cruise fast in the air. With a constant speed, I could control the pitch of the propeller while flying. I also wanted an airplane that could land and take off in a shorter distance than the PA-20. I was willing to sacrifice the reduced cabin space to accomplish this. Going from a four-place to a two-place airplane had both advantages and disadvantages.

As soon as the floats were installed, I loaded Jenny, Michael and Toklat into the new airplane and flew to Echo Lake, where I had staked my home site. Flying an airplane on floats is much different from wheels or skis. The airplane is heavier and has much more wind resistance. Besides being slower in the air, a completely different method of getting the airplane airborne had to be followed. The floats sank lower in the water when the airplane was not moving. After advancing the gas for takeoff, you have to rock it back and forth to get the floats flowing over the top of the water, much like a water skier being pulled by a boat. This is called getting on step. From that position the airplane could gather the speed necessary to fly. The opposite is true on landing. Floats do not have brakes so you have to come off step to slow down. I had learned how to fly floatplanes while working for Fish and Game.

The first several weeks were spent building a platform for a wall tent, and digging a hole in the permafrost for an outhouse. Completing these chores and flying in camping supplies took two weeks. The location I choose to build my homestead on was, unbeknownst to me, in forest fire alley. These destructive fires blanketed the area ever twenty years or so. I had looked the lake over before staking a claim there and knew there were not enough large trees to build a log house, but did not realize the reason. The lake was about 5,000 feet long and offered the advantage of an outlet, so I hadn't looked for another site.

After looking over the tree situation I decided to build a modern house out of lumber and thermal pane windows, instead of a log house. With my bad back, I figured it would be easier than cutting and moving large trees. I knew nothing about building a house. That and how I would get the supplies out to the lake did not bother me. I did not know how to build an airplane either, when I had bought the wrecked 58E long ago in Yakutat. Ignorance always lost the battle to arrogance when they conflicted in my mind. I wanted to do it so I would.

Talking to veteran bush pilots as well as the Citabria dealer who sold me the airplane, I was told it was dangerous if not impossible to fly full sheets of plywood on an airplane as small as the Citabria. I would need a Cessna 180 at the very least, or have the supplies flown in by an Otter on floats. I could not afford a Cessna 180, nor did I want one. I was proficient in flying the bigger Cessna as well as the even larger Beaver, but did not want the expense of either one. They were too big and expensive to maintain and fly for the lifestyle I had planned.

For once I followed the advice I had received and cut the eight-foot plywood sheets in quarters. I could only carry three sheets of plywood at a time this way inside my new airplane. It quickly became a pain in the behind. Flying between Echo Lake and Nenana took over three hours when combined with the time it took to load the building material and refuel the airplane. This did not include the time it took to drive to Fairbanks to purchase and cut the wood. I flew the full length two by fours and two by sixes for the foundation and wall on the airplane floats with little problem.

I started hauling the longer pieces of wood for the foundation and walls' frames a few pieces at a time. The airplane would not fly when I tied too many to the floats, so I would take some off until it would get off the water and stay in the air. A tried and true Stultz method of flying. Things like weight and balance, cg (center of gravity) and maximum legal load for flying an airplane safely were for sissies and FAA thugs. I learned during this give and take process that it was not just the weight of building supplies I was carrying on the floats, but the wind resistance to the material tied on that made the difference of getting in the air or not. At a certain point the thrust of the engine could not overcome the wind resistance and weight to allow the wings to generate enough lift to fly. Weight was a big consideration, but wind resistance was the major factor.

Predictably, after a short while I got awful tired of cutting plywood to fit inside the airplane. At this rate I would still be building my house three years from now. Thinking I was better a pilot than those who had failed before, I decided to fly full sheets of plywood on the floats. Stultz arrogance and obstinacy were again plaguing reasonable thought processes. Instead of hauling full sheets of heavy plywood three-quarter and one-half-inch thick, I would start with the lighter one-eighth-inch paneling for the interior walls. I knew generally what amount of surface resistance I needed to stay within to get airborne. I was a little nervous, but decided to give it a try.

I roped six sheets of interior paneling to the cross struts of my airplane floats. They did not weight that much and there was no turbulent wind that day to affect the flying characteristics of the airplane, so I did not see any problems to prevent me from flying them into Echo Lake. N8689V jumped up onto step as I applied takeoff power without any hesitancy. I eased the airplane off the water and flew ten feet above it while I tested the effects the paneling had on N8689V in the air. Airspeed only dropped 5mph below normal. The airplane turned and flew normally. The nerves evaporated as the airplane answered every control movement I asked of it, so I felt confident as I lifted over the trees and started my flight back to the lake.

Vibration is a nasty word in an airplane. On the ground while driving a car you can stop and change a tire or go to a service station to fix the problem. Flying in the air, vibrations meant your happy flight was about to become a nightmare. It could be the engine, propeller, wings or other necessary parts to keep you in the air going bad and about to ruin your day. Vibrations immediately get a pilot's attention.

The vibrations I first felt through my control stick started very gently. I was considering turning back to Nenana to see what was wrong when things got violently worse. The tiny vibrations I first felt was the paneling tied to my floats flexing as I reached cruising speed. The chaos that shortly followed was the small but increasing vibration loosening the knots of the ropes with which I had tied the paneling to the floats. The airplane soon was jerking all over the sky as the ropes holding the paneling became untied. I had almost no control as the airplane headed to the ground at a steep angle. Trying to pull up on the stick had little effect. I was going to crash. There was small slough hardly wider than my wings underneath me. Just before we hit it I gave full power to the engine, pulled on all forty degrees of wing flaps while jerking the control stick back as hard as I could. Somehow this worked and the nose lifted just before the floats came into hard contact with the surface of the slough.

The landing was not pretty or well executed. A short while later, as I lay on the banks of the slough regaining my breath, I reflected that maybe those people who told me not to fly plywood on my floats were not only better pilots, but smarter than me as well. This experience should have killed me like it had so many others. Only instinct and luck had again saved me.

After I regained my breath I looked at the paneling on the floats. One sheet was missing entirely. The rope on the front strut had a foot of slack in it. The rope to the rear cross bar was missing entirely. I removed the rest of the panels and tossed them onto the bank, thinking I had wasted money buying them. I certainly had no intentions of flying them out of there.

Stultz obstinacy does not allow giving up so easily. Each time I flew over the discarded paneling the following weeks, I thought back to what had happened. I decided the reason the sheets of paneling had vibrated loose was because there was no support for them in the middle. The middle of the thin sheets started to flex in the wind, slowly working the knots of the front and back ropes loose. I thought if I put a two-by-four dead center underneath and on top of the paneling it would prevent it from vibrating loose. The airplane had flown fine before they worked loose. Problem solved. The rest of the paneling made it safely to Echo Lake. I even landed back at the slough and flew out the paneling I had left there. I never did find the missing sheet.

Flying building supplies out to Echo Lake continued uneventfully with one exception until Jenny left. She and Michael had gotten along very well over the summer. Jenny did an excellent job taking care of him. I worked all day on the cabin and then would fly supplies from Nenana each night until the increasing darkness of fall prevented it. I had told Jenny that if I was flying in the fog at night, just put a Coleman lantern on the shore of the lake. I could use that to guide the airplane onto the lake. The fog was a thin lake mist as the cooler water mixed with the warmer air above.

If I could see where the shoreline was I would be able to land the heavily loaded airplane with an instrument approach and landing.

Inevitably the shrinking daylight hours of fall caught me flying in the dark as the lake fogged over. But instead of putting the lantern on the shoreline as requested, Jenny had tied it to a two-by-four and stuck it upright on top of the bank, bracing it against our wall tent. In her mind, the higher it was above the lake the easier it would be to see. It was a good thought and would have worked fine if I had been expecting it. I easily saw the light from the lantern through the fog as I flew over it later in darkness. The lake itself was completely invisible. I had been fighting a heavily loaded airplane all the way from Nenana and was exhausted from that and working on the house all day. I set an instrument approach and cut power to the engine as I passed over the light thinking the lake was only inches below it.

The wind resistance to the stack of plywood on the floats slowed the aircraft quickly. Expecting a drop of inches, I let the airplane approach a stall, only adding power when I realized we were dropping way too long. Having no visibility, I did not expect the drop to be that far. I hit the lake with such downward force it threw my back out. Luckily, there was no damage to the airplane.

Two weeks later, Jenny and I parted the same way we started. I was carrying her across the water on the Yukon River. It had been a hot interior Alaska day, reaching up into the mid-eighties. Michael was in Fairbanks visiting David and Sharon, so we decided to fly down to the Yukon River for a picnic and to sun bathe. I had been working long days on the Echo Lake house and flying supplies most of the night. A little relaxation was in order. We spent several hours relaxing on a sandbar on the Yukon. Jenny did not want to get wet on the way back to where the airplane was anchored in deeper water. Being the gentlemen I am, I told her not to worry, I would carry her.

We had almost reached the anchored airplane when her camera fell into the river. Her screaming at me that I was a so and so and had to replace her camera ended with a gulp as she joined the camera in the cold murky water. There is only so much abuse a gentleman can take. Enough was enough. I took her back to Fairbanks where she worked as a waitress in a bar until she left for school back in California. During that year she took Bob Widmann's scuba class but quit it midterm, telling him he was as bad as I was: a nice compliment even if she did not mean it that way.

A Glutton for Punishment

I HAD A MAJOR DECISION to make concerning Sharon. I was worried about David; he seemed depressed whenever Michael and I visited them. I either had to contact a lawyer for a prolonged court battle over guardianship of David, or bring Sharon along with me if I were to get any control over how David was being raised. After many mental battles weighing the merits of both options, I approached Sharon. She would not let David come with me without her accompanying him. Biting my tongue and keeping my feelings to myself, I agreed to take her to Echo Lake and later Ruby when the school year began.

Sharon cancelled her rent of the Fairbanks apartment. Loading all four of us and Toklat into the airplane, we headed to Echo Lake to finish the summer working on the house. David and Michael were happy. Sharon seemed contented living at the lake. I was the only one not happy with the situation, but decided again to put my personal feeling aside for the sake of my family.

The State of Alaska wanted to experiment with a one-teacher high school. Up until that time in Alaska, all the Native children in the state's small remote villages were shipped off to a school on the coast after finishing grade school, to complete their education. Very few of the students would stay away from their villages long enough to earn a high-school diploma. The State wanted to increase the graduation rate by seeing if local one-teacher high schools would work. As far as I know, Ruby was the first such attempt to do so.

I arrived in Ruby for the start of the school year in my two-place Citrabria airplane packed with the two kids, Toklat, Sharon, and a few belongings, in the middle of a wind storm. We were on floats. The wind had created three-foot waves on the river in front of the village. The only place to land was across the Yukon in the calm water near the bend in the river. It was all I could do to keep the airplane from tipping over while trying to taxi it back across the river in the high waves and 40 mph winds. The waves would force one wing up into the air where the wind would grab it, giving that wing flying speed. Only a burst of power and full rudder would bring the flying wing back level with the other, keeping us from flipping over and drowning. I held my breath all the way across the Yukon until we reached the shore. I tied one float to a river boat and the wing to a large dead stump further up the bank. I spent the night on the banks of the Yukon River protecting my aircraft as much as possible. By morning my new twelve thousand dollar floats looked like they had been roughly used the past twenty years, but the airplane survived the night. The river bank did not fare as well. What had been a gentle inclining sandy beach was now an abrupt five-foot cliff. Not an auspicious arrival.

The Yukon River freezes every fall, so one of the most important tasks prior to flying to Ruby was ordering a year's supply of food and household items to be delivered to the barge company in Nenana. Along with our pickup truck, these supplies would be floated down the Tanana River to the Yukon, and then down to Ruby. There was a small trading post in Ruby that had some items we could use, but the prices were so high the only realistic option was to buy them in Fairbanks and ship them by river. The only real error Sharon and I made in ordering our year's supply was alcohol. I only ordered one case, thinking it would take far more than a year to consume it, given how seldom I had a drink. Wrong! It was gone by Christmas.

The school sat on a plateau about 800 feet above the river, with houses containing the Natives of the region spread below and around. The school complex contained living quarters for the families of both the grade and high school teacher, as well as a classroom for each. There was also a separate structure outside containing the school generator.

The principal at Ruby was the teacher I had replaced in Circle. She had taught in Circle for many years before going to Ruby. She was also good friends with the owner of the trading post in Circle, so I was not certain what kind of a reception I would receive from her. Surprisingly, we got along. We were not to become friends, but had a professional relationship for the one year she remained there.

The first day of school was unique. The kids were excited that they got to stay in Ruby to start the ninth grade. The average academic level of the students was low, around the fourth grade. I started off with reading just to get some idea of what I could expect out of them. My thought, that they were not going to be able to perform academically above their ability to read, proved correct. So we reviewed reading, math and other disciplines that morning prior to lunch break. At lunch I joined them for a softball game on the narrow gravel road that ran outside the school.

After lunch break I had a confrontation with an older male student who did not want to be there. I knew after the first four hours that there was going to be an inevitable clash between us. At the start of the first class period after lunch this guy kept talking with other students after I asked for their attention. Instead of getting quieter, his voice rose in volume, telling the other students to ignore me. I walked over to his chair and put my hand on his shoulder to ask him to quiet down. This guy's reaction was to tell me, "Mind your own fucking business and leave me alone." When offered the choices of walking out of the classroom or being tossed out on his head, he chose to depart on his own two feet while offering his colorful opinion of white people. I think the principal had spent a long time convincing this student to join the high school classes. She was not happy when I told her of the encounter. To address her concerns, I replied that he was welcome back at any time, but he needed to follow instructions. He never came back.

I could tell from the other students' reaction that this incident had been expected. So I quietly sat on my desk and asked them if there was anyone else who wanted to question my ancestry, intelligence or looks. If so, this was a good opportunity to express themselves. If not, I would then explain what I expected out of each of them for the coming school year. Everyone was quiet, though most did not make eye contact with me.

In the coming months I was able gain their trust and raise their measured academic skills five levels to about the ninth grade. I used the same methods I had found successful at other schools. Kids love learning if they are not made to fail. I had fun teaching them.

Over the ensuing winter, Michael, David and I would drive the single road out of Ruby toward the mining claims the road had been built to service. David would shoot his first grouse, scratching gravel on the road's surface, before school started. Sharon made friends with the local Natives and used her nursing skills to help them through sickness and injury. I made friends with the many of the locals. The preacher of the solitary church in the village was from Snohomish, close to where Dad taught school. We got along well until a serious discussion of religion took place.

I explained to the preacher that I did not believe God saved his grace for one brand of religion, but was much more cosmic in his understanding and love of humans. The door slammed in his quick departure. A good friend I did make that winter was a local gold miner with the last name of Kangas. He figured out where the previous miners in the district had gone wrong, and along with his three sons, successfully mined gold during the summer months.

In late February, as darkness was falling, I saw two Piper Super Cubs land on the frozen surface of the Yukon next to where my airplane was tied down. I got on my snow machine and drove down to them. There was no hotel or place for the them to stay in Ruby. As it was dark, I wanted to talk to them and offer a place to sleep the night if I was comfortable with their demeanor.

They were two physicians from Anchorage on their annual wolf hunt. They would take time off each year to hunt wolves north of the Alaska Range. Their names were Joe Chandler and Bill Rienbold. They accepted my offer of dinner and a place to stay for the night. They were such delightful company I told them they were welcome to stay as many nights as they were hunting in the area. They hunted the area for wolves, with good results, before flying back to Anchorage for a break.

They came back several weeks later to continue their hunt. While they were out hunting, Joe's wife arrived on a commercial flight to join him in Ruby. It was a bit crowded, but we had a great time eating the New York steaks they had brought with them. Several nights later Bill flew back into to Ruby just before dark, without Joe. Bill said they had become separated while hunting. He was afraid Joe had crashed. Dark arrived and Joe did not appear. His wife was really concerned, so I told her I would go out and find him even if it was dark and cold.

I prepared survival gear to drop out of my airplane for Joe if we were able to locate him. I had Bill point out the location on a map of the Melozitna River where he had last seen Joe. With Bill in the backseat of my airplane, I took off in pitch black skies hoping the rising moon would provide enough light to see Joe if were able to locate him.

We flew up the Melozitna to where Joe was last seen and started searching. It was not long before I spotted an upside down airplane on the top of a ridge. We flew over the wrecked Super Cub and saw Joe waving to us, indicating he was not hurt. It was dark but the now fully risen moon reflecting off the snow on the ridge showed this was not a night landing location. I had Bill drop the tent, sleeping bags and food I had prepared for him with a note saying we would be back in the morning.

I could have kicked Bill when the first thing he told Joe's wife upon returning to Ruby was that Joe had bought the farm. This is a term used by pilots when someone had died in an aircraft accident. I hurriedly explained to her that Joe had wrecked and was cold, but in good health. I also explained that it was too dark to try landing on the ridge at night to pick him up, and Bill and I would fly out in our separate airplanes in the morning and bring him home. I also explained that we probably would not return immediately, but would work on Joe's airplane that day and camp at the crash site. Color returned to her face as we all sat down for a strong drink.

After dinner I told Pat, the Ruby School principal, I was taking the next couple days off to help rescue Joe. Sharon would fill in for me in my absence using the lesson plans I provided. Pat agreed I needed to help my new friend.

Bill and I flew our airplanes out to Joe's crash site after first light in the morning. Upon reaching it, I saw that Joe had stamped a landing path steeply uphill in the snow to the ridge top his crashed airplane laid on. I called Bill Rienbold on the radio and told him to follow me and land in my ski tracks. He refused, saying it was too dangerous. I had wondered the previous evening why Bill had not seen Joe's plane and rescued him then. The airplane crash was visible for miles. If I could locate it in the dark, he must have seen it the previous day and chosen not to land. To be fair, he could also have been flying in the wrong direction and not seen the crash site. I did not push Bill to land, but had him follow me back down to the Melozitna River where I found a safe place on the river.

Landing on the steep upslope of a ridge is fairly tricky. If he did not feel comfortable doing so, I would not force him. Putting Bill's 250 pounds in my back seat, I flew back up to the crash site. I carried an extra 20 mph speed so when I pulled the airplane into a climb upslope to land we would not stall. When the skis broke the crust of the snow, my airspeed dramatically slowed. Once the skis were in the snow, I gave the aircraft full throttle to power our way up the hill to the top of the ridge.

Joe was very happy to see us. He had shot two wolves on the ridge the day before, and hit a large rock while landing to pick them up. Joe was not surprised that Bill had not landed here, as he knew far more about Bill's flying proficiencies than I did. In the succeeding weeks, as Joe's friends brought in parts to repair the upside-down airplane, I would repeat this process many times. They all refused to land on the deeply sloping, crude landing path up to the ridge by the crash, so I would ferry them and the repair parts up to the wrecked airplane.

That first day was spent getting the Super Cub ready to flip over, and taking notes on all the parts we would need to repair it enough to fly it out to a shop where the repairs would be completed. To get a helicopter to come in and lift it out was extremely expensive. Besides that, you had to sell the helicopter company your airplane for one dollar and sign a "hold harmless" waiver in case something happened. If the helicopter pilot ran into wind or other conditions that made hauling the airplane too dangerous, he would just hit the release and drop it, after which the wreck would be an unrecognizable ball of crumpled metal, making any further repairs impossible.

The temperature was approaching -45 degrees by the time we crawled into our sleeping bags that night. The next morning, as I was in the process of scraping snow away to build a fire for coffee and eggs, I noticed a green tint to the lower layers. All the fuel from Joe's airplane had drained out, saturating the snow closest to the ground. The fire Joe had started the day before my arrival had luckily been built on a small hill the fuel drained around. Still, it was amazing it had not ignited the aviation fuel, burning up Joe's airplane and camp.

Having accomplished all we could, I flew Bill down to his airplane and then flew back to the ridge to get Joe. Upon arrival in Ruby, they decided to head back to Anchorage to gather the parts and people needed to get Joe's airplane airworthy enough to get it to a repair facility.

A week later Joe arrived back in Ruby with friends and parts for his Cub. Taking time off from teaching again, I flew with them to the crash site. The two other pilots opted not to land on the ridge, so I spent the morning transporting people and parts. Once the landing gear was replaced, the task of getting the airplane right-side-up started. It was a delicate process, using pulleys, cables and rope. We needed to make sure we let the tail wheel back onto the ground as gently as possible when it flipped over. Once that was accomplished, we discovered the frame inside the cabin holding the wings on and the aircraft cabin together was broken in two places.

The mechanic Joe brought back with him used cables and turnbuckles to pull it back together. This temporary repair would have to hold the wings and cabin together until Joe could land somewhere to get them welded. The next concerns were the propeller and engine. All the oil had leaked out, so we replaced that and the bent propeller. The mechanic was concerned about the crankshaft being bent from the force of the crash. The only way to check that out here was to place a stick of wood underneath the propeller and start the engine. We all breathed a sigh of relief as both ends of the propeller tracked identically over the stick.

Here Joe earned many points with me. All other pilots I had helped to recover aircraft had me fly it out, not trusting themselves to do so. Expecting Joe to do the same, I was surprised when he jumped into the idling Cub, saying he would meet us on the river below. We all watched, with concern over Joe's wellbeing, as he added power and took off down the sloped runway. The airplane bumped and rocked side to side in the uneven snow until gaining enough speed to lift off. The wings stayed on and the engine did not falter as we slapped each other on the back in congratulations and relief on a difficult job well done.

The rest of the winter went smoothly. I selected a place on the hill overlooking the Yukon River above the school to build a house in Ruby for my family. My friends, the Kangas, used heavy equipment from their gold mine to level it out for me. I ordered lumber from Fairbanks to be delivered to Ruby on the yearly barge. After school ended for the year, we all loaded into the airplane to fly back to the homestead and finish building our house there.

John and Eric Peterson visited us that summer. I was on the second year of building my home on the Echo Lake homestead. They drove up to Nenana from Anchorage in John's pickup. I landed on the Tanana River and flew the two back to Echo Lake. Eric got sick on the flight in from Nenana and had to throw up into his hat. The chamois leather filter covering the funnel used to put gas into the airplane still reeked of gasoline fumes and nauseated him. I felt badly that I had not more tightly wrapped it in a plastic bag after using it in Nenana. I was so used to the smell of gasoline inside the airplane that it never occurred to me to do so.

The next day I flew Sharon, Michael, David and Toklat from Echo Lake to Ruby, and then returned to the lake to get John and Eric. It was windy with lots of turbulence, but Eric was a trooper and fared well in the rough air. We still lived at the Ruby school house in the teacher's quarters. John and I went hunting in the flats bordering the Yuki River the following day. We shot three black bears for their meat and hides.

The next day I first flew John and Eric to the Melozitna River, and then back to Ruby to get Michael and join them. David could not come, even though this was his favorite fishing spot. He was recovering from being bitten by about a thousand mosquitoes. I had had to fly him into the hospital for treatment earlier in the week because of his severe reaction to the bites. It seemed as if he had picked up my penchant of running around naked whenever possible, but without applying the prerequisite mosquito repellent first.

The Melozitna River empties into the Yukon close to Ruby, and had one of my favorite grayling fishing holes three miles up from its mouth. It was intimidating for passengers their first time landing there, because you had to land right into the rock face of a mountain. It was one of those Alaskan places where, once you committed, you either landed or crashed. The river takes an abrupt ninety-degree turn between two opposing cliffs, each 1,500 feet tall. The Melozitna is a small river without much room to maneuver an airplane. I had taken the family and other people to fish there many times, and invariably they would comment, "Well that was fun," after their bodies unclenched and they got their breath back.

The technique for landing there was to fly high over the river looking for any conditions that would affect the landing. I did not want to be surprised by turbulence accompanied by up and down wind drafts, or anything in the water. I could easily check this from 2,000 feet. Turbulence would be shown by swirls and gusts of winds going in different directions on the river's surface. I could also see if any logs were floating down the river. I would then fly back down to the Yukon, cutting across the Melozitna bar, angling for a right turn into the canyon. At 60 mph and twenty degrees of flaps I would make the turn, apply full flaps, reduce power, and let the floats sink down into the river. Done correctly, the floats would settle into the water about 1,000 feet from where the river made the abrupt turn east between the two opposing cliffs.

We fished for several hours, using light spinning rods with a bobber and fly. The grayling were not large there, and ran between ten and sixteen inches. There was not a lot of room to fish, as the stream running into the Melozitna was pretty narrow and shallow. The grayling run up it to spawn. I did not fish but watched Eric and Michael as they had a ball hauling in grayling. It was readily apparent from watching them that they would grow up to be better fishermen than their fathers. We had more fresh grayling than we could eat that evening for dinner.

We fished the Koyukuk River for sheefish the following day, but they were not running yet. The day after, we flew to a slough off the Yukon thirty miles above Ruby that was Michael's favorite pike area. We routinely took large five to fifteen-pound pike, and Dad would catch a twenty-eight-pound pike there several weeks later.

I had an Otter on floats scheduled to fly lumber into Echo Lake, and needed to fly to Fairbanks to check on it. I made two flights to and from Ruby to Echo Lake to get everyone back to the homestead. The following day I flew into Nenana and drove to Fairbanks to purchase the lumber, and delivered it to the airport to be flown out to the homestead. The Otter is a very large single-engine airplane that could haul long and heavy loads. It would save me weeks of flying it out myself.

We woke up at Echo Lake the following morning to smoke from a nearby forest fire blotting the horizon. From the ground, it looked like it was between Echo Lake and Nenana. John and Eric were scheduled to go home that day. I had planned to fly them into Nenana, but with a fire on the horizon, I could not safely leave my family at the lake. John, Sharon and I discussed it and decided to fly her and the kids back to Ruby before flying John and Eric into Nenana. Once I was in the air I could see that the fire was by West Twin Lake, heading my direction. I would be able to fly John and Eric around the northern end toward the Tanana River when I returned to pick them up.

Flying back after dropping my family at Ruby to pick up John and Eric, I saw that the fire had rapidly grown in size, but if I climbed high enough I could still skirt around the north end and make it into Nenana without too much of a detour. It was either that or fly them back to Ruby. John wanted to head into Nenana. It would be a rough flight with the smoke and heat from the fire, but I could see nothing to cause concern.

I landed at Echo, where John and Eric were packed and ready. I asked John to put more gas in the airplane while I got the belongings I did not want destroyed by the fire if it made it to the lake. The BLM did not fight forest fires on federal land but let them burn, so there would be nothing to stop the fire from coming all the way there.

After loading everyone into N8689V, I was concerned about how far the floats were sinking into the water. If I could get on step I could power around the lake on the water surface until I had enough speed for takeoff. The GCBC on floats had a legal useful load of about 420 pounds. Which was me, full fuel and forty additional pounds. Looking at the floats, I estimated we were a good 700 pounds over that.

Unfortunately, it was too much weight for the GCBC to make it off the lake. I tried every trick I knew to no avail. The aircraft would not get on step. I taxied back to shore, taking out John's heavy tackle box and some other stuff before we were able to get off the water and fly toward the forest fire and Nenana.

The takeoff was uneventful after removing some of the excess weight. I kept the aircraft at full power to gain as much altitude as possible. I could see the fire was growing, and was getting more concerned it would reach my homestead. Climbing over the north end of the fire, the engine coughed at 7,000 feet. Quickly looking at the gas gauges, I was shocked to see that both the right and left wing tanks were on empty. They both should have been almost full. The only thing that made sense was that when John had put gas in at the lake, he had not put the gas cap back on and the wind over the wings siphoned gas from the tanks.

This was not John's fault, but mine. I was the pilot and it was my responsibility to check and make sure everything was in order prior to flying. He probably left the cap off so I could visually check the gas level. In my haste to take off and get John and Eric safely out of the fire's path I had made a cardinal pilot sin in not checking to make sure everything was ready for takeoff. We were about to run out of gas 7,000 feet in the air skirting the edge of a large forest fire, halfway between Echo Lake and Nenana, with nothing but wilderness below us—which was much better than being at 700 feet in the same circumstances.

I looked for a place to land and saw Duck Lake about four miles behind and to the left of us. I had previously stashed fifteen gallons of aviation gas there just in case of emergencies like this. Banking and descending to Duck Lake seemed to take forever. I was used to air emergencies happening real close to the ground and being over in seconds, not this long dragged-out affair.

The engine quit running at 2,500 feet. Duck Lake is fairly large and probably has 4,000 feet of water to land in. Even though there would be no go-around, I was not concerned. We had plenty of altitude and a good place to set down. You practice for this type of situation when earning your pilot's license. I had landed on thousands of lakes without needing to add power on landing.

I kept the airplane fairly high and fast in the air. I crossed over the edge of the lake way too high and fast. I steeply side-slipped to lose as much altitude and speed as I could before touching down. I was surprised when the engine started again as I leveled out of the slip, but held my breath, as we were going so fast the floats skied across the water instead of coming off step and sinking down into it to slow us down. We were not going to crash, but I was worried we would skid so far up the fast approaching shore that we would end up in the willows lining it. Just when I was bracing myself for hitting the shoreline, the floats came off step and we gently bumped into the sand close to where I had stashed the gas.

Sure enough, the left gas tank cap was missing. I kept a spare in my emergency kit, as I had heard of this same thing happening to other bush pilots. We gassed up and uneventfully flew the rest of the way to Nenana. The only casualty of the trip was John's tackle box. It filled with water before I could get back to the lake, ruining thousands of dollars of fishing gear inside.

* * *

Dad and I were getting along well, so after John and Eric left, I called him and asked if he wanted to come up to Alaska for the summer and help me build my house. He seemed excited about the prospect and agreed to come. Dad flew into Fairbanks, where I picked him up, and we drove to Nenana. After gassing up the plane and storing Dad's stuff inside, he asked where the seat belt was after he climbed in. I told him I had been flying building stuff and my family, and had taken the belt and seat out—and if he needed a belt, it would not do him any good. Airplane crashes are usually fatal whether you are wearing a belt or not. Was I needling him a little? Sure; he had put me through hell growing up.

From there we flew out to my home site on Echo Lake. I had taken the rear seat out of N8689V so I could haul building material. Everyone who flew with me that summer had to sit on an empty wooden box that had held two-five-gallon cans of aviation fuel. Even though Dad and I got along well now, I had not completely forgiven him. Reaching the lake, I was flying at 1,500 feet. I told Dad to hang on, and raised the nose of the aircraft straight up into the air. Before we stalled, I kicked full rudder and pushed the control stick forward and to the side as far as it would go. I still remember, with pleasure, the terrorized look on Dad's face as he was pinned to the ceiling while the airplane rolled on its back and plummeted straight down toward the lake's surface. Paybacks are a bitch. Neither of us mentioned the incident after landing. We both knew what had taken place. He would remember his first flight with me for the rest of his life, like I remembered so many encounters with him, growing up.

Dad was an experienced carpenter. The house quickly took shape after his arrival. We had the siding on and were laying the plywood on the roof when I received a certified letter from BLM telling me I was building a house illegally on federal land. The BLM had landed at Echo Lake during the forest fire and set up a large camp for their firefighters. I was glad they were there because they stopped the fire right at the foundation of my house. They would not fight the fire, but would save most of the home-steads in a fire's path. Seeing my house, they reported it to the Fairbanks office. Checking their records, the Fairbanks office determined I was building on the wrong lake.

I took the flight map with the original marking of Echo Lake I had used in filing the home site, and flew into Fairbanks to talk to a BLM agent. I figured it was a simple clerical error that could be easily corrected. Like everyone else who has had to deal with federal bureaucracy, I quickly found out there is no such thing as a small problem. They told me I had two choices. Move the house to the lake they believed I needed to be on, or they would burn it down in sixty days.

I mean, come on. How in the hell do you move a house to another lake in the wilderness of Alaska? I tried to convince this overzealous moron it would just be a far simpler process to amend the BLM records to show where the house was located. No, according to this enlightened bureaucrat; I had to move it five miles over a hill and creek to where it should be. Hiring an attorney to straighten the mess out accomplished nothing. Several weeks later I received another certified letter saying my appeal was denied and I had sixty days to remove the Echo Lake house or they would burn it down.

First there was Fish and Game, followed by the FAA, and now BLM. I became convinced our government was staffed with crooks, liars and in-competent morons. I was evolving into a complete Alaskan. I developed an acute distrust and dislike of all government officials.

Dad and I discussed the situation and came to the conclusion we had to tear the house down piece by piece and fly it to the new location. We got in the airplane and flew to where the BLM had decided, in all their divine wisdom, I needed to be. First we had to find a site suitable for building on the lake I named Stultz Lake. I briefly considered naming it the "Stultz Confederacy" in my anger over governmental incompetence, but Dad, being older and wiser, convinced me not to do so. He was right. I had enough ongoing battles with these idiots already.

We started the process of cutting trees off the selected building site and preparing it for construction all over again. Dad and I started dismantling the original house. I marked each piece of lumber so we would know how to put the building back together again. Unfortunately, the indelible ink pen I used was not indelible, and lake water washed the marks off during takeoff and landing, making the process of reassembling it like putting together a puzzle.

I needed all the help I could get to complete the building before winter. Everyone was given a job. Sharon cleared brush while Michael and David carried building material from the lake shore and stacked it near where the house would be reconstructed. Dad tore down the old house and, after enough material had been removed, I flew it over to Stultz Lake. Everyone worked hard and, before I knew it, the walls and roof at the new location were up and Dad was cutting holes for new windows by what would be the kitchen counter with a panoramic view overlooking the lake. I could not have accomplished this within the sixty days given by the BLM if it were not for Dad's help and expertise. It was a frantic summer, with everyone involved working their tail off, no matter the weather, mosquitoes or fatigue.

I wanted this house to have electrical lights and outlets, as well as propane heat and lights. Dad was no more an electrician than I was. The electrical wire I ran through the walls for outlets and lights shorted out each time I tried to use the generator. Throwing my hands up in the air in disgust, I flew over to Becky Lake to ask Bill for help. It took him about ten minutes to figure out what was wrong and correct it.

We finished the house just about the same time the two gallons of Everclear alcohol that Dad had brought with him was consumed. Before bed each night, Dad, Sharon and I would have a good shot of Everclear mixed with Tang to help us sleep. It was potent stuff, this Everclear. One drink and everyone was blissfully snoring.

I would add another room to the house each summer until it was complete. The kids had a bedroom upstairs. In the bedroom downstairs I built the bed high off the floor, even with the bedroom window, so we could see out over the lake. In subsequent years it would become the nightly location where I read to the kids. It was where they developed their love of reading. They must have had me read J.R.R. Tolkien's series, *Lord of the Rings*, five times. The boys would, laugh, cringe or clap as I acted out each character's voice, while outside the snug, warm cabin, the northern lights swirled in their colorful dances beneath bright stars, undiluted by city lights.

* * *

The principal at Ruby had retired and the state school system, in its wisdom, had replaced her with a man from Georgia. His wife and two kids accompanied him. I was distinctly unimpressed upon meeting him and his family. Deciding to get along with the skinny nervous little redhead, I invited him for a fishing trip to the mouth of the Melozitna River where sheefish were running. Sheefish are a variety of whitefish that can reach twenty pounds. Though they did not have the nutritional value of salmon, they were prized for their delicate white flesh. Putting fishing gear and my new boss into the airplane, I flew the short hop to the Melozitna. He complained there was neither a seat belt nor comfortable seat on the way over. Thus we began the matrix of our relationship. He whined and complained while I mostly ignored him.

We caught seven sheefish between three and ten pounds. I did not want to clean them at the school, so I gave him a knife and explained we would remove the guts and heads here. He looked at me as if I were insane and asked if he had to get his hands messy. I thought, "My God this is going to be a long year." Little did I know how difficult our relationship would become as there was no common ground in our interests or personalities.

The man had absolutely no control over his classroom. His students screamed, yelled and moved around the classroom as he, unsuccessfully, tried to teach. The noise was so great that, even with my classroom door closed, I could not eliminate the noise to conduct my own classes with the quiet decorum I preferred. It was not surprising that Sharon and his Georgia Peach wife did not hit it off, either. Michael and David had no use for his sons, as well. Sharon had her Native friends, and the Georgia Peach only associated with the Anglo Saxons of the village.

The guy was so irritating I had a hard time communicating with him. When I requested that he keep the noise down in his classroom, his reply was that he was the principal and would set the standards of the classroom. It was exactly the wrong approach to take with me and was met with resentment and a look of disdain that could not be concealed.

Joe Chandler and a fellow physician from Anchorage named Jack Frost had planned a wolf hunting trip in the spring. I had already cleared it with the previous principal, but when I brought it up with the current one, he said he would have to think about it. I explained to him that it was already approved. Sticking his thin needle nose in the air, this prime specimen of southern inbreeding explained that he was now in charge, and would decide what days I could take off. Keeping my incredulity and anger in check, I told him, "Fine, I will clear it with your boss, who has already approved it."

Turning even further red-faced, he shouted at me, "Go ahead and leave, but do not expect to take any more time off." I smiled at his loss of control, saying Sharon would have my lesson plans to make sure the high school students continued their academic progress. This was the last straw for him. Seeing something he could control, I was informed that he would decide who would replace me. It was his decision that the preacher would teach in my absence. I asked him if he was certain the man could read and understand math and science, or should I prepare lesson plans to equal the intelligence of the preacher's sermons? I was told to leave his office immediately. Leaving teaching and moving to Stultz Lake full time was becoming more enticing.

By now my Stultz temper had had enough of this little southern rat, so I smiled at him, stood at attention, gave a crisp military salute, did an about face, and marched out of my commanding officer's room. I did not slam the door, a fact of which I am proud. Punching him in the nose would come the following year. The only other interaction we had that school year was when he told me to keep Michael and David out of the classroom when school was out. My reply, that I would as soon as the same rule applied to his sons, was not met with his divine approval.

The school year progressed well. The students continued to grow academically, but at a slower pace as the material became more difficult. About a third of the students were from other villages. One of these students was a boy from Koyukuk, a remote village on the North Slope. I had been in his village several times, and would discuss his people and their lifestyle with him when he became lonely enough to overcome his shyness. He was in the tenth grade and did well at his studies. He was very quiet in the classroom and only participated when called upon, like many Native students. Also, like many Native children who had never left their small villages before, he was very homesick.

One night about 1:30 a.m., I heard a loud crash in the school house attached to the teacher's quarters. Getting up to investigate the noise, I encountered this student in the hallway between classrooms. He was extremely angry. He also appeared to be very drunk. His hands were in his coat pockets so I could not see what was in them, but all my police instincts told me something was seriously wrong. I tried talking to him with no response but a glare and grunt. He moved toward me but stopped when, in a commanding voice, I told him to do so. I could see dark stains on his coat, but the lighting was not fully on, and I could not discern if he was injured.

At this point I had two main concerns. He was drunk and angry, but the main focus, as I talked to him, was his health. I wanted to know if he needed medical attention. Sharon was out sleeping with someone in the village and I was home alone with the boys, but I wanted to help him if I could. I think that got across to him as he gruffly turned and left out the broken door he had entered through. Thinking I would deal with the issue in the morning, I shut the door, blocking it with a chair, and returned to bed. My fearless principal had not made an appearance, despite all the noise.

Several hours later Sharon returned home, all distressed, telling me that my student had killed several people in Ruby with a knife and injured others in a drunken fury that evening, and was hiding somewhere. I replied that he had broken into the school earlier but had left. That morning an Alaskan State Trooper from Galena arrived to investigate the murders and take the kid away to jail in Fairbanks. It was a prime example of the effects of alcohol on Alaskan Natives. Here a boy's life was ruined, far away from the home and people he loved, because the State of Alaska would not provide education for him in his home environment. Several villagers in Ruby with whom I was friends lost their lives in this tragic incident. Murderous rampages were not uncommon in remote Alaskan locations, especially in the middle of the long cold winters, when fueled by alcohol or the lack of social interaction.

I was sad for the kid and his victims as I answered the Trooper's questions the following day. Upon hearing of the crimes and of the boy's breaking into the school, my fearless leader's only concerns were that the kid was in jail, and that he and his family could have been murdered in their sleep.

First Summer at Stultz Lake

THE MOST EAGERLY AWAITED PHENOMENON of the Alaskan Bush was when the Yukon River, or whatever river the village was located next to, melted and started flowing again. It meant salmon would return to replenish food for dogs and inhabitants alike. It also allowed people living along its banks to resume safe travel and hunting for ducks, geese, moose and bears. Some people traveled on the Yukon during the winter, but enough people died doing so that it was not a universal method of winter travel. It was dangerous. Three years later one of my first students in Ruby died while snow machining on the Yukon.

As life in Ruby picked up to its summer pace, I replaced the snow skis on my airplane with floats and flew the family back to Stultz Lake. I planned to build another room onto our house. It would be a fifteen by twenty-five-foot front room, with rugs on the floor, suspended ceiling and a picture window. I would also add an oil heater as a second heat source to supplement the wood-burning Yukon stove.

This summer construction went much smoother, as I was more familiar with flying construction materials and building. Michael helped me with the heavier lifting, while David's job was to pick up scrap wood for the fire. David also perfected his duty of shutting off the generator when it was not needed to save fuel. The prior year he had shocked himself as many times as he had shut the generator off safely.

I had been thinking all winter of moving the trapping and other items stored in the Toklat River cabin to Stultz Lake, with the exception of the snow machine. This thought process included possibly flying the twenty-foot square-stern canoe that Jenny and I had used on our trip from Nenana to the Toklat River. After having completed that summer's construction project, I removed everything from the back of N8689V and flew over West and East Twin lakes to the Toklat River. I landed on the Toklat and tied the floats to a tree. Looking around, I saw there was no way I would be able to fly the canoe out from there, even if I were to get airborne with it tied outside on the floats. The river was just too narrow and crooked, with high trees lining the banks.

I took off again and landed on a long straight stretch of the Kantishna. Approaching the cabin on foot after the six-mile trek back up the Toklat, I saw a black bear trying to break into the log structure. I quickly shot the bear and dragged it to the banks of the Toklat. I saved the meat and hide, while the rest went into the river where it would finally wash up somewhere downstream as food for other animals.

After hauling the canoe from where it was hidden in the trees, I loaded my traps, spare gas, bear and rifle into it. The 10 hp Mercury outboard started on the second pull, but I shut it off. I wanted to paddle slowly and quietly downstream to enjoy the peace, beauty and tranquility of my second Alaskan cabin for the last time. However, as much as I enjoyed the quiet trip to the Kantishna, I could not pass up the opportunity to add more food to my winter larder, and soon added six geese to the bear meat and skin on the bottom of the canoe.

Arriving at my airplane on the Kantishna, I loaded everything inside the cabin except the canoe. Originally I had planned to fly all this stuff out first, and come back for the canoe. The more I looked at the size of the canoe in comparison to the size of my airplane, the more concerned I became that the airplane would not get on step, let alone fly with all the drag and added weight.

The part of my personality that my son, David, inherited took over. I decided to tie the canoe on, and if I could not get into the air, I would just fast taxi the airplane and canoe on step, all the way back up the Toklat river to our cabin. This would save me another long twelve-mile walk.

I could not open the aircraft door after tying the canoe on to the floats and fuselage because the canoe was so big. I had to enter by climbing in the left side window. Debating whether to take off upstream or downstream, I decided to head down river. I was really surprised, after pushing the throttle forward, that the floats jumped right onto step well before they would normally with just me inside. I figured that when I pulled back on the stick, the back of the canoe hitting the water pushed the airplane up onto step. Soon I was speeding over the water at 45 mph. I applied twenty degrees of flaps and tried to get off the river. The airplane did not lift off, so I applied full flaps.

The floats lifted off the surface of the river but would not climb above ground effect. The drag of the canoe and the weight loaded inside was too much for the engine to overcome and create flying speed. I thought about landing, but was afraid of what would happen when the back of the large canoe dug into the water if I did. If I was going to crash, I wanted it to be at my lake, where I could get help, not on some river so full of glacial silt I would not be able to swim to shore before drowning.

I thought as I struggled to stay in the air, I had really messed up again, and cussed myself for even trying to fly the canoe. Flying at full throttle with full flaps I could not gain more than 55 mph. Every time I tried to reduce the flaps' setting, I sank back toward the river. I was more than five miles downstream before I was able to raise the flaps to twenty degrees. Slowly trading air speed for altitude in tiny increments, I was more than fifteen miles downstream before I was flying at the level of the pine trees lining the bank. I was over the Tanana River before attempting a turn toward Stultz Lake.

It had taken me over fifteen minutes at full power before trying the turn. I lost a precious 200 feet completing it. The aircraft just did not want to want to fly or turn with all the weight inside the cabin and the wind resistance, caused by the large canoe, outside. The cg, center of gravity, was so far out of kilter it was probably back by the tail. I had fifteen miles to gain another 800 feet in altitude to clear a small ridge between the East and West Twin Lakes leading to Stultz Lake. Trading my excess 10 mph over stall, I gingerly coaxed the airplane over the ridge with 100 feet to spare. It was like flying a pregnant elephant with small ears. By the time Stultz Lake came into view a short time later, I was bathed in sweat. Making a long, slow, gentle turn into a landing, I pushed the nose of the floats down with the elevators and power as the floats touched the lake surface. I wanted to stay on step as long as possible, fearing what would happen when the rear of the canoe, sticking out beyond the end of my floats, dug into the water.

Thinking the canoe had pushed me onto step at the beginning of the flight, I was afraid the opposite would happen on landing. That is, the rear end of the canoe would dig into the water as I came off step. I was anxious; it could flip the airplane over if it happened at too great a speed. Sure enough, as the floats settled into the water and the end of the canoe dug into Stultz Lake, there was a violent jerk to the right. I thought for sure the right wing would dig into the lake flipping me over as the airplane tipped precariously toward the float holding the canoe. Thankfully the wing tip only skimmed the surface before we lost enough forward momentum to allow the airplane to again settle on both floats. The canoe was at the lake. It would damn well stay there. I needed a bath and a good shot of Yukon Jack.

Immediately upon removing the canoe from my airplane, Michael and David took possession of it to start exploring Stultz Lake. It was almost an impossibility to keep them in life jackets on those journeys. They would invariably ground the canoe on some sandbar, take off the life vests, and go exploring and swimming. After a while, we gave up arguing with David to keep his on. He could swim a little bit and got better as the summer progressed. The boys came back one afternoon, saying there were no fish in the lake to catch. We decided it was time to stock the lake with whitefish and pike. Both were hardy species that would live through the lower water oxygen content caused by the lake being covered by ice and snow during the long winter months.

At this time in their lives, Michael was the better fisherman. David was more interested in art, throwing rocks, exploring and getting into trouble, while Michael lived for fishing. All three of us hopped into the float plane and flew to Wien Lake to begin the stocking process. It was not long before we had a twenty-gallon barrel full of fish for the first transplant into our lake. It would become a daily routine for the next two weeks, until it was time to head back to Ruby for the start of the next school year.

Stultz Lake in foreground with Echo Lake in background.

Setting corners for Echo Lake house.

David running the generator.

Forest fire burns to the foundation of Echo Lake house.

Dad building Echo Lake house.

Stultz Lake house completed.

Black bear that tried to break into Stultz Lake house.

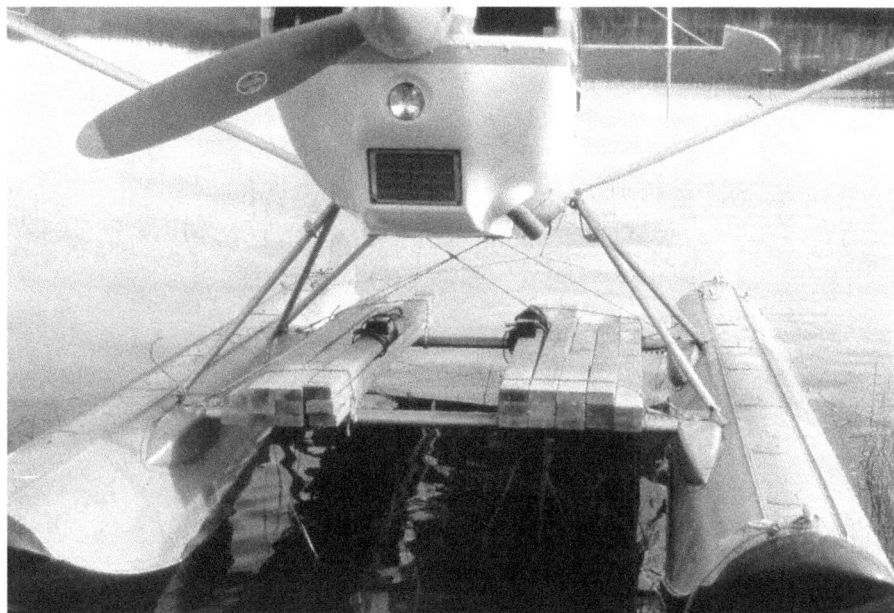

Flying building supplies into Stultz Lake.

Michael and Toklat fishing at Stultz Lake.

Winter at Stultz Lake.

David in Ruby before school.

Moving to Stultz Lake

THE SUMMER VACATION AT STULTZ LAKE was fulfilling but uneventful, other than the flight with the canoe. I spent some time helping Bill and Becky haul firewood and some other chores, as Bill had had a serious back injury and could barely walk. I flew Becky into town for supplies several times, and built another room on my house. This addition was a place to work on equipment and store frozen meat during the winter. While I had not yet decided on moving full time to our homestead, my subconscious was already working on me to do so.

All too soon the summer was over and it was time to head back to Ruby for the school year. I was not looking forward to it. The impasse between myself and the principal was reaching critical mass. The slightest disagreement could set off a major confrontation. He wanted respect because of his position, and I was equally of a mind only to respect someone who deserved it. Not a good way to start the year trying to open the minds of young students.

The year started off normally, with the kids reluctant to get back to serious study. The moose season arrived, and I was busy getting a moose for myself as well as flying others in Ruby out for their winter supply of meat. I met Charlton Heston and his family, who were staying with the trading post owner. I was impressed with them. They seemed like an ordinary family who would make good Alaskans. They were very down to earth and unpretentious.

On one of these trips I spotted N1416H, an Aeronica Sedan I was familiar with, parked on a slough. I landed beside the Sedan and got out to talk to the pilot. Hank worked for Veterans Affairs in Fairbanks. He had a hunter with him from Fairbanks named T.D. They were moose and bear hunting, but had had no success. I invited them to stay the night with me in Ruby if they remained in the area.

Later that evening, in Ruby, I saw Hank's Aeronica Sedan land on the Yukon and taxi to shore, where I met them. They explained over drinks later that they had seen moose, but were unable to land anywhere close enough to shoot one. Hank then requested that I take T.D. out the next day, as Hank wanted him to get a moose. Hank knew my reputation as a hunter and pilot, and felt I could land in places he couldn't, and in doing so could help his friend out. I agreed to take T.D. the next morning.

We took off after breakfast, and Hank followed us in his Sedan. T.D. was a large man over 250 pounds; not much of it was muscle. He had a hard time getting into the airplane, let alone exiting. I saw several bull moose that I could have landed and taken but, with T.D.'s weight, passed them up. Receiving a radio message from Hank that he had developed engine problems and was going down, I immediately abandoned moose hunting and started looking for his blue and yellow airplane.

I spotted Hank just as he touched down on a big slough, and flew over to land beside him. He had blown a cylinder and lost power. We discussed his situation for a while, after checking the engine. Hank decided he wanted me to fly him back to Ruby where he could catch a commercial flight back to Fairbanks to get the parts he needed to repair his airplane. I had T.D. stay at Hank's airplane while I flew him back to Ruby. T.D. was so large I did not think both of them would fit in the back seat area.

I returned to pick up T.D. several hours later to continue his moose hunt. Within an hour he had a nice sixty-inch bull down. By the time we cleaned and loaded the moose into my airplane and were tying the rack onto my floats, we were running out of daylight. I had originally planned to haul the meat in first and come back for T.D., but the darkness and settling fog changed that plan. The slough we were on was fairly large. If I could get the 1,100 pounds loaded into my airplane on step quickly enough—almost three times what my airplane was designed and licensed to fly—I felt I could get into the air and fly back to Ruby instead of spending a cold night camped here.

N8689V was capable of hauling three times its legal load. The trick was to get up on step so the engine could overcome the drag of the floats and pick up flying speed. I looked at the floats as I taxied to the end of the slough preparing for takeoff, and noticed the rear three sections were under water. This would be the maximum weight I had ever tried to fly when on floats. There was no way to tell how much weight I was carrying, so I had a habit of looking at the floats. Two sections under water, I could get off with. Three, I had my doubts.

I told T.D. to get on his knees and crawl over the still-warm meat, and hug my pilot's seat. I wanted his considerable weight as far forward as possible. The airplane struggled, but got on step quickly enough to take off before the water under us met the shoreline. Luckily there were no trees here, so I only had to clear the five-foot embankment. However, the fog in the fast cooling late fall evening was forming everywhere from the numerous small lakes and sloughs in the area. I climbed up through it on instruments and headed toward the Yukon to follow it back to Ruby. I could not see the river itself but knew the surrounding country well enough to follow the fog-obscured river to Ruby. Parts of the village were above the fog when we flew over. Using the lights from the village, I set up an instrument approach to land on the Yukon beside the village.

The landing through the fog was uneventful for carrying such a large load. Soon I was taxiing, looking for shore. When it appeared fifteen feet in front of me I cut power to the engine and was reaching for the door handle to jump out onto the floats and dock us when I was violently pushed forward, crushed against the dashboard. I saw T.D. rush headfirst out the door into the Yukon River with a huge splash. I screamed at him to grab the floats as I quickly exited the cabin and ran to the front of the floats, jumping onto shore to anchor us before the current swept us back out into the main channel. Behind me I could hear laborious breathing and splashing as T.D. struggled to shore.

I did not know whether to laugh or scream at him for needlessly endangering himself. You can't swim in the Yukon with clothes on. The heavy glacial silt quickly seeps into your clothing, weighing it down and dragging you to the bottom, no matter how strong a swimmer you are. In the end, I just helped him up onto the bank. The panic on his face needed neither mirth nor chastisement. He later told Hank that I was a crazy pilot flying an overloaded airplane at night through the fog, and made an instrument landing when not even the propeller could be seen. He may have been right, in some respects. However, I was never crazy enough to jump into a silt laden ice cold river instead of calmly walking on floats to shore. T.D. never wanted to fly with me again.

That fall, as the family settled into school life, I helped many of the villagers put in a winter's supply of moose and bear meat, as well as teaching. The boys and I hunted the road system in the morning before school. They had increasingly become targets of discrimination from the Native children in Ruby. They used Michael's dog, Toklat, as their personal protector when being ganged up on. Sharon was increasingly acting out, sometimes disappearing for weeks at a time. The situation with the principal and his family deteriorated as well. It was not a pleasant start to the year. Neither the boys nor I were comfortable or happy with the situation.

After Thanksgiving, the principal and his wife banged on my living quarters door, screaming about some perceived wrongdoing on my part. I'd had enough of the red faced idiot, so when he shoved me in the chest after spraying my face with spittle while shouting at me, his nose met the end of my fist.

Picking himself off the floor, holding his bleeding and rapidly swelling nose, he promised to get rid of me. The Georgia Peach stayed for a bit after her husband ran away, to rant about Sharon and what a disgrace she was to other proper women of the village. She was right, of course, about the disgrace part, but I am not so sure about the proper woman stuff. I growled at this proper woman and stepped toward her. She fled, following her husband's trail of blood marring the newly waxed school house floor, shouting invectives that were certainly unladylike.

I was not surprised to receive a letter several weeks later telling me that my performance was on the agenda of the next meeting of the school board. The night of the school board meeting, Toklat had somehow gotten loose from his chain and was terrorizing villagers. The Native children loved to tease him while he was chained up by throwing stuff at him. I was really concerned he would seriously hurt them. He was certainly capable of mauling one or more of the kids, so I went to look for him, along with Michael and David, while telling Sharon to sit in for me at the school board meeting. I told Sharon to tell them I would attend as soon as Toklat was safely chained again.

We had not located Toklat before Sharon came running up to, me saying the principal was telling a bunch of lies about me in the meeting and I needed to get there quickly. Entering the meeting, I was met with silence. The head of the school board, a nice fair man who ran the village trading post, said the board had received some serious allegations about my behavior. I asked him to make me acquainted with these supposedly dastardly deeds. After consulting the written page in front of him, he began listing the things Mr. and Mrs. Georgia had complained about.

I interrupted him by standing and stating that, yes, I had spanked his son. Not for malice, as stated, but because he had shot an arrow through the open windows of my pickup as I was driving past his store one afternoon. The barbed arrow had barely missed us by a few inches. I also suggested he take a firmer hand in raising his out-of-control child. The audience snickered, as the behavior of this kid had been an irritant to many in the village. And, yes, I did assault the principal after he almost knocked my door down, yelled at me, spit in my face and shoved me in the chest. However, I did not get the chance to discipline him as much as he deserved, as the little rat ran away, crying, after one punch. This brought outright laughter from the audience, but stern looks of disapproval from members of the school board, who had been well prepared by the principal and preacher prior to the meeting.

As the chairman began to reply to my response, after quieting the room, I interrupted him again. I stated that the principal was a liar and the worst teacher I had ever associated with, and had zero management skills. His classroom was a zoo, without any semblance of control. I concluded by resigning immediately from my position as a teacher at this school, before I did something more than punch the preening clown in the nose. The crowd was quiet as I got up to leave the meeting. I had taken many of them hunting, free of charge in my airplane, and they had no love for the principal. He and his wife's attitude of being above the village people had also grated on them. Before I got to the door, I was offered a free house to live in, and help moving out of the school house.

I breathed a real sigh of relief and looked forward to moving to Stultz Lake full time. We lived in Ruby until spring approached before moving. I gave the lumber and home site I was preparing at Ruby to the Kangas. I wanted to be away from people, and yearned for the quiet solitude of Stultz Lake.

* * *

It was fifty below zero when I quit teaching at Ruby, so we moved into the free house that had been offered until the weather became more moderate. I never saw the principal again, but friends in the village informed me later that he became a further laughingstock in Ruby, after ordering an emergency flight to pick him up and fly him to Fairbanks because he was having a heart attack. There was nothing wrong with him physically, only a bad case of indigestion. The villagers told me it was his wife's cooking that had upset his stomach. He was later transferred to Tanana to be the principal there. The last I heard was that people in Tanana were mad at him because he stated at a public school board meeting that women would no longer be hired as janitors in the school, as that was man's work, but they could continue to apply for teacher's aide and cooking jobs.

It was a big relief to be completely out of civilization and at home on the homestead. The process that had started by moving to Alaska many years before and slowly but surely moving further away from civilization was now completed.

Homestead living in an isolated setting sounds like an idyllic and carefree lifestyle. It is in a way, but in reality, it is also very hard work. Now you are working for yourself and your family. You still need shelter, food, medical and dental care, heat, and a way to procure all of them. Our life at the homestead was much easier than for many others in the bush of Alaska, because of our airplane. I could earn money flying, guiding and trapping that many could not.

After my yearly spring wolf hunt with Joe Chandler and Jack Frost we were visited by a writer and photographer from Paris, France, writing an article on Alaska homesteading for *Geo* magazine. The advantage of an airplane became abundantly clear. The writer and photographer from *Geo* visited four homesteading families for their article, staying with each family for extended periods over a two-year span to get a clear picture of what it was like to homestead in Alaska for their European readers. They were amazed during their visits with us at the creature comforts of our house and our food supply compared to the other homesteaders they visited. When the article was published for their European audience, this difference was glaring. I was a school teacher and pilot. Sharon was a Registered Nurse. The schooling and care Michael and David enjoyed far outreached that afforded to children in other homesteads featured in the article. We had a multi-room house with various light and heating sources, rugs, suspended ceiling, picture windows, and a grass lawn bordering our lake. This was compared to the others who barely survived on a diet of rice, beans and whatever meat supply they could find. The other children did not have medical and dental care, except in cases of severe injury. They all did home schooling like Michael and David.

You had to be very independent to live on a homestead. There was no one to hold your hand if you got lonely, something needed to be repaired or built, or if you got sick or injured. You handled it yourself. I never got lonely, so that was never a problem for me, or Michael or David. If we needed something, I built it. If it broke, I fixed it. Sharon handled medical problems and schooling. A teacher from Tanana would fly in twice a month to check on the kids' school work and provide the needed books and supplies. I flew and guided Glenn Straatsma and Bob Jordan, physicians in Fairbanks, in exchange for treatment of medical problems.

The silence of the far north was a real problem for some people who moved to Alaska. Away from civilization, the silence was so loud it really bothered people used to some type of noise in their life, whether it was from traffic, radio, other people, or other sounds of city life. I loved the solitude and silence, and would sometimes stop what I was doing to just appreciate the big, wonderful, quiet world I inhabited. Sometimes the lack of noise was so great that, in the middle of winter, the cracking of the lake-ice as it expanded sounded like shots from a rifle. It was loud enough to wake out of a deep sleep. Most of all, I loved lying in my bed at night, watching my private showing of northern lights as they performed their delicate ballet just for me and my family, lighting up the entire sky with ever changing, colorful movements.

* * *

Sharon and I met Dr. Glenn Straatsma during the Fairbanks flood of 1967, while I was at the University of Alaska getting my teaching degree. I had been helping Don Roberts sandbag his house to protect it from the rising waters of the Chena River. Done with that, I met Sharon at a local grade school where she was helping to organize medical treatment for people being displaced by the rising waters of the Tanana and Chena Rivers. The shelter mainly housed Native Athabaskans, Aleuts and Eskimos who were living on the streets of Fairbanks or visiting friends in town. Many of the displaced Natives in the shelter were alcoholics, and in various stages of intoxication.

Sharon expressed her concern to me that this would become a serious issue. No more alcohol was available, as the city was rapidly going underwater. I told her to bring it to the attention of whomever was administering the shelter. I was shocked to learn there was no one in charge. No one from Red Cross, City, County, State, or the school itself was inside the school to run and provide for the people in the shelter.

I took control and became responsible for managing the fast-developing crisis. I immediately ordered that all containers in the kitchen be filled with water, and the toilets bagged with plastic sacks. I left all drinking fountains on, not knowing if the water was contaminated or how long they would flow, with instructions to Sharon and written on the fountains to immediately report any instance of diarrhea. My experience in the Aleutians taught me that we needed water before anything else. I figured we could boil it later if need be.

Glenn's house was underwater, so he had come to the nearest shelter to offer his assistance. When Sharon brought him up to introduce us, I could have hugged him. He immediately became our Medical Director.

Between Sharon, Glenn and I, we got people settled for the night as much as possible without the beds, sleeping bags or other conveniences you would expect a shelter to have. Most of those housed in the school were from the bush and used to living under harsh conditions, so there were few complaints.

Later that evening when things quieted, we discussed what was needed to run the shelter. Food was the prime concern, followed in order by sleeping bags, clothing and alcohol. The National Guard and other emergency agencies arrived the next day. They told me the Red Cross was setting up a distribution station at the Fairbanks International Airport for emergency supplies. The previous evening an Aleut had arrived at the shelter in a river boat. I talked to him about using his boat to get supplies from the Red Cross. He agreed, as long as he was the boat driver. I dispensed him and Sharon to the Red Cross at the airport to get some badly needed food and supplies.

They returned a few hours later, stating the Red Cross had refused to give them anything unless everyone signed a statement that they would reimburse the Red Cross at a later date or made a $50 donation. I was stunned. Going to the Red Cross myself, I demanded to meet the person in charge. I was introduced to a gentleman who seemed much more interested in erecting fences and storing the food and supplies arriving by air than hearing my concerns. He eventually provided me with a stack of Red Cross donation papers for people to sign, as well as an official Red Cross requisition book. He told me to return the following day with the signed document, and he would then authorize release of the emergency supplies I was requesting. Informing him that most of the residents of the shelter were penniless indigents living on the streets of downtown Fairbanks did not move him at all. If I wanted Red Cross supplies, I needed to return with the signed documents tomorrow.

This was my first dealing with the Red Cross. I do not know if this was a universal Red Cross practice, or a once-in-a-lifetime situation. It certainly changed my perception of the renowned organization forever.

Returning to the shelter empty-handed, I met with Dr. Straatsma. He explained DTs were becoming a problem for many of the shelter's residents, due to the rapid withdrawal of alcohol. Looking at the Red Cross requisition book in my hand, I signed several requisitions and gave them to Sharon, telling her to take the boat and find the nearest liquor store still on dry land, and get a boat load of whiskey. She returned an hour later with fifteen cases of whiskey, some of it pretty high-end stuff. She did not find a store on dry land, but she did find one partly underwater whose owner was busy loading his products into his own boat to save as much as possible. He was more than happy to take the Red Cross requisition.

One problem was solved, but food, clothing and bedding were still needed. I decided a midnight invasion of the Red Cross stockpile at the airport was indicated. I recruited three fit Native men staying at the shelter. I explained we would wait until everyone at the Red Cross compound was asleep, then cut a hole in the back fence farthest away from where people were sleeping, and steal what we needed. They were more than happy to help, as they had fathers, mothers, wives and children sleeping on hard floors. The food in the school cafeteria was running out and needed replenishing quickly. The boat owner took us as close to the airport as possible. The other four of us jumped overboard and started swimming the boat to shallower ground. After cutting a hole in the back fence, we proceeded to locate and load what we needed. It took three trips back and forth from the school before we had enough to last us through the duration of the flood.

Our DT problem was solved when Glenn set up a distribution location for those people who needed alcohol to prevent violence or medical issues. We passed out sleeping bags and clothing, and restocked the cafeteria with food. I did not know what to expect from the Red Cross, but the following day a Red Cross nurse showed up. I tried to be gracious and kind to her. In turn she was defiantly unfriendly. A day before I would gladly have given her control of the shelter, but after my encounter with others of her kind and their expectations of donations, I assigned her to work under the direction of Sharon and Dr. Straatsma. She was not happy, but acquiesced to my directions. It was not long before I got complaints from families who brought the Red Cross contracts to me, saying the nurse demanded they sign papers of subsequent donations to the Red Cross before she would provide treatment. After tearing up the contracts I went down to the nurse and explained we would force no one to sign the contracts before rendering aid or service.

She was livid. She told me she had represented the Red Cross in over twenty disasters around the world, and had never seen a shelter run in such a negligent manner. Furthermore, when this disaster ended, she would report me to the national office of the Red Cross for theft and buying liquor with their requisitions. I offered her a boat ride to the airport so she could make her complaints in person. She gladly took me up on the offer but returned later, somewhat subdued, to continue her work in the shelter.

She would never forgive me, and later wrote a long detailed letter to the national office. Red Cross sent me a letter months later, asking if the charges were true. I wrote back telling them that they were, and why I had acted as I had. I never heard back from them. We were at the shelter for over a week before the water began to recede and normalcy returned to Fairbanks. During the flood our shelter became the most popular meeting site for government officials responding to the flood, as we had the only open bar in town.

The one lasting friend I did make during the flood was Glenn Straatsma. I would later take him hunting and fishing. In return, he gave medical treatment to our family. We would frequently stay in his house when going to Fairbanks on trips lasting more than a day. So it was not unusual when, ten years after the flood, in the fall of 1977, he asked if I would take him and a friend out for a moose hunt. I told him I would be happy to do so when the hunting season arrived.

The second full summer at our homestead was quiet and peaceful. The pike we planted the year before became common table fare. I noticed lots of baby pike in the shallow water around the lake's edge. The pike were proliferating in the lake, so the main problem would be food for this voracious predator. The pike ate the whitefish we planted almost as soon as they hit the water. I guess we should have planted the food source before the predator. A biologist I was not.

* * *

Bill flew over to Stultz Lake and asked if I would fly his small canoe into Becky Lake. I explained all the problems I had had flying mine. Bill stated his canoe was much smaller, and that our friend, Hank, was letting us borrow his Aeronica Sedan for the trip.

Hank and his wife were in Hawaii for a vacation and had agreed to let Bill use his airplane if I did the flying. The Sedan was the big brother of my first airplane. It was a four-place airplane, much larger and more stable than my Citabria. There were 561 of them produced between 1948 and 1951. I had never flown a Sedan, but they were a common Alaskan bush plane. Hank's Sedan was on floats, so there was a place to tie the canoe. I knew from watching it perform during my prior hunt with TD that it would probably be able to handle a small canoe.

I agreed to do the flying. You may know the saying, "There are old pilots and bold pilots, but no old bold pilots." Unfortunately, I had achieved the unpleasant ranking of a bold pilot. Smarter people contacted me to do their difficult flying. I was dumb enough to do it.

Bill and I flew in his PA-12 to Fairbanks to get Hank's Sedan. Getting into the pilot's seat of the Sedan I started the engine and reviewed the instruments on the dash. There was nothing there I was unfamiliar with. Taking off, I got a feel for the airplane as we left the Fairbanks float pond for Nenana to get the canoe. I liked the feel of the old girl as we plowed through the air at a stately 90 mph. It was not fast or fancy, just a solid old airplane built for rough handling. At Nenana we tied the canoe on, and took off down the Tanana River for Becky Lake. The flight was uneventful. The airplane hardly felt the canoe on the flight, and soon we were untying the canoe at Becky Lake.

After pulling the canoe up onto shore we, took off and headed back to Fairbanks. I was enjoying the flight as the winds picked up and started tossing us around. The Sedan's big wings caught every updraft and downdraft as we bucked toward Nenana. There was a solid line of thunder showers and lightning between us and Nenana that was causing the havoc. We were really being knocked around in the air when the airplane engine died.

There was no advance warning; the engine just quit. Bill looked around for a place to land while I applied carburetor heat, pumped the gas control, and tried to find the reason for the engine failure. Bill yelled to me there was a small lake behind us big enough to land on. I turned back toward, it letting the nose of the Sedan drop to keep up airspeed, as I fought the wind and turbulence. Nearing the ground, I could see we were being blown sideways by 50 mph winds. Sixty feet from the ground I quickly turned us into the wind, knowing if I touched down on the lake we would wreck. Bill yelled at me, "No! Land on the lake," as the Sedan floats hit rough tundra. I had kept enough airspeed through our journey to the ground that I was able to lift the nose of the sedan just before we hit. That and the heavy winds created by the thunder clouds slowed our forward progress enough that it was a fairly benign landing for a crash.

Bill was mad. He berated me for not landing on the lake. Getting agitated at his behavior, I asked him if he even bothered to look at the ground as we neared it. After he replied no, I explained to him why I had landed on the tundra. The violent winds were pushing us well over a hundred miles an hour when combined with our airspeed. The small pond he wanted me to land on was too small to attempt to land at our speed. Not only that, but the wind was blowing us sideways as well. I explained that if I had tried to land where he wanted we would have destroyed Hank's airplane and maybe our lives as well. Bill was making a classic mistake that killed many pilots with engine failures—trying to land where he wanted instead where the airplane and conditions would allow.

We got out and examined the airplane after setting off our emergency locater beacon. The only damage was a single float strut wire that had snapped. Climbing back into the Sedan out of the wind, Bill stewed to himself until the Civil Air Patrol out of Fairbanks flew over us, answering our emergency beacon. They complimented me on my successful landing on the tundra, saying they had seen many airplanes wrecked and pilots killed trying to do so. After telling us a helicopter would be dispatched to pick us up, they circled a few times then headed back to Fairbanks.

Bill began to see I was right to land where I had after the Civil Air departure. He asked me how I had made the decisions I had, and how I kept us from crashing. I explained the wind again, and the low stall speed of the Sedan touching down softly on the rough ground with the aid of fifty mph headwind versus landing downwind at over 100 mph in a quartering tail crosswind. How one would have crashed us into the trees bordering the small pond while the other allowed us to walk away unscathed. Again, Dad's upbringing and my subsequent flight training allowed me to keep my wits under difficult circumstances.

When the thunderstorms passed, we got out to see how we could get the airplane off the tundra. There was no way to take off from the tundra itself, so we walked over to the small lake Bill had wanted me to land on earlier. It was only about a half mile away. I figured if we took everything out of the Sedan we could power and push it back to the lake after replacing the broken strut wire. I was surprised to see that the small slough I had made an emergency landing on when flying paneling several summers ago was also within a half mile of our landlocked seaplane. We made plans to get the part we needed and come back out to land on the slough with our personal aircraft. The small pond was not big enough for all the airplanes.

The helicopter out of Eielson Air Force Base picked us up a short while later, dropping us off at Fairbanks. Hank and his wife returned from Hawaii the following day. The front page of the Anchorage newspaper he was reading featured a colored picture of his airplane sitting on the tundra. The paper explained that the airplane had experienced an engine failure and crashed on the tundra outside of Nenana. The Civil Air Patrol had taken the picture and given it to the newspapers. Hank was pretty upset until after he landed at Fairbanks and found we were all right, and there was only minor damage to his airplane.

Neither Bill nor I could figure out why the engine quit. There was no obvious damage to it. We restarted the engine about two hours after we made the emergency landing. It ran fine. There was no oil leakage nor was there any foreign material in the gas line filter. The gas gauges registered a quarter full. It did not make any sense, until Hank told us that the Sedan had rubber gas tanks that could decompress and shut off the fuel to the engine under extreme turbulence and air pressure changes. That fit our circumstances at the time of the engine failure. Most Sedan owners had converted to metal gas tanks because of it. Hank had not. He said he would in the future, if we could get his airplane home.

In the following days all three of us discussed getting the Sedan over to the lake. Bill and I flew our separate airplanes with Hank in the back of mine and landed on the small slough bordering the stranded Sedan.

We took all weight except the pilot's seat out of the Sedan, and drained all the remaining gas into the empty gas cans we had brought along for this purpose. We added five gallons of fuel back in before I powered up the engine. Hank asked me to be the pilot while he and Bill pushed on the floats. It took us a little over an hour before the floats were resting on the small pond's surface. I was in good shape as I sat inside, adding and reducing power while moving the control wheel back and forth. The same could not be said of Hank and Bill.

They were both sweaty and dirty by the time we got the airplane to the pond. Blasts of air from me gunning the engine blew dirt and grass, coating their hair, faces and clothes. Resting on the bank of the pond with the first phase of our plan successfully completed, we discussed flying the Sedan out. Hank wanted me to do the favors. I balked. I did not have much time flying it and figured Hank should do the flying as he was much more familiar with the aircraft. Besides, he was the owner. The pond was small, no more than 500 to 600 feet long, counting the shallows. There was no wind and the temperature was around 75 degrees. We could not get the Sedan into the slough where Bill's and my airplanes were parked because of the steep banks.

Finally, I relented, telling Hank I would try to fly it out expressing all the concerns I had. I asked him point-blank if he wanted me to just try to get it off the pond, or go for broke. Explaining to Hank that if I went for broke and held the airplane on the water to the last second, it would crash into the trees if it did not fly. Hank said he understood, and to go for broke. Here was that old/bold pilot thing again. Shaking my head, wondering how I allowed myself to get into such predicaments, I climbed into the pilot's seat.

We pulled the back of the airplane onto as much ground as possible. I had Bill and Hank hold onto the tail as I gave the Sedan full power. They released the tail when the engine reached maximum rpm. I had only flown this airplane off the water twice. When it did not immediately get on step as we left shore and seemed to be dragging in the water, I was really concerned. The shoreline was rushing toward me before I felt the floats begin the rotation onto step.

The shore filled my windshield. The airspeed indicator was still not registering flying speed when I ran out of water and jerked back as hard as I could on the control wheel. The old airplane shuddered and just got airborne as I crossed over the shore line toward the trees 200 feet ahead. The airspeed indicator was still not registering flying speed. I was flying on the compressed air between the wings and the ground, and not on lift generated by the curvature of the wings. Knowing I could not climb above the trees, I used the rudders to angle toward a small opening between them, hoping it was bigger than the span of my wings. It was so close I could not tell if one or both of my wings would hit trees until I was on the other side, flying over the tundra.

Slowly the airspeed indicator began to register, and I gently climbed into the air. Landing on the slough a few minutes later, I was greeted by my smiling friends who had thought for sure I was going to crash twice. Once on takeoff, and the second time, getting through the trees. Bill said he did not know how the airplane flew, as it had never really got on step. I don't know how it flew either. It surprised the hell out of me. I think the old girl was just making up for trying to kill us in the storm.

Life at Stultz Lake

WHEN GLENN STRAATSMA CONTACTED ME during the fall of our first full year at Stultz Lake about moose hunting, he said he wanted to bring a friend along as well. This was no surprise, as my passion for hunting and flying led me to guide many of my friends. The man Glenn asked to bring along was Dr. Bob Jordan, who was also a physician at Glenn's Medical Clinic in Fairbanks. He was a pediatrician and, following this hunt, would provide pediatric care for Michael and David.

They both said they wanted to hunt moose. At the time, no one hunted the Melozitna River, so I figured it was a good place to take them. I had seen many moose along the river while hunting wolves there. The Natives in Ruby feared that Big Foot lived along the river, so stayed away. The problem was to find a safe place close to the river where I could land and fly out heavy loads. The Melozitna is a narrow tree-lined stream, so the river itself presented some problems. There were places to land on the river, but I wanted to be out of the current and in the protection of a slough.

I located a U-shaped slough. It was smaller than I would have liked. I could only land and take off in one direction because tall pine trees lined three sides. I could get the airplane on step on one arm of the slough, ski around the corner and then take off on the other arm. It was also advantageous that the Melozitna Valley narrowed there, making any animals traveling up and down river accessible to hunting from camp. Small rapids right above camp allowed hunters to wade across the river itself.

I had Glenn and Bob drive to Nenana, where I picked them up. It would take two trips to get both supplies and people into the camp. That evening, as fog rose from the cooling river, we sat around a comfortable fire discussing the next day's hunt over glasses of good scotch. We decided that I would fly one of them out of camp to search for moose while the other hunted around the camp on foot.

The following morning, after a hearty breakfast and strong hot coffee, I flew Bob down river. It was not long before we spotted a nice bull moose about a quarter mile off of the river, feeding in a small lake. Telling Bob not to shoot the moose in the lake but wait until it was on dry land, I landed and let him out onto a small gravel bar. I then flew back to camp to help Glenn, figuring Bob could handle shooting the animal by himself. Moose are easy to hunt so I did not see any problems, as Bob had said he was an experienced hunter.

Glenn had only seen a cow moose with a calf around camp, so we both got back into the airplane. Guiding Glenn to a bull up river, we made a short stalk on it before he put it down with one shot. The rest of the morning and a good part of the afternoon was spent getting the meat to the airplane and hanging it up back at camp. It was around 3 p.m. when I took off to find Bob. I had expected him to shoot his moose and pack it to the gravel bar where I had left him. He was not there.

I spotted him two miles below where I had left him, about a half mile off the river. I flew low over and motioned him back to the river. When we got together, Bob explained that he had wounded the bull and it had run off. He was trying to track the animal down. It was getting late into the afternoon. I did not want Bob, a person I barely knew, wandering alone in the fast approaching dark. He was also exhausted and dehydrated from a day of walking over tundra searching for the moose. I told him to get in and we would look for the moose from the air.

Taking off, we searched the entire area where Bob had shot at the moose from the air. By the time dark closed in and we could not see to search any more, I was convinced the moose was not hindered by injury, and headed back toward camp. I soon saw the reflection of a large camp fire among the pines lining the river and began a turn to land.

It was a dark cloudy night with no light from the moon. There was also fog coming off the river, so I assumed the slough would be foggy as well. I could not see it but knew from the gap in the trees where it was located. I debated with myself whether or not to use landing lights, as visibility would be further reduced if there was fog on the water. Finally, I decided I needed to see the opening in the trees and could shut off the lights if I encountered fog.

Flipping the switch for landing lights, I saw a brief flash of light followed by darkness. Re-flipping the switch did no good. The landing lights had burned out. I added power and climbed above the fast approaching trees. I needed to be very careful in my landing, as there was no go-around. Once I committed I had to land in whatever was ahead of me. Heading the airplane at the gap in the trees I hoped was the slough opening, I set up for an instrument landing. Landing in a dark hole is unnerving at night. You cannot tell water from dry land, as many Alaskan pilots found to their dismay while their wheeled aircraft sank below the watery surface of what they had thought was a dry landing strip, but was in reality a wet float pond beside the runway.

Setting my doubts aside, I descended between two dark lines of trees. I had to land quickly before the slough made a U-turn. The jar of the floats hitting the water much harder than normal did not bother me, as it would have under normal circumstances. I held the nose of the airplane up in the subsequent bounce off the water and reduced power. It was going to be a real stall landing. After contacting the slough's surface again in a spray of white water, I was soon trying to keep my wingtips out of trees I could barely see, as we slowly taxied toward the campfire reflecting through the dark trees.

The next day Bob and I again unsuccessfully searched for the moose he thought he had wounded. There was no blood or hair at the spot the animal had been standing when he had fired. From Bob's description of the animal's behavior after he pulled the trigger, I thought instead of suffering a wounding shot, the moose had merely reacted to the loud noise and a bullet narrowly missing it or grazing its hair. By the time darkness fell that evening, Bob had really shot a moose and it was hanging in camp alongside Glenn's.

I had developed a reputation among people who knew me as a competent and successful hunter. A reputation that was built on the fact no one I took out hunting came home without meat or a good shot at the animal being hunted. They told their friends, and requests for guided hunts came in faster than I wanted or anticipated. Within a year I had requests from people who wanted me to take them hunting, from across the nation and overseas. All from word of mouth. I had never advertised my availability for guided hunts. I had decisions to make. Was I going to take the test to become a licensed guide? Was I going to hire additional assistant guides to help me handle the number of requests I was receiving?

I finally decided I would not receive fair treatment from Fish and Game if I pursued the licensed guide route. All I would accomplish would be letting them know I was guiding hunters for hire. If I did not get a guide's license, I would be taking hunters out for money illegally. I finally decided

I did not want anyone else involved in this illegal operation. What began as a love of hunting and seeing my friends getting the meat and trophies they wanted had evolved into a serious business. The knowledge that I was on a collision course with Fish and Game enforcement did not bring doubts, but a small smile to my face. I had been taking hunters out for over a decade, free of charge. Now it was time to get some of those expenses back.

* * *

I had also earned additional income from my airplane by flying supplies and mail to homesteaders in this area of Alaska, as well as from trapping and wolf hunting. The Carlsons lived on a homestead about ten miles away from us on Wilderness Lake with their four kids. Bill and Becky Spear lived about the same distance away on Becky Lake. Bill and Becky had moved off their homestead full time, and Bill was now working in Nenana as the School District's business manager, only spending weekends at Becky Lake. We visited the Carlson family the most, as Michael and David loved playing with the kids. There were other families within a sixty-mile radius. As word of mouth got out, I was soon flying for them as well. A normal charter service out of Fairbanks cost $1,200. I would provide the same service for $400. Also, I would pick up their mail free from Nenana and deliver it to them. Many times these homesteaders did not have the cash for a trip so I would provide the service for an unneeded rifle, sewing machine, water pump or other items that I often did not need, but my accepting them made both parties feel better.

That year as Christmas approached, Michael told me the Carlson kids did not get presents as their Mom and Dad were too poor to afford them. Sharon and I decided that we could become the flying Santa Claus for bush families with children. That Easter we also became the flying Easter Bunny. Michael and David would wrap presents and tie long sections of surveyor's tape onto them. We'd fly over the homesteads and drop the presents from the air when someone would hear the engine and come outside to investigate. I did not want to land to give the gifts, as this might embarrass the parents. Besides, Michael and David loved dropping them from the air.

The first year, the kids receiving these gifts or candy did not know what was going on. We hardly saw them when flying over and dropping the gifts. It did not take long, however, before the sound of my airplane engine brought kids running from their cabins without properly dressing for the cold to receive these gifts from the air. It was Sharon's and my way of giving back something to our neighbors who did not have the resources we enjoyed.

*   *   *

When I was not flying there was wood to chop, haul and stack. The Yukon stove took about eight cords of wood a winter to keep us warm, as the fire was never allowed to go out. The only time to efficiently accomplish wood gathering for me was during the winter. I had an Otter fly in my two snow machines, an oil stove, and fifty gallon barrels of gas as soon as the ice was thick enough to support the large aircraft's weight. My wood source was half a mile away across the lake. In the spring, I would ring the trees that I wanted to use for the next winter's wood. The tree would die and start drying out while upright. When winter set in, I drove a snow machine over to the dead trees to cut down and drag to the cabin. The boys would do the stacking while I cut and split.

Water was gathered each day as well. This was Michael and David's job. The water hole in the five feet of winter ice covering the lake had to be reopened each morning before all five feet solidly refroze. The boys would cover the water hole after getting the thirty gallons of water we used each day. Michael would do 95 percent of the work while David pretended to be helping. I had flown in a washer and dryer, so on wash days the kids had to bring sixty gallons of water for Sharon to use washing our clothes.

David also provided some excitement for us later that winter when a ball he was playing with rolled underneath our propane stove. Despite my yelling at him to stop, he pulled the lit stove up, reaching under it for his ball, severing the propane line. The resultant ball of flame erupting into his face caused screams from everyone in the house while I ran frantically outside to shut the propane off. The house did not burn down, thankfully. You would have thought David had learned about the dangers of fire after he put a can of Off insect repellant in a propane portable oven we used during the construction of the house. He wanted to see what would happen when it exploded. It did explode after Sharon lit the stove to cook dinner. Sharon's hands, face and hair suffered painful damage while part of the tent burned before I could put out the fire. Maybe my sister was partially correct saying I was troublesome growing up. Whatever deviltry gene I had, David inherited it in spades.

We had five separate trap lines to operate. The boys had their own short line near the house, where they mainly caught marten. Michael also had a mink line around the lake. One day as I was landing after flying to Fairbanks for supplies and mail for a neighbor, I saw him kneeling at one of his mink traps. I could not tell what was going on with him, but it was odd, so I taxied over and jumped out. He had caught a mink that was still alive. The mink got out of the trap just as Mike grabbed to kill it. The vicious animal was biting and scratching Michael's ungloved hands in its attempt to regain its freedom. It was a battle of wills. Michael was just as determined to keep his prize as it was to escape. I was proud of him. Not many people have the intestinal fortitude to hold on to an angry mink with bare hands. Later that evening, after his mom had tended to his injuries, I carefully guided him through the process of skinning his mink, and showed him how to put it on a fur stretcher to dry.

Both of my boys showed a lot of courage and tenacity while living in the bush of Alaska. Michael's efforts were more visible, as he was the eldest. David had the same Stultz traits of being stubborn, resilient and resourceful. How they accomplished things was completely different. Michael was thoughtful, and studied situations before fully committing himself. David's approach was to jump in head first and damn the consequences. Take their approach to driving a snowmobile. After the Otter delivered the snow machines to us on Stultz Lake, I decided to take the boys out on the lake for a lesson in how to safely start and drive them. I had made a trail around the lake for them to follow. We were using the smaller snowmobile I had bought for Sharon to use around the homestead while I was out on the more powerful one getting wood or trapping.

Both machines were idling on the lake as I explained the throttle and brake operations. I had intended for them to take turns on the small machine until they got comfortable. Michael got on the lower powered one and was slowly making his way around the path I had made. I heard the larger one's engine suddenly revving up. I looked behind me to see David grinning as he gave it full power and took off, until hitting a tree at the end of the lake stopped him. They each had parts of my personality. The Michael part would figure out how to accomplish a task like safely flying plywood on floats. The David part would tie flimsy paneling on the floats and damn the consequences.

They had a great life on the homestead. It taught them self-reliance, and that hard work was rewarded. Their school lessons were the same as any student's in Alaska. The difference was they did not have to sit in a classroom for eight hours. When they completed the daily lessons, they got to go out on their trap line or play on the snowmobile.

I had a rifle range for sighting in my guns right next to the cabin. I would use it to sight in our weapons at the beginning of each year. Usually it took more ammunition to sight them in than to down all the Alaskan game animals we lived on. The boys learned to shoot there, as well as to handle weapons safely. All guns in the house were loaded for instant use, as Toklat had the disturbing trait of chasing bears. When the bears got tired of Toklat's game the tide would change, and the bears chased Toklat. Being no fool, Toklat would bring the enraged bears back to the homestead. More than once I heard Toklat's chasing bark turn to one of a frightened yelp, and then silence. The kids knew when this happened to drop whatever they were doing and get safely in the house behind a closed door. Toklat was on his own unless I could shoot the bears. I shot three bears chasing Toklat while we lived at the homestead, and another five that wandered around the lake onto our property. Many other times his barking would let us know bears were nearby so we could get into the house and let them wander away. The only time I shot them was when the bears were endangering property or lives.

When trapping or hunting close to the homestead, I would take the boys with me. One winter morning while looking at a series of long lakes to trap beaver, I found a bear hibernation hole. It was close enough to the homestead that it could have been the black bear that was causing havoc when we left the homestead for any period of time. It would never show up when we were in residence, but was smart enough to come around when we all departed for some time in town. It had eaten part of my snowmobile seat and caused other minor damage.

When I found the bear hole, I decided to shoot the animal inside it. Waking a hibernating bear is not easy. I tried shoving a burning rag tied to a limb down the hole, but could not get it far enough down the hole to wake the bear. I decided to crawl down the hole, with the burning brand in one hand and my pistol in the other, to wake and shoot the bear. Michael thought this was decidedly uncool and tried to prevent me from doing so. David thought it was a grand idea.

I wrapped a rope around my waist to tie around the bear after I had shot it so we could pull it out with the snowmobile after it was dead. After stationing the boys on the running machine pointed down the trail toward the homestead with instruction to leave if the bear got past me, I crawled into the small hole. I could hear the bear growling and could see far enough ahead of me by the flickering flame to shoot if it came toward me. Unfortunately, the tunnel rose and then dropped sharply downward again in a narrow constriction I could not pass. Finally, the smoke from the oil and gas-soaked rag got to me instead of the bear. I had to back out, gasping for breath and coughing. I shoved the burning rag as far down the hole as I could before backing out. I stood away from the bear hole after exiting, waiting for the smoke to chase the bear out as well. I could hear growling and other noises inside the den, but the bear never came out.

Living there made teaching the boys safe gun practices mandatory. They had to learn to shoot one proficiently, and how to care for it, as well. Guns are only a dangerous tool if a fool, criminal, or unschooled person is mishandling them. Neither the boys nor I ever experienced a problem with weapons, even though they were always loaded. The kids each had .22 rifles. They received ten shells for their weapons each week. If they shot a squirrel, which I used for marten bait, they got an additional five shells. Voles and small rodents netted them two shells. Limiting their ammunition and rewarding only successful shots taught them to shoot carefully and straight.

Toklat had another disturbing habit. He hated porcupines. How such an intelligent animal could consistently be so stupid was beyond me. He would come whimpering back to the homestead after a porcupine encounter with his face and mouth littered with embedded quills. The painful removal of quills with their barbed tips never stopped him from trying to eat the next porcupine he saw. The same was true of ducks on the lake during the summer. He would swim after them for hours while the ducks would let him get just close enough to think he had a chance before swimming thirty feet away again. Finally, the exhausted dog would struggle back to our lawn and helplessly watch the ducks swim in the distance. Toklat never learned, as the next day he was at it again. Never, in hundreds of hours of swimming, did he ever get a duck snack.

Toklat would also run ahead of me while I drove the larger snowmobile up the trap line. This line was fifty miles long. It ended at a Chet's cabin twenty-five miles away before curving back to the homestead. We would spend the night in this cabin after a long, cold, grueling day on the trail before heading back home. If the weather turned bad, we would stay at the cabin until it cleared. Chet did not use the cabin during the winter and had given me permission to use it after I flew supplies and parts for him when he brought his Nodwell, a large rugged all-terrain vehicle used by oil companies and others to cross wilderness areas without roads, overland to his homestead several summers before.

Chet was a mechanical genius who invented the Warren Hub to lock the front wheel on four-wheel drive vehicles when he worked for Nodwell He was an older, portly gentleman who always wore grease stained coveralls and had a smile on his face. His birthday occurred during the overland journey from where the barge company dropped his Nodwell off on the banks of the Tanana River to his homestead, a rough thirty-mile journey over irregular virgin hills and creeks. I would fly out and check on Chet once a day during the trip. We communicated by aircraft radio. If he was broken down or needed something, I would fly into Fairbanks to get it for him. I could not land on the wild terrain he was traversing so had to drop what was needed from the air. When Sharon told me it was Chet's birthday we decided to bake him a cake. After the cake cooled and was frosted, I debated how to get it to him. I mean, how does a cake survive after being dropped a hundred feet from an airplane flying sixty mph? It doesn't! Finally deciding the thought and the taste of jumbled cake and frosting would have to be enough, I put the cake in a plastic container tightly wrapped shut with duct tape.

Loading Michael and David into the airplane, we took off in search of Chet and his Nodwell. Following a trail of broken trees and mud-churned tundra caused by the Nodwell, we found Chet parked in a small clearing working on his machine. He looked up as I flew over and waved. Answering his call on the radio I told Chet I was dropping something fragile for him. As we flew over a third time David shoved the cake with its tail of surveyor's tape out the window. We flew overhead until Chet got the package open. I could see a huge smile on his face as he took his first bite of the disorderly mess and waved goodbye to us.

All snow machines came with an evil demon embedded deeply within them. They never broke down at home or close to housing. Mine would always break a belt or have problems right in the middle of my line, making me walk back to Stultz Lake for parts if I could not fix it. A broken belt or bad spark plug was easily fixed, only resulting in painfully cold hands. Track, carburetor and engine issues were a whole different ballgame. Five times I had to walk over twelve miles through deep snow to get parts for broken machines that could just as well have acted up before I started out. But no, my snow machines had that evil mind and dark disposition.

Sled dogs were much more reliable. You could cuddle them on cold nights for warmth or eat them if you were hungry. The only drawbacks were that you had to feed them twelve months of the year, and they pooped all over. They also made a lot of noise, so I chose to use a snow machine instead.

Toklat ran ahead of me on the trail, and let me know if anything was in the next trap. He got his foot caught in one once, and never forgot that painful experience. He would bark at the trapped animal, which was usually dead, as I approached. He was a completely fearless dog that would attack anything alive. One day he started barking at the next trap and headed behind a tree where a cubby set was located. I was extremely surprised when he let out a yelp of fear and bolted back down the trail past me as fast as he could, with his ears pinned flat to his head. I knew something dangerous was in the trap or close by. It turned out to be a wolverine, but it did show he had some sense.

Wolverine are a relatively small animal weighting only thirty to sixty pounds. They were one of the few animals in Alaska that deserved their nasty reputation. They are mean, strong and extremely intelligent. They will chew their toes or foot off to get out of a trap if left in it long enough. If they escaped they could ruin the whole trap line by running from trap to trap, eating the bait and animals caught in them without setting the traps off.

I had a wolverine get out of one of my traps that made me abandon that line for the rest of the winter. Snares or traps freshly boiled and cleaned to remove any scent were avoided with ease, even if they were placed in the middle of the snow machine trail without getting off the machine and leaving human tracks and scent. I even tried a shotgun trap, with the trigger tied to a set line across the trail. Nothing worked. The wolverine tracks would run down the middle of my trail only to stop within ten feet of whatever kind of trap I had set. The animal would then circumvent the trap and go on to munch on the next bait or animal. It drove me crazy to think an animal was smarter than I was. The wolverine had the last laugh, as I abandoned the line and gave up in frustration.

I caught many more wolves and wolverine on my airplane trap line than the ones originating out at Stultz Lake. I used two kinds of traps there. One was an empty fifty-gallon gas barrel with one end cut out. I would put the bait in the back of the barrel and use a Conibear trap on the open end. This kind of a trap was much more humane, as it killed the animal immediately. The drawbacks were their cost and their extreme danger to the trapper. The traps were so powerful they could easily break a trapper's limb if he made one bad move while arming them. Being caught in a larger Conibear was life threatening. I was always extremely careful and nervous when using them.

The other traps I used for wolves and wolverine were cubby sets, made by constructing a small den and placing a normal jawed trap at the entrance, with the bait inside. Instead of attaching the trap to a stationary tree I always attached it to a cut log about ten feet long and five inches thick. Wolves would stay close to where they were caught, but wolverine would tear up everything for acres when trapped. I could see when I caught a wolverine from miles away by the torn-up terrain. The ten-foot log would often be chewed down to a sliver.

I can't say I enjoyed trapping. Using anything but a Conibear trap was cruel. The animals suffered, and many times froze to death. The fact that the animal being trapped was also a predator and cruel to his prey was no solace for me. However, it was one of the few ways to make money to support yourself and your family in the bush. It was like cleaning a toilet: an unpleasant but necessary chore.

*   *   *

In January Bill Spear landed at Stultz Lake. Over a cup of coffee Bill told me his meat supplies were getting low and wanted to know if I could go caribou hunting with him. I had just finishing clearing my longest trap lines of fallen trees from the latest batch of bad weather and only had wood cutting on my agenda for the rest of the week, so I told him sure. It was too late in the day, but we could leave first thing in the morning. Bill agreed to meet me at my lake an hour before sunrise in the morning. That would give us five hours to locate and shoot caribou prior to it getting dark again.

Taking off the following morning in the crystal-clear arctic air underneath a canopy of stars we flew over Moose Heart Mountain and headed toward Tanana. After that village passed under our wings we followed the Little Melozitna through the low hills to the rolling snow-covered plains beyond, where decent numbers of caribou could be found this deep into winter.

It is easy to see caribou tracks from a long distance away flying at 1,500 feet above the snow. We followed several such herds, but decided not to shoot any of the animals because of the large percentage of females. We could distinguish female from male caribou in January because the females still had antlers. They carry theirs long after the male antlers have dropped, to protect their calves from predators.

Bill called me on the radio after we crossed some wolf tracks, saying he had never shot a wolf and would like to try. I told Bill to drop back a quarter mile and follow me as I tracked them. It was easy to tell the direction they were heading, because wolves kick snow spray out to the side as they run. You cannot tell how many wolves are in a pack because they all step directly into the lead animal's tracks. Every once in a while, we would see a single wolf track veer to the side as the leader became fatigued and another pack member would take his place breaking trail.

I tracked this pack until we came upon a moose kill they had been feeding on for several days. Circling around the kill I saw six wolves resting in a large patch of willows digesting moose meat. I wagged my wings to let Bill know where the wolves were laying and dropped back behind his PA-12 so I could observe him. Bill would have to land first to shoot a wolf, but there was nowhere to land here, so he would have to get the wolves moving toward a clear area where he could land. I explained this to him as he buzzed the willows. The wolves did not budge. I asked Bill if he had a .22 pistol with him. When he came back on the radio and said no, I told him to climb to 2,000 feet and circle behind me while I got the wolves on their feet.

Getting my .22 Colt Woodsman out of the pocket of the airplane where I stored it, I circled in back of the wolves and fired three shots out my side window. The wolves immediately got to their feet and ran away from the direction of the shots. I herded the pack toward a clear ridge using this technique. When they were headed in the right way I dropped back and let Bill follow them. I told Bill when the wolves reached the next plateau to land just behind the pack and pick out one to shoot.

I watched the wolves crest the ridge with Bill about 500 yards behind. They continued straight toward a mountain peak half a mile ahead. Bill landed close to the end wolf and jumped out of his airplane with a rifle in his hand. I thought he was going to shoot a wolf, but Bill disappeared head first into the snow. He had tripped on the edge of the airplane's ski bending under the wing strut. By the time he gained his feet and cleared the snow from his eyes and rifle the wolves were long gone up the mountain. The wolves won this battle as they disappeared into the deep timber.

I landed beside my frustrated friend who filled the chilly air with hot profanity. He asked me as I waded through the deep snow toward him if there was any chance of going after them again. I said no, they were in deep timber and would not come out until we were long gone. Getting out thermoses of hot coffee and our lunches, we sat on a rock swept free of snow by the brisk wind and had a good laugh about his snow bath. I consoled Bill by telling him I could not count the number of times wolves had outsmarted me and gotten away.

Finishing our coffee and lunch we resumed our original goal of getting caribou. An hour later we had four caribou down. After dressing the animals out, Bill put the two he shot in the back of his airplane while I stored the final two in mine. We taxied back to our landing tracks to take off again in the deep snow and headed toward Tanana. I was concerned by how quickly ground fog was forming. By the time we reached Tanana, fog obscured the land below our wings. I called the Tanana Flight Service as we crossed over the airport to get the current weather forecast. They called back stating local pilots were reporting heavy icing and advised staying clear of clouds and layers of fog. They also reported that both Tanana and Nenana airports were closed due to icing and low visibility.

With rising anxiety Bill and I parted at Moose Heart Mountain to fly to our separate homesteads hoping the higher elevations of our houses would not yet be fogged over. I was disappointed five minutes later to see Stultz Lake and the surrounding countryside covered in thick clouds. Only the top of Stultz Mountain was visible. By looking at the mountain I could see the clouds were over a thousand feet thick. I called Bill on the radio to see if Becky Lake was clear, and received a reply back that he had a small opening in the ice fog and was attempting to land. Heading to Becky Lake intending to spend the night there, I arrived too late to take advantage of the small window of weather Bill had. He called me on the radio as I flew over telling me not to attempt a landing as his airplane accumulated over a quarter inch of ice getting through the small opening in the fog.

I left Becky Lake for Wien Lake, but that lake was completely fogged in as well. My gas gauges were too low to attempt flying to Nenana for an instrument landing with the aid of their guidance systems. Heading back to my homestead I set up for an instrument landing using Stultz Mountain as a guide. It was a crap-shoot with the odds heavily in favor of Mother Nature. I could only guess where my lake was located. The small lake was only 2,000 feet long and surrounded on three sides by trees and wooded hills. I would attempt my landing on the one open end so if the landing was short of the lake I would only have small brush and willows to contend with.

I had landed here a thousand times with the mountain visible and used those memories to set up for my descent. Slowing to 55 mph and pulling on forty-degrees of flaps I allowed my aircraft to sink into the liquid ice. Immediately my front windshield turned opaque with ice. Looking out the side window I could see the leading edges of my wings were also quickly accumulating a thick coating of ice. Pilots hate icing for good reason. It only takes a little bit of icing or frost to disrupt the flow of air over an aircraft's wings that allow it to stay in the air. You never know when one or both wings will quit flying. My altimeter had not reached half the altitude I needed to lose before coming into contact with the ground before it stopped functioning. My Pitot tube completely iced over, causing all my instruments besides my electric artificial horizon and compass to stop working.

Feeling a deep sense of dread creep into my body, I forced myself to breathe deeply and relax my hands and feet while I concentrated on my two remaining instruments. I had no idea of my airspeed or rate of descent. Relying only on the seat-of-my-pants feeling for my airplane, I continued down blind toward whatever fate awaited me to the sound of the propeller flinging off chunks of ice onto the side of the fuselage. I felt a faint nudge as my skis settled onto a snow-covered surface before I realized I had landed. All of the windows in the airplane were covered with a thick layer of ice preventing me from seeing outside. Not knowing where I was I shut off the engine, unfastened my seat belts and tried to get out, but both my door and side window were frozen shut. It took several minutes before I was able to force the door open and exit the airplane.

Looking at my airplane in the heavy fog, I saw that I had been flying wings of ice. Three inches of ice covered the leading edges and extended far back onto the cord of the wings. How they kept flying I had no idea. They should not have kept me in the air, and would not have much longer. Not seeing any brush, I hoped I was onto the frozen surface of Stultz Lake as I could only see several feet in any direction. Kicking the snow, I formed a hole in it to the surface below. It was ice. I was on my lake.

I undid the hinges of the airplane door to remove it and deposited it on top of the caribou so I would have some visibility when I restarted the engine. Hopping back into my pilot's seat, I used my electric compass to taxi toward the edge of the lake where my cabin was located. Shortly afterward, I saw indistinct shapes in the fog ahead and shut off the engine and electric system. Jumping out of the now-silent aircraft I could hear Sharon's voice yelling for me. I followed the frantic sounds of her voice into the arms of my frightened family who feared I had crashed and died in the fog. The cabin only became visible when we were within ten feet of it while following tracks in the snow back toward the warmth within. Taking off my ice-crusted outer clothes I allowed the breath I had been holding to escape. The boys had tears in their eyes as they hugged me. They knew as well as I did how close I had come to never reading or playing with them again. Two days later it took me five hours to eliminate the ice from my airplane. I used a blow torch attached to a five-gallon propane tank that I inserted into four-inch stove pipes to produce the heat necessary to remove it. The length of the stove pipes cooled the heat from the blow torch enough to avoid harming the fabric of the airplane while it melted the ice.

* * *

I received many request to guide fishermen during the summer months. I would rent myself and the airplane out by the day. The fisherman paid me a set wage for a day's guiding, and paid for the airplane by the amount of time we flew. They would choose where they wanted to fish by the type of fish they wanted to catch. Although expensive if we flew to Bristol Bay or down to Southeastern Alaska, is was still less expensive than staying at one of the well-known fishing lodges. It was also rustic and a real Alaskan experience, as we lived in tents and on supplies we could carry in the airplane. Some fishermen stayed at Stultz Lake if they wanted large northern pike. I would fly them out to areas off the Tanana River where I knew big pike hung out eating whitefish and grayling.

If I had more than one fisherman staying with us I would sometimes use Michael as a guide. The clients would look at me strangely when I mentioned Michael was going to guide them that day. Some of the dark expressions disappeared when I told them if they were not happy with Michael as a guide for any reason, they would not be charged for that day. Little did they know that Michael lived for fishing. It was his thing and he excelled at it. Not once did any fisherman he guided request a refund. They all marveled at his expertise at such a young age. At that time in his life, fishing did not interest David. He would later become an excellent fisherman in his own right, but back then he more enjoyed exploring his artistic talents.

The most memorable fishing guiding trip I had involved a coach from Wisconsin. I won't mention his name, as he was very well known. I will refer to him as Burt. Burt had stayed with us at the lake for periods of time over the past two summers. After a day of fishing, he loved to sit in a chair on our front lawn overlooking the lake, enjoying several glasses of excellent scotch and the beautiful scenery around him. I don't remember how many times he told us how lucky we were to be living there as he watched the ducks and swans swim on the lake's placid summer surface.

Burt told me one summer he wanted to see large bears the next year, and asked where we should go to do so. I explained that Bristol Bay was probably the best place for him to see big bears from the ground. Many of the rivers and streams had heavy salmon runs and large rainbow trout that bears ate, gaining weight for their winter hibernation. We agreed to schedule a trip to Bristol Bay the following summer.

When the time rolled around to guide Burt, I picked him up in the town of King Salmon, the closest airport to where we were going to fish. We flew down the Peninsula toward a stream I wanted to fish that emptied into Bristol Bay. We were late leaving King Salmon as his flight was delayed, so I landed on a small lake that had a good population of rainbow trout spawning in the outlet.

After setting up camp we walked to the outlet and spent several hours catching and releasing rainbows, only keeping two for dinner. Arriving back at camp, we saw that a bear had visited during our absence. It had tried, unsuccessfully, to reach our food supply tied high up in a tree, and taken out its frustrations by flattening the tent and leaving a big deposit of bear crap in the middle of it.

Burt's eyes were as big as the pile of poop in the middle of the tent as he took it all in. I reminded him he wanted to see bears up close and personal. I could see he was reconsidering his request. We cleaned up the mess and set the tent up again, but Burt's eyes were more on the surrounding brush than the job at hand. My favorite bear rifle for these excursions was my .444 Marlin. However, at night when camping in bear territory, I kept a twelve-gauge shotgun loaded with double 00 buckshot beside me in the tent. It was the most effective weapon for stopping a bear within twenty feet. My night encounters with bears were usually closer than that. Yet, I never had to shoot one at night when they entered my camp sites, as they usually ran away quickly after I fired once into the air. I don't think Burt slept that night, waking me many times, asking if I heard one noise or another. I would tell him to go back to sleep. If a bear was in camp, he would know it. It would not be the rustling of brush in the wind or other minor noises. He slept closer to me than I felt comfortable with, but we survived the night, even though Burt had puffy eyes from the lack of sleep as he drank his morning coffee.

The next day we flew to the river on Bristol Bay. I stayed away from the popular tourist sites, like McNeil River, on that bay. Not only did the site draw a lot of tourists, but the bears there had mostly lost their fear of humans. Upon landing and setting up camp I asked Burt if he wanted to go back to Stultz Lake, as he was still unnerved by yesterday's experience. He said no. He wanted to see big brown bears.

After we secured our food supply from roving brown bears, we walked down to the river to film brown bears feeding in it. I don't know how many rolls of film Burt shot of bears fishing and eating salmon, but it was a lot. We did not fish. We just watched and shot pictures of bears. The cubs were comical, trying to imitate their mother's fishing methods. One boar thought we were getting too close and charged in a spray of water, but stopped thirty yards from us. He was just warning us to stay out of his fishing hole. Burt had dropped his camera and was backing away until I told him to remain still. He forgot to shoot photographs of the charging bear. Bears have that effect on many people. I often wondered if the attraction/fear many people had toward the animal was a result of some imprint upon the brain by long ago ancestors. I did not fear bears, but I had a very healthy respect for them.

Walking back to camp on a bear trail, a three-year-old female and I met face to face rounding a sharp corner, to the surprise of both of us. As her face came within a foot of me I yelled and hit her on the head with my camera. The bear took off back into the woods. The blurry picture the camera took as I inadvertently pressed the shutter while reaching to smack the bear entertained guests at the lake for years. Almost as much as the picture of a wolf biting my snowshoe I took as I lay on my back in the deep snow.

Burt was grey faced after the encounter. I was not surprised. Humans seemed to have an intrinsic fear of bears. Like any creature, they had moments of rage, but mostly they just wanted to eat and be left alone. Around the fire as we consumed our evening meal along with a drink of our favorite beverages, I asked Burt if he had seen enough. His fear of bears was readily apparent. I did not want him to run away from one at an inappropriate time, causing the bear to charge for real. Burt replied that he had paid for a week here, and by God, he was going to get his money's worth. The next day changed his mind.

We hiked upstream, where most of the brown bears were feeding on spawning salmon, to fish the following morning. I loved fly fishing and wanted to get away from bears as much as possible so I could concentrate on catching some large rainbow on my light fly rod. Burt preferred to fish with his spinning rod for larger salmon. We fished for three hours before taking a break for lunch. During lunch I asked Burt if he was comfortable enough for me to cross the narrowing stream to fish a hole on the other side, where I could see a large rainbow trout feeding on floating insects. I would only be gone for thirty minutes and would be in plain sight the whole time. Burt urged me to cross over, saying he was fine. Before leaving, I reemphasized to him to not panic if he saw a bear. I also reminded him that sometimes lazy brown bears would lie in the willows lining the stream waiting for a fisherman to catch a fish. These bears would wander out toward the fisherman as he landed the fish, expecting to be fed. This was more common on streams that were popular with tourists, but bears have a large migratory path and could be here as well. If that happened,

I told Burt to simply unhook the fish and toss it to the bear. The animal would leisurely pick it up to take back to the willows to snack on while the fisherman caught another fish for him.

I crossed the stream on a log that had fallen over it. I had just made my first cast when I saw a large brown bear walk out of the willows behind Burt. It did not show any signs of aggression as it sat on the rocks fifteen feet behind Burt to watch him reel in a salmon. I had my .444 Marlin on my back but did not want to shoot it, as the animal was not showing any signs of anger. I shouted and motioned to Burt that the bear was behind him, but because of either the loud rushing stream or his concentration on landing his fish, he did not hear or see me. I started toward the log to cross back over when Burt landed his fish and saw the bear sitting behind him.

He let out a horrific scream as he threw his fishing rod in the air and dove into the river. The bear slowly walked over to the flopping fish, picked it up and disappeared into the willows. Burt was not so fortunate. He was wearing chest waders that quickly filled with water, dragging him down the deep, fast-flowing stream. He was never in danger from the bear, but was in real danger of drowning. I ran down my side of the river and shed my boots as I dove into the river and swam across to the struggling Burt. By the time we safely reached shore, both of us were shaking. Me from the cold; Burt from fright. As we lay on the sun-warmed rocks regaining our breath, Burt asked me if I thought the pike were biting in the Tanana River. He'd had enough of bear and wanted to sit on our homestead lawn, drinking scotch and watching the sun set.

Unfortunately, that was my last trip with Burt. He died of a heart attack the following winter. I missed his sense of humor, taste in good scotch and love of fishing.

David paddling wash tub on Stultz Lake.

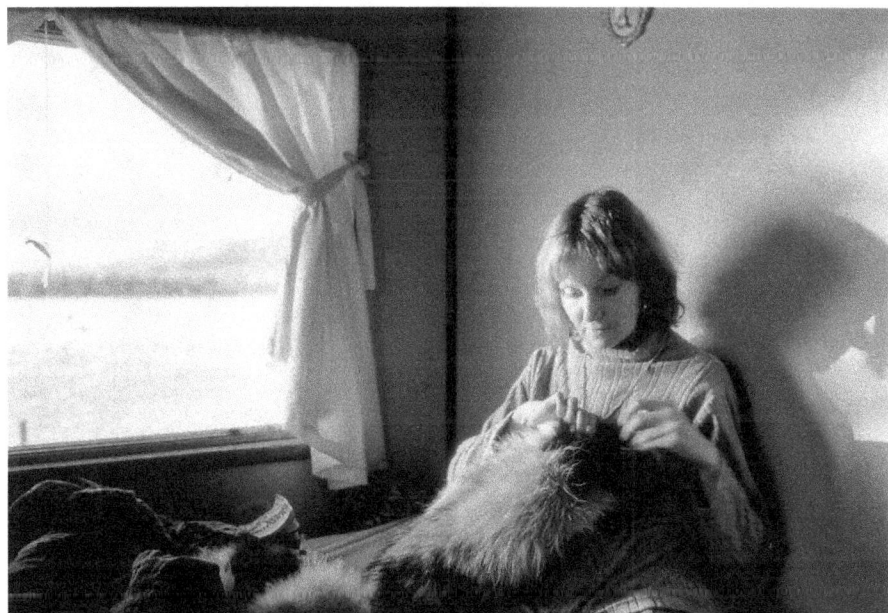

Sharon sewing gloves from wolf I trapped.

263

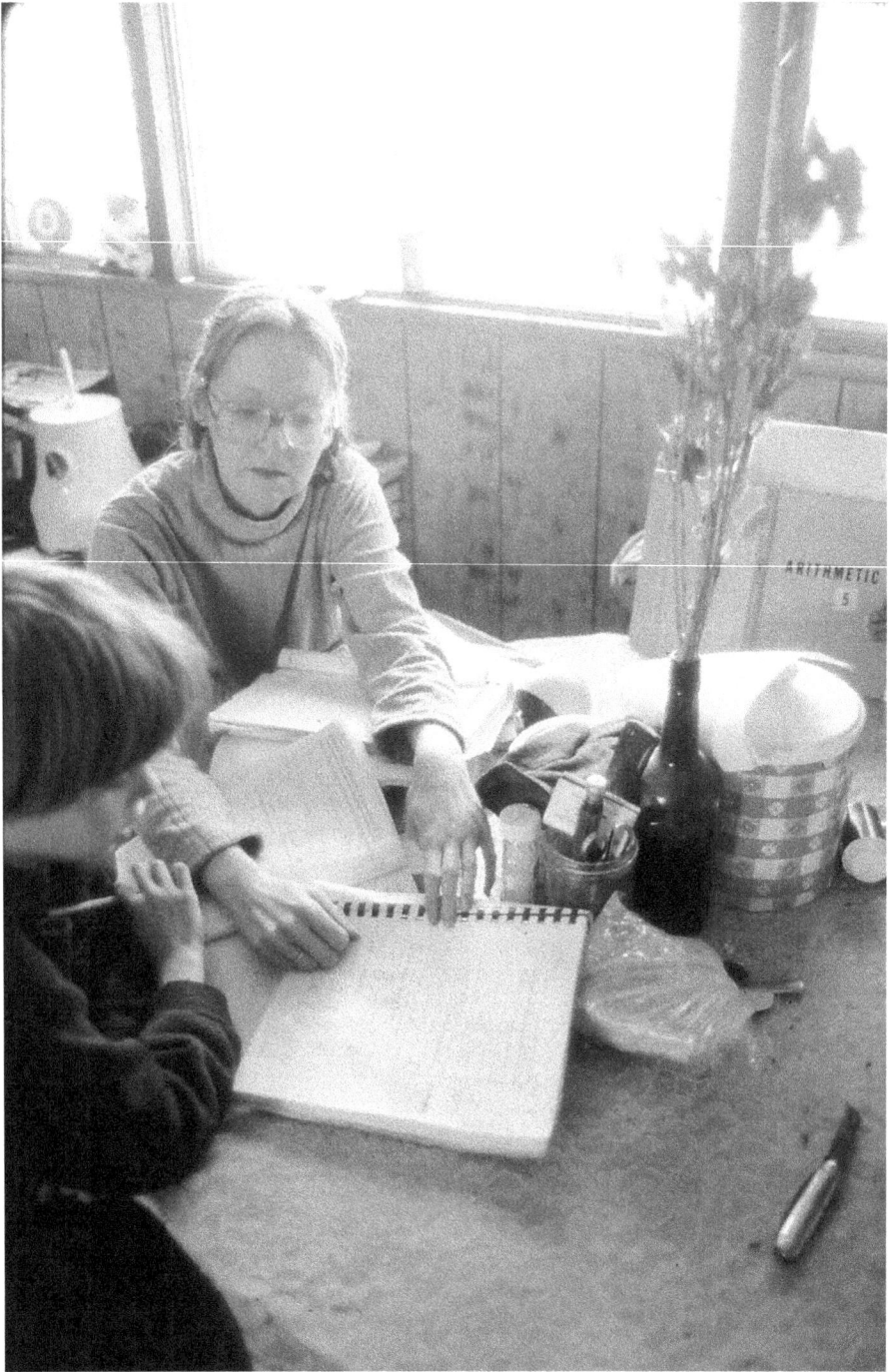

School time at the lake.

Boys taking a bath at Stultz Lake.

Evening wrestling match before bed.

Boys playing in snow storm.

Evening book reading session.

David trapping voles for extra .22 shells.

Michael and Sengic getting my trapping sled ready.

Family at Stultz Lake.

Michael hauling water while David gives instructions.

Stultz Mountain surrounded by ice fog.
I had three inches of ice on airplane after instrument landing.

Author and Joe Chandler on wolf hunting trip.

Changing from float to skis in the fall.

Sharon cutting off moose roast for dinner.

Family admiring a hunter's grizzly bear at Stultz Lake.

Hank's Sedan has engine failure in Ruby.

Taking off from the Kantishna River.

Al approaching his Brooks Range caribou.

Harry's Hunt

THAT COMING FALL I WAS SWAMPED with requests to guide hunters. The requests came from California to New York. I had no idea how these people got my name or how to contact me. When asked, they invariably said they had heard about me from a friend. There were only so many weeks in a hunting season, so I turned most of them down. One request I could not deny was from Dr. Bob Jordon in Fairbanks, who oversaw the health of my two boys. Bob stated that his father had been on guided trips for moose and bears in Canada and Alaska without success. The main reasons for him not being able to successfully complete these hunts were his age and health. He was eighty-two years old and had a hard time walking. Harry lived in Oakland, California, where he owned a specialty wood store. He sold exotic hardwood to discerning customers. Harry had dreamed of having moose and black bear mounts in his store for years. Bob asked me to get his Dad one before he passed. That sounded like a difficult task as his walking, let alone shooting ability, was compromised. I agreed to take Harry out, so I flew Harry as well as Glenn Straatsma and Bob to my Melozitna hunting camp. This time I had them drive to Manley Hot Springs to be picked up, as it was closer to the hunting camp. After meeting Harry, I was glad I had agreed to try to help fulfill his hunting dreams.

Harry's eyes twinkled, and he shook my hand with a huge smile on his aged face. He was gregarious, friendly and impossible to dislike. I noticed how hard it was for Harry to walk on the floats of N8689V and to get inside the cabin. If it was hard for him to walk on an even surface and climb up into an airplane, I had my work cut out for me.

I had camp set up prior to the arrival of my trio of hunters, so we all settled in around the campfire after my three trips into Manley and back. The evening was cool. That was a good sign for hanging meat to cool and age. It also meant winter was not far off. We discussed how the hunt was going to progress. I could not guide all three at once. Both Glenn and Bob had gotten a moose the previous fall, so they knew the basics of how to hunt them. They would need help dressing their moose, but I figured

I could check on them often enough to prevent any meat from spoiling if they brought down an animal. We agreed that Harry had to be my primary focus.

The following morning, I dropped Glenn and Bob off at locations that had a good viewing area for spotting moose. Back at camp, I got Harry ready to hunt. I went over what the terrain was like, where to shoot the moose, and how to handle his rifle inside the airplane. Harry was excited and told me again and again how much he appreciated me guiding him at his age and condition. Who could refuse a gentleman like this?

Getting Harry into the airplane before handing him his empty 30-06 was easy, compared to getting him out. Soon after takeoff we spotted a nice bull moose about a quarter mile off the river. We landed and exited the airplane before Harry loaded his rifle. Soon after beginning a stalk I could see this was not going to work. Harry just could not walk on the uneven surfaces of the Alaska tundra. I took his rifle, deciding to carry it myself to prevent its accidental discharge. Looking around, I found a dead tree limb I could trim for a walking stick to help Harry. It helped, but not enough. We never got close to the bull before Harry gave out.

We sat and rested while I tried to figure out how Harry was going to get near enough to a moose to shoot one. I would have to find an animal sleeping close to the river for Harry to have a chance. It was clear he could not walk on tundra. The forest floors around the river also presented challenges. I thought we could go slowly and remove dead branches in our way. Landing on one of the small lakes and sloughs was out. The moose would hear us and leave before I could get Harry ready to shoot one.

Harry had had enough for one day, so I took him back to camp to rest while I checked on the other hunters. I showed Harry where to sit to view passing moose if he felt up to it later, after he rested.

Bob was close to where I had dropped him, and waved to me as I flew over. He hadn't shot anything so I continued on to where Glenn was hunting. Glenn had a bull down, so I landed to help him dress it out and haul it back to the airplane. It was dark before I had Bob and Glenn back in camp and the moose hanging on the meat rack. After a dinner of moose backstrap, potatoes and biscuits covered with butter and honey, we discussed the day. I could tell Harry was resigning himself to not having a successful hunt by the way he was withdrawing from the conversation. He was thinking his age and disabilities were going to forever prevent him from harvesting his dream animals. Talking to Bob later, out of Harry's hearing, he told me how disappointed and depressed his dad was. That conversation cemented it in my mind; Harry was going home happy. I would use all of my flying and hunting expertise to make sure it would happen.

Bob decided to hunt around camp the following day while I took Harry out. We flew the entire valley for several hours before I spotted a bull moose laying in timber within fifty feet of the river's edge. Looking at the wind pattern on a nearby small lake, I saw I would have to land downriver to keep our scent from the moose's sensitive nose. I landed and floated about a quarter mile downstream from the animal before tying off on a tree. I did not want to power the floats up on shore, as it would probably spook the moose. It took a while to get Harry out and on shore before the stalk began.

It was a slow stalk before I saw that the moose was still laying where I had first spotted him. I could only see its antlers. They were moving around like he knew something was not quite right and was trying to see what disturbed him. It took another five minutes to get Harry in a position to shoot when I got the moose on its feet. Getting Harry braced with a tree to steady his aim, I told him to put a shell in the chamber. I just stepped to the side to grunt and get the moose up when Harry's 30-06 fired. The moose immediately jumped to its feet and disappeared, unharmed, into the brush.

Harry had had his finger on the trigger with the safety off when he chambered a round, causing the rifle to fire. From talking to him and his son earlier, I knew that Harry was an experienced hunter, so these errors puzzled me. Looking back to Harry to ask why, I could see tears of frustration and disappointment in his eyes. Instead of lashing out, I told Harry this was just a practice run. He would get his animal. He did not believe me, but said thanks anyway for the effort.

Now that I am in my mid-seventies writing this book I understand the frailties of the human body more than I did at that time. The damn thing just does not do what you tell it to anymore. At the time I was guiding Harry, I could only guess what he was going through. It was not pretty. The worst part was not his physical limits, but the effect they had on him mentally. I could work around his physical limitations, but only successfully getting a moose would strengthen him psychologically. He had failed so many times over the years he had come to accept that he would do so again. I was damned determined that his last hunt would be his most successful.

Bob had not gotten his moose hunting around camp, so we decided I would guide him in the morning while Harry rested. We were back, tired, bloody and thirsty from packing his moose to camp the following day before I had time to think again about Harry.

That evening I took Harry aside. We sat by the bank of the river looking at a sky full of bright stars undimmed by the lights of civilization. Harry started off the conversation by saying how sorry he was about his failures. I stopped him in mid-sentence. I put my hand on his shoulder and looked him in the eye as I said in a reassuring voice, "Harry, I have never guided anyone who was not successful in their hunt. You will not be the first. We found out the day before how we could get close enough to a moose for you to shoot it. What you did by misfiring your rifle was a mistake, but easily corrected. I just need you to calm yourself and follow my directions. Before you know it, your moose will be hanging beside your son's." His eyes took on a misty look in the full moon as he thanked me for my efforts. I could tell he did not believe me, and the emotions he was showing were because I was trying so hard.

Day three of the hunt we tried three more stalks without getting a shot off. Once Harry slipped from the floats as he tried to step off them, and shouted as he hit the cold water. Luckily, he was not hurt. The other times the moose heard us and took off before we could get in range.

Bob took me aside again that evening and asked if Harry was going to be able to get a shot at a moose. I told him I did not know, but I would try. The odds were against us, but if Harry held out, we would have a chance.

The following morning after breakfast, Harry gave me a big grin as I helped him into the airplane. He told me he could feel that this was his lucky day. He was right. We again found a bull laying down next to the river. I landed downwind and got Harry out of the airplane. I took his rifle and checked it, telling Harry I would carry it for him. It took us more than an hour to walk what should have been a fifteen-minute hike along the shoreline. I carefully removed all branches and helped Harry over fallen logs, but finally he was situated for a shot. Carefully chambering a round in the 30-06, I handed it to Harry, reminding him to keep his finger off the trigger until he was ready to shoot. He was hyperventilating and a little red in the face. I took the rifle back and had him sit down and breathe deeply.

When normal color returned to his face, I told him to rest his rifle across a nearby fallen log and get ready to shoot his moose.

When Harry was situated with the rifle pointing in the direction of the moose, I patted him on the shoulder and said to him, "You were right. This is your day. Just think of the moose as a paper target on the range." He nodded as I moved into position to get the moose on its feet. Just as planned, the moose got up at my mating grunt, giving Harry a clear shot. Harry killed it where it stood with one shot. Tears were rolling down the seams in his face as I hugged and congratulated him. Harry was speechless, but his joy was evident all over his body as I positioned him for a camera shot next to the sixty-four-inch bull he just killed. Bob also had tears in his eyes later as his animated father related the events of the hunt. Mine were not dry, either. Some people think hunting is just going out and proving yourself a man by killing some defenseless animal. To Harry, that was the furthest thing from the truth you could get. He overcame his physical disabilities and mental doubts to successfully complete his dream of a lifetime. The odds were all in favor of the moose.

Now we had to get Harry a black bear to make the final portion of his dream come true. I was shaking my head, staring into the campfire, when Bob asked if it were possible for Harry to shoot one. I told Bob a black bear is much more difficult for someone like Harry. We could keep an eye on the kill sites of all three moose we had taken on this trip, but it was much more likely in this valley for grizzly bears to claim the remains. I said the best chance for Harry was over on the Kantishna or Toklat Rivers.

The next few days were spent flying meat and gear to Manley Hot Springs where it would be driven to a butcher. Completing that, I picked Harry up and we started our pursuit of a black bear. The Harry that met me at the float pond in Fairbanks was much different from the man of a week earlier. He had a glint in his eyes again, and a more youthful spring to his step. I knew that if fate and the hunting gods allowed, Harry would shoot a bear. I was surprised at how easy the hunt was. We landed and set up camp on the Kantishna River where I had seen many black bears on prior flights. In the morning, as we were draining the last of our coffee out of the cups, a nice black bear boar came walking up the banks of the Kantishna toward camp. Harry killed it with one shot.

Bob told me later that Harry had both trophies mounted and standing in his shop, where he regaled buyers with tales of the hunt until his failing health made him retire. It was probably the most rewarding hunt that I ever took part in. Money could never compare with the tears and joy Harry blessed me with.

* * *

My first two hunters that fall, after Harry, were from Wisconsin. They had been referred to me by a friend living in Nenana, and they wanted to hunt caribou and Dall sheep. The best place I knew to get both was in the Brooks Range, it is the most northern mountain range in Alaska, and stretches some 700 miles until it enters Canada. Alaskans considered the Brooks Range an extension of the Rockies in the lower US, while Canada has a completely different name for it. Most hunters I took there were dumbfounded to find sea shells embedded in the exposed rocks. Scientists think these mountains had been an ancient seabed 126 million years ago, before being formed by shifting plates and volcanic eruptions. I chose the Brooks Range to set up hunting camps; because of its remoteness, fewer registered guides hunted it. There were no moose in the Range itself, but it was home to Dall sheep, caribou and grizzly.

I flew over an area out of Anaktuvuk Pass where I had previously seen good sheep numbers, looking for a place to set up camp. I found a small lake at the top of one of the minor passes in the central portion of the range. The lake was 4,300 feet in elevation, higher than ideal. It would freeze sooner than many of the other lakes in the area. This was always a concern when hunting sheep. You could go to sleep one night to the gentle ripples of water washing on shore and wake up to a lake solidly encased in ice. Ice and float planes do not coexist favorably, as ice can cut holes in the floats during takeoff if the pilot is unlucky or careless. The only options beside cutting a path through the ice by gently taxiing the airplane through it are to wait for the wind and sun to create a takeoff area, or wait for the lake to freeze more solidly: all bad options, as the temperature this far north hardly rose above sixty-one degrees in the lower elevations, even during the summer. It was best, this high, to get in early, shoot your animals, and get out quickly.

I set up camp on a platform some previous hunter had made on the shore, and then flew back to Nenana to pick up Al and Dan, my hunters. It was a long day of flying people and supplies into the high lake spot. The weather was overcast, with occasional areas of turbulence. The mountains usually had turbulence, but it was tiring to have to fight it all the way to Nenana and back.

The guys were excited by the number of caribou crossing over the pass where we were camped. I had a hard time calming them down enough to eat dinner. They just wanted to take pictures of the passing animals or take shots at them. Finally, darkness fell suddenly, and they consented to dinner and sleeping bags.

Up early the next morning before the guys shed their sleeping bags, I fixed the fire and made coffee. The aroma got Al and Dan up as I prepared a breakfast of pancakes, eggs and bacon in darkness only lit by the fire. I could not see stars, so I knew it was overcast. I hoped it would not turn to snow, as we hunched over our breakfasts, close to the small fire.

I didn't like taking two hunters out at the same time. It overtaxed my airplane and there was always dissension over who got to shoot first and at what. I only agreed to take the two together because of the friend who had referred them. I went over my rules for hunting with the two men. We flipped a coin to see who would shoot the first caribou. Dan won the toss, meaning Al would get first shot at a sheep. They each had a nonresident caribou and sheep tag.

There were numerous caribou in small herds of ten to forty animals around us on the flats of the pass, and on the ridges to the higher mountains surrounding the lake. Being from the Lower 48, they considered anything with antlers fair game. This was not true of caribou. Female caribou also have antlers, to protect their young from predators. Their antlers are much smaller than the ones the males grow. Time after time I would tell Dan no, the animal he wanted to shoot was a female and too small. Even the females had far larger antlers than the deer he was used to hunting back home.

Rain had started falling and mixed with the blowing fog before I spotted a small group of male caribou about a half mile away. They were feeding as they marched north toward their winter grounds. Now both Dan and Al saw why I had stopped them from shooting before. These were not exactly trophy class, but respectable enough to harvest. Caribou are judged by how close their antlers come to their rear ends when they put their heads back. That, the number of points on the antlers, and if they had a double shovel down the front of their faces gave the guide a fair idea of the size of the animal without resorting to a spotting scope. The animals in this small herd would not make my hunters a Boone or Crockett, but would hang proudly on the walls of any hunter.

I had explained previously to the guys how we would stalk the caribou. We walked in single file, bent over. I stopped whenever one of the animals raised its head to look around. Al and Dan were to do the same. Slowly we closed the range between us to 200 yards, using whatever small cover this open pass provided. I looked at Dan as he was getting set to take a shot at the largest buck. He was calm and his breathing normal. He was under control, so I readied myself to shoot only if he wounded the animal and could not bring it down before the animal escaped to suffer a lingering painful death.

Caribou moved very fast and could easily disappear far enough away and into terrain where we could not retrieve them. I believed in a fair hunt, in which my hunter would have the chance to first down his animal. I would not allow the animal to escape wounded, however.

Dan's rifle barked once and the big caribou fell in its tracks without rising. The others quickly disappeared over a ridge and out of range. Carefully approaching the animal and touching the end of my rifle on its eye to make sure it was dead, I turned to congratulate a jubilant hunter. They were both surprised at how easy the hunt was. They did not know of my first caribou hunt in Alaska and how easy it was to make a supposedly easy hunt into a nightmare if you did not know what you were doing. I had learned a lot in those years long ago; it enabled me to find the right area and approach for Al and Dan so they would have a smoother time with their first caribou. We quickly dressed out the caribou. I had them haul the meat back to camp while I worked on preparing the cape for mounting. My hunters worked. They got bloody and sweaty, the same as I did. At times I would also have them cook meals if I had to prepare a cape or skin a skull prior to bedding down.

It was raining hard by the time we got the meat, antlers and cape into camp. I was glad to see the rain, as it usually meant warmer temperatures and no snow, but that could change instantly. That evening we enjoyed a meal of caribou steaks, baked potatoes and camp made biscuits.

The next day it was Al's turn. We could have shot another caribou the day before as Al wanted, but none of the males had been mature enough to meet my minimum standards. He would have been happy upon shooting one of the animals he wanted to harvest, but his elation would soon turn sour as he watched much larger animals pass by camp in the coming days. He had one tag and would only get one animal. I would not be bribed, like some guides, to calm a disappointed hunter by claiming the animal as mine for the right amount of money. As I had explained to both of them before we started hunting, if you shot it, you took it home.

Al's hunt was a repeat of Dan's, only differing in that Al was a little more excitable. He was breathing more heavily as we got into position. I had to stop him from shooting until he got his breathing under control. When he pulled the trigger, the large caribou dropped dead in its tracks with a nice shot through the heart. We quickly dressed the animal and carried it to camp. That night over dinner I told the guys I was going to fly the meat and antlers into Nenana the following day. They were to stay in close proximity of camp, and not shoot their rifles unless it was in self-defense from a grizzly.

They agreed to follow my instructions. I really hated to leave hunters alone in the Alaska wilderness. Too many bad things could happen, but it was the price to pay for taking out two hunters at one time. They still had a sheep to get, and wondered why I was taking the day to fly the meat into town. I explained that flying two caribou, two sheep and two hunters at the same time was impossible for my valiant little two-place airplane. Especially at this altitude. I was not going to take a chance on the spoiling meat being eaten by a grizzly bear while we hunted sheep.

After flying the meat into town and refueling, I took the time to fly the mountains and canyons around camp for sheep. I found them bedded down above a shale slide about two miles from camp. There were two nice rams among them. With luck I could get both Al and Dan a sheep on the same day, and we could get out of the mountains before the snow fell or the lake iced over.

Getting everyone up and moving before daylight, we started hiking back down the pass to the side canyon where the sheep were. It was tough walking over the slippery rocks and crossing the stream numerous times. Daylight came an hour before we started up the canyon. We sat behind rocks as I took out my spotting scope to locate and measure the sheep. They had split into two groups with one of the largest rams in each small cluster. The older, more mature rams liked to keep younger ones around them as an early defense warning against predators. They have better eyesight and sense of smell than the older ones do. That and the terrain make them one of the most difficult animals to hunt in Alaska. The only animals more difficult to hunt, in my experience, were mountain goats.

We waited in our cover for the sheep to stop grazing and lay down for a nap. It was several hours before we started carefully moving up the mountain. We would have to cross one small shale slide to get to the small outcropping where I thought we would be within range. Thus far the sheep had not spotted or smelled us in the shifting air currents of the canyon. We all made noise crossing the shale; it was impossible not to. Hoping the sheep had thought it was just a natural rock slide or some other animal causing the noise, I carefully raised my head above the small hill we were to shoot from. I was relieved that the one group of sheep was still where I had last seen them thirty minutes ago, but they were intently watching where I was crouched. Easing back down out of sight, I motioned for everyone to be quiet and sit against the slope.

When the sheep settled down again I got Al in a position to shoot, pointing out the best legal ram. Dan and I crept farther up the canyon to where we could see the second group of sheep. I spotted the largest ram and pointed it out to Dan, cautioning him not to shoot until he heard Al's shot. Dan would have an easier shot of about 150 yards slightly upslope. I was relieved it was Dan I was leaving by himself as he was the more composed of the two.

I silently crept back to where I had left Al. I estimated the distance Al would have to shoot at about 250 to 300 yards: a long shot across the canyon to the opposing slope and slightly uphill. Wind currents affect the flight of bullets, and in canyons these high winds were very unpredictable. I was really concerned whether Al would be able to make the shot cleanly. He was shooting the same rifle I was, a Remington 7mm Magnum loaded with 150 grain Nosler bullets that were plenty capable of bringing the sheep down at this distance if the shot was placed correctly. After giving him his aim point, corrected for range and elevation, I positioned myself to help him if he needed it.

I saw rocks ricochet two feet below the resting ram as the sound of Al's shot reverberated around the canyon. It was closely followed by another shot from the direction I had left Dan. Al fired again as his sheep jumped to its feet. This time he missed a foot to the right. Telling him to take his time did little good and he missed every shot until his rifle was empty.

Almost unbelievably the ram stood still before heading straight up the cliff while Al hurriedly reloaded his rifle. Telling him how to correct his aim, I was both surprised and relieved when his next shot of over 400 yards connected. The sheep lost its footing and slid downslope about twenty yards before getting to its feet again, and started running more slowly up hill. Now that the animal was wounded, I placed a shot in the struggling animal's lung area just as Al hit it again. The ram laid down for final time.

Al was beyond happy as we congratulated each other. Dan approached us as Al was regaining his breath, saying he had also shot a sheep. Some guides will not help a client and let wounded animals get away. Some will shoot and not let the client know they did so under the same circumstances. I always told my hunters beforehand that if they wounded an animal it was my responsibility to not let it suffer. If they did not agree I would not take them out hunting. This was especially important for dangerous game like brown or grizzly bears. Anyone who has ever had to enter the brush after a wounded grizzly or brown bear know how dangerous this is. I always used a twelve-gauge shotgun with double .00 buckshot when going into the brush after a wounded brown or grizzly bear, and usually smelled it before I would see it.

It is uncanny how well large bear can conceal themselves in brush. Several times I have had brown bears get up within ten feet of me in an area I had already looked at closely. In two instances there had been no time to raise my shotgun and I had to shoot from the hip. Friends under the same circumstances had been killed and partially eaten by the animals.

We started the back-breaking process of dressing and packing out two large Dall rams before darkness closed in. Everyone was out of breath with heavy loads on our backs as we made our way back up the pass toward camp. Al said he saw someone glassing us from the direction of camp. I did not see anyone but was surprised to see the reflection of a camp fire as we crested the final ridge. Our tents were gone and in their places were several large white walled tents. I finally saw our tents and supplies thrown into a heap about 300 yards from where we had left them that morning.

Seeing this, I felt two conflicting reactions. One was to go up and confront the person who had dismantled our camp and thrown it into a heap. At least it could have been stacked neatly. The second thought was to tread carefully. I was illegally guiding two out of state hunters and did not want to call unnecessary attention to myself. Deciding to take the second route,

I led us to our crumpled tents and made camp again as best I could in the darkness. I had Al and Dan take care of the meat. I told them if they were asked, to say we were three instate friends on our yearly sheep hunt. When they shook their heads in agreement I left to approach the individual who had so rudely dispossessed us.

The man introduced himself as John as I walked up to him, and stated he was a registered guide who had built the platforms our tents were on and guided this area every year for caribou and sheep. I apologized, saying my friends and I were on our yearly sheep hunt and did not know anyone else hunted the area. I told John we would be leaving the next day so he would have the area to himself. We talked for a while in increasing comfort. John was surprised and impressed that we had gotten two sheep on the same day and asked who was in charge.

I told John that I was the more experienced hunter and owned the airplane. Every year I would take my friends out for sheep and caribou in the fall. After asking several questions about my hunting and guiding experience, John asked me if I would be an assistant guide for him. I explained that I was booked this year but would consider it for the year following. We exchanged addresses and amicably parted. I went back to my two concerned hunters around our campfire, and explained everything was settled. We would be flying out in the morning.

The rest of the fall hunting season went smoothly and soon I was back with my family at Stultz Lake. I was surprised when checking N8689V before winter set in that my engine was overdue for a replacement or overhaul. It had more than 2,300 hours on it. The cost of a new engine was about $2,500. I had not planned on this expense in my flying budget, but had the money to cover it. I was even more surprised to discover that I now had more than 10,000 hours of bush flying experience. Deciding to get a new engine to replace my 160 hp Lycoming before winter hit for good and the lake froze, I flew off to Anchorage to have the work done.

Michael's Sheep Hunt

IN NOVEMBER THE LAKE WAS FROZEN solidly enough to change from floats to snow skis. In the past I had to fly to Fairbanks to do the conversion and then wait several weeks for the ice and snow to get deep enough to land back at Stultz Lake. That summer I had cut down some of the larger white pines around the lake and made an A-frame on the edge of the lake so I could do the conversion myself at home.

Winter set in and the family adjusted to the winter schedule of school work, hauling water, preparing trap lines, boiling and cleaning traps and hauling a winter's supply of wood. John and Heather visited again from Paris to put the final touches of their article on Alaskan homesteaders. John told me later that one of the pictures taken of Sharon and me had won national honors in Europe. It was a picture of us in full face masks with a dusting of snow and frost, kissing in the fading light of sunset. They sent me a copy of the article that had featured us, but it was published in German and I could not read it. The pictures were great.

Looking across the cabin, I watched Michael and David playing with toys they had made with their own hands. They were on the floor having a mock battle and laughing as they scurried around. I thought about the Alaska Native Land Claims Settlement Acts and the effects they would have on hunting in Alaska, and how they might prevent my two sons from enjoying the wonderful bounty of Alaska as I had. I decided to take them on a sheep hunting trip the following fall. Sharon and I discussed it. She firmly put her foot down, saying that David was just too young: thinking about it, I had to agree. He was only six years old and his legs were too small to climb the steep mountains Dall sheep called home. I promised myself to make it up to him when he was eleven, as Michael was.

I glanced over the fifty-gallon barrel wood stove. The boys were sitting at the table alongside it, looking across the frozen lake that was our front yard at the northern lights dancing over Stultz Mountain. Speaking quietly, I informed Michael that I was thinking of taking him on a sheep hunt this coming fall. The peaceful quiet of our cozy home was shattered with Michael's shouts of joy, and the toy in his hand went flying across the room when he understood what I had said. My heart broke as I saw David withdraw into himself when he learned he was too young to come with us. I made another promise to myself to make it up to him.

Michael had shot his first moose the previous fall and was an expert marksman, having handled guns soon after he learned to walk. Both boys were tough and independent, having lived most of their lives in the bush of Alaska. We had worked together as a family to carve out our Toklat cabin and house on Stultz Lake. Our life-style had become comfortable in this wilderness setting. We each had our assigned tasks that we completed without complaint, except for David, who continued to challenge all attempts to work without day-dreaming.

After finishing the months-long season of guiding for fish on the Alaska Peninsula that summer, I landed my airplane and taxied up the lake to the front of my house, where Sharon greeted me with relief. She had many faults, but to her credit, she could take care of herself and the boys during my frequent long absences. Many women would not have been able to handle the isolation. Both boys held a barking Toklat back as I slowly got out of the airplane to give them all hugs. My back was killing me from the long hours of flying in the Peninsula weather. I wanted to do nothing more than lie down on our bed overlooking the lake and rest for a few days.

The boys would have none of that and tackled me as soon as I was on dry land to begin a boisterous round of wrestling. As soon as I was on my back with the kids swarming over me, Toklat joined the fracas as well, getting in little nips to go along with his growls. It was a great feeling, being home and having the boys in my arms again.

After beating me into submission they agreed to let me up and climbed on the bed with me. David held out *The Hobbit* for me to continue reading from where we had left off four weeks previously. Sharon busied herself in the kitchen making lunch as I acted out the characters in the book, and the boys laughed or cringed at my reading.

Sharon told me later that Michael had driven her crazy all summer with questions about sheep hunting. He had shot his complete supply of .243 ammunition practicing for the hunt. His bright shining eyes contrasted with David's darker, disappointed ones. Michael questioned me incessantly about hunting sheep. I told him I needed to rest up and get the airplane's oil changed before we could even think about it. I looked at Michael and asked how he intended to shoot a sheep, as he had no shells left for his rifle. He quickly disappeared and came back with the expended brass saying he had saved every one he shot so we could reload them before leaving. I rumpled his hair and gave him a big hug, saying we sure could.

Before I had completely recovered from the long summer of guiding, Michael stamped his foot and said, "Damn it Dad, let's go hunting." Soon after the airplane was loaded we were heading north to the Brooks Range.

I was taking Michael to one of my favorite sheep hunting locations northeast of Bettles deep in the Brooks Range. Three hours later I pointed out the high mountain valley that would take us to the lake where we would make camp. Michael wanted to see some sheep so I increased power to gain altitude and flew the ridgetops surrounding this beautiful valley. We spotted a large group of mature rams, several bands of caribou, and a lone wolf in the next half hour. Our gas was getting low, making it imperative that we land soon. To the disapproving groan of my son, I headed north to our camping spot.

As we topped the crest of the valley, I was relieved to see the lake's surface was unruffled by wind and turbulence. The lake we were landing on was very small and, at 5,200 feet in elevation, dangerous to land on. That made it an ideal place to hunt as few pilots were willing to land here. The lake is only about a thousand feet long and surrounded on three sides by steep slopes. There is only one way in and out.

Taking one last look at my touchdown point, I took a deep breath, eased on full flaps, and flattened the pitch of the propeller as I began a steep descending turn into the lake. N8689V slipped gently between the shoulders of two opposing monoliths like a colorful bird of prey flaring just above the mirrored lake surface. The bottoms of the floats gently kissed the wet translucence, destroying the smooth perfection as they slowly settled into the still, cold water. Thousands of arctic grayling darted beneath the floats as Michael and I looked in silence at the wilderness paradise that would be our home for the next week. The floats nudging the shoreline brought us back to the reality of having to quickly set up camp before darkness.

We emptied the plane of our gear and pulled it as far out of the water as possible onto the rocky shore. After partially filling the floats with water to keep the aircraft anchored in the fierce winds common to this lake, we pitched our camp on a shelf 100 feet from the lake. I had camped there with hunters before and knew it would offer us some protection from the wind while affording a breathtaking view of the mountains surrounding us.

In a short while we had the tent up and the rest of the gear sorted and put away. I was working on a cooking space and a place to store our food. If we were visited by one of the many nocturnal grizzlies in the area, I wanted to be awake before they investigated the tent. This done, I searched for firewood. Michael, thinking we had worked long enough, said impatiently that he wanted to fish instead. Ruffling his hair and giving him a shove toward the airplane and our fishing equipment, I told him to go ahead and leave the hard work for the old man. Laughing at me, Michael unpacked his fishing rod and headed for the lake to catch supper.

My son would willingly walk across ten miles of frozen tundra to catch a fish. He was not going to let this opportunity to fish a virgin lake full of grayling go by. I soon had a small campfire going next to our cooking area and settled back against a pack sack to relax with a glass of Yukon Jack mixed with the pristine icy lake water, to enjoy the colorful sunset. The peace and silence of the cooling evening was too quickly interrupted by a yell from Michael to get the frying pan ready.

I readied the cooking utensils and the Coleman stove as Michael walked into the light of the flickering fire with six small, cleaned, grayling trout. The lake was so shallow and cold that fish seldom got above seven inches in length. What the fish lacked in size they made up for in numbers. Many evenings I had caught and released fifty of the small fish on a light fly rod while guiding other hunters. Both Michael and I were starved after the fast pace of the previous days and the long flight, so we quickly got down to the serious business of preparing dinner and eating.

The following morning, we were greeted by a white frosty landscape as we crawled from the tent several hours before daybreak. The airplane sat imprisoned in a skim of ice at the edge of the lake. Its orange paint was hidden beneath a thick frost glittering with a diamond's brightness in the pale moonlight. The chill discouraged conversation, and puffs of frozen vapor punctuated our efforts to restart the previous night's fire. Success with that task brought warmth back into our hands and faces as I cooked a hearty breakfast to sustain us against the rigors of the coming day.

I would not be taking a sheep. This was Michael's hunt. Yet even my heart beat a little faster the closer we got to leaving camp. A boy's first serious hunt provides a lifetime of memories, so I wanted everything to go right for him. It was neither the birthing sun nor the low flames that put the sparkle in the serious, intent hazel eyes across the fire from me. We were both excited to get going. By silent consent we finished our packing in the quickening light and started up the steep gray mountain.

We had just topped a high ridge when cold white clouds came tearing up the mountain from behind and quickly shrouded us and a small band of sheep we were watching in a thick ocean of tormenting wind and mist. All thoughts of hunting left my mind as I quickly dove for protection from the icy brush of these frenzied arctic gusts behind some rocks, pulling Michael with me. This storm that had appeared without warning was a common occurrence in the fall this far above the Arctic Circle. Michael and I huddled together for warmth among the large rocks to wait for the storm to blow itself out.

Weather was always a major concern that a wise hunter prepared for this far north and at 7,200 feet in elevation. I had been trapped by storms before and had learned to prepare for and survive them. We were lucky this storm was short lived. Within thirty minutes we resumed hunting. The sky was no longer a bright blue, and had clouds racing across mountain tops, but I figured it was not snowing and we could continue the hunt.

After an hour and a half of walking and glassing we spotted five large rams about a half mile away from the west facing slope we were walking on. We closely looked the rams over with my 40X spotting scope. I was surprised that all five were a legal three-quarter curl. Two looked to be better than a full curl. Mature sheep like these seldom banded without some younger rams, with better eyesight, to act as an early warning system.

I explained to Michael how we would try to get within shooting distance. Winds that high are fickle, but favored us at the moment. We spent the next hour getting within comfortable shooting distance and had a final 200 feet to climb to top the ridge behind the resting rams. If they hadn't moved, they should still be laying down about 200 yards below us.

In hushed whispers we went over our plan one last time. I explained to Michael that the sheep would be about 150-200 yards below and to our right when we topped the ridge we were climbing. I cautioned him to take his time and not dislodge any rocks or make sudden moves while we got into position. I checked to make sure he had no rounds chambered in his .243 Mauser before starting up this last hill.

The slope was typical shale and loose rocks held tenuously together by lichen, moss and thin loose dirt; we carefully worked our way up the hill, taking one slow step at a time. Twenty feet from the top of the ridge was a steep patch of loose shale that would be impossible to walk through without making a lot of noise. We veered to the right toward a small rock abutment that offered better footing. I was holding onto the rock face, bent awkwardly backward around it, when I stepped on a piece of loose shale hidden underneath some lichen that caused my foot to slip sharply downhill as I put weight on it.

The rock clattered loudly downhill as I grabbed the rock face for balance. It slipped from my hands as I fell backward, and my right knee collapsed beneath me with a loud pop. My Remington 7mm Magnum banged hard against the rocks, causing another small avalanche.

When I stopped sliding downhill my knee was screaming in pain. I lay there several minutes to get my breathing under control while fighting the searing pain. From previous knee injuries, I knew I was in trouble. It would be days before I would be able to bear weight or walk on it again normally. Twenty minutes went by before I was able to hobble back up the slope far enough to help Michael around the rock face. He was obviously worried that I had hurt myself as he looked anxiously at my face, twisted in pain. I put my finger to my lips telling him not to talk.

I was sure the racket caused by my misstep must have been heard by the rams. I thought there was no way they would still be where we last saw them and they were probably miles away by now. When we finished the last few feet of the climb and looked down the slope on the other side of the ridge I was dumbfounded to see them laying just where we last saw them. I have had sheep spook at the slightest sound or movement, and looked in amazement as all five lay calmly, chewing their cuds.

The monarch of the bunch was a magnificent ram of over forty inches. It was one of the best rams I had ever seen in the Brooks Range. Michael found a good rest for his rifle and chambered a round as previously instructed. He slowly began to line up for a shot at the largest ram. Sick at heart, I put my hand on his shoulder to stop him. I knew how much he had been looking forward to this moment but could not let him continue. I knew it would be extremely difficult just to get myself back to camp. There was no way I could carry a sheep out, too.

Motioning for Michael to follow me out of sight of the sheep, I crawled backwards in agony. When we stopped I explained to him how badly my knee was hurt, and that I would not be able to carry the weight of a sheep on my back. I also told him there was very little chance of hiding the meat from predators until I was healthy enough to come back for it.

This was Michael's hunt. Although he was only eleven years old, I wanted him to make the decision on what we should do. If I had been guiding anyone but my son I would have ended the hunt as soon as I realized the seriousness of my injury. But boys do not grow into men by having others making hard decisions for them. Michael and David had both been raised this way. They made decisions and lived with the consequences. I believe it is one of the main reasons they grew into responsible adults.

After listening to me, Michael leaned back against the hill and thought for a while. Having the personality, he does, he had to think things through carefully before coming to a decision. After about five minutes he looked me in the eyes and said, "Dad, you have always told us that when we shoot an animal the meat comes out before anything else. That sheep is too beautiful to waste. Let's go back to camp before you get worse."

My eyes stung as I realized how hard that decision was for this man-child beside me. It brought tears to my eyes that no knee injury ever could. He had waited so long and had been so excited when he learned of the hunt, to have it end this way was beyond a major disappointment. Yet Michael made the decision not to waste his beautiful sheep. Hunting etiquette and doing the right thing were far more important than his dreams. I reached over and gave him a big hug as tears of pride, not pain, ran down my face.

The trip back to camp was a nightmare. It takes several grown men to help a football player with a knee injury off a perfectly level field, but in this case there was only my son to accomplish the task of getting me off this rugged mountain. The ups and downs across three and a half miles of mountain ridges, slopes and loose rocks was more than I could bear. There were no trees or branches to use for a crutch as I painfully hobbled along, concentrating on putting one foot in front of the other. Putting any weight on my knee or moving it in any way was like someone sticking a red hot knife in it. The pain so infused my body and mind that I began to lose direction.

After several hours of slow progress, I felt my body going into shock from the excruciating pain. I was getting confused and could not figure out where camp was. Almost delirious from pain, I had to stop. Michael came running back to me when I did. I could see he was both scared and concerned over our predicament. I told him I was in so much pain I did not know where camp was or how to find it. I could no longer think clearly.

Michael looked around for a bit before pointing to where he thought camp was. I was sure it was not in that direction and told him so. He looked around again and said he knew exactly where it was. Both my sons have a good sense of direction and the Stultz trait of being really stubborn when they feel they are right. Michael was exhibiting both now. I thought, "Dear God, do I trust this young boy with both our lives?" We were high in some of the roughest terrain in America and hundreds of miles from help. The slightest mistake could easily end both our lives. I had never been so disappointed in myself as I was for having put us in that position. I was supposed to be Michael's protector, not the other way around.

Going through our limited options, I finally decided I had no choice but to trust his judgment. We could spend the night on this ridge without camping supplies or water and risk being covered in snow by morning. This is what I would have done if Michael was not there. I also knew that by morning my knee would be so swollen and stiff I might not be able to walk on it at all, forcing me to crawl if I wanted to move anywhere. For the first time in my life, I was in no condition mentally or physically to look after myself.

I told Michael to take both our packs back to camp but to be careful to mark his trail so he could get back to me whether he found camp or not. I also told him if he did not find camp within an hour, to come back immediately. I gave him my watch so he could keep track of time. I also told him if he found camp within the hour, to get my pain pills out of the airplane. If he saw a stick I could use as a cane or crutch to bring it back with him. Michael grabbed my pack, gave me what little was left in his canteen of water, and quickly disappeared.

I lay on the cold rocky ridge cursing myself for putting my son in this position. I had gotten myself out of many difficult situations during my life in Alaska, and now was completely reliant on an eleven-year-old boy to bail me out of the current one. Alaska could be a hard cruel place. I hoped for my son's sake that we would get out of this dilemma.

I don't know how long I lay there before I heard Michael climbing rapidly back up the slope. I thought it was way too soon for him to have found camp and to have returned. I said a silent prayer thanking God for sparing my son when he came into sight, holding a long stick and my pain pills. Michael told me we had been heading the right way all the time and that camp was almost directly below us a half mile away. I gulped down some pain pills and, leaning on Michael and the crutch, we started making our way slowly downhill to camp.

Upon reaching camp I had Michael help me take off my boots and pants. I was surprised to see that I had sprained my ankle as well. It was swollen to twice its normal size. The ankle was mostly blue from blood leaking out of broken vessels. My knee was so painful I had not even noticed the ankle. I saw that my knee was also very swollen. It was extremely painful to touch, let alone move. Grabbing the tree branch crutch and holding onto the airplane floats, I moved deeper into the ice cold lake water, immersing my knee and ankle, hoping to slow the swelling and bleeding. I looked at a very concerned Michael watching me from the edge of the lake as I rested against the floats. I told him to get a fire started.

I knew we were both dehydrated and needed food and water. Some of the shock had left since taking the pain pills and resting. I instructed Michael about preparing hot coffee and our evening meal. I carried back, knee and ankle braces with me in the airplane everywhere I went, so I had Michael get out the knee and ankle braces. When I could no longer stand the cold water I hobbled back out and had him help me put the braces on. I needed Michael's help to put on fresh warm socks, winter underwear and warm outer clothes followed by a heavy winter jacket to warm my body back up again.

Lying next to the fire absorbing its warmth, I helped with dinner as much as possible. It was the most delicious tuna fish sandwiches, cookies and hot coffee I could remember. I wondered for a while if my body was going to chuck it back up as my stomach rebelled, but it stayed down long enough that I convinced myself that a cup of Yukon Jack would be a great nightcap. Finally laying back against a pack board watching my son fish under a vividly colored sunset, I consoled myself with the thought that I may be out of commission, but I was not out of Yukon Jack. I toasted my son and thanked God for getting us safely through the day.

There was no way I was going to be able to fly the airplane with my knee the way it was. I could no longer even begin to bend it. I had previously flown with a broken leg by having the doctor cut the cast in half lengthwise so I could take it off when I was flying and tape it back on when I got out of the airplane. After an injury to my right hand, I had that doctor, Jack Frost, my wolf hunting partner, not only bivalve that cast so I could take it off, but form a hole between my thumb and first finger so I could hold my airplane control stick. I had also flown with a back so bad I had to have help getting out at the end of the flight. Sprained ankles were so common I just ignored the pain until one day I slipped off the airplane while putting gas in it and broke the ankle. The screws, ligaments from other parts of my body, and cast it took to put the joint back together did not long stop me from hopping back in my airplane. Pain was such a normal part of my life that I had learned to just ignore it for the most part. However, I had to be able to bend my knee to fly, and I could not. I hoped frequent soaking in ice water and time would heal it enough to allow me to bend it before the lake froze over.

Michael spent the next five days fishing and keeping the fire going. I was able to move a little more each day until, on the fifth day, I was able to climb in the airplane and fly out. I would have to tell John in Bettles I would not be able to guide with him that fall as planned. I only had some hunters from California on my books and a few friends from Alaska scheduled to take out. I had not accepted my normal number of hunters knowing I was going to guide for John. Medical attention would have to wait until I had time for it—if ever.

Michael had been such a good sport that I decided to enjoy the rare opportunity away from guiding others to give him a caribou hunt instead of heading back to the homestead. A major caribou migration was underway about forty miles to the northeast. We decided we would fly into one of the lower valleys and hunt them. I wanted to get off this high lake as soon as possible. It was already past the time it should have frozen over.

The takeoff from the lake was even more difficult than landing. I had to takeoff to the west, get airborne, and clear a 100-foot ridge within 1,300 feet. The altitude coupled with the short takeoff area makes this particular lake a challenge, even for someone like me who flew the Alaska bush twelve months of the year. Originally I had planned to make two trips out to a larger lake at a lower altitude to be as light on takeoff as possible, but a 10 mph easterly wind and the fact we didn't have any extra weight from a sheep changed my mind. I used the eastern shore to get the floats on step and turned into the wind for takeoff. We easily cleared the ridge and were onto the second phase of Michael's hunt.

We soon found numerous herds of caribou northwest of Anaktuvuk Pass. The herds were scattered throughout the valley floor. Now all we had to do was find a lake with lots of fish close to the caribou migration paths. My knee could not endure a tough hike across the tundra, so the caribou would have to come very close to our camp.

As we flew down an emerald green valley 500 feet above the ground, Michael tapped me on the shoulder and pointed out a grizzly bear standing in the outlet of a medium-size lake. We flew over the bear and were rewarded with the sight of thousands of spawning grayling in the shallow lake outlet. The large grizzly stood glaring at us, telling us to find our own fishing hole. There were caribou herds working their way up the valley floor on both sides of the lake. If our friend the grizzly wasn't too upset, the lake would be the perfect location for our new camp.

We landed and taxied toward the fishing bear as it stood on both hind legs defiantly watching the noisy invasion of his private fishing hole. It finally got nervous and dropped to all fours, heading for the nearest mountain three miles away. I knew the grizzly would not go far and would be back. Food is not something bears can afford to give up or forget easily. The Alaskan winters in the Interior are too long and cold.

We made camp far enough away from the outlet to allow him to come back at night without disturbing us, but close enough that I could hobble on the smooth shoreline to watch over Michael as he fished. For dessert we would leave the bear several caribou carcasses to munch on when we left, to apologize for our intrusion.

Michael was incredulous at the sight of thousands of large mature grayling fighting for every square inch of the small creek bed for a place to lay their eggs. The next year he would work on a commercial fishing boat in Prince William Sound for my friend Bob Widmann and see salmon do the same thing. But for now it was a first. The grayling were twelve to twenty-one inches long and put up a good fight. I had to drag Michael away forcibly several hours later. He caught a trout on almost every cast and did not want to stop. I could not set up camp by myself yet, and I did not want him near the creek without me standing watch. The grizzly would be back; it was just a matter of when.

Caribou of every size and description kept interrupting the tent-raising with their close passage. It was all I could do to keep Michael's attention on the task at hand. I did not want to teach Michael bad habits, so we would follow the law and did not hunt until the next day. After setting up camp, taking care of the airplane and making our food supply as safe as possible, I unpacked my fishing rod and headed back down the shoreline to catch more grayling with Michael. My .444 Marlin was slung over my shoulder for protection. We were using #12 black gnat flies I had tied before heading out on the hunt. The fly was tied two feet behind a bobber, as John Petersen had taught me to do years before in Anchorage. Every cast resulted in hooking a fat, mature grayling. We soon removed the barbs from the flies to make the battle more sporting for the fish. After catching and releasing about seventy of these feisty northern trout, I retired to the bank to rest my knee and ankle and watch my son. With the grizzly about I could not leave him alone, but neither could I convince him it was time to go back to camp. When he finally showed signs of tiring I had him clean two fat eighteen-inch grayling. Bribing him with the promise of fried fish, hot biscuits, and hot chocolate I got him to follow me back to camp.

We enjoyed another leisurely meal cooked over an open fire under the canopy of bright stars. I found myself wishing again that David was with us as well. That would have made the evening complete. It was not long before we climbed into our sleeping bags. I placed my twelve-gauge shotgun between us as we murmured good night.

Constant pain was exhausting. I fell asleep as soon as I crawled into my sleeping bag. Michael woke me several hours later by saying there was a bear in camp. Groaning, I struggled out of my sleeping bag. Without putting on clothes, I grabbed my shotgun and opened the tent flaps. The grizzly we had seen earlier at the creek was standing fifteen feet away, chewing on my packsack. I shouted at it and fired into the air, chasing the grizzly out of camp.

I was really tired. My body needed a lot of rest to recover from its injuries. My objective was to sleep the rest of the night while Michael's was to get the morning here quicker. Throughout the night we were awakened by the clicking ankle joints of passing caribou. Each time Michael woke me up it became harder to get him to lay down and go back to sleep. Once more during the night I had to get up and chase our grizzly friend away from our food supply and back to his fishing hole again. The critter was really ticked at us for taking over his fishing station and wanted to eat whatever we were having.

I hadn't gotten much sleep before a bright-eyed, fully dressed son was shaking me, telling me it was time to get going. My sleeping bag was so comfortable that normally I would have made some caustic remark about there being enough caribou around to last for a couple more hours, but I just did not have the heart to do so after the disappointment of the sheep hunt.

Trying to dress with a knee that screamed "don't" each time I bent it inside our small dew-drenched tent was not my idea of starting the day off right. I finally managed to dress and put my boots on with the impatient help of Michael. He handed me my 7mm Magnum as I struggled upright outside the tent, pulling on a coat. Michael pointed out two caribou bulls about 400 yards away. They were quartering away from us, leisurely eating lichen as they went. There was a good chance if we got to the lakeshore unseen we could intercept them as they rounded the lake.

The hunting Gods, being fickle and mischievous that morning, urged the two animals away from the lake before we had a chance to intercept them. The two bulls swung out from the lake shore, making us follow them across the tundra. Stalking caribou across open tundra is not easy under the best of circumstances and demands patience. There are differing philosophies on how to get close enough for a shot. I preferred to keep as low to the ground as possible and move quickly when the animals' heads are down feeding. My knee was preventing me from either bending down or moving quickly. Caribou, like other members of the deer family, have excellent eyesight and sense of smell. It is important to freeze in place when they look up, because any movement will spook them. It is a game the hunter is bound to lose sooner or later. The trick is to make it last as long as possible. We lost this encounter faster than I wanted.

The youngest bull saw us about 200 yards away. It instantly whirled toward us on stiff front legs, alerting his companion in the process. Neither animal could identify us by smell as the wind was blowing in our faces. They both raised their heads high in the air and started their odd stiff-legged circling maneuver to get our scent.

I got out of Michael's way and told him to shoot the larger bull behind the shoulder. I flinched at the sharp report of his .243 Mauser and heard the bullet strike the animal as I prepared my own weapon. The light was not good enough to see where the bullet hit. The bull gave a short hop into the air and started running. A second shot from Michael quickly followed the first, and the bull immediately fell to the ground. When I was sure Michael's caribou was down I shot the second one before it could get out of range.

Michael shot a respectable bull caribou. Mine was much smaller, but we were after meat and not a trophy. His proud beaming eyes and broad smile as I turned toward him attested to his elation at downing the bull and contributing to our winter's supply of meat. Walking up to his animal, I saw he had hit it once in the lung and once through the heart, both excellent shots for any hunter. I was proud of my young son standing beside his first caribou. He was growing into a man right before my eyes. At his young age he was already an accomplished shot and outdoorsman. Yet all this paled compared to the pride I had felt the day he decided not to shoot at all.

Living Alone at Stultz Lake

UPON ARRIVING BACK AT THE HOMESTEAD, I was mystified and furious to discover that Sharon had decided to move back to Washington State to live by her sister in Lake Chelan and was taking David with her. She had done well the last two and a half years at the homestead; from experience I knew what would happen if she left. As we argued I was thinking that this damn woman was insane to leave the bush of Alaska and our wonderful homestead. We were not married, but even if we had been, I couldn't stop her or convince her it was in David's best interest to stay, as well as hers. Even though I had cancelled the hunts I had planned to work for John, I still had hunters from California and Alaska I needed to guide. Knowing there would be no one to watch Michael, I allowed him to go with David and Sharon as they departed on a charter flight to Fairbanks. I was mad, sad, and lonely as my family disappeared in the thinning daylight of that fall evening. Toklat was my only companion as I sat nursing Yukon Jack in a dark cabin built with such joy and expectations. Toklat was mournful as well, with no boys to play with.

A week later I picked up the Kiely brothers in Manley Springs for their moose hunt, but couldn't guide them. With my knee still swollen and sore, I would take them out as promised and drop them off to hunt on their own. I think they were from somewhere around Sacramento, California. John was a fireman and Hugh a veterinarian. They were pleasant guys referred to me by Glenn Straatsma. It took two trips from Manley to get them to my Melozitna hunting camp.

I told them I would check on them in several days and left. Coming back later, I discovered one of them had shot a monster bull moose right across the river from camp. I had seen the moose from the air many times in the lower portion of the valley. It was huge, measuring more than eighty-two inches in width with many points, wide palms, and massive beams. It was so large I was concerned about flying it on my floats. The brothers discussed how to handle the situation between themselves before finally deciding to cut the antlers in half so I could fly it out. I convinced them not to, as it would ruin the trophy value of the animal. It was a Boone and Crockett level trophy. The antlers would go far up the record book, if not to the top.

There was no way I would be able to take off in the small horseshoe slough by the camp with the antlers tied to the floats. I would have to use the narrow winding river. It would not be pleasant. The Melozitna is a small stream by Alaskan standards and had 150-foot pine trees bordering its banks. Wind would be an issue, as well as the narrow stream itself. It was blowing about 15 mph. The strength of the wind didn't bother me, but the turbulence generated by it boiling over the tops of the trees did. I would not need any downdrafts or wind direction changes as I struggled to get the sluggish airplane into the comparatively smoother air above the trees.

Putting half the moose inside, I took off from the slough and landed on the river just below the rapids above camp. Just tying the antlers on was a problem. When they were finally attached to the float and wing braces to my satisfaction, I had to climb into the airplane through a small side window on the opposite side of the aircraft, still hobbled by my knee. The antlers were so large they blocked my door. Just looking at them tied on to my airplane gave me pause. The wind resistance they would generate would be significant and possibly cause control problems. They were not an extra set of wings but a huge anchor.

I decided to take off up river as I needed to get on step quickly to navigate the rocks in the rapids on each side of the camp. The airplane got on step before I reached the rapids. Staying on the water, I avoided the rocks as N8689V sent a white spraying plume high into the air. The airplane slowed some as it nosed into some of the larger waves but all too soon I was at the head of the rapids gaining speed as the first sharp corner blocked my windshield. A large pine tree whose roots had been eroded by the spring floods leaned dangerously close to the river surface on the inside corner of the turn. Keeping the floats firmly in contact with the water, I used rudder and ailerons to navigate the bend.

Getting around the corner and under the leaning pine without my wings hitting the tall trees on each side of the river, I lifted off on the short straight stretch ahead before taking another sharp turn only fifteen feet above the water. The airplane was lethargic because of the drag of the antlers but made the corner without any problems. In each straight stretch ahead in the river, I lifted the airplane higher in the air until I could climb above the trees. I was able to maintain an airspeed of 70 mph as I climbed out of the Melozitna Valley toward Tanana.

I swore when I flew within eyesight of Tanana. The Tanana River merges with the Yukon a short way above the village. Sand blowing from the mixing winds of the Tanana and Yukon was reaching hundreds of feet in the air. The turbulence from the mixing winds would be horrific. I climbed as high as I could above the blowing sand, but it was not high enough. My airplane shook and bounced so hard I was afraid of losing a wing. After safely making it across the convergence of winds from the two rivers I lowered to thirty feet above the Tanana River, hoping the ground would break up some of the turbulence of the winds gusting down the river. I bounced and swerved up the river, plowing my way slowly toward Manley.

Having to clear the trees to get to Manley, I again climbed to 500 feet, only to have the airplane's horizontal elevator jam. It only did it once in a while under certain wind and load conditions, but it was a pain to deal with, especially loaded as I was. I could horizontally control the airplane pitch with the trim tab and power if I did not allow the nose to raise or lower too much. With plenty of room to land on the river in front of Manley, I made a wide gentle approach and landed without any issues. I was relieved to get the antlers and meat out of my airplane.

After loading them in the back of the Kielys' truck, I checked my horizontal stabilizer. It worked fine again. The demon residing within it decided to be nice until it saw a chance to ruin another day. I had replaced the bushing within the hinges attaching the horizontal stabilizers to the tail, hoping, without success, to solve the issue. I also had mechanics check the stabilizers and try and fix the problem that had started two years before, after I had landed on a rough snow-covered hillside to pick up a wolf I had shot. Nothing had worked and periodically the tail stabilizers would freeze for no apparent reason. Not a happy or safe flight condition.

Slowly my knee healed over the fall and winter, but it would pain me the rest of my life. I really needed to have it operated on. I could not stop flying, so the operation would have to wait for another forty years until it gave out completely. The knee would have to join the growing list of body parts that complained every time I moved. I could deal with the pain as I did with the pain in my back, neck, ankle and shoulders. Pain had been my constant and unwanted companion since my first year of college.

* * *

Overnight the leaves on the cottonwoods turned yellow and started blowing across the cooling water of Stultz Lake. It would soon be frozen over. I needed to get the airplane ready for converting from floats to snow skis. The conversion was much harder without the helping hands of my family to stop the gently swinging airplane dangling from my A-Frame to line up bolt holes. Toklat, now my constant companion, wanted to help. He ran around the swinging airplane, barking and attacking it like it was a giant airborne predator, occasionally knocking me over in his enthusiasm to protect me. A normal two-hour process took twice as long before N8689V, finally on snow skis, sat on the thickening ice along the lake bank.

Waiting the two to three weeks for the ice to get thick enough to support the weight of the airplane used to be a happy time. I would be with my family reading stories or playing with them while getting ready for the long winter ahead. Now there was only getting ready for winter as I cut wood and prepared traps. Even Toklat would whine once in a while and look around for the boys.

The Call

THE CALL FOR HELP CAME over the radio program, "Trap Line Chatter," out of a station in Fairbanks about 120 miles east of my remote homestead in the Yukon-Koyukuk District of the Kuskokwim Mountains in central Alaska. Tom, a man I barely knew, was requesting that I check on his wife, as he was stuck in town and could not get a flight out because of weather. It was not an unusual request, and was the reason I listened to this program every evening if I was home and had enough power in the batteries to turn on the radio. This radio message happened before the advent of computers, satellite telephones and other messaging devices, and was the only way people living in remote locations could receive messages from town.

I knew where Tom and his wife lived as I had made several grocery and postal air deliveries to their cabin, something I did for most of the homesteaders in this remote area of Alaska. Walking outside and looking at Stultz Mountain, I observed that clouds had covered the top half and the wind was blowing a light snow at about 15 mph. I had about a 1,200-foot ceiling and what looked like about five miles' visibility—plenty good enough for flying this January morning if the storm descending on Fairbanks did not come this way overnight. Also, I had a trap line for wolves, wolverine and fox that had to be checked by airplane. This trap line was eighty miles long and ran within fifteen miles of where Tom and his wife lived. Deciding to fly in the morning, I walked out onto Stultz Lake to light the small kerosene heater inside my airplane's engine compartment so the engine oil would heat enough overnight to allow the aircraft engine to start the next day.

The following morning the weather had warmed up twenty degrees but was still good enough for flying, as visibility was still five miles or better. The weather pattern moving into Fairbanks was obviously affecting my local weather for it to warm up this much. Removing the engine and wing covers from my Citabria GCBC, I checked the fuel gauge and saw the tanks were about three-quarters full, much more fuel than needed for this flight. I briefly debated putting in more fuel as the nearest aircraft fueling station was in Nenana, more than sixty air miles away, but decided not to further deplete my precious gas supply. I was only going to notify Tom's wife that he would be delayed a few days until the weather cleared, and check a few traps close to their cabin.

After removing the kerosene heater from the aircraft I rocked the wings to free the skis from the blocks of wood they rested upon, then started the engine. The oil had warmed enough overnight that the oil pressure gauge was in the green. I set the rpms to 900 and walked back inside the house and banked the fire to keep things warm for the two hours I figured I would be gone. I then dumped the rest of the morning's hot coffee into a thermos and headed back outside.

Inside the airplane cockpit I again checked oil pressure, magnetos, controls, and carburetor heat, then cycled the constant speed propeller before adding power and flaps, heading down lake for takeoff. When the airspeed reached 45 mph I lifted and released the flaps as I headed northwest toward East and West Twin Lakes to intersect my trap line.

I checked a few traps on the way, picking up a red fox before heading in a general westerly direction toward Lake Minchumina. The couple's rustic one-room log cabin lay east of Minchumina on a small slough. As I approached their cabin, I was relieved to see a nice plume of smoke coming out of the chimney, as that meant Sara was alive and keeping warm. I did notice that the wind had increased and was coming out of the east. I was taxiing up to the cabin after landing on the small slough when the door opened and Sara walked outside, dressed in a nightgown and heavy coat and boots. I noticed that she had put on a lot of weight since I last saw her about seven months ago. After shutting down the engine and electronics I walked up to her.

My first thought, as I greeted Sara, was that she was not fat but pregnant. My second thought was that she was really far along. My third thought was the panicked realization that she was acting like she was in labor, as she was holding her stomach and grimacing. Sara grabbed tightly onto me as I came close, crying and smiling at the same time saying over and over, "Thank God, thank God my prayers were answered." I don't know about her prayers, but delivering a baby certainly was not on my bucket list.

I got her back inside the cabin and helped her lay back on the bed while informing her that Tom was stuck in town because of weather. A large cat of some unrecognizable breed jumped on the bed as Sara explained between sobs and contractions that this was her first child and it was coming about three weeks earlier than expected. She and Tom had planned on a natural birth here at the cabin—a really dumb idea, I thought. Many young couples come to Alaska and settle somewhere in its vast wilderness expecting idyllic life without the stresses of civilization. Few make it for very long and some of them die in the process. Wilderness living is tough and mistakes are not mere inconveniences, but life-threatening.

Tom had evidently gone to town several weeks earlier to wire for money from his family in the Lower 48. He was also going to get supplies and books on delivering a baby. I was thinking while being told this that my estimation of this couple's sanity on a scale of 1 to 10 had shrunk to about minus 300. I mean, no one loves the Alaska bush more than I do, but that did not stop me from shipping my wife, Sharon, off to the nearest hospital to have both our sons, something every sane person should do if they had the opportunity.

It was obvious while I was comforting Sara that she was really scared and had reason to be. She had changed her mind about having the baby there, and wanted me to fly her to Fairbanks to her husband and a hospital. Good thinking on the first part, very bad thinking on the last.

Here I made the second bad decision of the day. I explained to her that if Tom could not fly out to where we were, flying into town to him might be difficult if not impossible. I told her that the warming temperature and increasing wind strongly indicated a low-pressure system was approaching. I was in a real quandary. Having a baby without proper medical help was dangerous for both Sara and the baby, but I did not want to fly into bad weather with a woman about to have one.

In the end her tears and fright and the very real risks to her and the baby of a home delivery made me agree to take her to Fairbanks, and overcame my reluctance to fly. I had flown hundreds of hours through some really miserable weather that should have killed me and was so bad that birds had given up flying for walking, but I had never delivered a baby nor did I ever want to. I knew a lot about making babies but next to nothing about delivering them.

Books I had read and movies I had seen portrayed this birthing routine as a lengthy and difficult process from which husbands were thankfully excluded. The father's job was to call for a midwife, then get out of the way. The midwife and helper would heat lots hot water and collect clean rags while the woman giving birth lay on the bed screaming, calling her husband every bad name she could think of. One of the ladies would sit by the bed holding her hand, saying over and over in a calm voice, "Take a deep breath and push." What the hell does push mean? The only push that came to my mind was pushing the cabin door open and getting the hell out of there. It only got worse in this delivery thing when someone would kneel between the woman's legs and stick their hand up inside her to feel the dilation of something called the cervix. I had taken high school and college biology and seen diagrams of naked women showing where these female parts were located, but I was a young adolescent male at the time. Then my mind was really on other things than how to deliver a baby. But believe me, as much as I like women, that was not going to happen here if I could help it. I was a bush pilot, not a physician.

Telling Sara to pack, I went back out to the airplane to check my maps and fuel. From what I could figure, it was about 140 nautical miles on an approximately 61-degree heading to Fairbanks. My fuel gauges registered over half full. If the headwinds did not pick up too much, I had enough gas to get to Fairbanks with over forty minutes to spare. I decided to stop in Nenana for more fuel anyway, as flying to Fairbanks would take me almost directly over the Nenana airport. I was concerned about the weather in Fairbanks. I had no way to check it until I got close enough to Nenana to call the Flight Service Station (FSS). The Nenana airport could give me both the Fairbanks weather and what was being reported out of Nenana by local pilots.

No matter how much bad weather a pilot experiences, flying a single engine airplane by visual flight rules (VFR) is not fun when you are in an aircraft going over 100 mph, and can see neither the ground nor what lies ahead of you. Besides not being able to see the rocks in the clouds, it is illegal to fly in these conditions unless you are Instrument Flight Rated (IFR). I had flown many hours on instruments when forced to do so but was not licensed for it, as I did not want to be tempted to do so.

To legally fly VFR, especially near an airport where the FAA (Federal Aviation Administration) heavies are located, you need five miles of visibility and a thousand feet clear of clouds and in sight of the ground. Aircraft icing is a big concern. Icing coats your windshield, making forward visibility impossible. That is the good part. The bad part is that it coats the leading edge of the wings, interrupting the airflow over the camber of the wings that allows an airplane to stay in the air. Though conditions were above VFR minimums here, I was intending to fly into an area where they might not be. A wise pilot in a normal situation would not do so. Not if he valued his life and wanted his airplane to stay in one piece. Even if the pilot survived, he was likely to receive a nastygram from Big Brother inviting him to meet with one of the FAA shrinks or enforcement people.

I had already removed the back seat in my airplane to better accommodate trapping and flying supplies, and needed to take out the dead fox, traps, bait, and other nonessential items, leaving only emergency gear to make a fairly comfortable bed for Sara out of the sleeping bags and pillows from her cabin. It would be a tight fit, as a Citabria cabin is only about ten feet long by two feet wide. The pilot needs about three feet of that space, and emergency equipment needs another foot. Sara walked up to the airplane with a small pack of clothes and a metal cage containing her cat.

I HATE CATS! I mean, what in earth are they good for besides sometimes catching mice? They will not retrieve game birds or fetch on command. They don't welcome you home after a long day on the trail or flying. Besides that, I am allergic to them. Cats make me sneeze and my eyes swell up and water.

I explained to Sara that I would fly her to Fairbanks, but not the cat. She starting crying again and looking at me as if I was some monster instead of the savior who stood in these boots twenty minutes earlier. Sara told me through her tears that the cat would freeze to death if I did not take it, and that she had raised it from a kitten. I wanted to say that freezing was the general idea, but that I would be happy to give it a quick death if that made things easier. Finally, after much hemming and hawing and feelings of guilt, I agreed to take the cat if it stayed in the cage, thereby making mistake number three in this very young day.

I helped Sara climb into the plane and get settled in her makeshift bed. I explained that this was probably going to be a very rough flight, taking well over an hour to complete. If the baby came while we were flying I would not be able to help her. I showed her a can if she needed to urinate and where the backseat gas and trim controls were located and cautioned her not touch or lean against them. I then handed her several barf bags in case her stomach rebelled. I tied the cat cage above the emergency gear on the rear cabin braces.

Taking off was uneventful and we headed toward Nenana to refuel. As we bumped and dipped on this air highway, I was thinking that if the weather was too bad to fly the rest of the way into Fairbanks we could terminate the flight at Nenana where I planned to land and refuel. Sara could get a ride into Fairbanks by vehicle from Nenana if the weather was worsening. If no ride was available, I would hand her off to Wayne Walters, the town cop. He could find her a midwife or deliver the baby himself. I mean, he was the local authority. The more I thought of this the better Nenana sounded to me. I was not being insensitive to Sara's needs. I did not want to endanger her and the unborn child needlessly, I told myself to ease my sense of guilt.

By the time we reached the Kantishna River twenty minutes later, air turbulence had increased from mild to moderate and we were fighting a head wind of over 25 mph. The temperature gauge in my windshield registered zero. The pilot in me realized that there was a large low pressure ahead and to the south of me, and that I was heading into its downwind flow. The visibility had decreased to about two miles with heavy snow. I tried calling Nenana flight control to get a weather update but could not climb high enough to reach them with my VHF radio, as the clouds had descended to less than a thousand feet above the ground. My bad feeling about this flight were intensifying.

The weather worsened in the direction of Nenana, forcing me to angle toward Clear Airforce Base and the Parks Highway. In a very short time we were flying only 500 feet above the ground, and I was fighting to stay in sight of the road. The turbulence was making it extremely uncomfortable for Sara. I was hoping all the gasping, moaning and groaning back there did not mean the baby was coming.

By the time I was able to reach Nenana Flight Service by radio the storm had pushed me about fifteen miles south of my intended route. I was over the Parks Highway following it to Nenana when FSS told me that Nenana airport was closed due to weather. They were reporting an estimated 200-foot ceiling and less than a quarter mile visibility, with icing.

Nenana Airport was remotely operated out of the Fairbanks tower and did not have FAA personnel onsite. I would have snuck into the airport and landed anyway, because I really liked the Wayne Walters idea, except for the icing. The 200-foot ceiling was okay if it was really 200 feet. I only needed 100 feet to clear the trees. The railroad and vehicle bridges over the

Nenana River and the hills on the opposite side of the river were another issue. They required more altitude, and I needed to stay clear of them. Icing was the issue here. I needed to be able to see all of that quarter mile. The controller continued to report that Fairbanks had improved to 1,500-foot ceilings and more than three miles' visibility with light snow, no icing, and winds out of the northeast at 15 mph. They were forecasting worsening conditions in about an hour's time.

I briefly considered heading back up the Parks Highway to Clear Air Force Base. However, landing there was not a legal option, as they reacted badly to private pilots landing on their fancy concrete. I thought about landing on the highway and taxiing up to a house, but decided not to as I might not be able to see electrical wires or road signs soon enough to avoid them.

I hoped the improving weather in Fairbanks would hold for another forty to fifty minutes, and I made the fourth stupid decision of the day and headed toward Fairbanks. Even if Fairbanks International Airport weather was below VFR minimums when I arrived, I could land at one of the local runways in the area that were not controlled. I figured as the weather improved the closer I got to Fairbanks, I would turn the aircraft to the left to intersect the Tanana River and follow it to the Fairbanks Airport. I filed a flight plan by radio from my approximate position into Fairbanks International Airport, stating that I intended to land there within forty minutes.

Looking at my fuel gauges, I realized the head wind cause me to burn more fuel than anticipated. I leaned the fuel flow mixture to the engine even more, keeping an eye on the EGT (exhaust gas temperature) so I did not over-lean the fuel mixture to the point it would cause the engine to overheat. Rechecking my gas situation, I thought I would have enough for the flight, but with a smaller reserve upon arrival than I was comfortable with. I informed Flight Service of this and that I was carrying one passenger who had been in labor more than eighteen hours. They asked if I wanted to declare an emergency. I replied no, but that we would require an ambulance upon arrival. I requested they send the ambulance to the ski strip and not the main runway when I got closer.

I yelled to Sara over the noise of the airplane that it looked like we would be able to get her to a hospital soon. She replied back between gasps of pain that she hoped so because her water had broken. Lovely!

I put myself into survival mode, excluding all thoughts of Sara and everything else outside of the weather and keeping the airplane in the air and headed in the general direction I wanted to fly. The warmer air temperature and moist air was causing the engine to sputter and cough when I applied carburetor heat, meaning ice was forming in the carburetor. Not a good thing, but manageable if it did not start collecting on my wings and windshield.

By the time we were an estimated twenty minutes out of Fairbanks our fuel state was critical and the weather was so bad I was only 200 feet above the ground. Visibility was less than a half-mile at best. The white snow and clouds were occasionally broken up by brush and stands of trees, allowing me limited forward visibility. Turbulence had increased from moderate to occasional bouts of severe. It took all of my experience of thousands of hours of flying in Alaskan weather to keep us from crashing into the trees or going on instruments into the clouds. My arms and legs were burning from the strain of fighting the weather. My back was starting to spasm from being jerked around the cockpit. I had gone from keeping the airplane straight and level to reducing airspeed, trying keep the wings on and just averaging the wild swings of my flight instruments. I was a mess, the weather was a worse mess and Sara the biggest concern of all.

The weather kept me from steering toward the Tanana River to get a pathway into the airport. I had to fly to the right of the river, as the left side had hills much higher than the altitude I was flying. Unfortunately, my side of the river did not have any distinguishing landmarks in this weather to allow me to identify my location. I had no idea how far this storm had blown me off course.

Thankfully I had an electric compass, artificial horizon, and turn and bank instruments, and did not have to rely on a wildly fluctuating traditional compass and needle and ball. I dialed a Fairbanks radio station into my ADF. An ADF is an inaccurate instrument that only gives the directional heading to the station dialed. This gave me the direction to a radio station in Fairbanks somewhere ahead and to the left of me. That was where it should be. My VOR was unable to pick up the Vortac signal from the airport, which would have given me precise directional information to the airport. The radio station could change without notice, as you have no doubt discovered when trying to tune a radio in your car on a trip away from a population center. Without knowledge of wind direction and intensity to compensate for the real path of the airplane, a direct line heading might not take me to the station's location before I would run out of fuel.

My fuel gauges had been bouncing off empty for a while. I was still unable to raise Fairbanks Approach Control on the radio. We had been flying for almost an hour since filing the flight plan. Fairbanks FSS would be trying to contact me, as I was overdue and flying in very hazardous conditions with a medical emergency on board. My fuel gauges were spending more time on empty and less time bouncing. In normal weather conditions this flight should have taken about an hour and forty minutes but was now approaching three hours from the time I had taken off from Stultz Lake. I did not know where we were exactly. Constantly fighting the flight controls was exhausting me mentally as well as physically. Our situation was looking more likely to go from critical to all pilots' most dreaded condition—out of airspeed, altitude and ideas at the same time.

Just when I thought things could not get worse they did. Either the turbulence or Sara's thrashing had somehow unlocked the cat's cage. My first inkling of this was when the large cat jumped onto my head, sinking its claws into my neck and forehead in its acute fright. Without thinking, I ripped the cat off my head, opened the side window and threw it out of the airplane. Now on top of everything else, I had blood running into my eyes and a woman in the back whose pet had just met a horrifying death at my hands.

I was beginning to seriously consider making an emergency landing while I still had the fuel to control the plane and wait out the weather and rescue helicopter, when I heard a faint voice in my earphone calling out my aircraft number. I responded, but they did not hear me. The few minutes before they returned my call seemed like hours. The voice belonging to the Fairbanks Flight Service Station (FSS) called back again, asking my position, direction and situation.

I replied that I did not know exactly where I was, but we were 200 feet off the ground somewhere in the flats west of the airport, flying VFR on an 057 heading in severe weather with a critical fuel situation. They informed me that the airport was closed because Fairbanks had less than a 200-foot ceiling and a quarter mile visibility. I responded that I was declaring an emergency.

Declaring an emergency would allow me to enter airport airspace even when it was closed. I also requested a DF steer to the airport. In a DF

(Direction Finder) steer, the pilot holds down his radio transmitter at various intervals and headings, allowing Flight Service (using some magical formula), to determine his direction and distance from the airport. When it is needed Alaska pilots love their FSS buddies. When not, not so much love.

I was passed to another radio frequency and was requested to hold down my radio transmit button for fifteen seconds, change heading for a minute and then transmit for another fifteen seconds. Flight Service came back on requesting that I climb and transmit again. I replied negative; my fuel situation was critical, and I wanted to maintain visual contact with the ground in case I ran out of gas and had to make an emergency landing. They came back and requested I gain as much altitude as possible, and transmit for another fifteen seconds. I climbed about 150 more feet before all visibility suddenly dropped to zero. I repeated the DF steer process and reported I was now IFR.

I was on instruments whether I wanted to be or not. Flight Service came back and told me I was about six miles from the airport, and gave me a heading to fly. I replied that both my fuel gauges have stopped bouncing, and I did not know if I had enough fuel to reach them. I also wanted to know if the heading they had given me included a wind correction component. I could have hugged them when they said yes.

I informed the person giving me the DF steer that I was a VFR pilot flying on instruments. I told my radio contact I would turn to the given heading then drop down until I had visual contact with the ground. I would transmit for fifteen seconds every minute whether they requested it or not so they could see my direction from the airport in case I ran out of gas. They acknowledged and stated they were turning on the airport approach lights for me and that there was no other known aircraft traffic in the area. My altimeter read 180 feet above ground when I caught a glimpse of trees flashing beneath me. I had not adjusted my altimeter when they gave me the current barometric pressure, so I was not sure of my current actual height above the ground.

As I regained downward visibility, I saw I had a thin sheet of ice on the upper half of my windshield and leading edges of the wings. That meant no more climbing. The only altitude change from here on was down. When I saw the white blaze of the airport approach lights through the blowing snow several minutes later, it was like seeing a halo on an angel. I did not realize until then that I had been holding my breath, and had not heard anything from Sara for a long time. I yelled back to her that we would be landing in one minute and that an ambulance was waiting for her.

The landing on the ski strip adjacent to the main runway was uneventful. The EMTs removed Sara from the airplane. My back hurt so much I was unable to assist them. She did not say anything about her cat when they asked her if the empty cage belonged to her, nor did I volunteer any information about what happened to it. She had glanced at the deep, still-bleeding scratches on my face and neck as she got out of the airplane, and must have known what happened. I gave her a hug and wished her well. She hugged back and thanked me profusely.

At the fuel pump I put 35.5 gallons of fuel in tanks that held 36 gallons. I had Flight Service call a taxi for me. When it arrived I told the driver to take me to the nearest tavern. During the taxi ride, I thanked God for delivering me from my bad decisions one more time, and keeping Sara and her unborn child safe. I should have flown Sara to Tanana instead of trying to fly into bad weather. Tanana had a Native hospital and could have delivered her baby.

Tanana was an Athabaskan Indian village just below where the Tanana River converged with and became the Yukon River. It was about the same distance from Tom and Sara's cabin as Nenana. As aircraft crash investigators are fond of pointing out, a deadly flight is usually not the result of one bad decision, but of many. I had made four questionable decisions that day, and the flight could very well have ended tragically. At the bar I set about seriously trying to deaden my memories of the day. This never works, but the headache the following day makes the recollection more acceptable. The fact that I was alive was a positive, but I needed to quit getting myself into these situations. I never heard from Sara or Tom about the delivery of their child. I hoped they had a happy and healthy baby.

Breaking My Back for the Third Time

AFTER THE COLD OF MINUS FIFTY DEGREE temperatures settled over the still land and daylight shrank to a dim three to four hours a day in February, I broke my back for a third time. I was cutting down cottonwood trees on the opposite shore from my cabin for firewood in the -45 degree temperature. Because of the long summer flying the Aleutians and the injuries during Michael's hunt, I had not been able to ring trees to allow them to die and dry over the summer, so I was cutting living trees frozen by the cold weather. I had been told never to do this, as trees being cut down in this extremely cold weather could shatter from the chainsaw vibration and fall on the man operating it. This was especially true of cottonwood, as they could have hollow interiors. I had been leery of this after being told it killed several Alaskans every year and was really careful the first three winters of harvesting wood. Unfortunately, this day I was engaging in my well-practiced technique of daydreaming instead of paying attention to what I was doing

I came quickly back to reality as I heard an ominous crack. Looking up I saw the large cottonwood I was sawing through had shattered into several big chunks that were falling directly down on top of me. I thought, "Of course the damn things could not fall the other way," as I let go of the saw and made a desperate leap to get out of the way in the deep snow. One of the large sections of the falling frozen tree hit me on the head and back, driving me deep into the snow. Sometime later I came back to consciousness to the soft putting of my idling snowmobile. A heavy weight was on my back pressing me face first into the snow. I tried to move but could not. The intense pain in my back and head competed with the numbness of my frozen face for attention.

I could move my hands and feet and breathe. That was the good part. I slowly began to put together what had happened. My desperate leap and flight as I tried to get away from the falling tree had brought me close enough to the snow machine that, when a piece of the heavy tree fell across me, the machine had absorbed much of the energy. The idling machine had saved me from being smashed into the frozen ground.

I tried inching closer to the machine to get clear of the tree pinning me, but met with resistance and pain. I could move, but it hurt like hell. Slowly, by grasping the side of the snow machine with my hands and shoving my feet against the frozen tundra, I was able to wiggle clear of the tree. I tried to stand up but could not. The pain nearly made me black out as I tried. That, combined with the fact my legs buckled every time I tried to stand, told me I was again in real trouble. I became aware, as I tried to lift myself, that I had also broken some ribs. With every breath and movement, I felt a hot knife driving into my chest in an orchestrated symphony of pain combining with the protests from my head and back. Just holding my head up above the snow was enough to almost make me pass out.

The snow machine was pinned under a twenty-foot section of broken tree. I could not use it to travel the half-mile to the warmth and safety of my cabin. Unable to get to my feet or walk, I blocked out as much pain as I could, got on my hands and knees, and wondered how many more of these violent accidents I would survive. I remained in this position until my breath slowed enough to begin the seemingly endless crawl back to safety. I was worried more about going into shock than the extreme cold, as I was warmly dressed. The good thing I noticed on one of my lengthening rest stops during this travail was that the drool and spit dropping off my face into the snow did not contain any blood. My ribs had not punctured a lung. The bad thing was that Toklat thought this was one of his favorite wrestling games and kept bumping into me, wanting to play. I could not breathe deeply enough to shout at him to go away. Eventually his warm tongue licking the snot and sweat off my face was annoying enough to get me moving again.

I do not know how long it took me to get back to my cabin and crawl inside. It must not have been as long as it felt because it was still daylight outside. I crawled into the living room and turned my oil stove on high as I cuddled around it. The sweat pooling under my clothes woke me up sometime later in the night to the somber eyes of Toklat again licking me on the face. He was thirsty and hungry, but I could also see he was worried. So was I.

On top of the pain, my body had stiffened from the trauma of my injuries. It took me a long time to shed my heavy coat and painfully crawl to one of the crutches I kept in the cabin. Using it, I knocked a bottle of pain pills off the kitchen counter to the floor. My mouth was so dry I could not swallow. I crawled again, this time to the water jug on the floor, where both Toklat and I had a long drink shared from the same container. It hurt to swallow but I managed to get several potent pills down before crawling back to the oil stove where, using my discarded coat for a pillow and Toklat for a blanket, I went into another deep sleep.

With the help of the pain pills and crutches I managed to get to my feet the following day to fix something for Toklat and me to eat, and put on my back brace. I thanked my lucky stars for the doctor who made it for me long years past, as it brought a bit of relief from my back pain. The firmness of the brace across my entire chest also managed to stabilize my broken ribs. I struggled to get onto my bed for another long period of rest. Toklat jumped up to join me and cuddle the pain away.

It was a long week before I was able to hobble out to my airplane to light the engine heater. The following morning Toklat and I flew into the hospital in Tanana. He stayed with friends while I recuperated in the hospital. Four days later, with heavily taped ribs and my back brace back on, we flew back home to Stultz Lake. The doctor knew me enough to know I would not follow his well-meant advice to rest for several months and let my injuries heal. I had wood to cut and haul and a trap line to run. With a new supply of pain pills and rolls of medical tape, Toklat and I flew back to Stultz Lake.

*   *   *

During that spring's wolf hunt with Joe Chandler and Jack Frost, Joe told me one of his friends was a high-ranking Federal Aviation Administration official in Anchorage. He had discussed my lack of a flight physical with the guy, asking him to reinstate it. The friend called Joe back after checking into my case. He told Joe that the FAA had tracked me at every staffed airport I had landed on in the years since they had revoked my physical and were astounded that I had flown into almost every airport in Alaska. He stated that most pilots who were licensed stayed within several hundred miles of their home airport, but that I flew from Point Barrow to Ketchikan and down the Aleutian Chain. Was Joe sure of my mental stability? I am glad Joe was because I sure wasn't, considering everything I had gotten myself into.

Joe's conversation resulted in the FAA agreeing to administer their own physical and mental health evaluation in Anchorage later that spring, prior to making a decision about giving me back my flight physical. Before the physical testing I had to meet with a psychiatrist and pass a psychiatric evaluation and then an intelligence test. The psychiatrist must have been low grade as he passed me even though I could not make any sense of the pictures he asked me to look at. The person administering the intelligence test said my IQ measured out at 114. Whatever in the heck that meant.

I guess I was smarter than a dog because they scheduled me to meet with an FAA physician the following day for the physical part. The male physician asked me to strip and put on one of their funny gowns. Why put the damn thing on? It did not cover anything. Having me lay down on the examining table he put on gloves. I knew I was in trouble. Inserting two of his long fingers into my rectum and wiggling them around, I swear he smiled at my discomfort. The doctor withdrew his fingers after what seemed like an hour of painful humiliation and immediately took my blood pressure and pulse. What kind of a fair physical was this? I was sure my blood pressure was up but not high enough to disqualify me, by the frown that replaced the smile on the doc's face as he read the results. Not trusting the first reading, he rechecked it.

At the end of the FAA examination the only things they found wrong with me were my eyesight and hearing. I was color blind to green/grey, and my hearing was marginal but passable. After taking and passing the colored light test a tower would give me if my radio failed, they told me to meet with an FAA official the following day at their headquarters there in Anchorage.

The man I met the following day had the official government disapproval look on his face that must be issued to all government employees upon being hired. The first thing he asked me was how such an intelligent person as myself could be so stupid? I liked the intelligent part, but not so much the stupid. The stupid struck too close to home. He told me my IQ of 114 was in the low-level genius category, but my actions were solidly moronic. No one in his right mind would fly an airplane following the head injury I suffered in my car accident years ago when the FAA revoked my medical. He obviously did not know that my Stultz head was the hardest thing on my body, as squishy grey matter was held to a minimum. I did not remind him that following the revocation of my flight physical, I had extensive neurological examinations performed, and those physicians had not found anything wrong with me.

I listened to the graduate-level lecture with a contrite face, looking as guilty as a four-year-old caught with his hand in the cookie jar, hoping this damn farce would be over soon. I was genuinely surprised when he handed me my FAA flight physical license signed by the doctor who performed my exam the day before. Gee whiz, could I have been wrong about Big Brother? No, I concluded, as I walked out of the Air Gods' palace. If they hired a psychiatrist who thought I was a low-level genius, they were as incompetent as I figured all along.

David and Michael on the Alcan Highway coming back to Alaska.

Sharon in Trouble Again

As SUMMER APPROACHED and guiding sports fishermen commenced, I received a letter from Sharon's sister in Lake Chelan saying she was worried about Sharon and the kids. Sharon had taken to associating and riding with a local motorcycle gang. The letter included a statement from David's teacher reporting she was really worried about him, as he was drawing pictures of people being stabbed and rarely participated in class. I cancelled the rest of the sports fishermen I had scheduled to drive all the way to Lake Chelan to see for myself what was going on. This one woman was causing me more trouble than a harem full of them would.

Arriving at Lake Chelan a week later, I again confronted my ex-wife about her behavior. She admitted both Michael and David were having problems she could not handle by herself. She also admitted she was good friends with the motorcycle gang and often rode with them. I convinced her after several hours that the life she was living was both dangerous to her and harmful for the boys. She agreed to move back to Alaska where I could be more involved with the boys' upbringing. I did not want her living with me anymore, but wanted her close enough I did not have to drive thousands of miles to monitor my sons. I had some wonderful relationships with women and pondered why this one was like a heavy weight around my neck. Each time I lifted the anchor off the bottom, it would eventually drag me back down into troubled waters.

We agreed to travel back up the Alcan together. The boys were beside themselves with joy to see me and to be going back to Alaska. The trip back up the Alcan was far different from our adventure of years past. We finally arrived in Fairbanks, where I helped Sharon get an apartment. Michael flew off to Cordova to be a deck hand with my friend, Bob Widmann, on his commercial fishing seiner. I flew up to Bettles to start assistant guiding with John.

* * *

After landing in Bettles I walked over to John's house to discuss the upcoming hunting season. He told me his clients were mainly from Germany and Austria. He had hired a local pilot with a large capacity plane to fly all the gear, food, supplies, and equipment needed at the hunting camp out to the high lake location where we had met two years prior. I would help him with guiding his clients for caribou, sheep, moose and bear. John was also a pilot and had a Champion AC, like the first airplane I owned in Yakutat. It was on wheels so he used it sparingly.

On this first meeting we were like two alpha male wolves circling each other with our tails out and neck hair raised. John because we had only met once, and me because I really did not know if I wanted to work for another guide. I was the outcast coming into the pack for the first time. After a period of sniffing each other's rear ends, things relaxed as I explained to John I would do as he requested within certain limits. If he wanted to use my airplane to guide with I would do the flying and it would cost him $200 an hour. I alone would decide if the weather or landing site was safe. John questioned me about my hunting and flying experience. We were both satisfied after an hour of questions and answers and agreed to meet the next morning where he had torn down my camp. I was spending that night with a lady friend, but would be staying with him if we were overnighting in Bettles during the time I guided for him.

When the clients joined us at the sheep hunting camp a week later, everything was set up for their arrival. They shared white wall tents, as did John and I. The hunters were serious and respectful. They had all taken advanced hunting courses in their native lands. Unlike our hunting classes, they learned to have respect for the animals hunted as well as the environment in which the animals lived. I was impressed. It was an intelligent and thoughtful process that made the hunter part of the stewardship of the land. There were four hunters, one of whom had brought his wife along. John went over his expectations with the men, including the instruction that hunters were never to fire their weapons without the consent of either John or me. I was impressed with John after his talk. We shared many of the same attitudes about hunting and guiding. I began to relax about assistant guiding for him.

Caribou were again using the pass as a migratory path to their winter grounds and small herds were constantly seen on the shore and skyline around us. We took the men caribou hunting first. Both John's and my client each got a nice caribou the next morning. The man I was guiding was careful with his weapon and respectful to the animal he killed, putting a sprig of food in the dead animal's mouth and thanking it for his sacrifice. It was a happy camp when everyone called it a night and headed to their individual tents.

I was awakened by a loud rifle shot the next morning. Jumping out of my tent after dressing, I went to see what was going on. I figured it was a grizzly bear eating the caribou we had shot the day before. I saw John angrily gesturing at the Austrian hunter. Walking up to the hot discussion, I learned that the Austrian had awakened early and seen a herd of caribou close to his tent and had shot one. Not only was this against John's camp rules, it was also stupid, as the man had shot a female caribou. John was red in the face as he shouted at the befuddled man. I parted them to allow a cooling off period.

The Austrian was extremely disappointed when his small female antlers were placed next to the male antlers taken the day before. They were less than a quarter the size. When he complained he wanted to shoot another one, John angrily told him no, that he had filled his one tag. The man puffed up in self-importance and reached into his billfold and pulled out several gold coins worth over $500 each in an attempt to bribe John. I was delighted when John refused them. After being rebuffed, the hunter turned his back on us and stamped back to his tent in self-righteous anger. He was like a little child who had been told to get out of the sandbox by his friends because they did not want to play with him anymore.

I took the last German hunter out for caribou after breakfast while John took another for a sheep hunt. My hunter and I hiked several miles away from camp to the edge of a mountain to glass over passing caribou. Unfortunately, most were females with their young. Later in the afternoon we spotted a herd of eight bulls walking and feeding on lichen across the pass. We attempted to get within range without success. Lichen on which the caribou feed takes over 90 years to mature. Through natural selection, caribou do not stop and feed as do horses and cows, but continue walking as they forage, stopping only to take a few bites before moving on. If they stopped and grazed like domestic animals, they would destroy large portions of their feeding grounds because it takes so long for lichen to grow back. This makes it extremely hard for hunters to catch up to them. Caribou, with their broad hooves, walked easily over tundra and muskeg that humans struggled over. Looking back at my red-faced, sweating hunter, I decided the caribou won this round and turned toward camp. Besides, my feet were hurting badly and felt like I had developed blisters. I was having an increasingly difficult time walking. I had worn the same White's boots for years. They were well broken in and unlikely to cause a problem.

Taking off my boots back in my tent, I saw my socks were bloody as I peeled them off. Both feet were blistered so badly they were bleeding. I wear boots the year around and should never have blisters. I doctored them as much as possible and put on softer shoes to wear around camp. I decided that my knee was causing the problem. It had never healed completely and had changed my stride as I walked. This was going to be a doubly painful season.

The next morning my hunter was successful. We returned to camp where the guy was met by a smiling wife and a big hug and kiss while I hobbled around and hung the meat. Sitting down with a sigh of relief, I started the tedious process of preparing the antlers and skull for a European mount. European mounts don't contain the skin but only the bone of the animal skull. John and I preserved the cape from the animal's head and shoulder to either sell to a taxidermist or to a hunter who needed one. Many hunters do not skin an animal correctly for mounting later, so taxidermists were always looking to buy the capes of trophy animals.

John was unsuccessful again, guiding his hunter for a sheep, and asked me to take the guy out the following morning to another canyon about five miles from camp. I cringed thinking of my injured feet, but said I would do it. It would be a long day hiking the ten miles to and from camp, not including climbing the canyon to get a shot at a sheep if there were any there. I talked that evening over the camp fire with Eric, the guy I would be guiding. I asked if he was up to a long hike after the two days he had already spent hunting sheep and caribou, or if he wanted to take a day off to rest up. Eric assured me he was up to the challenge, as he was disappointed with sheep hunting so far.

My valiant effort to get a day off for my feet failed. John noticed I had changed shoes and was limping. He asked if I had injured myself. I explained the problems with my feet and told him to ignore it. I would continue hunting even if I had to crawl. If, as a seventeen-year-old I could continue throwing sixty pound bales of hay for another eight hours after a fellow farm hand put two tines of a hay fork through my hand, I would not be stopped by mere blisters.

Getting up before dark to make coffee and breakfast I was met by Eric, who helped me do both. We ate and picked up our packs containing lunch, water, and first aid kits, as well as some lightweight survival gear in case we got caught in a storm. The hike to the mouth of the canyon was downhill through alder patches, uneven tundra, and rocks. We stopped to glass a large male grizzly bear on a side hill and discussed taking it instead of a sheep. While Eric was trying to make up his mind, the bear made it up for him by leaving the area. It was walking away from us and over a mile away. The chance of catching up to the bear with the wind blowing in the wrong direction was almost nil, especially with my bad feet.

Continuing on to our targeted hunting area, I set up my spotting scope on a large, grey rock splotched with lichen to see if there were Dall rams in the area. At first the slopes seemed empty of activity, although there were many sheep trails crossing the vertical shale slides. We moved higher into the canyon and up the right side slope to get a better vantage point for glassing. Once set up, I could see rams bedded down on a slope hidden from our previous location. Only one was legal. The eldest of the group was a full curl. Dall sheep rams have to be a minimum of three-quarters curl to be legal. It is fairly easy to determine if a ram is legal or not. If the animal's horns curl past the eye, it is legal.

Wind in mountain canyons is extremely difficult to sort out. It swirls and moves around without any set pattern and can change from one breath to the next. Dall sheep have six times the eyesight humans do, and their sense of smell is uncanny. There was a slight breeze blowing. A lot of things were against this hunt being successful, mainly due to the wind. To compound the problem, we would be in plain sight of the animals on several occasions.

I led us back down to the canyon floor before making our way slowly up to the sheep. The rocks littering the floor were larger than those higher up and were easier to step over and around without making a noise. The rattle of falling shale above us made me stop and look up. The sheep that had been bedded down were now walking back toward the canyon's mouth. I quickly got out of Eric's way, pointing out the sheep I wanted him to shoot. They were standing still about 250 yards above us trying to determine what we were. Eric brought the rifle to his shoulder, took a deep breath, and pulled the trigger. The large ram never knew what hit him as he immediately collapsed and rolled down hill toward us.

I congratulated Eric and took the obligatory photographs before dragging the animal the last fifty yards to the valley floor to prepare for packing the meat and horns back to camp. We started the long uphill walk back toward camp when the grizzly bear made another appearance. I shooed it away by shouting and throwing rocks at it. The rest of the way back to camp Eric was looking over his shoulder, worrying about being attacked by the curious bear. He was not mollified by my explanation that the bear would be more than pleased with the remains of the sheep we left behind.

Arriving back at camp, exhausted by the day's efforts, we were met by the rest of the hunters and John. John and his hunter had been unsuccessful again on their hunt. John gave me a peculiar look upon examining the sheep, as if he were surprised we had shot one. I shrugged the look off and together we hung up the meat and horns. That evening I was approached by several other hunters, who requested I take them out next. This was always done out of John's hearing. I clarified each time that I was working for John, and that he made that decision; they should ask him. Several replied that they already had. That explained the questioning look John had given me earlier. From everything I had observed, John was a competent hunter and guide. The only difference between my hunter's success and his was chance, I explained to each of them. It was very early in the hunt, so I cautioned them to be patient.

If John and I had known each other better, I would have teased him about it. I always followed his requests, as this was his camp. I did not want to upset him or the clients, so I did not argue with John, even when I felt him to be wrong. There was an uneasy truce between us that night as we sought out our sleeping bags. My head barely hit the mattress before I was soundly asleep.

I was rudely awakened by the loud thumping of helicopter blades shortly after dawn. I had planned to get a few extra hours of sleep because of the physical demands of yesterday's hunt, and groaned as the helicopters circled back around and landed in camp. This was really out of the norm. No one had helicopters up here, except the government and oil companies. Neither had any reason to be landing here. Struggling into my cold clothes, I stumbled outside to see a sight out of bad war movies taking place. The United States Forest Service SWAT team was rousting our hunters out of their tents with sawed-off shotguns. One of the SWAT team members made John and I back up to an area away from the clients with a shotgun pointed at our chests. I was both incensed and flabbergasted.

Our angry demands to know what was going on were ignored. The SWAT team were all dressed in black and equipped like they were invading a foreign nation. My puzzlement was replaced by growing anger as I watched our clients being rudely ordered about while their passports and hunting licenses were examined. This was the United States of America, not the domain of some third-world dictator. We do not treat people this way. I was wrong. That morning our government treated us as if we were criminals.

Prior to departing, the Park Service leader of the raid told John they had moved a large contingent into Bettles to monitor all hunting activity in the Brooks Range. He stated all hunting in this area would be outlawed with the passage of the Indian Land Claims Settlement now being voted on by the various tribes. They were making sure hunters and guides got the message.

I interrupted the preening ass to point out that he had no right being there. The Land Claims had not yet passed, and this was certainly not a National Park. The Park Service also had no right to treat us or our clients like they were criminals. The arrogant prick looked down his broad black nose at me before coldly stating we were on federal land and he could do whatever he wanted. My response, that some of our military had thought the same during the Vietnam War before they landed in prison for killing innocent civilians, so infuriated him that he bumped his armor and bullet laden chest into mine, sneering what did I think I could do about it. After disdainfully glaring at me again, he motioned his men back into the helicopters. They took off leaving a very shaken and angry camp behind.

Besides being angry, I was astonished, as we tried to calm everyone down. The clients felt that if the United States Government treated people like this they wanted to leave. John was as angry as I was and later asked me if I would fly to Fairbanks and complain to Alaska's governor about the incident. I told John he should do it, as he was the Registered Guide. That was true, but I also did not want to reveal my presence to Fish and Game authorities, either. I still had hunters of my own to take out after I finished with John.

John convinced me that he was too nervous talking to high-ranking government officials and newspapers. He felt I would do a better job.

Reluctantly, because I did not want the incident to go unreported, I agreed to do so. I prepared my airplane for a flight to Fairbanks. I stopped at Bettles after leaving the Brooks Range to fill my gas tanks for a direct flight to Fairbanks. There was indeed a large encampment of Forest Service personnel, complete with helicopter, camped around the Bettles airstrip. Just the sight of them made me angry all over again.

After fueling up, I walked to the only lodge/store in this small community to see what was going on and get something to eat. The owner was furious over the "Federal Invasion," as he termed it. He stated the same black man I had confronted had waltzed into his lodge, demanding he kick out all of his guests for the rest of the hunting season, and rent the rooms to the Forest Service. He had kicked the guy out of his establishment, telling him not only would he not rent a room to them, but he would not sell anything to them, either. They were not allowed in his lodge or his bar.

Flying on to Fairbanks, I called the governor's office in Juneau, asking to speak to the governor. The call was answered by an aide who explained the governor was not available and asked what I wished to talk to him about. I tried without success to get beyond this telephone screening, and finally told him why I was calling. He asked for John's and my names, as well as those of our clients. I only gave him mine and John's, stating we would be glad to introduce our clients to any Alaskan official who wanted to speak to them about the incident if they would fly out to our camp and do it in person. Finally, after repeating the series of events several times to him, I hung up, unconvinced any of this would reach the governor. At least this was a new governor I thought, and would not be upset about the helicopter incident years before after hearing my name.

I then called the Fairbanks *Daily Miner*, the only newspaper in Fairbanks, to make sure the actions of the Park Service were known and not covered up by my own state government. Speaking to the editor, I told him what had happened. The editor told me he had heard rumblings of other incidents of this type, but it was the first time they had gotten a first-hand account. I gave permission to use my name in any article relating to the incident. I explained I would be out of contact guiding in the Brooks Range for any follow-up questions. After another half hour of questions and answers, we hung up.

After returning to the Brooks Range, John told me he was moving camp back to Bettles to operate out of one of his other camps that he could

reach with his airplane on wheels. He asked if I would take one of the hunters out to my homestead and get him a moose, black, and grizzly bears. I
agreed after settling the terms for the use of my airplane and homestead.

I was met on the banks of the Koyukuk River by Fish and Game the
next time I landed. The Koyukuk runs right by the outskirts of Bettles.
Officer Dick Hynman, who used to be stationed in Delta Junction while I
was an officer in Fairbanks, walked out to my airplane as I was tying it to
the banks of the Koyukuk. I was right. Talking to the press about the Park
Service brought Fish and Game right to my doorstep. Dick would meet me
and whoever I was guiding every time I landed in Bettles for the rest of the
hunting season. I liked Dick. He was fair minded and hardworking, what
every game warden in Alaska should aspire to be. However, now I was on
the other side of the badge, and our relationship changed. Although I was
legally guiding for John in Bettles, I had my own hunter to look out for
later, a completely different proposition.

Peter, the hunter John next assigned to me, and I loaded the airplane
and took off southwest toward Huslia to hunt black bears feeding on
blueberries around the thousands of small lakes that dotted the low lands
between there and Galena. Seeing seven black bears close to one large patch
of blueberries, we landed a half mile away on a lake and set up camp. It was
getting close to evening. I was tired from flying all day. The camp was set
in a small copse of pines that provided wood for a campfire. There was no
wind and the camp was inundated with hordes of mosquitoes. I used some
green wood for the fire, but that was only marginally successful in keeping
the pesky mosquitoes from sucking us dry of blood.

We did not get up early, but stayed within the mosquito-proof confines
of our tent until the sun was well up. There was no hurry, as the black bears
would not start feeding until later. Black bears are mostly nocturnal and
would not be up until they finished their morning naps. I was puzzled as
to why Peter wanted a black bear. Most of my clients never mentioned
them. To me, shooting black bears was so common it was like going to the
neighborhood grocery store. I usually shot around ten bruins a year for
their meat and fat. Peter explained that black bears were prized in Europe,
as they did not exist there. Europe had brown bears but no black bears.

After eating a leisurely breakfast and packing a lunch, we hiked over
the rough tundra in hip boots to a location where we could keep an eye
on the blueberry patch. I did not pack my spotting scope, as binoculars

would be sufficient. Soon after we settled down, a black bear sow with two cubs walked into the patch and started feeding. Peter enjoyed watching the antics of the cubs while I kept a looking for a larger boar. Eventually the sow had her fill and wandered off with her cubs. Peter was getting anxious, as we had only seen three bears, and wondered if we should move. Finally, a mature black boar suddenly popped into sight, feeding on berries. I had not seen him approach, so he might have been bedded down right in the middle of the blueberries and just woken up.

I went over how we would stalk the bears with Peter, and made sure he knew where to aim to hit the bear's heart. It was an easy stalk. The bear was busy feeding on berries. They have terrible eyesight and he did not see us as we approached him from upwind. When Peter was ready, I had him steady his rifle against an upright pack board and put a bullet in the chamber. I readied my own rifle and told him to shoot.

Peter put a bullet from his 8mm Mauser right at the top of the shoulder. The bear dropped immediately. He was excited as we approached the animal, which I made sure was dead before letting him get near. He said a prayer of thanks for the spirit of the dead animal. This moment of reverence for the animal they had taken from European hunters always brought a feeling of respect and satisfaction to me. American hunters mostly celebrated themselves when they viewed an animal they had just shot. We could learn something from our European brothers.

Soon we were back in the air headed to Ruby, the closest native village, to get some gas. While gassing up, two of the Kangas boys with whom I was friends when teaching there came down to say hello. They explained that the principal had made an ass of himself after I left and finally was transferred to Tanana. They also asked if I was the guide the newspapers and radio were talking about, who had his camp invaded by the Park Service.

After having a good talk and saying goodbye to them, Peter and I took off heading to Stultz Lake. I planned to stage our hunts for moose and grizzly bears out of the homestead. It would be much more comfortable than camping out. I was getting tired of washing dead mosquitoes down with my coffee. Peter was impressed with our house on Stultz Lake, having envisioned a crude log cabin. We feasted on bear steaks along with fresh potatoes and vegetables from my garden that evening.

In the morning we headed past Tanana Village to a small lake below Wolf Mountain in the Korine Hills where I had seen grizzly bears in the past. We saw several bull moose along the Little Melozitna River, but I did not want to hunt that close to Tanana. The villagers needed moose meat for the winter. I was friends with many of them and did not want to make their hunting more difficult. I would drop off the meat from this hunt if we were successful, to help feed the elderly of the village.

Finding and landing at a suitable lake to camp took until almost dusk. I was just getting ready to cook dinner when Peter rushed over to me, saying there was a large bull moose on the hill above camp. It was late. I was concerned about shooting an animal and getting it to camp before dark. Peter's infectious urgency to hunt overcame my common sense. I put away the food and got out my rifle and pack. The moose was bedded down about a half mile from camp. He was large enough that his antlers were visible from where we stood, but we would have to go into the surrounding forest to approach it without being seen by the sleeping animal.

The climb up the steep hills to get on a level with the moose brought sweat to my face and glee to the swarming mosquitoes. Attracted by our puffing breath, they made the climb more miserable. We stopped to apply fresh mosquito repellant that had not been needed in camp. I explained to Peter how we would approach the bedded moose. I also told him that if the moose had moved we would not pursue him this evening but go back to camp. Thankfully my feet were almost healed and no longer bothered me. It took precious daylight to creep silently through the pines before I caught sight of the moose. He was still laying where we had last spotted him. I got Peter ready to shoot before calling to the moose, using their mating grunt. Peter downed the moose with one shot as it jumped to its feet searching for the bull who had invaded his territory.

This time I was impatient while Peter placed a branch of pine in the moose's mouth and paid the slain animal his respect and thanks. It was getting dark and we had a dead moose half-a-mile from camp in an area where I knew several grizzly bears lived. Their eyesight might be bad, but they could smell dead prey from a long way away. We quickly removed the stomach and intestines from the animal before quartering it, but it was pitch black dark before I hoisted a hind quarter to my shoulder. Peter started to pick up the antlers to carry back to camp. I made him put them back down and pick up a front quarter. He was not happy with my telling him the meat came out first. We would come back in the morning for his trophy and the rest of the meat. He reluctantly picked up the front quarter I pointed to and we started downhill to camp in the darkness. I kept a round chambered in my .444 as we noisily made our way through the brush and rocks. There was no sense trying to keep quiet. I wanted the dead meat off my back as quickly as possible.

Peter fretted about leaving the antlers behind as I tiredly made dinner. He finally quieted and accepted my decision when I explained that Europeans had their special way of paying respect to the animals they hunted. In America we, too, paid our respect to animals, by making sure the meat they provided was not wasted and came out before or with the trophy. Since we could not carry it all out at once we would get his antlers and skull in the morning along with the rest of the moose meat.

Morning came way too early. My back pain made it hard to roll out of the sleeping bag to start the morning fire and coffee. Upon exiting the dew-covered tent, I was greeted by a sea of fog. I could not even see my airplane as it floated on the lake sixty yards from camp. Walking over to the moose meat we had hung-up before retiring the night before, I was relieved to see it had not been chewed on by bears. I sat around the fire watching the fog lighten as the sun rose, drinking coffee. I did not awaken Peter from his deep slumber as I was sure he was even more worn out than I was. Besides, there was no hurry. I did not want to approach the moose carcass we left behind last night in the fog. The interior of Alaska this summer had been fairly dry, only wetted by the occasional thunder showers during the late afternoon. There must have been more precipitation in this area than normal for this much fog. I waited patiently for the sun to raise the morning temperature enough for the air to absorb the fog as I tried to get the kinks and pain out of my back and knee.

By the time Peter got out of his sleeping bag to join me for coffee and breakfast, most of the fog was gone. It still clung to parts of the mountain in which the dead moose lay. When we had finished breakfast, we began the hike back to get the rest of the moose meat and antlers. I made as much noise as possible as we neared the site of last night's kill. As we closed in the wind pushed one of the few remaining banks of fog over us, reducing our visibility to less than fifty yards.

The hackles on my neck raised the minute I saw the carcass of the dead moose. It was covered with moss and tree branches. A grizzly had found the kill during the night and had covered it after eating its fill. It would be close and protective. As we had made noise approaching, it knew exactly where we were. I moved a couple feet away from Peter after telling him to chamber a round and back slowly downhill. Before he could begin to move, a large grizzly bear charged us from the brush thirty yards away with a deep roar.

I brought my rifle to my shoulder and fired a shot at the base of the bear's skull the same time Peter's rifle barked. The bear immediately dropped, not more than ten yards in front of us. We each shot it once more before it stopped moving. I knew from first sighting the charging bear it was him or us. His ears were flat against his head. He was not fooling around, but protecting his food supply. My first shot had severed the spine, dropping it before it could maul us. It was an extremely lucky shot. Peter had hit it in the middle of the chest. The last two shots were fired into the bear's heart.

After looking at the bear, Peter slumped down to his butt, holding his head in his hands, shaking with delayed nerves. My heart was pounding as well. It had been too damn close. A bear skull is very thick and angled. That and the tough skin covering it made penetrating the skull area with a rifle bullet a chancy proposition. If I had hit the skull instead of the spinal column behind the large head, it was more than likely one or both of us would have been dragged to the pile of moss and branches and added to the bear's winter larder. The fact that the bear was slightly downhill, charging with his head low, had allowed me to take the only shot that would have stopped the fast-charging bear in time. A grizzly bear, despite its bulk, can outrun a quarter horse in a quarter mile. They are very fast, in short spurts.

It was a while before Peter regained his composure enough to help me skin the bear. He held the legs with a pale face and shaking hands. He looked at me and asked if the bear would have killed us. His face even got paler when I said yes.

Peter was quiet the rest of the day as we skinned the bear. The moose meat we left the night before had been ruined by the grizzly. We would not be packing it out. I put the bear skin and skull into my pack, while Peter tied the moose antlers and skull to his. They were heavy packs. Mine was close to 200 pounds while Peter's was over a hundred. Struggling downhill toward camp behind me, Peter asked if we were going to stay there or fly back to Stultz Lake. He was relieved when I said we would load everything into the airplane and fly back to my lake, after dropping off the moose meat we packed out last night at Tanana. Peter had had enough of bear hunting. He was going to see this one in his nightmares for years to come.

Killer Black Bear

AFTER BECOMING A GAME WARDEN years before, I had an encounter with a black bear that increased my respect for the species immensely. I had previously held them in little regard as to their danger to me. Don Roberts received a call from an official overseeing a camp of prisoners from the Fairbanks jail. The prisoners were cutting fire lines halfway between Fairbanks and Nenana. He told Don a black bear was attacking the prisoners and asked if he would send someone out to kill it. Don knew I hunted bears and asked me to go out to the camp and see what I could do.

Arriving at the camp, I talked to the camp manager. He explained that some of the prisoners had fed black bears from their lunches as they rode back and forth to where they were cutting trails. The camp supervisor made them stop this practice once he was made aware of it. One large black bear took exception to the fact that he was no longer being fed each morning and afternoon. The bear decided to take matters into his own paws, and jumped up onto the bed of the truck, severely injuring several prisoners before taking their lunches. The prisoners were afraid to go to work now. The bear had also located the camp and was breaking into tents and storage facilities. They had no choice but take the prisoners back to jail until the bear was killed.

The news of the incident spread, drawing a large crowd of hunters who came to kill the notorious bear. I looked at the hunters standing around with rifles. There was no way I was going to hunt with this many people nearby. They were talking and smoking as they walked off to where the large black bear was last seen. I informed the camp manager I would not hunt with this many people around. I told him I doubted they would be successful, from watching how they hunted. If the hunters were not able to shoot the bear, he was to call Fish and Game and I would come back. After I gave the manager my personal telephone number, I told him to call me, but only if I was the only one allowed to hunt.

A week later Don called me back into the office and said the manager had requested I come back and take care of the bear. No one had been successful in killing it. It seemed when the hunters were in the field, the bear snuck around them and raided the camp. The camp manager assured Don that he had sent all the other hunters home.

Returning to the almost deserted camp, I asked the manager to keep everyone left inside their tents for the night while I hunted. He agreed and I started tracking and hunting the rogue black bear. I saw two smaller bears prowling around camp that I shot within the first hour. The manager came out and ask if I had gotten the rogue. I told him I did not think so, as they were small and not like the bear he was describing. He helped me drag the two dead bears to some nearby trees where I dressed them and hung them up as bait for the larger bear. I then went to a nearby meadow with a mound of big rocks in the middle to set up an observation post. I heard another bear around the kills, but it never came into the open to give me a shot.

At 1:30 a.m. I was sitting at the rocks when the hair on the back of my neck rose. I could not determine why until I looked behind me. The large black bear was sitting five feet behind me, just watching me. I immediately rolled onto my back and shot the bear in the chest with my .338 Browning Magnum, killing it. How it had gotten across the open meadow without me seeing it was baffling. The taxidermist who later mounted it for me said it was the largest black bear he had seen in his twenty years of working in Fairbanks. They had to use a grizzly bear mount for the head, as the black bear mounts were too small.

This greatly increased my respect for the species. It could have easily killed me. I talked to many experienced Alaskans later about the episode and, to a man, they said the black bear was the most dangerous animal in the Alaska bush. They told me that black bears killed more experienced trappers and homesteaders than all other species combined. Most bears, except polar bears, attacked humans out of anger, or to protect their young or food supply. During prolonged warm dry weather when a bear's source of berries and other vegetation in its food supply dried up, or when the bears became diseased or injured, they became very dangerous. Black bears would patiently watch where you went and would ambush you without any warning or provocation. They did not want to chase you away from their cubs or food supply, they wanted to eat you.

I explained this to Peter as we flew to Tanana to drop off the moose meat we had salvaged. I dropped it off with a friend in the village to share with the older people who could no longer hunt. I did this at many villages when guiding hunters only wanted trophies and not the meat.

We then headed out to Stultz Lake. We spent two relaxing days while I fleshed out and salted the hide and prepared the skulls. I thought it likely that Fish and Game would check me again when I landed on the river at Bettles. When I asked Peter for his moose and bear tags to attach to the antlers and skulls, I was concerned when he said John had not given them to him. There was nothing I could do about the tags. There was also no way I could keep Fish and Game from seeing the untagged moose antlers as they were in plain sight on my floats, but I packed the two bear hides and skulls in duffle bags. On top of the hides I put some blood-stained clothes we had been wearing during the hunt. Arriving back at Bettles, Dick again met me as I taxied to shore. I was right; he was waiting for me to return. If this had been a normal Fish and Game patrol, Dick would have been flying out to the various camps checking on hunters. It seemed he was only interested in me. Someone had put him up to it.

Dick immediately noticed the moose antlers did not have a tag on them as he reached for the float rope to tie us off on shore. He asked me about them as I jumped off the floats. I told Dick it was my fault; I thought my hunter had them in his possession. I did not discover the tag was in Bettles until he shot the moose. John walked up at this time with the moose tag in his hand, apologizing to Dick for not giving them to us before we left. Dick could have issued a citation, as a guided out-of-state hunter had to seal the trophies immediately upon killing the animal. He watched John put the tag around the antlers. John looked questioningly at me behind Dick's back as he held the bear seals in his hands. I shook my head no, and he quickly put them in his pocket.

Dick might overlook one moose antler tag with only a warning, but not two additional bear tags. After examining Peter's and my licenses, Dick asked where the moose meat was. I provided the name of my friend in Tanana I had given the meat in case he wanted to check the story. Dick wrote down the name and asked why I had left it in Tanana. I could tell he approved when he learned I had left the meat for the elders in the village.

Knowing I was on thin ice, I asked Dick if he would help me unload the airplane. I knew full well he was curious as to what was inside. I held my breath as I handed the duffle bags to him. He glimpsed through the folded tops at the clothes underneath, but did not empty them. After helping me unload the rest of the camping gear he departed, telling me to always tag the trophy immediately. John almost fainted when I showed him the bear hides underneath the clothes after Dick's departure. I admonished him to never send me out with a hunter without tags again.

* * *

Things had heated up in Bettles during the week and a half Peter and I were gone. The Park Service had singled out the owner of the Bettles Lodge for special surveillance on his yearly sheep hunt. It seems as if his refusal to serve them in his lodge had greatly upset them. They declared the area he hunted in off limits for hunting. What gave them the power to do so, beside the fact that the federal government owned 90 percent of the land in Alaska, I don't know. John told me that evening that they had sent helicopters and float planes after the lodge owner when they learned he went hunting after being warned against it. A short while after the lodge owner downed a Dall sheep he saw a Park Service helicopter circling his airplane below, on the lake he landed on. He managed to bury the sheep meat in some willows that grew thickly around the lake under a blanket of moss before walking out to the Park Rangers standing around his airplane.

The Park Service questioned him when he walked over to them. They demanded to know where the dead sheep was. Not believing that he had not shot anything and only came out this far from town to target practice, they asked how he had gotten blood on his hands. Smiling, the owner climbed onto his airplane, saying he cut himself on some rocks, and took off back to Bettles. He hoped the Park Service would neither find the sheep carcass two miles away in a canyon nor the meat he hurriedly buried on the edge of the lake. It is not a testimony to their training or knowledge of Alaska that they found neither.

The guy was upset that the animal was going to waste. He was too much of an outdoorsman to let the meat rot. He did not care about the horns or cape, just the meat. He asked John if I could fly in and get it, as they were watching him and his float plane. I flew over the lake where he buried the sheep to discover that the Park Service was still looking for the sheep they knew he had shot. There were four large tents and about twelve federal employees within 500 yards of the buried sheep.

After flying back to Bettles, we came up with a plan for John and the owner to tie one of the large caribou antlers we had taken earlier at the high lake onto the lodge owner's airplane. They were to fly to the opposite end of the lake from where the Park Service had set up camp, land, jump out of their float plane, and fire several rifle shots in the brush at that end of the lake. I would be flying nearby out of sight. Fifteen minutes after they radioed me they were landing, I would swoop in and land at the other end to quickly get the sheep meat and fly out before the Park Service could get back to my airplane.

We photographed the caribou and antlers prior to taking off, and got sworn statements from residents the caribou was shot prior. John radioed me that, when they landed, the entire federal camp started running down the lake toward them. I timed my landing for fifteen minutes later. Quickly jumping out of my airplane, I saw several Park Service employees at the far end of the lake turn back toward me. It took me several minutes to locate the buried sheep and five more minutes to get the meat into my airplane. Two Park Service guys were within forty yards of me by the time I could jump back in my airplane and start the engine. They were waving their arms and shouting at me to stop. I waved back as I gave N8689V full power, and took off with the sheep meat safely stacked behind me.

The owner and John were questioned for over an hour before they were released. They explained they had landed on the way to a caribou hunt and needed to sight in their rifles, which was the rifle fire the Park Service heard. The caribou antlers on their floats were obviously taken at least a week before. The federal employees were just figuring out that they had been fooled and were extremely upset, promising all kinds of legal hell. Finally, John and the owner told them to talk to their lawyers, got in their airplane, and left the exasperated campers behind. I was later questioned in town about the incident. I could tell the two Park Service employees confronting me did not believe that I had landed just to relieve myself.

John and the lodge owner were still laughing when they landed at Bettles and retold the story to the delight of residents who had their fill of the arrogance and superiority of these representatives of the federal government. The owner was so pleased to get his sheep meat that he offered to pay me for my time and gas. I declined, but accepted a free meal that evening with all the drinks I could handle. That night, while celebrating, I met the chief of the federated tribes for the Brooks Range and spent the night with her. I knew the tribal representatives had to gather sometime fairly soon to vote on accepting the Native Land Claims. The next morning, I invited her to come spend time with me at Stultz Lake after the hunting season concluded. She accepted. We had three fantastic weeks together at the lake. She was a great cook and companion.

* * *

On the next moose and bear hunt for John, I took an industrialist and his wife from Frankfurt, Germany. They had informed John that they wanted to hunt with me. Everyone who hunted with me got trophies, while they went without. It was the last straw for John, and he shouted angrily at them showing them pictures of his successful hunts in the past. The coolness between John and me intensified. I made myself a promise not to come back again next year—if I was even asked.

They were a great couple. The husband had promised his spouse to include her in his hunts in Alaska, but John left her in camp most of the time and would not take her on daily hunts. She was offended and getting angry. When her husband explained what was going on and asked if she could come along, I said sure, if she was comfortable sitting on his lap in the back seat.

We enjoyed a wonderful week hunting. The couple were great sports and helped around camp. They never complained about the bugs or the hiking involved in getting their black bear and moose. We had two small adventures. The first was when I landed on a small lake surrounded by tall pine trees for black bears feeding on a nearby hill. Looking over the lake from the air, I thought there was enough room at the outlet for me to take off. After landing, I measured the distance between the small outlet and the trees and found there was not. I was wondering how I was going to be able to take off again. The trees were too close together and 150 feet high. There was only one way out, and that was to chop enough trees down for the wings of my airplane to fit between them.

That meant the couple got to help me chop down several trees with my camp axe before we could leave with their black bear. The blisters on both the wife's and husband's hands did not stop them from taking their turns at chopping. They were still happy and smiling at the end of a long day of logging as we hoisted a midnight toast in bloody and blistered hands to a successful hunt with great companions.

Leaving the small lake with the black bear, I moved our moose camp to the Kuskokwim River. Unfortunately, while we were out getting a moose, Natives from the nearest village raided our camp in their river boat, stealing supplies and the .22 Colt Woodsman pistol I used to shoot the heads off ptarmigan and grouse for dinner. I did not care about the supplies, they could be replaced, but I really missed the Woodsman. It was my fault for making camp within fifty miles of a Native village on a river. I knew better, but was pressed that evening to find a good camp with wood for my hunters before darkness. I was really surprised after the hunt to receive a brand new Colt Woodsman from them in the mail, along with a gracious letter inviting me on an all-expense-paid trip to visit them in Frankfurt, Germany during the coming winter. I had already made plans to go to the British Virgin Islands on a scuba diving trip with Bob Widmann and had to decline.

This couple and several other hunters told me how angry John got when they asked to hunt with me instead of him. This was silly as John was a competent guide, but I knew this would be the last year of my experiment of being a legal guide. I had gotten off the FAA blacklist, but had replaced that federal agency with the Park Service, who had begun to follow my airplane when I took off from Bettles. I looked for but could not locate a tracking device on my airplane. I was getting really tired of being a rogue and all the hassle it entailed.

I decided that after my trip to the Virgin Islands I would spend the winter with Kay Meacham, a lady friend who lived in Seattle, Washington. It was a wonderful, relaxing time; she was a great companion. I had met Kay and her sister, Carol, at Dad's house on a previous visit. Their brother, Pat, was married to my sister, Rozan. It would give me time to decompress and figure out the situation with Sharon and my sons. I knew that living full time at Stultz Lake would come to an end if I were to take the boys away from their mother. I liked women and being around them, but never again with Sharon.

While I lived with Kay, Carol, and their kids at their house in Ballard on the outskirts of Seattle, I had to have another engine put into N8689V.

I took classes I would need to complete my master's degree. It was nice adjusting to living in a city and with a lady who did not have mental and drinking issues. She put up with me, but was probably as happy as I was when spring came and I headed north again. Kay was fine, but civilization depressed me.

Grizzly Bear Mauling

I took the boys out to Stultz Lake upon arriving in Fairbanks after the winter with Kay. N8689V was spirited after getting a new engine. It was hard to believe I had flown that airplane almost 6,000 hours in such a short time. The boys and I fished for pike on the Tanana and up in the foothills of the Brooks Range, having a great summer together. David was older and now enjoyed fishing as much as Michael. They had many contests, seeing who could catch the most and the biggest fish.

As fall and the hunting season arrived, I took them back to their mother in Fairbanks. They were sad the summer was ending, and they had to go back to living with her. We had many discussions on why this was necessary, none of which ended satisfactorily. The drive from Nenana to Fairbanks where I dropped them off was a silent one. I knew this had to end. I needed to step up and be their father full time. I just did not know how to do it. My teaching license had expired and to renew it I had to meet the new qualifications that meant several years in school. How I would be able to do that and support the boys was a mystery. I did not want to go back to teaching, but I did not know what else to do other than teaching and flying.

The old saying there are old pilots and bold pilots but no old bold pilots is so true. There had not been any bolder pilots than me over the past thirteen years. I doubted I would live long enough to provide for my kids if I kept flying. I could not begin to count the number of times I should have been killed already, whether by flying, weather or animals. I did not know then that my closest encounter with the grim reaper was yet to come, and would change everything forever.

After taking the kids to their mother, I met Kay at the Fairbanks International Airport. I had invited her up for a trip to Alaska and a hunt in the Brooks Range. The trip did not go well. It was my fault. I had expectations for people living in the bush that no one could meet if they had not lived there. I got on her for the stupidest things. We parted, barely talking at the end. She was a good friend and deserved better.

After Kay left, I took Bob Jordan, our pediatrician, out on a grizzly bear hunt. We hunted the Melozie Valley and foothills of the Brooks Range before spotting a nicely colored small Toklat grizzly. The name comes from the coloration of their fur. The bear's feet and face are dark brown, with the rest of their body a bright blonde. It is my favorite color of all the bears in Alaska with the exception of glacier bear found around Yakutat.

It was feeding on spawning salmon in a narrow stream. The small river just barely had enough water for me to land on and clearance for my wings to fit between the trees. After landing we stalked the bear though the willows lining the rocky shore. The underside of the willow leaves was showing silver from the wind blowing down river, away from the feeding bear. We were able to get within 100 yards before Jim dropped it with a single shot.

The next two moose hunters were from out of state. It took several days of flying out of Stultz Lake to get their moose. The rest of that week was spent at the homestead fishing and relaxing before flying them and the meat into town.

* * *

My final hunter of the season was from out of the country. He had heard of me from one of the hunters I guided for John. We communicated over the winter by letter; he wanted moose, caribou, sheep and bear. I agreed to guide him for the two-week period I figured it would take to fill his tags. I won't give his real name or the country in which he lived, but will refer to him as Herr Cool.

I met Herr Cool at the Fairbanks airport. We flew out to Stultz Lake to sight in his rifle and let him relax from the long flight from Europe. I was impressed with his shooting ability. Not needing a rest, he put all his shots in the bullseye from both 100 and 300 yards, a very difficult thing to do. First on the agenda was a Dall sheep. I wanted to get it before the high lakes froze.

We really did not bond as I had with most of my hunters. Herr Cool was extremely reserved and standoffish. He never smiled or made small talk. He was all business about getting his trophies and leaving Alaska. He was the first foreign hunter I had guided that I had misgivings about, beside the one Austrian in John's camp who had shot a female caribou. I had no doubts about Herr Cool's shooting ability, but he was uncomfortable to be around. It was the first time I felt my client thought of me as a servant.

I flew him up to the small lake in the Brooks Range where I had taken Michael years before. Herr Cool was not interested in the beauty of the mountains and showed no inclination to help around camp. I had pointed out some Dall rams prior to landing. He wanted to immediately go after them, despite the lateness of the day. He did not grumble when I told him he would have to wait for morning, but turned his back on me and walked away.

The tent that night was as cool as the weather outside. After a silent breakfast and coffee, we started up the steep mountain side. The sheep were bedded down within a quarter mile of where we saw them the day before. The wind was in our favor. We completed the stalk without me injuring my knee and ankle as I had with Michael. One of the younger rams saw us move when we were more than 300 yards away. It immediately jumped to its feet, alerting the rest of the small group. I pointed out the largest to Herr Cool. It was starting to trot away uphill from us. My hunter downed it with one shot through the heart. It was an amazing shot. I was disappointed when he showed no emotion on approaching his kill. He never smiled or paid homage to the magnificent animal whose life he had taken. He acted as though he was just completing a chore and crossing it off the list. I was getting really annoyed and regretted I had agreed to guide him.

I dressed the animal and put the meat in my pack. I told Herr Cool to put the horns and cape in his. He refused, saying that was what he was paying me for. I told him in no uncertain terms he could either carry them out, or I would leave them here. The meat was coming out. I could give a damn about him or his trophy. He reluctantly put the cape and horns in his pack and followed me back to camp.

The hunt for moose and caribou followed the same pattern. He expertly killed each animal and balked at helping me with the tasks of caring for them. He was not interested in socializing with or assisting the hired help.

By the time we got to the grizzly bear hunt I was sick and tired of him. We would go hours without talking or interacting in any manner. I told him what to do. If he felt like it, he did it without an argument. If not, he ignored me. I decided I would not take him to any of my favorite bear spots and couldn't care less if he got an animal or not. I only had to put up with him for three more days.

We were camped on a small glacial stream about 100 miles from Bettles for the bear hunt. There were lots of bull moose entering the rut and wanting to fight all around camp. He had already crossed moose off his list, so Herr Cool paid them no attention. One evening after dinner and a day of trudging over and glassing the area, we saw a nice grizzly bear walk out of the willows 200 yards above camp. I don't know if it smelled the sheep steaks I had cooked for dinner or just smelled the camp and was coming to investigate. We both spotted the bear and grabbed our nearby rifles as it exited the willows and started downstream toward us at a slow walk.

I told Herr Cool not to shoot until I said to. I explained I would try to turn the bear to give him a shoulder shot. When it turned, he was to shoot it high on the shoulder. As usual he ignored me as we separated a few yards to allow each of us a shot if necessary. I whistled at the bear, who then stood before turning toward the willow. I usually shot a dangerous bear at the same time as my hunter to make sure it died quickly when it was this close, but because Herr Cool was a very competent shot, decided not to this time.

Instead, as I told him to shoot, I looked at him to make sure he was ready. What I saw was disconcerting. Cool he was not. His face was red and he was hyperventilating. The barrel of his rifle, instead of being steady, was wobbling all over. I yelled at him not to shoot and reached to push his rifle barrel up and away from the bear, but he fired before I could reach his weapon, hitting the animal in the stomach.

The bear immediately went down and then jumped back on its feet, charging us. I raised my rifle to fire at the charging enraged bear only to have Herr Cool jump in front of me, preventing me from shooting. Instead of pulling the trigger he panicked, and was jacking all the shells out of his weapon onto the rocks along the shore line. I had heard of hunters doing this, but never experienced it. They thought they were shooting but, in their fear, they were not.

I gave my panicked hunter a hard shove away from me as the grizzly hit me at full bore. The force of the blow was like being hit by a car. After flying backward several yards, I saw it biting me and slashing my arms and legs with its claws as it pummeled me, pinned beneath it. I did not feel any pain. I was surprised that I had held onto my .444 carbine after the bear crashed into me. When the bear's mouth opened next to my face to crunch my skull, I instinctively pushed my left hand as far down its throat as I could while bringing my rifle up to its neck and pulling the trigger. I never felt the bear's teeth biting into my arm as it dropped on top of me. My shot had luckily severed the spinal cord, but that did not stop it from continuing to bite me until I got my mangled arm out of its mouth and got out from under it.

After putting a killing shot into the bear, I looked for my hunter. He was over a hundred yards away. He had apparently run away as the bear mauled me. My body was a mess of claw wounds and bites underneath my shredded clothes. I was bleeding heavily. I immediately jumped into the ice cold stream to try and slow some of the bleeding and numb the pain that was starting to build.

Herr Cool stood by the dead bear, ignoring me laying in the glacial stream. I shouted at him to get my first aid kit out of the airplane until he finally left the bear and got the kit, leaving it on the bank of the river. I yelled at him that I needed help stopping the bleeding, but he turned his back on me and walked back by the bear. If I had had my rifle in my hands, I think I would have shot the son-of-a-bitch in the back I was so mad. I stayed in the stream until I was so numb I could stand it no longer. The frigid water had stopped some of the bleeding from my wounds as well as cleaned them. Opening the first aid kit, I spread the antibacterial cream over the most serious injuries until the tube was empty. Climbing into the airplane, I got fishing leader, a sewing needle, clothes and duct tape to sew the gaping wounds on my hands, arm and legs as much as possible. I tore my underclothes into strips and bound my wounds as tightly as possible, and then wrapped them even tighter with duct tape.

Naked and clothed only in blood and bandages, I grabbed my rifle and headed to the airplane. The nearest hospital was about seventy-five miles away. No one was going to come to my rescue. If I wanted to live I had to fly myself out. I yelled to no more Herr Cool that I was leaving, and if he wanted to come with me to get his ass in the airplane quickly. For the first time since the bear charged he looked at me, and then asked if I was going to skin the bear first. I won't print what I yelled at him, but for the first time since we met, he moved quickly into the airplane.

The pain was beginning to be overpowering. I took one of the pain pills I had for my back, hoping it would blunt my agony enough to allow me to fly to Tanana. I was worried about flying with the inevitable shock setting into my body, but had no choice in the matter. Getting off the water and heading to Tanana was easy compared to keeping myself awake and coherent during the flight. My control stick and seat were covered with blood before I got within radio range of the FAA station at the Tanana Airport. During much of the flight I hung my head out the open window to keep myself awake from the steadily increasing shock and pain. Telling the airport, I had been mauled by a bear and needed immediate medical assistance, I proceeded to the airport where I landed on the grass beside the runway. I did not want to take the time to land on the Yukon River. I needed medical help ASAP.

I don't remember much until the next day when I woke up in the small hospital. They had stitched me up properly and given me shots to prevent infection and ease the pain, but had no blood on hand for a transfusion. The doctor congratulated me on doing what was necessary to survive. He also wanted to know what to do with my hunter, who was driving everyone crazy. I contacted a friend in Fairbanks to come and deliver him and his trophies to the Fairbanks airport. I did not want to ever see the guy again. During the flight to Fairbanks, my friend later told me the guy tried to bribe him into going out to skin his bear. Herr Cool never once asked if I was okay. My friend told me that the guy finally shut up when he advised him to get out of the country before I got out of the hospital.

By the time I was discharged, someone had towed my float plane off the runway down to the Yukon River. It was another miserable flight back to Stultz Lake, where I took the next three weeks to recover. My body was a mess of scars from accidents, fires, surgeries, wrecks and animals. I had dislocated my shoulder several times, torn up my knees, and broken both ankles, one arm, one leg, back, and ribs several times. I could no longer move without constant pain, nor would I be able to do so for the rest of my life. I loved my life in Alaska, but conceded to the inevitability of having to find another occupation. As that fall slowly eroded into winter, I braced myself for the move back to the Lower 48 to find a way to support myself and my sons.

Anchored up while flying for Bob Widmann.

Bob Widmann with no room for more salmon.

Steve Edwards with salmon we caught in three hours outside of Cordova.

Wrecked airplane and I flew through a storm at the same time.
I made it, he didn't.

Flying for Bob Widmann

I DID FLY IN ALASKA two more summers while working as the Director of Security for Providence Medical Center in Seattle, Washington, after taking both boys away from Sharon for good. I had flown my airplane from Alaska to Seattle, and kept it at Kenmore Flying Service on Lake Washington. It kept me sane while adjusting to life back in civilization, knowing I could fly myself into the bush of Canada to camp and fish.

Bob Widmann convinced me to fly for him and several other commercial fishing boats in Prince William Sound during their summer salmon season. My boss at Providence agreed to give me the time off. I loaded a friend, Steve Edwards, a famous glass blower and artist from the Seattle area, and we headed north up the Inside Passage; a much easier trip when flying a float plane. Several days later we landed in Cordova where we proceeded to fish for red salmon until it was time for Steve to take a commercial flight back to Seattle and for me to get serious about flying for the boats I had contracted with for the summer.

My son, Michael, was still working for Bob on the *Orion*. Over the preceding five years he had worked his way up from a confused, lowly deck hand into a top-notch skiff driver. Prince William Sound borders on the Gulf of Alaska. The gulf spawns the storms that regularly hit Alaska, Canada, and the West Coast of America, so the weather was unpredictable and challenging, but I was no longer the new pilot that moved to Yakutat years before and was able to handle the weather. On clear and calm days, the mountains, islands, and glaciers are breathtaking, but the other 75 percent of the time, it is difficult flying. The summer went smoothly, and before I knew it I was flying back to Seattle.

I had not intended to fly in Alaska the following summer. Bob flew to Seattle that winter to talk to a ship builder outside Everett, Washington, about building a newer and bigger *Orion*. I flew him to the builder's shop, landing on the slough nearby. Staying at my apartment, Bob convinced me to come back to Alaska for one more summer. The only reason I agreed was so I could spend an entire summer flying and camping with David. He had missed out on so much while growing up in Alaska due to his young age. I always felt bad about that. This was a chance to make it up to him.

When the time came to head north, David and I loaded N8689V and took off for Alaska. It was a great summer of fishing, flying and camping out. I even taught him to fly the airplane again. David, being David, did not listen to instructions well. To teach him a lesson, I let him get into a death spiral and only took over control of the airplane when he was sure we were going to end up dead. From then on he was serious, and listened more attentively, and flew with a greater respect for our health.

Being a part-time bush pilot in Alaska is dangerous. That summer the weather was very uncooperative with lots of storms, wind, rain and fog. Despite the pleasure of being with David, I saw why I was reluctant to come back. One day early in the season while looking for a cannery boat that would take Bob's salmon, David and I ran into a vicious storm. There was no hope of trying to climb above it, nor was there any place we could land, even on floats.

The closest safe harbor was the bay where Bob and the other fishing boats in the area were anchored. It was miserable trying to see in the fog while getting bounced around by severe turbulence. I was not used to this anymore, and was really concerned about our safety. I could see David's hands clenched white to the support bars above my head as I fought the weather. He was quiet in the back seat with large eyes as the storm bounced us around. We finally made it safely back to our camp. I had to land sideways to the wind and in between large ocean waves instead of across them before taxiing and anchoring in a more protected area. Another pilot, also flying a Citrabria GCBC, was flying in the same area and, while looking for the cannery boat, crashed and destroyed his airplane in the storm. He had major injuries and had to be evacuated to a hospital in Anchorage.

Several days after that storm David and I were flying for Bob again, looking for cannery ships, when we hit a seagull in a bank of fog. There was a loud bang as something covered my windshield and hit my vertical stabilizer. There were several tense minutes until the weather cleared enough to see my windshield was covered with guts and blood. We landed in a nearby bay to clean the airplane and inspect the aircraft, tail assembly and propeller. The last incident happened late in the commercial fishing season. One of the five commercial fishing boats I was flying for that summer wanted me to fly into Valdez from where he was fishing in Prince William Sound. His wife wanted to fly into town for supplies and some parts for their skiff.

I left David with Bob Widmann and flew to the other boat. The wife of the captain requesting the flight was a real fishwife; she was loud, demanding, vulgar and a complete bitch. I disliked her as much as she disliked me, but I was under contract to fly for them so could not avoid the trip. I was not looking forward to the flight as the captain radioed for the current weather in Valdez. Hearing it was clear, with unlimited visibility and light and variable winds, I resigned myself to flying to Valdez.

My gas supply at David's and my camp on one of the small islands in the Sound was getting precariously low, so I did not refuel the airplane. I had plenty of gas for the trip, with a reserve of forty minutes. Taking off with the wife glaring at the back of my head because she had to sit on a wooden box instead of a comfortable seat, we headed for Valdez. Approaching Valdez Arm about an hour later, I was met with a solid wall of fog. I climbed above it thinking is was clear closer to Valdez. I reached Valdez but the fog was still solid underneath my wings. The airport reported the weather had just moved in and was forecast to last another four hours. The airport was closed with less than a quarter mile visibility and heavy fog. I advised them I was running low on fuel and did not have enough reserve to reach Cordova, and that I would attempt an instrument landing on the salt water of Valdez Arm.

This was a desperate maneuver. Valdez Arm is the main traffic lane for commercial and private boats into and out of Valdez. The Alaska Oil Pipeline terminated there. They loaded oil onto massive oil tankers that transported it to refineries in the lower United States.

Flying back out the Arm, I set up for an instrument landing. I told the woman in back to tighten her seatbelt and put away any loose items. She demanded that I fly back to her husband's fishing boat. I replied that was impossible as I lowered us into the sight-eating fog. Most non-pilots do not know how dangerous this is, as they are used to commercial airlines doing the same thing routinely. However, commercial airlines are riding a tight radio wave guiding them away from danger and to the airport. No such thing here, as I put myself and my passenger into the hands of fate.

Locking my vision onto my instruments and electric compass to ensure I maintained the correct heading and airspeed, we sank into oblivion: a small speck of life in a world of suffocating white. When the altimeter told me we were nearing the surface of the water, I divided my time between looking out the windshield for fishing boats, water, and at my instruments.

I had just glanced outside after once more looking over my instruments when I saw an enormous bow wave of white water rushing toward us. My mind screamed oil tanker as I frantically pulled up and banked the airplane left to get out of its way. I missed the oil tanker somehow, but was back in the heavy fog in an airplane that had run out of airspeed. Fighting to regain control of the faltering aircraft took more time on instruments than it would in clear weather because I had to maintain as much altitude as possible, not knowing what was ahead and below me.

When my breath and airspeed returned, I started climbing back up toward the top of the clouds on a heading I thought would take us back out toward Prince William Sound. At 1,500 feet the fog lightened, telling me we were about to break out into the sun-filled blue skies above, until suddenly rocks and trees filled my windshield. One of the few of my pilot friends who survived this type of situation had told me earlier that trees flashing before him were the last things he had seen before crashing and waking up in a hospital. With this in my mind, I again violently jerked the airplane to the left, pulling up and away from the rocks and trees.

This time I lost the battle of physics. My battle to prevent a crash resulted in an advanced stall and spin toward the ground. Trying to recover from a spin on instruments is difficult without visual references. I had no idea if I had gotten far enough away from the mountain before the airplane stalled and entered the spin. Not knowing what was below me or how far below it was or in what direction, I shut all of that out of my mind and concentrated on the instruments in front of me. I don't remember much of what happened next, other than releasing back pressure on the control stick and using the right rudder to stop the spin. I concentrated on making sense of the whirling instruments on the dashboard. When they finally steadied, I reduced power to slow my rapidly increasing speed and started pulling the aircraft up into level flight. N8689V's nose had just risen past where my rate of climb and artificial horizon instrument told me I was again in level flight when my floats hit the water. We came to a jarring halt, in a spray of salt water after several hard bounces across the small waves, surrounded by a thick blanket of fog.

We survived, but much clearer and sterner than any letter from the FAA, I saw the message flow firmly across my mind, "Thou Shalt Fly No More!" as if God had finally grown tired of saving me from myself. When the fishing season ended, and after David and I spent a last week at Stultz Lake, I left N8689V parked at the Nenana Airport, never to get in it again.

Epilogue

Leaving Alaska for the last time was bittersweet. I knew if I stayed I would never live to see my sons grow up and have families of their own. I had planned to finish my master's degree in education and start teaching again when I moved back to Seattle, but while I was taking classes, I took a job as a security officer in a Seattle hospital. Not that I wanted a career in security; I was just showing a friend how easy it was to get a job. She was in a difficult phase of her life and seemed unable to find work. She looked at me and said, "Okay, show me how easy it is," handing me the classified ads in the *Seattle Times*. I opened the jobs section and pointed to an ad by Northwest Security. I called them and set up an interview. I was hired to work at Providence Hospital as a security officer the following day.

Distressed by the lack of professionalism among my fellow security officers and by the amount of crime in the hospital that was not being handled in any meaningful way, I complained. Northwest Security did not take me seriously, but the hospital did. They hired me to become their Director of Security to address security issues.

That position challenged me to develop policies on procedures, training, and report writing that allowed security personnel not only to handle security issues but also to interact in a more positive way with other medical professionals. That effort was so successful that when the University of Arizona in Tucson became the first healthcare institution in the United States to perform a heart transplant and had problems handling the media, they hired me to come and fix their security issues.

After I trained the security personnel at University Hospital in Tucson, my supervisor confounded me by introducing me to the first computer I had ever seen. He told me to write a parking program for the thousands of employees, patients and visitors who used the Medical Center's many parking lots. The knowledge I gained struggling through dBase to write that parking program gave me the computer knowledge to write a program that would measure security personnel productivity. The program was used to demonstrate to other employees that security officers did not just stand around talking to nurses all day. It also told me which of my employees were doing their job. Recognition of my efforts to modernize and improve security professionalism led to my election as the President of the International Association of Healthcare Security and Safety (IAHSS), where I helped establish national standards for security officers and directors.

My last job was at Sacred Heart Hospital in Spokane. I moved to Spokane because my mother was dying of cancer, and I wanted to be around her for her final days. The best part of the Spokane job beside being at my mother's side was meeting Colleen Dea, the love of my life, who became my wife. Both of my sons eventually migrated to Spokane, Michael as the lead electrician for a major security firm, and David, who spent twenty-four years in the Army doing a multitude of demanding jobs in war zones across the globe. We still get together to fish and hunt many times a year.

Unfortunately, Sharon's life continued its downhill spiral. After many admissions into mental institutions, she died as a ward of the State of Alaska.

Do I miss my home on Stultz Lake? Yes, sometimes. I miss it more than I miss flying. I console myself with memories of a life full of adventure few get to experience, and the fact that I got to raise my sons. Someday I might win the lottery, buy another airplane, and fly back to the home I still own on Stultz Lake. But then, maybe not. I am happy and contented with who and where I am. I am surrounded by a loving wife and our large combined family of children and grandchildren. Colleen's children Thomas and Kirsten Dea live in Spokane as well as Tom's two children, Kelsey and Cayleigh. David's two kids, Cassie and Justyn, live with their mom in Texas but visit when they can.

After retiring I spend my time making fly rods for family and friends as well as tying flies and teaching others, especially my grandkids, to fly-fish. I have a large woodshop attached to the house to fiddle around in making furniture or turning wood into bowls when not trekking around the streams of Idaho or Montana fly-fishing. There is little more a man could ask for than the life I once lived in Alaska and the one I now enjoy in Spokane.